Don't Cry for Us, SAIGON

Dynamics of the Second Indochina War
A Pragmatic, Poignant, and Provocative
Supplement to Vietnam History

*For readers who know virtually nothing
about the Second Indochina War*

MAJOR (RETIRED) STEVEN E COOK

Proud Vietnam War Veteran

Foreword by Dr. David Turner
Chair, History and Political Science Department
Davis and Elkins College
Elkins, West Virginia, 26241

ISBN 978-1-64349-434-0 (paperback)
ISBN 978-1-64349-706-8 (hardcover)
ISBN 978-1-64349-435-7 (digital)

Christian Faith Publishing, Inc.
832 Park Avenue
Meadville, PA 16335
www.christianfaithpublishing.com

Printed in the United States of America

DEDICATION

This book is dedicated to all veterans and gold star mothers.
Thank you for your service and sacrifice for America!

*****

My heroes did not wear capes and fly. My heroes are and will always be the young soldiers who faced the trauma of war and possible death and then weighed those concerns against obligations to America. These heroic citizen soldiers who interrupted their personal and professional lives at their most formative stage in life are exemplified in the timeless phrase of the confederate memorial in Arlington National Cemetery, "Not for fame or reward, not for place or for rank, but in simple obedience to duty as they understood it."

The why of the Vietnam War may never be answered and soldiers' sacrifices never vindicated. Soldiers are those which others cared not to be. We went where others feared to go and did what others failed or refused to do. We asked nothing from those who gave nothing. And reluctantly accepted the thought of eternal loneliness should we fail. Soldiers have seen the face of terror and fear and warmed to the touch of love. We dreamed; cried; felt pain, hunger, thirst; and witnessed death and carnage. But foremost lived in times others would say best forgotten.

No soldier stands alone, and our lives touched one another. When one soldier is killed in combat, our lives are diminished, and part of our lives, family, and team is gone. We learned from the Vietnam War to honor their professional and family sacrifices and to pray for peace.

At the very least, in later days and years, we will be able to say with great pride that we were indeed soldiers!

Soldier and Warrior Ethos

> If you will not fight for right when you can easily win without bloodshed; if you will not fight when our victory will be sure and not too costly; you may come to the moment when you will have to fight with odds against you and only a precarious chance of survival, there may be even a worse fate. You may have to fight when there is no hope of victory. (Author Unknown)

Contents

FOREWORD

Vietnam has attracted an enormous amount of work on the part of scholars and lay writers. Most follow a familiar pattern of citing the *Pentagon Papers* or *Foreign Relations of the United States.* Many are excellent and provide the reader a firm interpretive understanding of the conflict. However as the years go by, younger readers often have trouble relating to the narrative on the importance of the story of the Vietnam War.

Major Steve Cook has produced an interesting volume that reintroduces the conflict from the viewpoint of the field soldier. More importantly, it also adds a colorful cultural context important to readers who did not live during the '60s and would find some references difficult to understand. Popular music, the rapidly changing moral revolution, and the maturation of the baby boom generation have often been described in the light of the antiwar movement. Major Cook places these in the context of all-American culture at the time, regardless of one's opinion of the war; an antidote to the cultural stereotyping often accompanying the description of the home front and, for that matter, the battlefield.

Reflection of veterans, particularly from West Virginia, adds to the depth of the narrative. In addition, the leadership aspects of the war are expanded to include the acts of noncommissioned officers who learned much as they tried to win "hearts and minds" in South Vietnam. One aspect was the relationships with the tribal culture of the Central Highlands, which sheds light on the role of the field soldier as adviser. The book is refreshing in that it eschews the usual oral revisiting of the antiwar debate among veterans. The editorializing is at a minimum and does not distract from the contribution of those actively engaged on the battlefield. It is a war seen from many lights, and Cook emphasizes the confidence of those engaged. Remember, 80 percent of the US soldiers in Vietnam were enlisted, and many were volunteers. War protests were not on their minds as much as their assignments and responsibility were.

However, if one needs a rehash of the standard story, Cook provides a brief narrative. More critically though is the inclusion of testimony by soldiers, which gives another perspective, many of them surprisingly unique. If one needs a refresher, Cook supplies an excellent chronology, or more to the point, several chronologies that quickly would get younger readers up to speed on the movements of the war. If you needed a general reference book, you would find no better general source. For those simply wanting a statistic or name or two, Cook has an almanaclike glossary of terms and the names of those who played a major role in Vietnam.

Having worked alongside Major Cook in teaching the Vietnam War, I can attest to how students appreciate his somewhat unorthodox approach. It provides them with an in-depth picture of a war as experienced by those who served. Yet unlike many other works on Vietnam, it is not overly surreal.

Cook offers a view of soldiers who were products of an era and were not alienated or even bitter about their years in Southeast Asia. He brings with him the experience of war unadorned and real.

Dr. David Turner
Chair
History and Political Science Department
Davis and Elkins College
Elkins, West Virginia 26241

My Support Team

I decided to self-publish my book. Self-publishing is self-induced abuse, stressful, arduous, mentally taxing, exhausting, and unforgiving. I have always been daring and tackled every task and mission in life with zest, zeal, and vim. However, this protracted writing project left me wondering occasionally about my mentality, judgment, analytical skills, critical thinking, competency, and cognitive skills. Initial self-publishing is sailing in uncharted water. You don't know what you don't know. Anxiety and the fear of failing my fellow veterans were always paramount. Anyone who self-publishes will immediately incur high blood pressure!

I have been blessed by God. The good Lord blessed me with the following blue-ribbon, world- class professionals that provided expert support to me in preparing, writing, and self-publishing this book. Many times I wanted to throw in the white towel, quit writing for a while because of exhaustive research, apathy, mental blanks, and go honky-tonking. It was the easy thing to do. When I experienced those blues, and self-pity, I thought about my support team. My support team individually and collectively really got on my case when I had these juvenile and immature dumb attacks. Through trying times, my support team never failed me. They were vigilant, steadfast, loyal, always positive, and provided unequaled support in every situation. They were the stimulus and mutual synergy that kept the train going and on the right track. On behalf of all veterans, I thank you for supporting me in my writing endeavor. I apologize and repent for being cantankerous, contentious, consternate, stupid, and for acting like a zombie periodically. You are absolutely the best! My support team consisted of:

1. *Deborah S. Cook.* Debbie is my business manager. I fell in love with Debbie at first sight and eventually married her.

My beautiful wife was always there for me and always the first one to detect a snag. Debbie's exceptional management, analytical skills, dynamic leadership, and high energy were the impetus and synergy that continuously achieved more than expected from the team and me. She used the full spectrum of encouragement from a gentle bear hug and a kind word to ball bat diplomacy to get me back into the game or to speed up the writing. I don't recommend ball bat diplomacy, but it was an incentive to keep me pounding those laptop keys! I love her and knew if I screwed up this book that she would personally kill me.

2. *My kids.* Steven and Heather, who grew up as military brats and always wanted me to write a book about the Vietnam War. Although I was never around much because of military duty when my kids were growing up, they were always in my heart and on my mind. Steven and Heather, I apologize and wish I could have spent more quality time with you. My kids are a blessing, my pride and joy, and helped edit my book.

3. *Chelsey Jones and her Tennessee Walking Horse Jean Luc.* These two are joined at the hip and are a marvelous composed riding team. Chelsey is my beautiful stepdaughter, and I am proud of her. She provided professional editing, insight, and was a morale booster. Every time I saw Jean Luc, he did more than just stand there and swat flies with his tail. He is high-spirited with energy to burn. His vitality, drive, and animation really impressed me; and I really desired to emulate his get-up-and-go demeanor. Indeed, animals can be inspirational. Big kudos to Chelsey for designing the front cover for me.

4. *Linda Nelson, Tammy Cook, and Ron Kuhl.* They provided excellent commonsense comments and recommendations. They are highly competent proofreaders. If I write another book, they will definitely be on my writing team.

5. *Cristin Dusenbury.* This beautiful lady was the executive editor in chief working overtime and above and beyond

duty. She was the muscleman converting perplexing and confusing military jargon into user-friendly reading. Cristin concealed my ineptness and stupidity; corrected my mistakes; cleaned up and bolstered the manuscript; and made me look blameless, respectable, and comparable to a seasoned author. Her specialized strong personal commitment, expert and exhaustive review and editing were without peer. Cristin is absolutely the best!

6. *Alexandra Jefferds.* Alexandra used her special and rare computer skills to develop and insert unsurpassed graphics, slides, and pictures into various chapters. She is a seasoned professional.

7. *Dr. David L. Turner.* Doc is a prolific strategic writer, eloquent speaker, and college history instructor. He wrote the foreword for this book. Doc is intelligent, visionary, articulate, savvy, my sage, and go-to guy when I needed anything. This book will enhance his Vietnamese history classes. Doc Turner is the best Vietnamese history professor in the world! He provided great insights, recommendations, and motivation. Best of all, he is my friend.

8. *Johnny Jacks.* Johnny was my Special Forces radio supervisor on a Special Forces A-team in Germany. He is the best radio and communications soldier and Green Beret to ever serve under my command or supervision in over fifty years of active military and federal civil service. He could establish commo anywhere in the world and probably the universe. Johnny provided technical publishing data and how to self-publish.

9. *Colonel "Hank" Harris, USA (Ret.).* Hank is a seasoned and veteran Special Forces officer. He is the consummate Special Forces warrior leader. Hank provided a comprehensive review, logical recommendations, and superb analysis. I would follow him anywhere. I wish we could have served in combat together.

CHAPTER 1

Introduction

> It was the best of times, it was the worst of times.
> —*A Tale of Two Cities*

Welcome home, Vietnam War brothers and sisters. This book is intended for a variety of audiences: veterans, family members, and gold star mothers. Other organizations, agencies, clubs, college students, faculty, and history buffs may have an interest in this book and gain new insights and unique perspectives into an unforgettable and misunderstood war. This book is succinct and not a complete book illustrating the Vietnam War. Hopefully, this book will correct many of those misconceptions about the Vietnam War.

I have a myriad of reasons for writing this book. Academically, I was disgusted with the two books used to teach Vietnamese history at a local college. These quick draw authors were premature and got it wrong! They were very negative, and in the first book I read and reviewed, the author states in his foreword that "the United States clearly lost the war." I took a strong exception to his statement. How can any author make such a statement? I read these books first with interest and hope, then with incredulity, and finally with anger. Books written on a war shortly after the war ends are usually inaccurate because the authors haven't had time to research and gather the facts. Because the Vietnam War was a new paradigm and venue for the US military, research may take a generation. No history of war is complete or accurate without data and writings from senior participants on the enemy side. Some of the most heroic and inspiring stories and facts do not become widely known until decades after the war. North Vietnamese tactics and facts have recently emerged through research and translation projects such as that currently underway at Texas Tech Vietnam studies center. Biographies, memoirs, after-action reports, and eyewitness accounts from key principles on both sides must be read and analyzed. These new documents and first-person accounts are more open, transparent, and have provided new and intriguing insights that characterize and portray the Vietnam War more accurately.

General Giap was a brilliant, highly respected leader of the North Vietnam military. His published memoirs confirmed what most Americans knew. The Vietnam War was not lost in Vietnam—it was lost at home. The following quote is from his memoirs currently found in the Vietnam War memorial in Hanoi: "What we still don't understand is why you Americans stopped the bombing of Hanoi. You had us on the ropes. If you had pressed us a little harder, just for another day or two, we were ready to surrender! It was the same at the battle of TET. You defeated us! We knew it, and we thought you knew it. But we were elated to notice your media was helping us. They were causing more disruption in America than we could in the battlefields. We were ready to surrender. You had won!"

Hoi B. Tran was a fighter pilot in the North Vietnamese Air Force. In his recently published book, *A Vietnamese Fighter Pilot in an American War*, he writes the following statements: "I want to say it clear to all my Vietnamese and American brother-in-arms that the US was never defeated militarily by the ragtag Army of the North Vietnamese Communist. There is absolutely no doubt in my mind that the US did not lose the war in Vietnam militarily. Ironically, politics dictated the outcome. Don't be bothered; only ignorant or misled individuals would buy into the notion that America lost the war in Vietnam militarily. The last advice I wish to convey to my younger generation is: Never trust the Vietnamese Communist!" These important facts were never mentioned in any of the previous Vietnam War history books that I read.

Most authors saw a chance to aggrandize, write a negative and biased book that reflected the majority of American antiwar dispositions. Researching facts was time-consuming and exhaustive. It was easier for authors to simply write from emotion, not facts to appease and ponder to their core audience. The authors knew their books would be an easy sell that would reap monetary benefits, establish a reputation, and tell the American public what they wanted to hear. But were these post–Vietnam War authors' versions plausible and accurate?

Veracity is important. With these inaccurate books, biased statements, lack of understanding and facts, I decided to write a Vietnamese history book with emphasis on the Second Indochina War to give readers a microcosm and basic dynamics of the Vietnam War, veterans, and veteran affairs. This book is not comprehensive or a complete book illustrating the Vietnam War. Hopefully, however, this book will correct many of those misconceptions about the Vietnam War. I will record and archive highlights of the Vietnam War and the accounts of American military heroes whose sacrifices and heroic exploits might otherwise be lost to history.

Public ignorance of the war is astounding and epidemic. High school history teachers and college professors often discussed the war and conveyed their personal perspectives rather than presenting the whole picture substantiated with facts. Most history books only gave a courtesy mention of the Vietnam War. Therefore, the stories of valor and sacrifice may perish with the Vietnam veterans. Most of the history books that I read and researched did not go far enough to explain our reasons for deploying and conducting military operations in South Vietnam. The books did not tell the reader about severe human rights violations, prolific communism, and blatant military aggression that jeopardized Southeast Asia, including the Philippines, and how North Vietnam invaded and violated the sovereignty of South Vietnam, Cambodia, and Laos. The history books also did not state that the Vietnam War was not a US-declared war.

America and the world did not understand why the US became involved in South Vietnam. The US deployed its military and support programs to South Vietnam to train the South Vietnamese military and to stabilize the country. The US also provided economic, political, civil affairs, and various other humanitarian programs to help the South Vietnamese government. Training the South Vietnamese military involved US and allied military ground offensive operations and several external strategic bombing campaigns against the North. These US military operations were limited and conducted for security and to buy time for the South Vietnamese to organize, train, and conduct limited offensive operations for confidence and esprit de corps. These short-range and initial goals were achieved through search-and-destroy operations in South Vietnam. The South Vietnamese military's brief successes were only cosmetic and nothing substantial. President Johnson later changed the name of search-and-destroy operations to reconnaissance in force for political correctness. His anomaly was futile, insidious, and mandated new constraints on US forces in South Vietnam. Our long-range goals were to train the South Vietnamese military and work ourselves out of a job. The US wanted to train a South Vietnamese military that could conduct unilateral military operations at will against an invading North Vietnamese Army. The US and the South Vietnamese military succeeded until Vietnamization. The US never intended to seize and hold any territory in South Vietnam except large base camps for security, logistics, and support. Vietnamization eventually resulted in diminishing returns for the US, and the US was ordered and negotiated out of South Vietnam three years prior to the South Vietnamese government losing the war. Later during the 1970s, training allied military and supporting foreign economic programs were adopted as a stability mission for the US military.

The worst atrocity of the Vietnam War did not occur in Vietnam at all. The worst atrocity of the Vietnam War occurred in the United States when America shunned its Vietnam War veterans! Our nation had a solemn duty to care for its native sons and daughters who served in South Vietnam. Because of politics and failed policies on the home front, the US government "copped out," took the easy way out, and viewed the Vietnam veteran not as heroes but as disgraced scapegoats and an imposition.

Discrimination was rampant and protracted. For example, several Vietnam War veterans were refused membership at a local Elkins Veterans organization. We were chastised and told that we did not qualify for membership because we were not in a real war. Several other Vietnam War veterans from various states shared similar stories about their hometown veteran organizations. They were told that they were losers and not in a real war also. In October 2014, I wrote an eleven-page document on the Vietnam War and delivered it to one of the editors of a central West Virginia newspaper for publication on Veterans Day. The intent of this document was to honor Vietnam War veterans. The editor read this document in my presence and asked me for a bio and a picture. I delivered the bio and picture the next day. For some reason, the paper did not print and publish this document, which I predicted, because the article was not politically correct but was factually correct. The editor's blarney substantiates that selective citizens, agencies, and institutions in central West Virginia are still discriminating against Vietnam War veterans. It is repugnant that this paper can publish pictures and stories of tasteless and disrespectful stories of tragic brutal murders but won't publish a story written by a veteran to honor veterans on Veterans Day. The integrity and character of this newspaper is reprehensible.

The Vietnam War–era gold star mothers experienced discrimination also. The American Gold Star Mothers (AGSM) was established in Washington DC in 1928. A prerequisite for membership includes a son or daughter killed while in service to America. When the Vietnam-era mothers petitioned for membership, they were disparaged, not welcomed, and denied. In an arrogant and vulgar manner, the national AGSM leadership told the Vietnam-era mothers that the Vietnam War wasn't a real war, and they were not qualified for membership. Slowly the stagnate attitude of the national AGSM changed, and several Vietnam War–era mothers became members. Dissension remains between the two groups, and although the AGSM has two thousand members, only ninety are Vietnam-era mothers—not a good ratio.

As a young man I had a special calling. I was called to be a soldier! This calling was a difficult challenge because of the inherent perils, hardships, and separation from family and close friends. After high school, I always selected the easier tasks and challenges in my brief premilitary life; but this time, a tough, difficult, and harsh challenge selected me. I served multiple tours in South Vietnam during the war and was engaged in direct combat or conducted combat operations almost daily. I served my first military tour in the Vietnam War as a squad leader in Company B, 3rd Battalion, 506th Airborne Infantry (Currahee) of the famed 101st Airborne Division during the years 1967–68. In my battalion we were known as the Bastard Brethren of Bravo Company. At a recent Company B reunion, several of my Vietnam War buddies asked me to tell their story. Their request and passion was a collateral reason that inspired me to write this book. Initially I was reluctant to honor their request; however, time heals, and it is time that I write this book and tell their epic story. American, allied, and enemy military operations conducted in the Vietnam War in Southeast Asia will be discussed in this book. I fought with, led, and advised US and allied, conventional, Pathfinder, and Special Forces. I will use my unit as empirical examples; however, Pathfinder and Special Forces combat operations will be discussed also. These units were elite for a reason. We were capable of doing extraordinary things very few could.

This book will enumerate and perpetuate the proud lineage and fighting expertise of Company B, 3rd Battalion, and 506th Airborne Infantry. The 506th Parachute Infantry Regiment (PIR) was activated at Camp Toccoa, Georgia, in July 1942 as the sixth parachute infantry regiment activated in the US Army. Initially, the 506th PIR consisted of the 1st, 2nd, and 3rd Airborne Infantry Battalions. The 506th PIR completed training and was assigned to the 101st Airborne Division in 1943. On D-day, the 506th PIR conducted a combat parachute jump behind enemy lines and later participated in the defense of Bastogne, Belgium. This was known as the Battle of the Bulge. One of the last missions for the 506th PIR during World War II was the capture of high-ranking Nazi generals and leaders in Berchtesgaden, Germany. Shortly after victory in Europe, the 506th PIR was inactivated. The unit remained dormant until it was reactivated in 1956 with the newly activated 101st Airborne

Division at Fort Campbell, Kentucky. However, only the 1st and 2nd Battalions were reactivated. Later, during the midsixties, the Vietnam War escalated, and the demand for more American military combat troops increased. In April 1967, the 3rd Battalion was reactivated for training and deployment to Vietnam. I volunteered for this new reactivated battalion and was among the first enlisted soldiers assigned in April 1967. Pathfinder and Special Forces operations will be discussed also.

The Vietnam War was the one of the longest military conflicts in American history and claimed the lives of more than fifty-eight thousand American military. Over three hundred thousand were wounded. The Vietnam War was the most unpopular war in which Americans ever fought; and the final toll in suffering, sorrow, and national turbulence can never be calculated. The Vietnam War polarized America and could be considered a modern-day contemporary civil war in South Vietnam. For more than two million veterans of the Vietnam War, the wounds never healed. Serving in the military, or especially the war, was unpopular especially among some veterans who fought it. I never heard any Currahees in Company B say anything negative about the war. Several of the Currahees and veterans experienced shunning in society and had profound physical and psychological difficulties including post-traumatic stress (PTS), homelessness, and substance abuse during the postwar period. Do not judge these heroes unless you have walked a mile in their jungle boots through the jungle in a combat environment. Vietnam War veterans saw and experienced horrific savage and direct combat repeatedly that humans aren't intended to see. Remember, once upon a time we were all like you!

The Vietnam War wasn't the war you knew; it was the war we fought! The majority of Company B Currahees were triple volunteers. We volunteered for the Army, volunteered for Parachute School, and volunteered for the newly activated 3rd Battalion, 506th Airborne Infantry. My unit was instrumental in developing airmobile; air assault; and counterinsurgency tactics, techniques, and procedures that would ensure and enhance success on the battlefield later in South Vietnam. Many of these combat procedures were later adopted and integrated into US Army doctrine. This book covers activation in the spring of 1967 through completion of my first year of combat in South Vietnam, October 1968. Although greatly outnumbered, Company B was one of three maneuver companies in the battalion that was a barricade that prevented a communist takeover of the key city of Phan Thiet during Tet 1968. Every Currahee in Company B earned the coveted Valorous Unit Citation, equating to the individual military award of the Silver Star for their heroic combat action during Tet. The Vietnam War wasn't the war you knew; it was the war we fought, and we fought it our way!

This book is a no-spin, grassroots epic snapshot of a time when young men were suddenly thrust into combat and the coming of age of these soldiers—many still teenagers. The chapters will show everyday common Americans who volunteered as elite Army Paratroopers conducting combat operations to the best of their ability with the goal of coming home alive and uninjured. These soldiers were America's best and could have chosen another profession that was safer or less demanding or more profitable. This book is a first-person account of high school teenyboppers suddenly answering the call for duty and turning into elite combat warriors virtually overnight and of their families who waited anxiously for them to return home. We learned our excellent work principles, ethics, and morals from our parents. Free government giveaways were not in our family plan. We were old-school in an era before political correctness. We carried our books and didn't need any sissy backpacks. The teachers believed in the Board of Education, which they kept in their desks to maintain order and discipline in the classroom. Most parents supported the teachers paddling and sometimes took us out behind the woodshed when we came home and doubled the corporal punishment. Any benefits parents received were earned by hard and honest work. We had to try out for little league sports. Playing little league was not a right; we had to try out for the team. If we did not make the cut, we went home. If we made the team, we played hard; and when the season was over, no one received a trophy just for showing up. Mama and Papa Bear taught us to use *sir* and *ma'am* when answering or addressing adults. *Time-out* was not in their lexicon. We didn't have calculators, computers, or cell phones. We used the stubby pencil method and slide rules to solve problems. It was mandatory that we learn our multiplication tables in school, and we stood and recited them frequently in class. We were meat and potatoes guys who never heard of quiche, granola, or lattés.

North Vietnamese Army and Viet Cong unconventional military operations in tropical jungles were a new crucible for the Currahees and the US military. The book will depict the adaptive unconventional warfare tactics, techniques, and procedures the Bastard Brethren learned quickly and developed by trial and error to fight and defeat the North Vietnam Army in every major engagement in the Currahees' area of operations in South Vietnam. Testimonies of seasoned combat Currahees whose average age was twenty-one will be depicted through empirical vignettes. The carnage of fire-fights, mortar attacks, the stench of human decay and flesh torn and broken, the camaraderie and bonds of men at war were part of the Currahee experience. These highly trained men of mettle had a strong sense of patriotism, pride, selfless service, and teamwork. Uncommon valor was a common virtue. This book encapsulates the warrior-leader ethos of these men, their almost impossible mission, and the quagmire of politically correct politics of the war and por-trays the American combat soldier at his best. They were the Bastard Brethren of Bravo Company who was duty and honor bound by an unspoken oath sealed with blood that by God fought and died for each other!

The poignant, riveting, and the gripping reality of war and the demons and misfortune of the Vietnam veterans will be depicted in the book. The book lays out the post–Vietnam War era; the mean-ing of honor; and the morbid, indignant, and arrogant way America treated its military during an unpopular, undeclared, and unconven-tional war. Graphic carnage and the trauma of war will be drama-tized. Actual combat pictures, after-action reports, and eyewitness accounts will be included. These were just ordinary soldiers doing extraordinary feats against superb North Vietnam Army Hard Corps Regulars in combat. Currahees of Company B soldiered hard, fought hard, and partied harder. We were perpetually under extreme stress, hot, wet, thirsty, pain and endured real sacrifices. Every Currahee knew and understood what real honor was.

Myths of the Vietnam War will be refuted, rebutted, and debunked. In addition, another objective is to educate the world about the plight of the Vietnam veterans. Myths suggest that those veterans who obeyed the call of duty later became alcoholics and drug addicts in disproportionate numbers or that they became convicts and unproductive losers, homeless, or suicidal. Most Vietnam veterans returned home and led productive lives. For example, some remained in the military and rose to the highest enlisted or officer ranks. Others continued their education and became entrepreneurs and became very successful. Most continue to have jobs, pay taxes, and are upstanding in their communities. Our national government statistics and governmental agencies' reputable studies substantiate these facts.

The meaning of the Vietnam War isn't told by statistics or body count; it is exemplified in the veterans that served! These American youth chose to serve a country that turned its back on them. How could America turn its back on its native sons and daughters? Future generations of young people may learn and be proud of their American heritage and freedom because of the valiant Currahees. Currahees of Bravo Company never broke any promise of their military oath and accomplished every mission, sometimes against overwhelming odds. Our US government, in its arrogance and miscalculation, broke its promises not only to the Currahees and other veterans but also to America, South Vietnam, and to the world. Perhaps our politically correct government should be more prudent in the future about the promises it makes to the military because when our government capitulates, it betrays American heroes such as the Currahees and other war veterans.

Agent Orange and other herbicides used in the Vietnam War will be discussed. Agent Orange was the code name for herbicides developed for the military, primarily for use in tropical climates. There were a total of fifteen known herbicides and possibly more used in Southeast Asia. Agent Orange and other herbicides were intended to deny an enemy cover and concealment in dense terrain by defoliating trees and shrubbery where the enemy could hide. Agent Orange was principally ineffective against broad-leaf foliage such as that found in dense jungle terrain in Southeast Asia.

Emotional wounds such as post-traumatic stress (PTS) will be discussed. These emotional wounds are not new, just a new name for a very old combat anxiety. Every war and combat operation in history has had its share of PTS. Even the ancients experienced PTS. Veterans of all wars including Vietnam veterans have PTS to some degree. PTS and other psychological trauma doesn't mean the Vietnam veterans or any other veterans are crazy. Quite the contrary! Major symptoms of PTS include the following: guilt, anxiety, depression, flashbacks, hyperalertness, difficulty being intimate, various sleep disturbances, nightmares, trouble concentrating, intrusive memories, psychic numbering, anger, distrust, low self-esteem, difficulty with authority, and self-punishing. We left Vietnam, but for a few, Vietnam never left us. The antiveteran media defined us as a generation of PTS and suicide. Liberals hold that vets with combat-induced PTS are prone to violence. According to recent government research, a 2014 study debunks this popular perception. The study found no hard evidence that confidently links PTS with a propensity for violence. The real issue and problem is the public predicates their reactions on perceptions, not reality. These fake perceptions were sobering because they made it difficult for veterans to find jobs. We only have a short time remaining before that is how America will remember us. This message is too often detrimental to Vietnam War veterans. If veterans hear this message that they need help often enough, they will start to believe it. To the vengeful media, Vietnam veterans are the embodiment of America. When you insult or vilify us, you smear all Americans. Your hate emboldens us to work harder to save our liberty from your ignorance and bigotry. Too often some of our Vietnam War veterans resorted to self-medication of drugs and alcohol to experience oblivion. Most Vietnam War veterans had their own methods to deal with their PTS dilemma and predicaments. Most psychologists tell us it is okay to recall some of the carnage and painful hardships we experienced, but we need to do it in moderation. Sometimes, sharing these war stories with other Vietnam War veterans also helps and is therapeutic. It is okay to seek professional help if our flashbacks tend to get out of control. Doctors, psychologists, and other veterans are there to help us. PTS is not germane to veterans; relatives and other Americans are affected too. Since more than a third of war veterans' wives meet the criteria for secondary traumatic stress, any treatment offered to veterans with PTS should address the traumatization of their families. Recently, research and experiments with acupuncture, yoga, animal interaction, learning to play a musical instrument, and homeopathic cures have shown great potential in helping veterans recover. These alternatives to prescription drugs are better and have positive collateral effects on veterans. Another controversial treatment is psychedelic drugs found in molly and ecstasy. Recent tests have showed great utility and value in these psychedelic drugs. Treatment and usage gives people relief and the ability to revisit an event that's still painful without being overwhelmed.

This book will help all veterans, their families, and America to better understand and come to some closure and aid in catharsis. It is almost impossible for any veteran to have total closure. Total closure has two parts: forgiving and forgetting. I have no animosity to any foe, threat, or any people in Southeast Asia. As a Christian, I have forgiven them and prayed for them. Sometimes we are our worst enemy. Many of us constantly talk about the injustices we have faced and simultaneously talk about ourselves in a negative manner. I strongly encourage all veterans to look beyond the hate that binds so many of us together and realize that we must let it go, move on, and get on with our lives! Forgiving has been shown to reduce anger, hurt, depression, and stress. Forgiving can lead to an increased feeling of hope, peace, compassion, and self-confidence. The difficult part is forgetting. Forgiving does not mean forgetting. No Company B Currahee or other Vietnam War veteran will ever forget! I have learned to temper my feelings, think about other pleasant things, and get on with my life. The civilian environment and society is different from the military. You don't have that same sense of awareness that the person on your right and left is going to have your back. The camaraderie and sense of security is impossible to replicate.

In our era, the Army was great at training a soldier for combat. However, the Army failed when it was time to discharge soldiers and send them home. Currahees and Vietnam War veterans never had a transition and decompression period to readjust and learn some basic job skills to better prepare, integrate, and assimilate back into society. Psychologists should have counseled us also. Most Currahees were discharged and shuttled quickly back into a ruthless society. We were simply told to "man up" and get on with our lives.

Throughout America, we were treated as public piñatas, a beating and whipping post of society. The news media wasn't kind to the Vietnam War veteran. Often we were used as props for charity cases. Veteran charities are salesmanship. The more emotional a story, the more donations are received. Out of twenty major veteran nonprofit charities, only three discussed methods to empower veterans to achieve their potential. The remaining seventeen talked about helping veterans in need. Vietnam veterans must do a better job and demand that the nonprofit charities communicate better with the public and explain that the veterans are an asset to the community and not a liability. We finally determined that this narrative of helping veterans may actually be harmful to veterans by pervading a negative perception.

The Vietnam War was America's first television war. The news media exceeded its charter and attempted to develop and influence US foreign policy and tried to brainwash Americans on the home front. For the first time in history, families gathered around their television set and not around the supper table to have their family time. The news media revealed an aura of ignorance, apathy, and notably and intentionally withheld Vietnam War facts that were always there. The public and American families could only judge the war as revealed through television and other media information systems. Women and children were seeing mind-alternating worst-case actual combat footage edited by the biased news media showing only the "ugly American." The news media were the first to commit Stolen Valor because they stole our honor. America became a casualty of this first television war. In reality, the only part of the nightly news with any creditability and credence were the commercials. The press associated homelessness, psychological problems, and crime with the Vietnam veteran. The press was usually unfair. In 1975 for instance, the military wasn't in South Vietnam and hadn't been for two years; but we were blamed for losing the war. Hollywood portrayed Vietnam War veterans as having a long history of acts of violence. This characterization stigmatizes us and perpetuates the stereotype that we are inherently dangerous, misfits, and a menace to society. You never heard the good stories about Vietnam veterans; all you heard were the bad ones. The public saw and heard our struggles and pleas but never acknowledged our victories.

The American society and environment wasn't the status quo when Vietnam veterans returned home. The Age of Aquarius American society and environment often branded and called returning veterans entering college or the workforce as baby killers, murderers, and outcasts. Discrimination against us sometimes was rampant. Often the Vietnam War veterans weren't ready for the culture shock of readjustment to American life. Sometimes a veteran had only four days to adjust prior to being back in "the world." We learned very quickly that the world is cruel, brutal, unforgiving, and that only the strong survive.

The Vietnam War affected every American directly or indirectly. Many Americans have a relative, friend, or know someone whose name is etched into the Vietnam Veterans Memorial Wall. America must come to grips with the perils of not only the Vietnam War but also future wars. Some Vietnam War veterans and their relatives are still fighting the war. Sometimes these relatives endured hardships equal to or more arduous than those of the veterans.

I landed at both East and West Coast major airports several times when I returned from South Vietnam because of serving several combat tours. I did not see any blatant protestors, and no one accosted me or spit at or on me. I don't know of any Vietnam veteran returning home to a parade or hero's welcome, nor did I want or need any. All we wanted was just a little respect and a shot and opportunity at the American dream. In the fall of 2014, the mayor of Elkins and the city council organized and conducted a parade for veterans. I understood the intent of the parade, and the mayor should receive kudos for his initiative. After I read the parade lineup, I decided not to participate in this parade. The parade included past and present politicians. Why did politicians march in our veteran's parade? Were we honoring politicians or veterans? Another example of déjà vu.

The Vietnam War was the genius of a politically correct American government. No greater honor could be bestowed upon Vietnam veterans than to serve their country and fight communism. Veterans were engaging the enemy twelve thousand miles from home, not protesting, burning flags and draft cards, or defecting to Canada. They performed with a tenacity and quality of valor that America may never truly know or understand! Our path, mission, and faith were steadfast. Vietnam veterans deserve a far better place in history than now offered them by the self-proclaimed spokesmen of our so-called generation.

These self-respecting and dignified veterans have proven that they have high quality of character and should have been given the rite of passage back into society. Vietnam veterans are diverse and have made many significant and valuable contributions to America. These heroes are critical thinkers with superb work ethics that plan and execute difficult tasks out of the box. Vietnam veterans are the true grit and strategic reserve of America. They are multiskilled with diverse empirical expertise that "Got-R-Done" for top management in corporate America. Vietnam veterans are the consummate American citizens, responsible adults who support their communities and strive to make better lives for their families and country. They are the synergy that has solidified the American workforce with superb work ethics, managing and supervising skills, and savvy to do difficult jobs extraordinarily well. Regardless of any job or task, Vietnam veterans can be depended upon to carry through to completion the most arduous and demanding of assignments. Imagine the gaps in our character and honor if we had not served. America's general order number one should be to honor its veterans. Society must reflect upon, listen, learn, understand, and recognize the contributions and sacrifices of the Vietnam veterans. Vietnam veterans must never be forgotten. America must not think of its Vietnam veterans as part of the past but ones who made the present and future possible. All veterans' unselfish sacrifice in wars against enemies of freedom deserves recognition, reference, and gratitude. America should hold the memory of the Vietnam veterans close to heart because they are part of all we see around us. America should never abandon another generation of veterans again!

West Virginia had the highest casualty rate per capita in the nation from the Vietnam War. There are 711 West Virginia Mountaineers on the Vietnam Memorial Wall in Washington DC. Don't grieve them but remember the passing of an age when duty, honor, and country were common American traits and a way of life for Vietnam War veterans.

Every generation has its heroes. The greatest generation had the original Currahee Band of Brothers of World War II fame, and they were superb! Recently, pundits, historians, and real Americans have rediscovered this greatness in Vietnam veterans. We are awesome! It is chic and vogue to be a Vietnam veteran now! Our pain, sacrifice, suffering, hardships, and bloodshed together are without equal, peer, and bonded us as brothers. Our greatness never left us, and it never will.

Vietnam veterans have weathered decades of challenges. We never flinched or waivered when America called. Our finest hour was on the fields of battle. Diplomatically, we have made a positive difference in our community, state, and the world. Our trek continues. Our memories, solidarity, hopes, prayers, and legends live on. And by the grace of God, we are still fighting, caring, and praying for each other!

Chapter 2

Why the United States Went to War in South Vietnam

There is no such thing as a lost cause, because
there is no such thing as a gained cause.

—T. S. Eliot

For decades after the fall of Saigon in April 1975, pundits, historians, scholars, and veterans cannot agree on the primary reason the US went to war in South Vietnam. Evolutionary synthesis concluded the Vietnam War was a proxy conflict of the Cold War. A proxy war is a conflict between two states or nonstate actors where neither entity directly engages the other. While this can encompass a breadth of armed confrontation, its core definition hinges on two separate powers utilizing external strife to somehow attack the interests or territorial holdings of the other. This frequently involves both countries fighting their opponent's allies, or assisting their allies in fighting their opponent. Proxy wars have been especially common since the close of World War II and the rise of the Cold War, and were a defining aspect of global conflict during the latter half of the twentieth century. Much of this was motivated by fears that direct conflict between the United States and Soviet Union would result in nuclear holocaust, rendering proxy wars a safer way of exercising hostilities. A proxy war with significant effects was the Vietnam War between the United States and the USSR. In particular, the bombing campaign Operation Rolling Thunder destroyed lots of infrastructure, making life more difficult for North Vietnamese citizens.

The Cold War began soon after World War II and ended in 1989 without any direct combat between the US, USSR, and China. The Cold War was fought indirectly with surrogate countries, arms races, propaganda, economic embargoes, unconventional warfare, conflicts, crisis, and proxy wars in peripheral nations like Vietnam, Cuba, Korea, and the Berlin Airlift mission. Most American wars have obvious starting points or precipitating causes. However, there was no fixed beginning for the US war in Vietnam. The United States entered that war incrementally, in a series of steps between 1950 and 1965. The multiple starting dates for the war complicate efforts to describe the causes of US entry. The United States became involved in the war for a number of reasons, and these evolved and shifted over time. The US didn't deploy to South Vietnam to fight a war or to conquer a nation, nor did the US desire to remain as an occupation force. The Vietnam War began as a United States military crusade rather than a detailed coordinated military force on force protracted operation. The US sought to avoid major combat engagements through a plan to create a durable, functioning, democratic, and prolonged South Vietnamese military, government, and society. Initially, our national strategy was to help the South Vietnamese win their war and prevent the toppling of dominoes in Southeast Asia. Later, our strategy changed, and our mission was to obtain a negotiated peace. Our military ensured both missions were successful. The US government insisted on this negotiated peace agreement. However, after the peace agreement was signed, the US Congress abandoned the South Vietnamese government, allowed them to flounder and eventually lose their war.

Primarily, every American president regarded the enemy in Vietnam—the Viet Minh; its 1960s successor, the National Liberation Front (NLF); and the government of North Vietnam, led by Ho Chi Minh—as agents of global communism. US policymakers, and most Americans, regarded communism as the antithesis of all they held dear. Communists scorned democracy, violated human rights, pursued military aggression, and created closed state economies that barely traded with capitalist countries. An accurate and truthful interpretation emerged recently that the Vietnam War can be studied dispassionately by analysts and experts with greater and unlimited access to North Vietnamese war records. The Vietnam War was by definition a major proxy conflict in the Cold War. Historians, scholars, and documents conclude that "the Vietnam War was the second of three wars in Indochina during the Cold War." I disagree. Evidence suggests that there was only one protracted Indochina War planned, directed, and prosecuted by Ho Chi Minh. The scholarly three wars were mere conflicts, phases, or milestones in Ho Chi Minh's master strategic quest and plan to unify all of Vietnam and make the Southeast Asia domino theory a reality. After Saigon and South Vietnam fell to the North in April 1975, the North invaded and conquered Laos and Cambodia. Ho Chi Minh was a revolutionary, but his tactics, techniques, and procedures were evolutionary. The US military, when engaged in wars, thinks in terms of months and years. Ho's plan called for decades—and even generations—of war, conflicts, and strife for unification. Ho's lifelong goal of achieving communism for Indochina almost became a reality.

The roots of the Vietnam War were derived from the symptoms, components, and consequences of the Cold War. The foundations of the Vietnam War revolved around the simple belief held by America that communism was threatening to expand all over Southeast Asia. The US policy of worldwide containment gained momentum, energy, and allies because of fear of the domino theory. The domino theory is the belief that when one country abdicates to communism, a chain reaction will occur in neighboring countries. According to the domino theory, losing one country to communism meant more communist governments would come to power in other countries. The interventions of the United States, Soviet Union, and China turned civil wars in Vietnam, Laos, and Cambodia into proxy wars. This intervention substantiates to those who claim that the United States, by its intervention, mistakenly turned a pure civil war in South Vietnam into part of the Cold War. The United States shared its belief that Indochina was a major theater in the global Cold War with the Soviet Union and China. Lien T. Nguyen writes in *Hanoi's*

War: An International History of the War for Peace in Vietnam, "While Moscow desired to see Soviet technology defeat American arms in Vietnam, Beijing hoped to showcase the power of Mao's military strategy on the Vietnamese battlefields."

The Soviet Union emerged from World War II as a major world power with strong influence over Asian countries. The Soviet Union's chief tactic was to intimidate countries into appeasement after convincing them that the US lacked the resolve and/or ability to defend its interests. The US considered communism as the greatest postwar threat to democracy and capitalism. The US police of communism began with the dislike and bitterness that occurred between the US and the USSR during the end of World War II and in the postwar period. Neither the Soviet Union nor the United States could risk an all-out war against each other—such was the nuclear military might of both. However, when it suited both, they had client states that could carry on the fight for them. In Vietnam, the Americans actually fought; therefore, in the Cold War "game," the USSR could not. However, to support the communist cause, the Soviet Union armed its fellow communist state, China, who would, in turn, arm and equip the North Vietnamese who fought the Americans.

The Vietnam War began as a result of US strategy of containing communism during the Cold War. George F. Kennan was the architect and engineer of communist containment. He was a US diplomat stationed in Moscow from 1944–1946. Kennan knew the Soviets were a prolific and potent force obsessively committed to destroying democracy and capitalist societies. His lengthy telegrams to the US State Department caveated the perils of Soviet objectives and communist philosophy. Kennan's essays emphasized and recommended US resolve and to remain steadfast, firm, and vigilant in the containment of Moscow's domino goals.

The US government supported French colonialism in Southeast Asia because America needed France as a military ally to check and contain the Russians and communism in Europe. In May 1950, President Harry S. Truman authorized a modest program of economic and military aid to the French to fight and conduct military operations against Ho Chi Minh and communism in Southeast Asia because he was a Moscow and Beijing puppet. Truman hoped that assisting the French in Vietnam would help to shore up the developed, non-Communist nations, whose fates were in surprising ways tied to the preservation of Vietnam and all of Southeast Asia. Later the US established the Military Assistance Advisory Group (MAAG) in Vietnam to assist the French in the First Indochina War. Eventually, the French lost the war in Vietnam. The French were not as concerned about communism as the Americans were. After the historic Dien Bien Phu campaign, the French pulled out of Vietnam.

The 1954 Geneva Accords split Vietnam into North and South Vietnam. The United States did not sign the Geneva Accords and refused to accept the political settlement. The US decided that in order to check communism, they had to increase military support, economic aid, and advisers to the South Vietnamese government. The administration of President Dwight D. Eisenhower undertook an ambitious but cautious program to build a nation from the spurious political entity that was South Vietnam by fabricating a government there, taking over control from the French, dispatching military advisers to train a South Vietnamese Army, and directing the Central Intelligence Agency (CIA) to conduct unlimited psychological warfare against North Vietnam. Dwight Eisenhower restrained US involvement because, having commanded troops in battle, he doubted the United States could fight a land war in Southeast Asia and not get bogged down in a quagmire. The US still maintained major Cold War concerns and fears that if North Vietnam defeated the South that the rest of Southeast Asia would fall like dominoes.

After France was ousted, the Soviet Union and China had the most to gain in Southeast Asia. The Soviets and Chinese armed, equipped, and supplied the Viet Minh, Viet Cong, and the NVA in South Vietnam. President Kennedy vowed to not allow South Vietnam to fall to communism. The failure of the Bay of Pigs Invasion of Cuba, the building of the Berlin Wall, and communist incursions into Vietnam's neighbor Laos had convinced Kennedy that the US needed to stand firm against communist expansion. Kennedy viewed South Vietnam as the cornerstone of freedom in Southeast Asia. In early 1960, the South Vietnamese Conventional Army was not yet armed, trained, and ready to fight and sustain combat operations against the NVA. Kennedy told a *New York Times* journalist in 1961 that "we have a problem making our power credible and Vietnam looks like the place." Although reluctant to commit ground combat forces, Kennedy increased the number of US military advisers to sixteen thousand—up from nine hundred who had been there since President Dwight D. Eisenhower's administration. President John F. Kennedy rounded another turning point in early 1961, when he secretly sent four hundred Special Operations Forces–trained (Green Beret) soldiers to teach the South Vietnamese how to fight what was called a counterinsurgency war against communist guerrillas in South Vietnam. When Kennedy was assassinated in November 1963, there were more than sixteen thousand US military advisers in South Vietnam, and more than one hundred Americans had been killed.

Kennedy's successor, Lyndon B. Johnson, escalated the war and committed US ground combat troops. In August 1964, he secured from Congress a functional (not actual) declaration of war: the Tonkin Gulf Resolution. With the arrival of the Marines and the escalation of the air campaign, America's military role in Vietnam crossed the line from advise and assist to offensive warfare. "I am not going to lose Vietnam," Johnson told the US Ambassador to South Vietnam Henry Cabot Lodge soon after becoming president. "I am not going to be the president who saw Southeast Asia goes the way China went." Instead, the new president increased the number of US military advisers in Vietnam to twenty-three thousand. Johnson named Gen. Maxwell Taylor, who had urged Kennedy to deepen US involvement in Vietnam, as his ambassador to Saigon. With Taylor's support, Johnson named Gen. William Westmoreland as the top American commander in Vietnam.

Concurrently, the situation on the battlefield in South Vietnam was deteriorating. Allied intelligence detected regular North Vietnamese Army units in the South, fighting alongside Viet Cong guerrillas. The US estimated that almost half of South Vietnam was under the control or influence of the communists. The options and choices for the US were mixed: escalate and go in deeper or get out. On February 7, 1965, the Viet Cong raided a US airfield near

Pleiku, killing eight American soldiers and destroying or damaging twenty-five helicopters. Within hours of the attack, Johnson ordered selective bombing of North Vietnamese targets. Three days later, the communists attacked the US base at Qui Nhon, killing twenty-three Americans. Johnson responded by ordering a sustained bombing campaign against North Vietnam—Operation Rolling Thunder—that would continue throughout his presidency. In a top-secret memorandum dated April 6, 1965, Johnson approved thousands more troops for Vietnam. He also changed the mission to allow "more active use" of ground troops—meaning offensive combat operations.

As presidents committed the United States to South Vietnam, little by little many of these ambitions were forgotten. Instead, apathy developed against withdrawing from Vietnam. Washington believed that a US withdrawal would result in a communist victory and begin the domino theory in Southeast Asia.

Along with the larger structural and ideological causes of the war in Vietnam, the experience, personality, and temperament of each president played a role in deepening the US commitment. The youthful John Kennedy felt he had to prove his resolve to the American people and his communist adversaries, especially in the aftermath of several foreign policy blunders early in his administration. Lyndon Johnson saw the Vietnam War as a test of his mettle.

The United States government withdrew with honor from the Vietnam proxy war in 1972. Shortly after America engaged the communists in South Vietnam, the US erroneously turned a civil war into a part of the Global Cold War. The US believed the Vietnam proxy war was a major sub theater and objective of the Cold War with the USSR and China. The Russians and Chinese endeavored to see communist arms and equipment defeat the US. As a sidebar, the Chinese attempted to showcase and evaluate Mao's military strategy in South Vietnam.

China and the Soviet Union played a much greater role in the Vietnam War than Americans realized at the time. Half of all Soviet foreign aid went to North Vietnam between 1965 and 1968. The Soviets supplied antiaircraft teams and weapons to the North that brought down dozens of US planes. Recently a former Soviet colonel, Alexei Vinogradov stated, "The Americans knew only too well that North Vietnamese planes of Soviet design were often flown by Soviet pilots."

Americans continue to draw and study the lessons learned from the Vietnam War. These lessons were short-lived. In the 1990s, the United States policymakers and military focused on swift, high-tech warfare against technologically advanced adversaries, only to painfully relearn forgotten lessons in Iraq and Afghanistan about counterinsurgency and nation building.

The Vietnam War was a historical event and unchanging part of the past. As a war, it will continue to evolve, reflecting the values and priorities of later generations. In discussing and debating the nation's most controversial war, Americans, historians, pundits, veterans, and history students would do well to remember the words of the poet T. S. Elliot: "There is no such thing as a lost cause, because there is no such thing as a gained cause."

Questions for Reflection

1. What is a proxy war?
2. What was the Cold War?
3. Who was Ho Chi Minh?
4. Describe Ho Chi Minh's protracted plan to unite Vietnam and his lifelong goal of attaining communism for Indochina.

CHAPTER 3

South Vietnam Maps, Climate, and Facts

Where the good guys were and where the bad guys were.

Map 1: Regions and Provinces of South Vietnam 1966
Map 2: The Vietnam War Military Corps Tactical Zones
Map 3: Size of Vietnam
Map 4: Ethnic Map of South Vietnam

Map 1
Regions and Provinces of South Vietnam 1966

Map 2
The Vietnam War Military Corps Tactical Zones

Map 3
Size of South Vietnam

DIGITS

Size of the Battlefield

American soldiers in South Vietnam were fighting in a place that covered 67,108 square miles, slightly larger than Florida, the 22nd-biggest state. Traveling South Vietnam from one end to the other, on a straight line, would be about the same as a straight-line trip from Pittsburgh to Savannah, Georgia, approximately 580 miles.

Postwar Vietnam encompasses 127,881 square miles, closest in area to somewhat smaller New Mexico, the fifth-largest state. The distance from top to bottom is about 1,000 straight-line miles. On a U.S. map, the country would fit roughly between Minneapolis and Dallas.

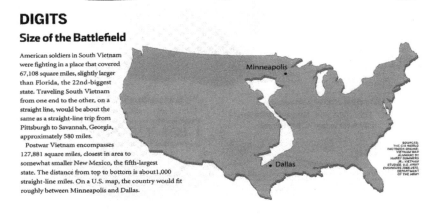

SOURCES:
THE CIA WORLD
FACTBOOK ONLINE;
VIETNAM WAR
ALMANAC BY
HARRY SUMMERS
JR.; VIETNAM
STUDIES, U.S. ARMY
ENGINEERS 1965-1970,
DEPARTMENT
OF THE ARMY

Map 4
Ethnic Map of South Vietnam

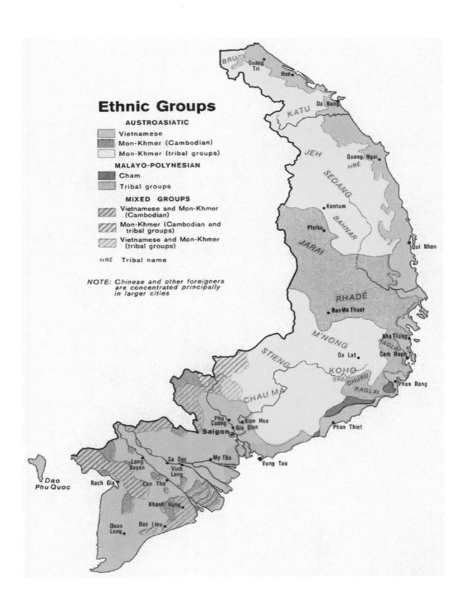

Ethnic Groups

AUSTROASIATIC

Vietnamese

Mon-Khmer (Cambodian)

Mon-Khmer (tribal groups)

MALAYO-POLYNESIAN

Cham

Tribal groups

MIXED GROUPS

Vietnamese and Mon-Khmer (Cambodian)

Mon-Khmer (Cambodian and tribal groups)

Vietnamese and Mon-Khmer (tribal groups)

HRÉ   Tribal name

NOTE: Chinese and other foreigners are concentrated principally in larger cities

Climate

Vietnam is located between nine and twenty-three degrees north latitude. Eastern Vietnam has a long coastline on the Gulf of Tonkin and the South China Sea. Vietnam is mountainous in the northwest and in the Central Highlands facing the South China Sea, with peaks reaching up to 8,000 ft. (2,450 m). In the North around Hanoi and in the South around Ho Chi Minh City, there are extensive low-lying regions in the Red River Delta and the Mekong Delta respectively.

It has a tropical monsoon type of climate; from May to September, the south monsoon sets in, and the country is dominated by south to southeasterly winds. From October to April, the north monsoon is dominant with northerly to northeasterly winds affecting the country. There is a transition period between each monsoon season when winds are light and variable.

Vietnam has a single rainy season during the south monsoon (May–Sept). Rainfall is light during the remainder of the year with annual rainfall exceeding 1,000 mm almost everywhere. Annual rainfall is even higher in the hills, especially those facing the sea, in the range of 2,000–2,500 mm.

For coastal areas and the parts of the Central Highlands facing northeast, the season of maximum rainfall is during the south monsoon, from September to January. These regions receive torrential rain from typhoons, which move in from the South China Sea at this time of the year. The weather at this time is cloudy with frequent drizzle. About 70 percent of Vietnamese live along the coast. Most of the population that lives along the coast is especially vulnerable to rising sea levels related to climate change.

During the north monsoon, northern Vietnam has cloudy days with occasional light rain, while southern Vietnam tends to be dry and sunny.

Temperatures are high all year round for southern and central Vietnam, but northern Vietnam has a definite cooler season as the north monsoon occasionally advects cold air in from China. Frost and some snow may occur on the highest mountains in the North for a few days a year. In southern Vietnam, the lowlands are sheltered from outbreaks of colder northerly air, and the dry season is warm to hot with much sunshine.

Facts
(As of 2014)

Land area: 125,622 square miles (325,361 square kilometers); total area: 127,244 square miles (329,560 square kilometers)

Population (2012 estimated): 91,519,289 (growth rate: 1.054%); birth rate: 16.83/1000; infant mortality rate: 20.24/1000; life expectancy: 72.41; density per square mile: 683

Capital (2009 est.): Hanoi, 6.5 million (metro area), 2.6 million (city proper)

Largest cities: Ho Chi Minh City (Saigon), 7,396,446; Haiphong, 1,907,705; Da Nang, 887,069; Hué 333,715; Nha Trang, 392,279

Monetary unit: Dong

The Socialist Republic of Vietnam is controlled by the Communist Party. However, the government encourages privately owned business.

National name: Công Hòa Xa Hôi Chú Nghia Viêt Nam

Languages: Vietnamese (official); English (increasingly favored as a second language); some French, Chinese, Khmer; Mon-Khmer and Malayo-Polynesian (mountain area languages)

Ethnicity/Race: Kinh (Viet) 86.2%, Tay 1.9%, Thai 1.7%, Muong 1.5%, Khome 1.4%, Hoa 1.1%, Nun 1.1%, Hmong 1%, others 4.1% (1999)

Religions: Buddhist 9%, Catholic 7%, Hoa Hao 2%, Cao Dai 1%

Literacy rate: 94% (2010 est.)

Economic summary: GDP/PPP (2011 est.): $300 billion; per capita $3,400. Real growth rate: 5.9%. Inflation: 18.7%. Unemployment: 3.6%. Arable land: 20%. Agriculture: paddy rice, coffee, rubber, cotton, tea, pepper, soybeans, cashews, sugar cane, peanuts, bananas; poultry, fish, seafood. Labor force: 48.23 million; agriculture 48%, industry 22.4%, services 29.6% (2011).

Industries: food processing, garments, shoes, machine building; mining, coal, steel; cement, chemical fertilizer, glass, tires, oil, paper. Natural resources: phosphates, coal, manganese, bauxite, chromate, offshore oil and gas deposits, forests, hydropower.

Exports: $96.91 billion (2011 est.): crude oil, marine products, rice, coffee, rubber, tea, garments, shoes

Imports: $97.36 billion (2011 est.): machinery and equipment, petroleum products, fertilizer, steel products, raw cotton, grain, cement, motorcycles

Major trading partners: US, Japan, China, Germany, Singapore, UK, Taiwan, South Korea, Thailand (2011)

Transportation: Railways: total: 2,632 km (2008). Highways: total: 180,549 km; paved: 133,899 km; unpaved: 46,650 km (2008 est.). Waterways: 17,702 km navigable; more than 5,149 km navigable at all times by vessels up to 1.8 m draft (2011). Ports and harbors: Cam Ranh, Da Nang, Haiphong, Ho Chi Minh City, Ha Long, Quy Nhon, Nha Trang, Vinh, Vung Tau. Airports: 44 (2012).

International disputes: Southeast Asian states have enhanced border surveillance to check the spread of avian flu; Cambodia and Laos protest Vietnamese squatters and armed encroachments. Communications: Telephones: main lines in use: 10.175 million (2011); mobile cellular: 127.318 million (2011). Radio broadcast stations: Government controls all broadcast media exercising oversight through the Ministry of Information and Communication (MIC); government-controlled national TV provider, Vietnam Television (VTV), operates a network of 9 channels with several regional broadcasting centers; programming is relayed nationwide via a network of provincial and municipal TV stations; law limits access to satellite TV, but many households are able to access foreign programming via home satellite equipment; government-controlled Voice of Vietnam, the national radio broadcaster, broadcasts on 6 channels and is repeated on AM, FM, and shortwave stations throughout Vietnam (2008). Radios: 8.2 million (1997). Television along border; Cambodia accuses Vietnam of a wide variety of illicit cross-border activities; progress on a joint development area with Cambodia is hampered by an unresolved dispute over sovereignty of offshore islands; an estimated 300,000 Vietnamese refugees reside in China; establishment of a maritime boundary with Cambodia is hampered by unresolved dispute over the sovereignty of offshore islands; the decade-long demarcation of the China-Vietnam land boundary was completed in 2009; China occupies the Paracel Islands also claimed by Vietnam and Taiwan; Brunei claims a maritime boundary extending beyond as far as a median with Vietnam, thus asserting an implicit claim to Louisa Reef; the 2002 Declaration on the Conduct of Parties in the South China Sea has eased tensions but falls short of a legally binding "code of conduct" desired by several of the disputants; Vietnam continues to expand construction of facilities in the Spratly Islands; in March 2005, the national oil companies of China, the Philippines, and Vietnam signed a joint accord to conduct marine seismic activities in the Spratly Islands; Economic Exclusion Zone negotiations with Indonesia are ongoing, and the two countries in fall 2011 agreed to work together to reduce illegal fishing along their maritime boundary

A Brief History

The Vietnamese are descendants of nomadic Mongols from China and migrants from Indonesia. According to mythology, the first ruler of Vietnam was Hung Vuong, who founded the nation in 2879 BC. China ruled the nation, then known as Nam Viet, as a vassal state from 111 BC until the fifteenth century, an era of nationalistic expansion, when Cambodians were pushed out of the southern area of what is now Vietnam.

A century later, the Portuguese were the first Europeans to enter the area. France established its influence early in the nineteenth century, and within eighty years, it conquered the three regions into which the country was then divided—Cochin-China in the South, Annam in the central region, and Tonkin in the North.

France first unified Vietnam in 1887, when a single governor-generalship was created, followed by the first physical links between north and south—a rail and road system. Even at the beginning of World War II, however, there were internal differences among the three regions. Japan took over military bases in Vietnam in 1940, and a pro–Vichy French administration remained until 1945. Veteran communist leader Ho Chi Minh organized an independence movement known as the Vietminh to exploit the confusion surrounding France's weakened influence in the region. At the end of the war, Ho's followers seized Hanoi and declared a short-lived republic, which ended with the arrival of French forces in 1946.

Paris proposed a unified government within the French Union under the former Annamite emperor, Bao Dai. Cochin-China and Annam accepted the proposal, and Bao Dai was proclaimed emperor of all Vietnam in 1949. Ho and the Vietminh withheld support, and the revolution in China gave them the outside help needed for a war of resistance against French and Vietnamese troops armed largely by a United States worried about Cold War communist expansion.

A bitter defeat at Dien Bien Phu in northwest Vietnam on May 5, 1954, broke the French military campaign and resulted in the division of Vietnam. In the new South, Ngo Dinh Diem, prime minister under Bao Dai, deposed the monarch in 1955 and made himself president. Diem used strong US backing to create an authoritarian regime that suppressed all opposition but could not eradicate the northern-supplied communist Viet Cong.

Skirmishing grew into a full-scale war, with escalating US involvement. A military coup, US-inspired in the view of many, ousted Diem on November 1, 1963, and a kaleidoscope of military governments followed. The most savage fighting of the war occurred in early 1968 during the Vietnamese New Year, known as Tet. Although the so-called Tet Offensive ended in a military defeat for the North, its psychological impact changed the course of the war.

US bombing and an invasion of Cambodia in the summer of 1970—an effort to destroy Viet Cong bases in the neighboring state—marked the end of major US participation in the fighting. Most American ground troops were withdrawn from combat by mid-1971 when the US conducted heavy bombing raids on the Ho Chi Minh Trail—a crucial North Vietnamese supply line. In 1972, secret peace negotiations led by Secretary of State Henry A. Kissinger took place, and a peace settlement was signed in Paris on January 27, 1973.

By April 9, 1975, Hanoi's troops marched within forty miles of Saigon, the South's capital. South Vietnam's president Thieu resigned on April 21 and fled. Gen. Duong Van Minh, the new president, surrendered Saigon on April 30, ending a war that claimed the lives of 1.3 million Vietnamese and fifty-eight thousand Americans.

In 1977, border clashes between Vietnam and Cambodia intensified, as well as accusations by its former ally Beijing that Chinese residents of Vietnam were being subjected to persecution. Beijing cut off all aid and withdrew eight hundred technicians.

Hanoi was also preoccupied with a continuing war in Cambodia, where sixty thousand Vietnamese troops had invaded and overthrown the country's communist leader Pol Pot and his pro-Chinese regime. In early 1979, Vietnam was conducting a two-front war: defending its northern border against a Chinese invasion and supporting its Army in Cambodia, which was still fighting Pol Pot's Khmer Rouge guerrillas. Hanoi's Marxist policies combined with the destruction of the country's infrastructure during the decades of fighting devastated Vietnam's economy. However, it started to pick up in 1986 under *doi moi* (economic renovation), an effort at limited privatization. Vietnamese troops began limited withdrawals from Laos and Cambodia in 1988, and Vietnam supported the Cambodian peace agreement signed in October 1991.

The US lifted a Vietnamese trade embargo in February 1994 that had been in place since US involvement in the war. Full diplomatic relations were announced between the two countries in July 1995. In April 1997, a pact was signed with the US concerning repayment of the $146 million wartime debt incurred by the South Vietnamese government, and the following year, the nation began a drive to eliminate inefficient bureaucrats and streamline the approval process for direct foreign investment. Efforts of reform-minded officials toward political and economic change have been thwarted by Vietnam's ruling Communist Party. In April 2001, however, the progressive Nong Duc Manh was appointed general secretary of the ruling Communist Party, succeeding Le Kha Phieu. Even with a reformer at the helm of the party, change has been slow and cautious.

In November 2001, Vietnam's national assembly approved a trade agreement that opened US markets to Vietnam's goods and services. Tariffs on Vietnam's products dropped to about 4 percent from rates as high as 40 percent. Vietnam in return opened its state markets to foreign competition.

The government highlighted its efforts to crack down on corruption and crime with the June 2003 conviction of notorious criminal syndicate boss Truong Van Cam, known as Nam Cam. He was sentenced to death, along with 155 other defendants, and executed in June 2004.

Prime Minister Phan Van Khai visited the United States in June 2005, becoming the first Vietnamese leader to do so since the Vietnam War ended. He met with President Bush and several business leaders, including Microsoft chairman Bill Gates. The US is Vietnam's largest trading partner, buying about $7 billion in Vietnamese goods each year.

Questions for Reflection

1. Identify the military corps tactical zones in South Vietnam.
2. What was the capital of North and South Vietnam during the Vietnam War?
3. What is the current capital of Vietnam, and where is it located?
4. Identify two economic industries of Vietnam.
5. Identify two major economic trading partners with Vietnam.
6. Identify two major coastal water systems that border on Eastern Vietnam.
7. Where does 70 percent of the Vietnam population live?

CHAPTER 4

The Gulf of Tonkin Incident/Enigma

A smoking gun? You don't say. What happened and why?

The Gulf of Tonkin Incident occurred during the first year of the Johnson administration. Johnson supported military escalation as a means of challenging what was perceived to be the Soviet Union's expansionist policies. The Cold War policy of containment was to be applied to prevent the fall of Southeast Asia to communism under the precepts of the domino theory. After Kennedy's assassination, Johnson ordered in more US forces to support the Saigon government, beginning a protracted United States presence in Southeast Asia. Johnson was looking for a smoking gun to escalate the war. On August 2, 1964, the USS *Maddox* reports that it is under attack by North Vietnamese torpedo boats in the Gulf of Tonkin. This was Johnson's legal justification for America to enter the war.[1]

The Gulf of Tonkin Incident is the name given to two separate confrontations involving North Vietnam torpedo boats and United States Navy destroyers in the waters of the Gulf of Tonkin. The first incident occurred on August 2, 1964, as the US Navy destroyer *Maddox* performed a signals intelligence patrol as part of DESOTO operations. DESOTO operations were part of the US Operations

---

[1] Edwin E. Moise, *Tonkin Gulf and the Escalation of the Vietnam War* (1996). Also see Lyndon B. Johnson, Operation Plan 34A; and James B. Stockdale, Tonkin Gulf Resolution.

Plan 34-ALPHA, a black-classified operation. During this attack, the *Maddox* engaged several North Vietnamese Navy torpedo boats of the 135th Torpedo Squadron. The ensuing sea confrontation resulted in the *Maddox* firing over 280 3-inch and 5-inch shells. The Navy also strafed the torpedo boats with Navy jet fighters. One US aircraft was damaged, and three North Vietnamese torpedo boats were damaged. Several North Vietnamese sailors were killed; there were no US casualties. The *Maddox* failed to sink any torpedo boats, broke contact, and sailed back down the gulf to link up with the US Navy destroyer *C. Turner Joy*. This brief sea encounter was the first open fighting between the United States and North Vietnam naval forces.

On August 3, both US destroyers resumed patrolling in the gulf and were under strict orders to keep farther from the coast and out of the extreme northern part of the gulf. By nightfall, thunderstorms and fog had rolled in and affected the accuracy of electronic instruments of the destroyers. Tensions were high, and both destroyer commanders predicted an attack. The perceived attack occurred for several hours on August 4 when crew members reading their electronic instruments saw some nebulous radar blips and believed that they were under attack from North Vietnamese torpedo boats. Inclement weather skewed the instruments and gave faulty readings. *Maddox*'s sonar picked up sounds that could not be substantiated. Both destroyers reported renewed attacks against them and opened fire on Tonkin Gulf Ghosts. Tonkin Gulf Ghosts are false radar blips.

President Johnson, denouncing "hostile actions against United States ships on the high seas," ordered retaliatory bombing against North Vietnamese naval bases. President Johnson asked Congress for a joint resolution approving his orders. The resolution passed almost unanimously in the heat of the sea battle; this became the Tonkin Gulf Resolution. This resolution was the charter and legal justification for President Johnson to retaliate with air strikes against the North. This brief air strike was officially called Operation Pierce Arrow.

After fifty years, the Gulf of Tonkin incident remains an enigma and still has Americans confused, and some don't understand what actually happened and why. Many details and aspects of the initial Gulf of Tonkin attacks are questionable. Serious suspicions arose.

The National Security Agency originally claimed that the second Tonkin Gulf incident occurred on August 4, 1964, as another sea battle between US and North Vietnamese naval forces. Later investigations suggest that the US destroyers may have engaged invisible targets based on false radar images and not actual NVN torpedo boat attacks.

In 2005, an internal National Security Agency historical study was declassified; it concluded that the *Maddox* had engaged the North Vietnamese Navy on August 2, but that there were no North Vietnamese naval vessels present during the incident of August 4, 1964.

On August 2, 1964, as the North Vietnamese torpedo boats approached within ten thousand yards, the *Maddox* fired three rounds to warn off the communist boats. This initial action was never reported by the Johnson administration, which insisted that the Vietnamese boats fired first.

North Vietnamese General Phùng Thế Tài later claimed that the *Maddox* had been tracked since July 31 and that it had attacked fishing boats on August 2, forcing the North Vietnamese Navy to "fight back."

During the night of August 4 and the early morning of August 5 in bumpy rough weather and heavy seas, the destroyers received radar, sonar, and radio signals that they believed signaled another attack by the North Vietnamese Navy. For some two hours, the ships fired on radar targets and maneuvered vigorously amid electronic and visual reports of enemies. Despite the Navy's claim that two attacking torpedo boats had been sunk, there was no wreckage, bodies of dead North Vietnamese sailors, or other physical evidence present at the scene of the alleged engagement.

At 1:27 a.m. Washington time, Patrol Commander Herrick sent a cable in which he acknowledged the attack may not have happened and that there may actually have been no Vietnamese craft in the area: "Review of action makes many reported contacts and torpedoes fired appear doubtful. Freak weather effects on radar and overeager sonar technicians may have accounted for many reports. No actual visual sightings by *Maddox*; suggest complete evaluation before any further action taken."

One hour later, Herrick sent another cable, stating, "Entire action leaves many doubts except for apparent ambush at beginning. Suggest thorough reconnaissance in daylight by aircraft." In response to requests for confirmation, at around 4:00 p.m. Washington time, Herrick cabled, "Details of action present a confusing picture although certain that the original ambush was bona fide."

At 6:00 p.m. Washington time (5:00 a.m. in the Gulf of Tonkin), Herrick cabled yet again, this time stating, "the first boat to close the *Maddox* probably launched a torpedo at the *Maddox* which was heard but not seen. All subsequent *Maddox* torpedo reports are doubtful in that it is suspected that sonar man was hearing the ship's own propeller beat."

Within thirty minutes of the August 4 incident, President Johnson had decided on retaliatory attacks. That same day he used the "hotline" to Moscow and assured the Soviets he had no intent in opening a broader war in Vietnam. Early on August 5, Johnson publicly ordered retaliatory measures stating, "The determination of all Americans to carry out our full commitment to the people and to the government of South Vietnam will be redoubled by this outrage." One hour and forty minutes after his speech, US aircraft reached North Vietnamese targets. On August 5 at 10:40 a.m., these planes flying from US aircraft carriers bombed four torpedo boat bases and an oil-storage facility in Vinh.

Shortly before midnight on August 4, President Johnson made a speech by radio in which he described an attack by North Vietnamese vessels on two US Navy warships, the USS *Maddox* and USS *Turner Joy*, and requested authority to undertake a military response. Johnson's speech repeated the theme that "dramatized Hanoi/Ho Chi Minh as the aggressor and which put the US into a more acceptable defensive posture." Johnson also referred to the attacks as having taken place "on the high seas," suggesting that they had occurred in international waters.

He emphasized "commitment to both the American people, and the South Vietnamese government." He also reminded Americans that "there was no desire for war." A close scrutiny of Johnson's public statements reveals no mention of preparations for overt warfare and no indication of the nature and extent of covert land and air measures that already were operational. Johnson's statements were short to "minimize the US role in the conflict"; a clear inconsistency existed between Johnson's actions and his public discourse.

While President Johnson's final resolution was being drafted, Senator Wayne Morse attempted to hold a fund-raiser to raise awareness about possible faulty records of the incident involving the USS *Maddox*. Morse supposedly received a call from an informant who has remained anonymous, urging Morse to investigate official logbooks of the *Maddox*. These logs were not available before President Johnson's resolution was presented to Congress.

After urging Congress that they should be wary of President Johnson's coming attempt to convince Congress of his resolution, Morse failed to gain enough cooperation and support from his colleagues to mount any sort of movement to stop it. Immediately after the resolution was read and presented to Congress, Morse began to fight it. He contended in speeches to Congress that "the actions taken by the United States were actions outside the constitution and were acts of war rather than acts of defense."

Morse's efforts were not immediately met with support, largely because he revealed no sources and was working with very limited information. It was not until after the United States became more involved in the war that his claim began to gain support throughout the United States government. Morse was defeated when he ran for reelection in 1968.

Evidence was still being sought regarding the night of August 4 when Johnson gave his address to the American public on the incident. Messages recorded that day indicate that neither President Johnson nor Secretary McNamara was certain of an attack.

The use of the set of incidents as a pretext for escalation of US involvement follows the issuance of public threats against North Vietnam, as well as calls from American politicians in favor of escalating the war. On May 4, 1964, William Bundy called for the US to "drive the Communists out of South Vietnam," even if that meant attacking both North Vietnam and communist China. Even so, the Johnson administration in the second half of 1964 focused on convincing the American public that there was no chance of war between North Vietnam and the US.

North Vietnamese General Giap suggested that the DESOTO patrol had been sent into the Gulf to provoke North Vietnam into giving an excuse for escalation of the war. Various government officials and men aboard the *Maddox* have suggested similar theories. American politicians and strategists had been planning provocative actions against North Vietnam for some time. George Ball told a British journalist after the war that "at that time . . . many people . . . were looking for any excuse to initiate bombing."

Provocative action against North Vietnam was considered after the August 1964 incidents. John McNaughton suggested in September 1964 that the US prepared to take actions to provoke a North Vietnamese military reaction, including plans to use DESOTO patrols of the coast of North Vietnam. William Bundy's paper, dated September 8, 1964, suggested more DESOTO patrols as well.

Secretary of Defense Robert McNamara failed to inform US President Lyndon B. Johnson that the US naval task group commander in the Tonkin Gulf, Captain John J. Herrick, had changed his mind about the alleged North Vietnamese torpedo attack on US warships he had reported earlier that day.

By early afternoon of August 4, Washington time, Herrick had reported to the Commander in Chief Pacific in Honolulu that "freak weather effects" on the ship's radar had made such an attack questionable. In fact, Herrick was now saying, in a message sent at 1:27 p.m. Washington time, that no North Vietnamese patrol boats had actually been sighted. Herrick now proposed a "complete evaluation before any further action taken."

McNamara later testified that he had read the message after his return to the Pentagon that afternoon. But he did not immediately call Johnson to tell him that the whole premise of his decision at lunch to approve Herrick's recommendation for retaliatory air strikes against North Vietnam was now highly questionable. Had Johnson been accurately informed about the Herrick message, he might have demanded fuller information before proceeding with a broadening of the war. Johnson had fended off proposals from McNamara and other advisers for a policy of bombing the North on four separate occasions since becoming president.

President Johnson, who was up for election that year, ordered retaliatory air strikes and went on national television on August 4 and addressed the nation. Although *Maddox* had been involved in providing intelligence support for South Vietnamese attacks at Hòn Mê and Hòn Ngư, Johnson denied, in his testimony before Congress, that the US Navy had supported South Vietnamese military operations in the Gulf. He thus characterized the attack as "unprovoked" since the ship had been in international waters.

As a result of his testimony, on August 7, Congress passed a joint resolution (H.J. RES 1145), titled the Southeast Asia Resolution, which granted President Johnson the authority to conduct military operations in Southeast Asia without the benefit of a declaration of war. The resolution gave President Johnson approval "to take all necessary steps, including the use of armed force, to assist any member or protocol state of the Southeast Asia Collective Defense Treaty requesting assistance in defense of its freedom."

In 1965, President Johnson commented privately: "For all I know, our Navy was shooting at whales out there."

In 1981, Captain Herrick and journalist Robert Scheer reexamined Herrick's ship's log and determined that the first torpedo report from August 4, which Herrick had maintained had occurred—the "apparent ambush"—was in fact unfounded.

Although information obtained well after the fact supported Captain Herrick's statements about the inaccuracy of the later torpedo reports as well as the 1981 Herrick/Scheer conclusion about the inaccuracy of the first, indicating that there was no North Vietnamese attack that night, at the time US authorities and all the *Maddox* crew stated that they were convinced that an attack had taken place. As a result, planes from the carriers *Ticonderoga* and *Constellation* were sent to hit North Vietnamese torpedo boat bases and fuel facilities during Operation Pierce Arrow.

Squadron commander James Stockdale was one of the US pilots flying overhead during the second alleged attack. Stockdale wrote in his 1984 book *Love and War*: "I had the best seat in the house to watch that event, and our destroyers were just shooting at phantom targets—there were no PT boats there . . . There was nothing there but black water and American firepower." Stockdale at one point recounts seeing *Turner Joy* pointing her guns at the *Maddox*. Stockdale said his superiors ordered him to keep quiet about this. After he was captured, this knowledge became a heavy burden. He later said he was concerned that his captors would eventually force him to reveal what he knew about the second incident.

In 1995, retired Vietnamese Defense Minister Vo Nguyen Giap, meeting with former Secretary of Defense McNamara, denied that Vietnamese gunboats had attacked American destroyers on August 4, while admitting to the attack on August 2. A taped conversation of a meeting several weeks after passage of the Gulf of Tonkin Resolution was released in 2001, revealing that McNamara expressed doubts to President Johnson that the attack had even occurred.

In the fall of 1999, retired senior CIA engineering executive S. Eugene Poteat wrote that he was asked in early August 1964 to determine if the radar operator's report showed a real torpedo boat attack or an imagined one. He asked for further details on time, weather, and surface conditions. No further details were forthcoming. In the end he concluded that there were no torpedo boats on the night in question and that the White House was interested only in confirmation of an attack, not that there was no such attack.

In the 2003 documentary *The Fog of War*, the former Secretary of Defense Robert S. McNamara admitted that the August 4 attack never happened.

In October 2012, Ret. Rear Adm. Lloyd "Joe" Vasey was interviewed by David Day on *Asia Review* and gave a detailed account of the August 4 incident. According to Admiral Vasey, who was aboard the USS *Oklahoma City*, a Galveston-class guided missile cruiser, in the Gulf of Tonkin and serving as Chief of Staff to Commander

Seventh Fleet, the USS *Turner Joy* intercepted an NVA radio transmission ordering a torpedo boat attack on the USS *Turner Joy* and the USS *Maddox*. Shortly thereafter, radar contact of "several high speed contacts closing in on them" was acquired by the USS *Turner Joy*, which locked on to one of the contacts, fired, and struck the torpedo boat. There were eighteen witnesses, both enlisted and officers, who reported various aspects of the attack: smoke from the stricken torpedo boat, torpedo wakes (reported by four separate individuals on each destroyer), sightings of the torpedo boats moving through the water and searchlights. All eighteen of the witnesses testified at a hearing in Olongapo, Philippines, and their testimony is a matter of public record.

In October 2005, the *New York Times* reported that Robert J. Hanyok, a historian for the US National Security Agency, concluded that NSA deliberately distorted intelligence reports passed to policymakers regarding the incident of August 4, 1964. He concluded the motive was not political, but rather to cover up honest intelligence errors.

Hanyok's conclusions were initially published in the winter 2000/spring 2001 edition of *Cryptologic Quarterly* about five years before the *Times* article. According to intelligence officials, the view of government historians that the report should become public was rebuffed by policymakers concerned that comparisons might be made to intelligence used to justify the Iraq War (Operation Iraqi Freedom), which commenced in 2003. Reviewing NSA's archives, Mr. Hanyok concluded that NSA initially misinterpreted North Vietnamese intercepts, believing there was an attack on August 4. Midlevel NSA officials almost immediately discovered the error, he concluded, but covered it up by altering documents to make it appear a second attack had occurred.

On November 30, 2005, NSA released a first installment of previously classified information regarding the Gulf of Tonkin incident, including a moderately sanitized version of Mr. Hanyok's article. The Hanyok article stated that intelligence information was presented to the Johnson administration "in such a manner as to preclude responsible decision makers in the Johnson administration from having the complete and objective narrative of events." Instead, "only information that supported the claim that the communists had attacked the two destroyers was given to Johnson administration officials."

With regard to why this happened, Hanyok wrote: "As much as anything else, it was an awareness that President Johnson would brook no uncertainty that could undermine his position." Faced with this attitude, Ray Cline was quoted as saying, "We knew it was bum dope that we were getting from Seventh Fleet, but we were told only to give facts with no elaboration on the nature of the evidence. Everyone knew how volatile LBJ was. He did not like to deal with uncertainties."

Eventually it became clear that Congress and the American people had been misled about Johnson's intentions. The public came to suspect that the Tonkin Gulf attacks had been a deliberate lie and ruse. The Gulf of Tonkin enigma reminds us that small events can have enormous consequences. It also challenged the North to strike directly at Americans in the South. The Tonkin Gulf Resolution would be stretched beyond its context to cover a war commitment that would result in diminishing returns. Any prewar actions can be crucial not just for their intrinsic importance but also as a golden opportunity for escalation. The Tonkin Gulf incident was one of the controversial issues and pivotal point of the Vietnam War. It was a well-planned covert military operation as part of Operation Plan 34 Alpha intended to put gradual pressure on North Vietnam that escalated and opened a Pandora's box. In addition, it was a plausible contrived scenario that served as a hair trigger for Johnson.

In a US Military Officers Association of America magazine article in 2014, it was stated that 84 percent of Americans agreed that LBJ purposely misled the nation. Admiral Jim Stockdale agrees because he was flying his F-8 Crusader overhead both US destroyers in the Gulf of Tonkin on the night of August 4, 1964. After the mission, he was debriefed in the USS *Ticonderoga* ready room and stated, "I didn't see anything except black sea and American firepower."

The Tonkin Gulf Resolution

On August 5, Johnson was enjoying an increase of public support. Opinion polls indicated that 85 percent of Americans approved and supported his bombing decision. The majority of the news media supported Johnson. In response to this new public support, Johnson's aides, including Defense Secretary McNamara, drafted a Gulf of Tonkin Resolution and lobbied Congress for quick passage.

On August 7, in response to the two Gulf of Tonkin incidents and the behest of Johnson, Congress overwhelmingly passes the resolution. This resolution will give President Johnson a free hand in the Vietnam War. In June 24, 1970, Congress repeals the 1964 Gulf of Tonkin Resolution.

Questions for Reflection

1. Why did the North Vietnamese attack the USS *Maddox* on August 2, 1964?
2. Why did the USS *Maddox* and *C. Turner Joy* link up on August 3 and resume patrolling together in the Gulf of Tonkin?
3. Was the Gulf of Tonkin a springboard to escalate the war?
4. Why was the Tonkin Gulf Resolution passed so quickly?
5. Was the Gulf of Tonkin Resolution the "smoking gun" that escalated the Vietnam War?
6. Was President Johnson too ambitious or premature when he retaliated against the North Vietnamese?

CHAPTER 5

United States Military Advisers 1950–1965

A paradigm shift and a change in venue.

The Vietnam Military Assistance Advisory Group (MAAG) was established in Saigon in 1950. The MAAG in Vietnam was joint and consisted of US Army, Navy, Air Force, and Marines. MAAG is a designation for American military advisers sent to other countries to assist in the training of conventional and unconventional armed forces. Although numerous MAAGs operated in various countries around the world throughout the 1940s–1970s, the most famous MAAGs were Vietnam MAAG before and during the Vietnam War. President Harry Truman sent the Military Assistance Advisory Group (MAAG) to Vietnam to assist the French in the First Indochina War. Its mission was to supervise the issuance and employment of $10 million of military equipment to support the French legionnaires in their effort to combat Viet Minh forces. By 1953, the amount of US military aid had jumped to over $350 million and was used to replace the badly worn World War II vintage equipment that France, still suffering economically from the devastation of that war, was still using.

The mission of the Vietnam MAAG was to

1. screen French requests for aid,
2. develop and provide combat training to the Vietnamese military,

3. recommend strategy to the Vietnamese military, and
4. provide limited field advisers to the Vietnamese military.

The French Army, however, was reluctant to take US advice and would not allow the Vietnamese Army to be trained to use the new equipment, because it went against French policy. They were supposed to not only defeat enemy forces but to solidify themselves as a colonial power, and they could not do this with a Vietnamese Army. French commanders were so reluctant to accept advice that would weaken their time-honored colonial role that they got in the way of the various attempts by the MAAG to observe where the equipment was being sent and how it was being used.

In 1954, the commanding general of French forces in Indochina, General Henri Navarre, allowed the United States to send liaison officers to Vietnamese forces. However, because of the siege and fall of Dien Bien Phu in the spring, it was too late. As stated by the Geneva Accords, France was forced to surrender the northern half of Vietnam and to withdraw from South Vietnam by April 1956. At a conference in Washington DC on February 12, 1955, between officials of the US State Department and the French Minister of Overseas Affairs, it was agreed that all US aid would be funneled directly to South Vietnam and that all major military responsibilities would be transferred from the French to the MAAG under the command of Lieutenant General John O'Daniel. A problem arose, however, because the French Expeditionary Force had to depart from South Vietnam in April 1956 pursuant to the accords.

The MAAG had the following problems and issues:

1. General de Lattre, the French general, often bypassed the MAAG for support
2. General de Lattre openly resented the MAAG and the US aid program
3. No helicopters to move Vietnam military in the field
4. French often refused MAAG training strategy

5.   French often refused to allow MAAG to advise or train Vietnamese military

6.   French had an archaic equipment record-keeping system[2]

February 1955, additional American advisers began arriving to train the South Vietnamese Army. In 1956, the US took over training of the Vietnamese military establishment and structured the South Vietnamese military after its own military. Under the direction and tutelage of the American MAAG, the new 150,000-man South Vietnamese Army gradually took shape. However, US officials misread guerilla activity, believing it to be a diversion for a conventional attack across the demilitarized zone. Thus, the new Army's mission and training centered on repelling a Korean War–type invasion from North Vietnam. The majority of training focused on fighting a mid-intensity conventional war against the North. The South Vietnamese military was only trained briefly in counterinsurgency. During this period from 1955 through 1960, the US had between 750 and 1,500 military advisers assisting the Diem government to establish an effective Army. Attacks on US military advisers in Vietnam became more frequent. In the summer of 1959, communist guerrillas staged an attack on a Vietnamese military base in Bien Hoa, killing and wounding several MAAG personnel. During this time, American advisers were not put in high-ranking positions, and President Diem was reluctant to allow American advisers into Vietnamese tactical units. He was afraid that the United States would gain control or influence over his forces if Americans got into the ranks of the Army. The first signs that his position was beginning to shift came in 1960, when the number of official US military advisers in the country was increased from 327 to 685 at the request of the South Vietnamese government.

Prior to 1960, US advisers were involved primarily in training and high-level staff work. In 1960, they began advising ground combat troops at regimental level in the field. In 1961, advisers were at the battalion level, and by 1964, they were with the paramilitary

---

[2.]   Ronald Spector, *Advice and Support* (1985), 118.

forces.[3] Gradually, US advisers became involved in combat, but by then, MAAG had been replaced by MACV. By 1960, MAAG was training more than 50 Army of the Republic of Vietnam (ARVN) ranger units. At almost the same time from 1954 through 1959, the Navy section of MAAG worked to develop a viable navy for South Vietnam. By 1961, the steady progress of the insurgency was near crisis levels. The new Kennedy administration increased American support to the Diem regime to prevent a collapse. President John F. Kennedy agreed with MAAG's calls for increases in ARVN troop levels and the US military commitment in both equipment and men. In response, Kennedy provided $28.4 million in funding for ARVN, and overall military aid increased from $50 million per year to $144 million in 1961.

By 1961, communist guerillas were becoming stronger and more active. This increased enemy contacts in size and intensity throughout South Vietnam. At this point, Diem was under pressure from US authorities to liberalize his regime and implement reforms. Although key elements in the US administration were resisting his requests for increased military funding, MAAG played a significant role in advocating for a greater US presence in the country. Throughout this period, relations between the MAAG and Diem were described as "excellent," even though the advisers were doubtful of his ability to hold off the insurgency. MAAG problems and issues were the following:

1. MAAG inherited poorly trained ARVN
2. ARVN had no national spirit and had low morale
3. ARVN had few or little technical skills or specialties
4. ARVN had legacy equipment and weapons
5. ARVN was apprehensive that Americans would remain as a colonial force and power
6. ARVN was trained for a conventional war, not counterinsurgency

---

[3.] David Hachberstam, *The Making of a Quagmire* (2008), 47.

7. President Diem micromanaged the military, didn't use the military chain of command, and promoted loyal officers over professional competent officers
8. President Diem constantly shuffled colonels and generals
9. No helicopters to move military on operations

In the first year of the Kennedy administration, MAAG worked closely with administration officials and the US Information Service to develop a counterinsurgency plan (CIP). The CIP's main initiatives included the strengthening of ARVN to combat the communist insurgency, which had the corollary effect of strengthening Diem's political position. At the same time, President Diem agreed to the assignment of advisers to battalion level, significantly increasing the number of advisers: from 746 in 1961 to over 3,400 before MAAG was placed under US Military Assistance Command Vietnam (MACV) and renamed the Field Advisory Element, Vietnam. By December of 1961, 3,200 US military personnel were in Vietnam as advisers, supported by $65 million in military equipment and $136 million in economic aid.

Military assistance was reorganized as the United States Military Assistance Command Vietnam (MACV), formed under the command of General Paul D. Hawkins in February 1962.[4] MACV was there to support the Army of the Republic of Vietnam (ARVN) to defend the country. In addition, MACV was a subordinate unified command under the commander in chief, Pacific controlling units and military personnel in South Vietnam. MACV included Special Forces instructors and CIA personnel organizing the Montagnards in the mountains. By 1963, US military advisers in Vietnam had grown to sixteen thousand.

At the peak of the war in 1968, 9,430 Army personnel acted as advisers down to the district and battalion level to train, advise, and mentor the Army of the Republic of Vietnam (ARVN), Republic of

---

[4] Graham A. Cosmas, *MACV: The Joint Command in the Years of Escalation, 1962–1967* (1991), 21–35.

Vietnam Marine Corps, Republic of Vietnam Navy, and the Vietnam Air Force.

Advisers may have been sufficient until 1975. However, due to deeply imbedded social and other reasons, the South Vietnamese were adamantly against and persistently resisted much of the recommendations from US advisers.

While Army Special Forces gained fame early on, that was not the case with MACV personnel. Unheralded MACV special detachment officers and NCOs, however, often bore the brunt of VC and NVA attacks while advising ARVN units in the field. In fact, they—not the Green Berets—sustained the highest number of killed in action in a single firefight during the official years of America's advisory campaign in South Vietnam.

MAAG Vietnam was commanded by Lt. Gen. Samuel T. Williams, November 1955–September 1960; Lt. Gen. Lionel C. McGarr, September 1960–July 1962; and Maj. Gen. Charles J. Timmes, July 1962–May 1964.

Questions for Reflection

1. Explain why the US alone could not prevent the spread of communism in South Vietnam.
2. Why were the French reluctant to take US advice and not authorize the Americans to train the South Vietnamese military?
3. Explain the consequences for the French when they lost the battle of Dien Bien Phu.
4. Why did the US military train the South Vietnamese military in mid-intensity conventional war and not counterinsurgency?

CHAPTER 6

The Air War
Helicopters and Fixed Wing

Those magnificent men and their flying machines.

Helicopters

The advent of the helicopter in the early twentieth century had a profound impact on transportation, communication, and myriad of other areas of human endeavor. Combat and warfare also experienced an important transformation at the operational and tactical levels as a result of rotary wing technology. Helicopters are diverse and afforded rapid transportation of fighting forces and logistics on the battlefield. They also evolved to perform a much larger role as an efficient and deadly weapons platform, and conducted critical medical evacuation and search and rescue operations. The evolution of the military helicopter mirrors the rapid changes of American society while still reflecting Americans' faith in technology and efficiency.

The United States military first employed and experimented with helicopters in combat during the Second World War. When downed American bombers in Burma could not be reached by the vaunted American glider forces, helicopters were called in and successfully extracted the flight crews. Military planners immediately recognized the immense potential of the helicopter and focused on developing a rotary wing force to bolster the American arsenal. The Korean War witnessed a much wider usage of helicopters, mostly with the H-13 and its role in the medical evacuation of wounded personnel to field hospitals. The H-13 helicopter is the MEDEVAC helicopter used on the TV series *M*A*S*H*. In addition, the H-13 was used in minor troop insertions and in a limited reconnaissance role also.

Air Mobile Warfare

During the Vietnam War, the United States relied on the helicopter as never before. The helicopter's role in combat expanded enormously in this war as thousands of "choppers" rapidly transported personnel throughout the war zone. Heavily armed helicopters offered a fearsome component to ground operations as close air support. Mobility and firepower would be the keys for American operations in Vietnam, and the helicopter provided an abundance of both. But the role of the helicopter in support activities in the Vietnam War must not be overlooked as thousands of missions were flown to resupply and reinforce troops on the ground, to evacuate American and allied wounded, and to offer countless other services in pursuance of the war effort.

Helicopters transformed combat in South Vietnam. Not only was Vietnam the first war in which the Army and Marines deployed armed helicopters, but bigger, faster, and more dependable helicopters revolutionized moving troops, evacuating the wounded, commanding the battlefield, and conducting search and rescue.

"The loss of 110 helicopters in Laos late in the war and improvements in hand-held antiaircraft weapons raised questions about future Army use of helicopters that wouldn't be resolved for years," says author and scholar Ed Raines Jr., a former historian at the US Army Center of Military History for thirty-one years.

US helicopters that began arriving in South Vietnam in 1961 had better engines, more armor, and better fuel range and carried more crew. These choppers were initially armed only with light machine guns. A year later, Army assault helicopters had 30-caliber machine guns and 2.75 rocket launchers. Later, the M-60 machine gun replaced the 30-caliber. The Army gunships became the first true attack helicopter. These attack helicopters could provide even closer air support than the Air Force. In addition, the Army attack helicopters could arrive on station sooner than the Air Force and remain on station longer than the Air Force.

Helicopters proved their worth under fire in Southeast Asia. Successes included the 1965 Ia Drang Valley campaign, the relief of Khe Sanh in 1968, and moving the 1st Cavalry Division from northern South Vietnam to the Saigon area during Operation Liberty Canyon in the fall of 1968.

Meanwhile, the Marine Corps deployed its first designated helicopter attack squadrons in Vietnam, says Hill Goodspeed, historian for the National Naval Aviation Museum. Introduced in the early 1970s, the HMA-369 squadron flew interdiction missions off the coast of North Vietnam using AH-1J Sea Cobras. The Navy's Seawolves used UH-1 and Huey HH-1K helicopters armed with machine guns and rockets to support its riverine forces in South Vietnam.

Helicopters made an even more remarkable difference in medical evacuations in South Vietnam. In Korea, almost all Army casualties were carried in litters strapped to the outside of helicopters. Bigger and better helicopters meant that Vietnam casualties were carried inside the helicopter and received in flight medical care from a corpsman, medic, or doctor. At the peak of combat in 1968, 116 Army air ambulances were performing medical evacuation flights. They often meant the difference between life and death, Major General Spurgeon Neel Jr., chief of the aviation branch within the Office of the Surgeon General, reported after the war. "The most seriously wounded usually reached a hospital within one to two hours after they were injured," Neel said. More than 97 percent of the wounded who made it to a medical facility survived.

In May 1972, UH-1C Huey gunships armed with the new TOW missile system brought a whole new dimension to the Army's use of helicopter airpower in combat. Two UH-1Cs knocked out eight of the ten North Vietnamese tanks that broke through South Vietnamese defenses during the siege of Kontum. Overall, the two Hueys were credited with knocking out twenty-four North Vietnamese tanks during a two-month tour.

This success however was overshadowed by the loss of 110 helicopters during Operation Lam Son 719 in southeastern Laos late in the war. That called into question the ability of helicopters to survive where the enemy had sophisticated air defenses such as the NATO central front, where the Army focused after Vietnam. Army aviation pioneer Lieutenant General John J. Tolson concluded that the most important lesson the Army learned from the Vietnam War was that helicopters and the air mobility they provided are here to stay. Despite doubts about survivability, Tolson was right. Truly, the Vietnam War was the Helicopter War.

The most common helicopters used in the Vietnam War are listed below.

UH-1 Iroquois: Known affectionately as the Huey. The Huey was the workhorse in Southeast Asia. It was used for troop transport, resupply, medical evacuations, and reconnaissance.

CH-47: Known as the Chinook or Hook. The Hook was a medium lift helicopter that was used for troop transport, cargo, and resupply.

CH-54: Known as the Sky Crane. The Sky Crane was used for moving heavy cargo.

AH-1: Know as the Cobra or Snake. The Cobra was a close air support attack helicopter.

OH-6: Known as the LOH, Loach, Flying Egg, and when equipped for combat, they were called Killer Eggs. The OH-6 was used for scouting, observation, personnel transport, attack, and escort.

OH-58: Known as the Kiowa. The Kiowa was used for observation, reconnaissance, and small-attack helicopters.

CH-53: Known as the Jolly Green Giant. The Jolly Green Giant could refuel in flight, had a special hoist and other special equipment. It was well suited for search-and-rescue missions in Southeast Asia.

Fixed Wing

The air war in Southeast Asia faced many challenges. The on-again, off-again bombing strategy of President Johnson's administration did more to enhance North Vietnam's defenses than it did to weaken the enemy's resolve. Commanders were reluctant to shift B-52 bombers from nuclear deterrence to attacking North Vietnam. And controversy over the bombing of North Vietnam and Cambodia fueled the protest movement at home. Vietnam also marked the end of an aviation era. It was the last time the United States sent significant numbers of propeller-driven aircraft into combat, from fighters such as the A-1 Skyraider to forward air control planes like the 0-1 Bird Dog and flying boats like the Navy's SP-5B Marlin.

Ultimately, the Air Force and Navy adapted to the demands of the day. Abandoned production plants were resurrected, and training was revamped. Jet pilots found themselves flying single-engine Cessnas at one hundred miles per hour. Training planes that served as fighter-bombers and transport planes were turned into gunships. However, the Air Force and Navy emerged from the Vietnam War armed with the first generation of smart bombs, better aircraft, and a renewed appreciation for aerial combat training. The Air Force and Navy had a complete makeover. They shifted from a massive retaliatory nuclear force to a force able to operate across the entire spectrum. That success ultimately led to overwhelming US success in the first Gulf War.

The Air Force and Navy flew missions in Southeast Asia well before the United States committed large numbers of ground troops to the war. C-47 transports ferried US military advisers and supplies around South Vietnam beginning in the mid-1950s. C-123 Provider transport planes were charged with spraying Agent Orange in 1962.

In the South, Air Force and Navy pilots continued to fly close air support missions. Forward air control controllers in small single-engine airplanes provided the link between the troops on the ground in contact with the enemy and the fighter-bombers in the air. The Air Force and Navy were turning into an all-jet force but was still having trouble finding targets. Other air missions included flying missions over Laos and Cambodia hunting North Vietnamese supply trucks, training sites, and storage sites and patrolling the sea-lanes off South Vietnam.

The Air Force and Navy also made significant technological strides during Vietnam. Three new models of the F-4 were introduced during seven years of aerial combat, each better than the previous version. Three different laser-guided bomb improvements were introduced in a three-year period. Both the Air Force and Navy pilots came away from Vietnam with the realization that jet pilots had to be experts in air-to-air combat. That prompted the creation of schools devoted to air-to-air combat tactics, techniques, and procedures. These new learned procedures speak for themselves. During the Gulf War, the Air Force had thirty-five kills and no aircraft losses. No Air Force or Navy fighter received a scratch from an Iraqi fighter.

Operation Pierce Arrow was conducted in August 1964 as a result of the Gulf of Tonkin incident. After the Gulf of Tonkin incident, President Johnson immediately ordered retaliatory air strikes against targets in North Vietnam. Sixty-four sorties were flown from the US Navy aircraft carriers *Ticonderoga* and *Constellation* against North Vietnamese vessels along the coast and petroleum storage facilities at Vinh. The Vinh petroleum storage facility was destroyed. Reportedly, twenty-five PT boats and their facilities were destroyed. Most of the coastal vessels attacked were Swatow boats. Pierce Arrow was a tactical success but not without cost. Two US aircraft were shot down. Richard Sather was the first naval aviator killed in the air war. Flying his A-111 Skyraider off the USS *Constellation*, Sather was hit by flak conducting an air mission near Loc Choc Harbor North Vietnam on August 5, 1964. Both sides claimed victory. The American public overwhelmingly approved of the air strikes. President Johnson's public approval rating soared to 72 percent.

Operation Flaming Dart began in February 1965 as a result of a Viet Cong mortar attack against a US helicopter base at Camp Holloway near Pleiku, resulting in 8 American military KIA, wounding another 109 and damaging or destroying 20 aircraft. President Johnson ordered air strikes north of the 17th parallel as a reprisal air raid. Subsequently, in February, Johnson ordered Flaming Dart

II. Flaming Dart II was a series of air strikes against the North in response to the Viet Cong killing twenty-three Americans at Qui Nhon. Flaming Dart II was the onset of Rolling Thunder.

Operation Rolling Thunder launched one of the first high-profile air campaigns against North Vietnam. Crafted by President Johnson and Defense Secretary McNamara, the bombing effort was stopped several times to induce North Vietnam to abandon its war against the South. Instead, the North Vietnamese used the intermissions to strengthen its antiaircraft defenses and move additional supplies into South Vietnam. Meanwhile, the Air Force and Navy were prohibited from striking North Vietnam's air bases, key ports such as Haiphong Harbor, and many power plants and industrial sites for fear of civilian casualties or inadvertent bombing of Soviet and Chinese boats. In the end, Rolling Thunder cost the Air Force 531 airplanes; and 547 airmen were killed, captured, or went missing in action. The air campaign also failed to dissuade North Vietnam. Pilots would state, "It is difficult when you are fighting with one hand tied behind your back."

President Nixon authorized Operation Linebacker I and II in 1972. The Navy's new A-6 dropped laser guided bombs on power plants and industrial sites while Navy A-7s mined Haiphong Harbor. Waves of B-52 bombarded Hanoi and other parts of North Vietnam previously off-limits. By early 1973, North Vietnam agreed to end the war and return the American POWs. American decided they were going to employ airpower without any restrictions for about five months. It was a superb demonstration of what airpower can do when properly allied.

I am Richard (Rick) Hedrick and enlisted in the United States Air Force in March 1967 while I was 18 years old. My technical school training was at Sheppard Air Force Base Texas. I was trained as an aircraft mechanic. After 7 months I was sent to South Vietnam. I served in South Vietnam from October 26, 1967-October 26, 1968 in the 458th Tactical Airlift Squadron (Air Force) at Cam Ranh Bay. After 2 months I was awarded the title of crew chief and assigned a Caribou to crew. The C7A Caribou was a light to medium cargo lift fixed wing aircraft. Our Caribous carried almost anything you could load into the aircraft. Our normal daily load consisted of ammunition, weapons, C-rations, soft drinks, beer, soldiers and paratroopers. Occasionally we carried live animals such as cows, pigs and chickens. These were airdropped by parachute to troops on the ground for fresh meat. These units were primary the 5th Special Forces Group operating on some far out isolated A camp near the Cambodian or Laos border.

My major duty was to keep my Caribou in the air flying. As a crew chief I supervised all phases of having my plane air worthy 24/7. I would arrive at the flight line at O dark thirty (day light) and prepare my Caribou for morning launch at 0600 (6 AM). I split my time preparing other planes for launch and flying missions in the cargo compartment. If we had an airdrop I would always fly and push the pallets and bundles out the rear of the aircraft. We flew into many primitive dirt airfields on hill sides and jungles. The Caribou was designed to land and take off on these rudimentary and austere airfields. Some of the airfields were Nha Trang, Phu Cat, Vung Tau, Da Nang, An Kne, Chu Lai, Tuy Hoa, Phan Rang and Pleiku. There were many others but I can't recall their names.

We usually returned to Cam Ranh Bay anywhere from 1700 (5 PM) to 2100 (9 PM). After landing I would do a post flight inspection of the aircraft to check for any damage from ground fire, oil or fuel leaks, hydraulic leaks, landing gear issues or bird strike damage. I also had to write up any requests from the pilots that required a specialist for engine, prop, instrument or flight control problems that could ground the aircraft. When all problems were corrected I had the plane refueled and it was released to fly the next day. After my ground duties were completed I went to the chow hall, then a cold shower because no hot water was available. If it wasn't too late I would down a *few beers and maybe a hand of Black Jack before I sacked out. After a very short night of sleep usually 4-5 hours I started all over again. The only break in the daily routine was an occasional mortar or rocket attack.*

Some of my favorite times in South Vietnam were spent on temporary duty at Nha Trang supporting the 5th Special Forces. While there I lived in a sandbag bunker, ate with the Green Berets and partied with them. These were a great bunch of guys. In the early morning we linked up with our Caribous, loaded them and flew the missions into enemy territory.

I completed my tour and returned to the United States where I was cross trained on C-141 Cargo Jets. The C-141 is a heavy lift cargo and long range jet aircraft. I was assigned to Norton Air Force Base, California. I remained there for 2 and ½ years as a crew chief on flying status flying in the C-141s.

My service in South Viet became the proudest time of my 4 years in the Air Force. I would do it all over again. No regrets.

Richard (Rick) Hedrick
Montrose, West Virginia

The most common US fixed wing aircraft flown in South Vietnam are listed below.

B-52: Known as BUFF. BUFF was a large strategic bomber and was reconfigured to drop large loads of bombs on the enemy in North and South Vietnam.

C-47: This airplane ferried troops and supplies in the '50s and early '60s. Later it was turned in a gunship that provided close air support.

C-123: Known as the Provider. The Provider was used to spray Agent Orange across South Vietnam. It also transported troops and cargo.

C-130: Known as the Hercules. The Hercules was the workhorse in the Vietnam War. It carried troops and cargo. Some C-130s

74

were converted to gunships that provided close air support to troops on the ground.

C-141: Known as the Starlifter. The Starlifter provided jet-powered capability to the Air Force. It could carry large loads of troops and cargo.

F-4: Know as the Phantom. The Phantom provided close air support, reconnaissance, and was a MIG killer.

F-100: An Air Force fighter and bomber that provided close air support.

KC-135: This jet refueled the fighter and bombers and kept them on station longer.

O-1: Known as the Bird Dog. The Bird Dog was one of the smallest aircraft deployed in Vietnam. The Bird Dog was used to find targets, direct fire and bombers for close air support.

O-2: Known as the Sky Master. The Sky Master was a push-and-pull small plane used to find targets, direct fire and bombers for close air support.

OV-10: Known as the Bronco. The Bronco was used by the Air Force, Army, Navy, and Marines in various roles but primary in directing bombers for close air support.

The most common North Vietnamese jet was the MIG-21. The subsonic Soviet MIG-17 was the premier North Vietnamese jet fighter that had defended the homeland astonishingly well since 1964. By the end of 1967, the North Vietnamese began receiving the new Soviet MIG-21. The new MIG-21s were heavily engaged in the climactic air battles of Operation Linebacker I and II. The North Vietnamese had thirteen known air aces. The premier air ace of North Vietnam was Nguyen Van Coca, who claimed to have shot down seven US jets and two drones.

Questions for Reflection

1. How did the helicopter change warfare as related to technology of war machines?
2. Was Operation Pierce Arrow a success?

3. Was Operation Flaming Dart a reprisal air strike or the onset of Operation Rolling Thunder?
4. Why was Operation Rolling Thunder a failure?
5. Why was Operation Linebacker I and II a success?

CHAPTER 7

President Johnson's Dilemma:
Escalate or Restraint and Détente

You have to know when to hold 'em and when to fold 'em.

"If we get involved in that bitch of a war, my Great Society will be dead," President Johnson said this to his biographer.

Decades after the fall of Saigon, Americans have asked why President Johnson committed troops, escalated the war, and propelled the US into a quagmire.

Initially, during the early to late 1940s, the US government did not view Ho Chi Minh and the communist movement in Vietnam as a threat to US or allied nations. However, in 1949, the White House had a new radical perspective of Ho Chi Minh and communism. Alliances and partnerships between the Soviet Union and the US began to erode and unravel. The new concern and threat to the US and her allies was the Cold War with all the ramifications. Although Ho Chi Minh was not a direct threat to the US and her allies, Ho was increasingly viewed as a puppet and proxy surrogate advised and supported by the Kremlin. The US decided to oppose Ho and defeat him at all costs.

Early in 1950, Ho Chi Minh went to Beijing, China, and brokered an agreement that provided Chinese advisers and military aid to the Vietminh for their struggle in Indochina. This aid included automatic weapons, mortars, howitzers, and trucks. With this new external military support, General Giap developed and deployed the first Viet Minh Army Division.

In January 1953, Dwight D. Eisenhower is inaugurated as the thirty-fourth president of the United States. President Eisenhower will greatly increase US aid to the French to prevent a communist victory. America's aid will include military advisers, military logistics, and financial support to suppress a new domino theory. This new domino theory will be used by future US presidents to justify increasing escalation and US involvement in Vietnam.

Later in 1953, the French construct a series of outposts to protect a small airfield in a jungle isolated valley near Dien Bien Phu. General Giap immediately masses troops, artillery, and logistics in the hills surrounding Dien Bien Phu. On May 7, 1954, the French surrendered. President Eisenhower refused any US military support for the French during the siege.

In July, the Geneva Accords divide Vietnam at the 17th parallel. Ho Chi Minh and the communists are in the North and Bai Dai is in the South. In 1959, the Second Indochina War begins as Ho Chi Minh declares a People's War to unite all of Vietnam.

John F. Kennedy is inaugurated as the thirty-fifth president of the US in 1961. Kennedy very quickly increased military aid and increased funds to increase the ARVN military. This aid included four hundred American Special Forces Green Berets to train the ARVN military in counterinsurgency tactics, techniques, and procedures. Kennedy later increases the number of US military advisers to sixteen thousand and in addition sends American military helicopter units to transport the ARVN forces directly into battle.

Kennedy was assassinated in 1963, and Vice President Johnson was sworn in as the thirty-sixth president.

Johnson is the fourth president that copes with the Vietnam dilemma. Johnson inherited a rapidly deteriorating situation in South Vietnam from Kennedy. Johnson will escalate gradually because he doesn't want to jeopardize his reelection in 1964. Johnson also knows that he must support the Kennedy commitment to South Vietnam. He will direct and oversee a massive escalation of the war. A US intelligence report said that the Viet Cong now had control of up to 45 percent of South Vietnam. At the Pentagon, the US Chiefs of Staff adamantly recommended a strong air strike against the North. Johnson rejected these air strikes and opted for Operational Plan (OPLAN) 34-A. OPLAN 34-A established the Military Assistance Command Vietnam-Studies and Observation Group (MACVSOG).[5] This was a highly classified multiservice US special operations unit that conducted covert unconventional warfare operations prior to and during the Vietnam War. By midsummer, senior Johnson administration officials realized that Congress and Americans had to prepare for stronger action to reverse the rapid deteriorating economic and ARVN military situation in the South. The new government under General Big Minh was inexperienced. Although popular, he lacked economic and military vision and leadership. In January 1964, Big Minh was overthrown. US intelligence sources reported that enemy attacks and raids were up and increasing in the South Vietnam countryside. The popular strategic Hamlet Program became lethargic, wasn't cost-effective, and was halted. In addition, intelligence sources reported that the Viet Cong controlled about 40 to 45 percent of the countryside. Internally, tensions increased between the Buddhists and Catholics, especially in Saigon and the larger cities. Mountain minorities in the Central Highlands exhibited tension and friction also. President Johnson was seeking a "smoking gun" to increase economic and military aid to South Vietnam and to inch closer to war. The pretext came in early August when North Vietnamese patrol boats attacked US naval destroyers in the Gulf of Tonkin. This blatant sea attack against US naval destroyers was the impetus for Johnson to escalate the war.

Shortly after the controversial Gulf of Tonkin attack, Johnson authorized limited air strikes against North Vietnam against selected targets.[6] With political prodding, the Gulf of Tonkin Resolution was passed soon with little discussion. This resolution virtually gave Johnson carte blanche for unlimited military action.

[5.] Larry Berman, *Planning a Tragedy* (1982), 32. President Johnson approved covert operations along the North Vietnamese coast. OPLAN 35A was a progressive escalation of pressure against North Vietnam.

[6.] Brian Van DeMark (1991), 17–18.

In Johnson's presidential bid, he did not want to appear to be "soft on communism," yet he desired not to be labeled as a warmonger concerning Vietnam. Johnson's hypothesis was that the US would be in a limited part-time war. After the Gulf of Tonkin bombing reprisal, American opinion polls were 85 percent favorable. During Johnson's campaign, he stated, "We are not about to send American boys nine or ten thousand miles away from home to do what Asian boys ought to be doing for themselves."

Johnson was naive and failed to understand the tenacity of the North Vietnamese. Prior to the November election, another South Vietnam Coup is thwarted, and Soviet leader Nikita Khrushchev is ousted and replaced by Leonid Brezhnev as leader of the USSR. Responding to US escalation, China tests its first A-Bomb and masses troops on its Vietnam border. The VC increase attacks in the countryside, including the first attack against Americans at Bien Hoa Air Base, about twelve miles North of Saigon. This night mortar attack kills five Americans, two South Vietnamese and wounds nearly one hundred others. Johnson refuses a retaliatory air strike against the North.

In November, President Johnson wins by a landslide. During the first several months of his new term, the situation in South Vietnam worsened as ten thousand NVA soldiers slowly begin arriving in the Central Highlands. The NVA infiltration is completed in December. These fresh NVA soldiers have modern weapons and arms provided by the Soviet Union and China. Their mission is to infuse with the VC battalions and provide arms and leadership. On Christmas Eve, the VC exploded a car bomb at the Brinks Hotel, a popular American officer residence in Saigon. The bomb explodes at 5:45 p.m. during "happy hour" prime time. Several Americans are killed, and fifty-eight are wounded. Johnson refuses a retaliatory air strike against the North.

In January 1965, Johnson is sworn in and states, "We can never again stand aside, prideful in isolation. Terrific dangers and troubles that we once called 'foreign' now constantly live among us." Senior administration officials and aides tell Johnson that the US is not winning in South Vietnam and to either escalate or withdraw. After several attacks against American facilities in South Vietnam, Johnson states, "I've had enough of this." Because of the drastic, almost catastrophic situation in South Vietnam, Johnson emulated President Kennedy and renewed an improved offensive plan a la an enhanced version of Project Beef Up.

Air Escalation

Operation Flaming Dart begins in February 1965 and is the beginning of escalation. Operation Flaming Dart bombs the NVA camp near Dong Hoi by US Navy jets.[7] Later in February, Johnson approves General Westmoreland's request for two battalions of Marines to guard the American air base at Da Nang. Operation Rolling Thunder begins in March. Planned to last for two months, Operation Rolling Thunder will continue for three years and includes air strikes against the Ho Chi Minh trail. Bombing the trail did little to stop or impede the tremendous flow of logistics and NVA soldiers from the North. Napalm was authorized by Johnson for Operation Rolling Thunder. Napalm is a petroleum-based jelly organic solvent explosive. Operation Rolling Thunder costs the US one thousand aircraft, hundreds of prisoners of war, and hundreds of airman killed or missing in action. Although the US flew almost a million sorties and dropped nearly three quarters of a million tons of bombs, Operation Rolling Thunder failed to achieve its two major political and military objectives: strategic persuasion and interdiction.[8]

There are five primary reasons for the failure of Operation Rolling Thunder.

First: North Vietnam was not an industrial or agricultural country and was not vulnerable to the World War II carpet bombing. General LeMay, the architect of Operation Rolling Thunder, equated bicycle shops, vegetable stands, and open-air flea markets to the Panzer factories of Nazi Germany and Zero factories of Imperial

---

[7] Ibid., 64–65.
[8] George C. Henning, *America's Longest War* (1979), 173–178.

Japan. In addition, North Vietnam had no war-making industries; they relied on Soviet and Chinese military aid.

Second: President Johnson did not trust his generals and imposed political constraints on the bombing, fearing the Soviets and Chinese may enter the war. China had just exploded their first atomic bomb, and Johnson was fearful of this atomic threat. China had no atomic delivery means and was not a nuclear foe to be feared. Analysts can only imagine China transporting an atomic bomb down the Ho Chi Minh with porters, oxcarts, elephants, or bicycles.

Third: President Johnson and his administration did not understand the Guerilla Stone Age environment. Although the North was a primitive society and a third world country, they were very innovative and tenacious. The North was united in its war goals, objectives and was a very determined foe. General LeMay designed an air campaign that would bomb the North "back to the Stone Age." The North was already in the Stone Age. Their "Stone Age" society was stoic and content with mere basic needs. From the onset of the bombing, the North mobilized and used active and passive defensive measures. The earth opened up in the North, and the guerilla society and culture moved underground. Oil and fuel were transferred to fifty-five-gallon barrels and cached underground and in caves. Some utilities were buried, and redundant systems were established and moved to suburbs. Tunnel complexes for living became common. Most of the populace had their own personal bomb shelter. Bunkers were built on main streets for protection. Manholes in the streets were redesigned to be emergency backup bomb shelters. The North built their defensive systems in depth and with deception systems. Smaller bamboo bridges were built faster than the US could bomb the larger highway bridges. They used ferries and small boats to transport military, logistics, and vehicles. Bicycles were reconfigured to transport supplies, arms, and logistics down the Ho Chi Minh trail. Approximately 170,000 Chinese and additional North Vietnamese women work crews repaired and maintained the Ho Chi Minh trail and roads in the North with basic pioneer tools. The "Stone Agers" were resilient, Spartan, and impervious to the bombing that lived under austere conditions and did not need much to survive. In the end, Operation Rolling Thunder emboldened and united the North.

Fourth: The Northern bombing plan was not commensurate to World War II bombing plans where the US and allies bombed both military and civilian targets. Operation Rolling Thunder did not include bombing all the key terrain targets. In both North and South Vietnam, the key terrain was the populace. In the South, the US did a commendable job stabilizing the economy and winning the hearts and minds of the population. If Operation Rolling Thunder had included bombing the population centers along with the military targets, the war would have ended in six months. General Giap's memoirs and Operation Linebacker I and II substantiate this statement. Johnson's bombing halts, and moratorium was impetuous for Hanoi to tough it out a little longer.

Fifth: It was common knowledge at Da Nang Air Base, South Vietnam, in 1966 and 1967 that the Viet Cong knew where and when the Air Force would bomb. Most of the F-105 pilots flew out of Thailand. They had to fly a given route, at a specified altitude, and at a specified time. President Johnson once bragged "our aircraft cannot bomb an outhouse without my approval." Nearly twenty years later, former Secretary of State Dean Rusk was being interviewed by Peter Arnett on a CBS documentary called *The Ten Thousand Day War*. Mr Arnett asked, "It has been rumored that the United States provided the North Vietnamese government the names of the targets that would be bombed the following day. Is there any truth to that allegation?" To everyone's astonishment and absolute disgust, the former Secretary responded, "Yes. We didn't want to harm the North Vietnamese people, so we passed the targets to the Swiss embassy in Washington with instructions to pass them to the NVN government through their embassy in Hanoi." As we watched in horror, Secretary Rusk went on to say, "All we wanted to do is demonstrate to the North Vietnamese leadership that we could strike targets at will, but we didn't want to kill innocent people. By giving the North Vietnamese advanced warning of the targets to be attacked, we thought they would tell the workers to stay home." No wonder all the targets were so heavily defended day after day! The

NVN obviously moved as many guns as they could overnight to better defend each target they knew was going to be attacked. Clearly, many brave American Air Force and Navy fliers died or spent years in NVN prison camps as a direct result of being intentionally betrayed by Secretary Rusk and Secretary McNamara—and perhaps President Johnson himself. I cannot think of a more deceitful and treacherous act of American government officials. Dean Rusk served as Secretary of State from January 21, 1961, through to January 20, 1969, under President John F. Kennedy and Lyndon B. Johnson. Perhaps Senator John McCain, POW for five years and presidential candidate in 2008, was one of the many victims of the irresponsible and flawed policy flowing from President Lyndon B. Johnson. Mr. Peter Arnett opined that "this would be a treasonous act by anyone else."

In March 1968, President Johnson scales back the bombing and restricts the air strikes to the southern panhandle of North Vietnam. Johnson ended the northern bombing campaign shortly prior to the 1968 presidential elections. This bombing halt was Johnson's attempt to bolster Hubert H. Humphrey's bid for president.

Ground Escalation

After Operation Rolling Thunder began, Johnson almost immediately began the ground buildup of Army soldiers and Marines.[9] Initially, these troop buildups were separate Army and Marine brigades deployed for the mission of protecting several major air bases. They also conducted limited security patrols around the air bases. During early 1966, additional Army troops and Marines deployed to South Vietnam. In 1966, large-scale search-and-destroy operations were conducted against the Viet Cong and NVA with success. Johnson later changed the search-and-destroy logo to reconnaissance in force to appease the America public and for political correctness. By year's end, US troop levels would reach 389,000 with 5,008 dead and over 30,000 wounded. In 1967, General Westmoreland continues requesting large sums of additional military to reinforce current

---

[9.] Spencer C. Tucker, Encyclopedia of the Vietnam War, 1998, page 195

military operations. Johnson refuses to send large contingents but opts to send an additional 45,000. By year's end, US troop levels reach 463,000 with 16,000 combat deaths. In January 1968, Johnson sends reinforcements to Khe Sanh, and General Westmoreland again requests several hundred thousand troops. Again, Johnson denies his request and sends a mere token of 13,500 troops. US troop strength topped out at 495,000 at the end of 1968 with 30,000 deaths. Richard M. Nixon is sworn in as the 37th president in January 1969. Johnson's dilemma and his prosecution of the Vietnam War ends.

Detente

Johnson halted the bombing of the North seven times prior to stopping the bombing in 1968. These pauses had the same objective, to bring the North Vietnamese to the table and negotiate a peace settlement. The North Vietnamese ignored these peace offerings and used the pauses to repair and replace air defenses and infiltrate more troops and logistics into the South via the Ho Chi Minh trail. The North Vietnamese denounced several of these bombing halts as a trick and continued Viet Cong and NVA operations and attacks in the South. In October 1966, Johnson conducts a peace conference in Manila with South Vietnam allies. The allies declare that they will withdraw from South Vietnam within six months if North Vietnam withdraws completely from the South. During a public speech in 1967, Johnson publically urges North Vietnam to negotiate a peace settlement. Later in the year, Johnson makes another peace request, which is immediately rejected by North Vietnam. In March 1968, Johnson ends the bombing of the North, and peace negations begin. The bombing halt only affects targets North of the 20th parallel and included Hanoi. In May, peace talks stall and will be on-again, off-again for the next five years. After Richard M. Nixon is inaugurated, he immediately gets the Paris peace talks on track with the US, North Vietnam, South Vietnam, and the Viet Cong in attendance.

Epilogue

Since the fall of Saigon to communist North Vietnamese forces in April 1975, Americans have not been able to agree on how to characterize President Johnson's involvement and commitment in the Vietnam War. Some Americans think the Vietnam War was a forfeit, a just war, and lost by Johnson, ingenious policymakers and a biased media. Others will say the Vietnam War was a tragic mistake brought about by Johnson, who exaggerated the influence of communism, feared the domino theory, and underestimated the tenacity of a guerilla jungle environment and culture.

The Vietnam War was a proxy sidebar conflict of the Cold War. The Cold War began and ended without direct military conflict between the US and Russia. Both countries used superior military forces and nuclear weapons as deterrents. Both countries used surrogate countries as Vietnam, Cuba, Korea, and Free China as hotspots for low-level operations through economic embargoes, arms races, propaganda, and proxy wars and conflicts. During the Cold War, the US and its allies responded to aggressive meddling by communist bloc nations with dramatic displays of American resolve.

Pundits and historians agree with other critics who claim that the United States should have been more aggressive toward North Vietnam. In 1978, Admiral William Sharp wrote, "Why were we not permitted to win?" The Vietnam War was an enigma, a protracted and intricate unchanging part of US history. The first casualty of the Vietnam War was truth. The first domino of the domino theory was President Johnson.

Questions for Reflection

1. Why did President Johnson not seek reelection?
2. Define the domino theory.
3. Define the South Vietnamese Hamlet Program.
4. Explain why Operation Rolling Thunder was or was not successful.

5. Define the North Vietnam Guerilla environment.
6. Why were Johnson's moratoriums a failure?
7. Define the North Vietnamese external military and economic support.

CHAPTER 8

Conventional Ground Combat Operations

We are not about to send American boys nine or
ten thousand miles away from home to do what
Asian boys ought to be doing for themselves.

—President Johnson

In March and April 1965, President Johnson committed US major ground combat forces to the war in South Vietnam. This escalation of combat forces was to bolster US and allied defenses in South Vietnam. Up to this point, American support and troops consisted primarily of financial, advisory, and logistics support to the South Vietnamese government and military. The first conventional combat troops were the US Marines and the Army's 173rd Airborne Brigade. Later in the spring of 1965, the US Army Chief of Staff General Johnson went to South Vietnam on a fact-finding mission. General Johnson returned home and presented the president a report that contained twenty-one recommendations. The number one recommendation was to deploy additional combat troops to South Vietnam.

Early reports on ARVN military operations were negative and stated that the ARVN could not survive without additional US combat forces. The US military began a steady troop increase in South Vietnam. In the summer of 1965, General Westmoreland devised a strategy of attrition, and his major tactic was search-and-destroy operations. According to the *Pentagon Papers*, American politicians and military brass lost total confidence in the ARVN, and the US military began to take on more of the war effort. General Westmoreland committed large multi-battalions to conduct these search-and-destroy operations. These search-and-destroy operations were very effective and successful. These search-and-destroy operations destroyed NVA and VC base camps, cache sites, hospitals, tunnel complexes, resupply routes, kept the enemy moving, and killed numerous NVA and VC. Then the 1968 Tet changed everything. The 1968 Tet Offensive was a battlefield tactical failure for the NVA and an enormous US and allied victory. The NVA and VC suffered severe personnel and logistics losses.

In 1968, General Abrams formally assumed command of MACV. After Tet, the US changed its policy and tactics from seeking a military victory using search-and-destroy operations to clear and hold operations. These scaled-back offensive operations attempted to limit major battles between the US and the NVA. General Abrams's goal was to prevent any American military unit from becoming decisively engaged with the enemy. These revised tactics involved the deployed battalions conducting thousands of small patrols daily during the day and ambushes by night. These small-unit actions continued to find and destroy the enemy, logistics systems, base areas, and resupply routes. General Abrams stated, "Supply caches were the foundation of the insurgency's capabilities. Feeding and arming a force under fire in a land the North Vietnamese and Viet Cong did not control meant every kind of supply had to be pre-positioned, stocked and moved under fire. Make war on the supplies, capture the caches, and you had a way to devastate the enemy." Some military operations were micromanaged by General Abrams and other top brass. For example, no ground commander could bomb or shoot artillery at any village, town, or city without General Abrams's approval.

This major policy change in tactics shifted and put the onus for major military operations back to the ARVN. In 1969, Vietnamization became the dominate theme and order of the day. Redeployment of US forces began in August 1968 and continued to dwindle until all troops were home in 1973.

Search and Destroy

The US military never lost a major battle in South Vietnam. From the demilitarized zone to the Delta, Cam Ranh Bay to Cambodia, the US combat forces searched for the enemy, found the enemy, and defeated the enemy. Long-standing enemy sanctuaries such as the U Minh Forest, Iron Triangle, Parrot's Beak, Fishhook, War Zone C and D, Central Highlands, Khe Sanh, Ashau Valley, and the Rock Pile were invaded, searched, cleared, and no longer remained enemy-safe havens. These search-and-destroy operations were never-ending and were conducted in third world jungle and mountainous abhorrent environments. The days and nights were either hot and dry or hot and wet. The nights were sometimes surprisingly cold, especially in the Central Highlands. We called these Four Dog Nights. Occasionally the trees, bamboo, and wait-a-minute vines were so thick that we had to crawl beneath them. South Vietnam had a variety of animals. Some of the existing animals were deer, bear, tigers, and large spiders. US combat forces faced the daily challenges and perils of moving through waist-deep mud and water with bloodsucking leeches; procuring water from stagnant water sources; venomous spiders, bugs, and snakes, rabid rats, man-eating tigers; diseases including malaria; filth; and the perpetual threat of snipers, booby traps, punji stakes, mortar, rocket and ground attacks. Sometimes our movement was disrupted by fire ants and bees. Some military C rations were mere mystery meat that some dogs would not eat. Beginning in 1969, the majority of artillery requests had to have the local Vietnamese district chief's initials included in the fire request. This additional requirement was unnecessary, redundant, added additional time to receive the artillery fire, lowered morale, and was detrimental to US forces. On occasions, US forces were ordered to operate outside of the artillery fan and range. Through these catastrophic dangers, hazards, risks, and political constraints, US combat forces prevailed and were superb.

Enemy attrition was General Westmoreland's goal and objective used in South Vietnam from 1965 to 1968. This war of attrition was Westmoreland's strategy and was his best ad hoc tactic to defeat the VC and NVA. US and allied forces used this directed dominate approach in their military operations. General Westmoreland knew that the enemy would not be able to withstand the massive firepower and technology the US could bring to bear against them. Search-and-destroy missions and operations were the US and allied primary offensive tactic against the enemy. Enemy forces, base camps, caches, and logistical systems were identified and located using a variety of intelligence systems. Once these targets were identified and located, ground forces were inserted by helicopters into landing zones on the targets or as close as possible. Several landing zones were usually used. Multi-battalions were involved in these large-scale search-and-destroy operations. Upon landing at these landing zones, the battalions assembled and conducted sweeps through their assigned area of operations. Occasionally a few battalions would form a blocking force on one end of the area of operations. The majority of these search-and-destroy operations killed many enemies and yielded massive caches, logistical systems, arms, ammunition, and material. Although several search-and-destroy operations produced only minor results, all were successful. The benefits of these search-and-destroy operations were the following:

1. Demonstrate US and allied resolve and tenacity.
2. Demonstrate that the US and allies could penetrate and attack any enemy base areas jointly.
3. Prepared the South Vietnamese government and military for Vietnamization.
4. Keep the enemy moving. If the enemy chose to fight, he knew that he would die. When the enemy moved,
   A. he could not train
   B. he could not plan an attack
   C. he could not construct booby traps
   D. he could not attack US or allied forces
   E. he was subjected to observation and attack
   F. he had to build new base camps, caches, commo sites, training sites, and logistical systems

    G. his old base camps, caches, training sites, and logistical systems were usually found and destroyed

    H. occasionally he had to evade back across borders into Laos or Cambodia

General Westmoreland was frequently criticized for using attrition tactics. After the 1968 Tet Offensive, the term *search and destroy* was replaced with *reconnaissance in force*. This term was a politically correct term that appeased the peaceniks.

I served five months of my first tour as a squad leader in the First Platoon, Company B, 3rd Battalion, 506th Airborne Infantry, 101st Airborne Division. My last seven months, I served as a squad leader in the third platoon. I was transferred to the third platoon because of critical squad leader shortages. We usually moved long distances by helicopter. The preferred choice for initial air assaults was the US UH-1D and H model helicopter (slicks). The flight time from the pickup zone (PZ) to the landing zone (LZ) was between five and fifteen minutes. I don't remember any helicopter flights over fifteen minutes. Once airborne, we usually just laid back and enjoyed the scenery and the cool air. Although the countryside below was littered with bomb craters, it was still a very beautiful country. The allowable cargo load was six, seven, or eight soldiers based on the air density, temperature, rucksack weight, and whether we were flying in the mountains or the flatlands. Usually five to seven slicks would conduct the mission and put the first lift on the ground. The turnaround time for the second lift to land with additional troops was usually about twenty minutes. It was simply a shuttle system. Twenty-minute turnaround time is important because a commander usually only has a platoon on the ground with no additional troops until the second lift returns. If the first lift had a hot or Red LZ, twenty minutes seemed a lifetime. Occasionally the medium lift CH-47 helicopter (Hook) was used after the initial air assault of the slicks. In the 101st Airborne Division and 1st Cavalry Division, the LZs were usually prepped with artillery prior to our landing. About one minute out, the artillery was lifted and shifted from the LZ to suspected enemy locations. I can't recall the 101st using any tear gas on the LZs; however, the 1st Cavalry Division did. Upon landing, we immediately exited the slicks on both sides and ran about 20–30 feet to the side and hit the ground. We hit the ground because the enemy may be near or on the LZ, and the prone position aided the slicks to exit the LZ in a fast matter. After the slicks exited the LZ, we moved to one side of the LZ and waited for the next lift. Sometimes the turnaround time was more than twenty minutes. Regardless of the turnaround time, my platoon was always vulnerable until the remainder of our platoon landed on the LZ. If the LZ was Green (no enemy contact), we moved to our assembly area and conducted a head count, checked equipment and weapons, received any last-minute instructions, and moved out to conduct the mission. This was accomplished quickly. If the LZ was Red (contact with the enemy), we laid down a base of fire with small arms while we determined where the enemy was located and his strength. We only maneuvered to cover and concealed positions on and around the LZ until we called in air strikes and artillery. Later, after the enemy withdrew, we moved out and conducted the mission. There was no established time to conduct these air assaults. We conducted these air assaults at various times during the day and night. The biggest problem I had with air assaults was command and control of my squad after we landed. My soldiers were often hard to see on the LZ because of artillery smoke, flying grass, leaves, dirt, sand, small pebbles, sticks, and brush from the helicopter rotor wash. The platoon leader or platoon sergeant was usually the first to start the movement off the LZ. After I located one of them moving, I followed, and then the remainder of my squad followed tactfully.

We moved from the LZ to a specified target or objective using our compasses and moving on an azimuth. My platoon did not wander around haphazardly; we always had an azimuth to guide us to our objective. The leading squad of the platoon had the compass man. His job was to navigate us to a specified target or location. This compass man was checked by his squad leader and platoon leader. The leading squad changed point men frequently during the day because of the stress. Occasionally, I walked point and was always up front in my squad. You get a different perspective on the war and life when you walk point. You feel isolated, vulnerable, and alone.

Everyone in my squad was cross-trained in infantry weapons. We had dedicated M-60 machine gunners; however, everyone in my squad carried the M-60 machine gun occasionally, including me. Every soldier in my squad carried two hundred rounds of M-60 ammunition (minus the grenadiers), Clay More mine (minus the M-60 gunner), trip flare, five hand grenades in a canteen cover, one to two smoke grenades, railroad flare, and a radio battery. The rifleman usually carried an average of forty M-16 twenty-round magazines. These twenty-round magazines were only filled with eighteen rounds to keep the magazine spring strong. Filling the magazines with twenty rounds would eventually weaken the spring and cause firing stoppages.

We did not have a standing operating procedure (SOP) for wearing our web gear. Each soldier configured his web gear for personal preference and ease of carry. Our web gear consisted of the standard US Army Olive Drab H harness, two ammo pouches, two canteens with covers, first aid packet, compass packet, flashlight, strobe light, and an entrenching tool with six inches cut off the wooden handle. Reducing the length of the entrenching tool reduced the weight and facilitated carrying. I carried four ammo pouches and three bandoliers. Each ammo pouch contained five twenty-round magazines. Each bandolier held seven magazines loaded. Our rucksack was the standard US Army jungle ruck. The jungle rucksack consisted of a light metal frame, and the cargo carrier was attached to the bottom. We removed the cargo carrier from the bottom and moved it up to the top of the frame. The ruck was easier to carry, and we wanted the majority of the heavy weight on top of our shoulders, not down on our lower back. I carried four additional canteens full secured to my ruck with snap links. We did not carry a sleeping pad or air mattress. The air mattress would squeak at night when you rolled or turned over. This squeak could be heard for about one hundred meters by the enemy on a quiet night. We were issued a poncho liner and poncho for sleeping at night. We rolled up in the poncho liner and poncho and lay on the bare ground. Sometimes during a rainy night, we would construct a poncho hooch high enough to crawl under for sleeping. These were one- or two-person poncho hooches. No matter what the sleeping conditions and hooches were, we always were wet to some degree in the morning.

Our uniform consisted of the standard US Army Olive Drab jungle fatigues, jungle boots, and a helmet. The jungle fatigues dried quickly when they became wet with rain, sweat, or crossing a stream. Our fatigue pockets were always full of letters from home in a plastic bag, chewing gum, candy, cigarettes, cigars, weapons cleaning material, iodine tablets, malaria pills, Kool-Aid packets, instant tea packets, and C ration coffee, sugar, creamer packets, and junk. The jungle boots were nylon and dried quickly also. The helmet was heavy but would protect your head from small shrapnel. The helmet would not stop a direct hit from an enemy AK-47 round. Some soldiers carried cigarettes, bug spray, some type of cross or religious medallion, and sometimes a personal lucky charm on the outside of their helmets under the helmet band.

In the jungle or thick brush, we usually moved in a file formation, one soldier behind the other. This movement formation facilitated movement. If we came upon a large open area, we changed our formation. In large open areas and rice paddies, we used a vee, wedge, or line formation. These formations spread out soldiers and made it more difficult for the enemy to engage and hit several soldiers at once. The file formation in the triple-canopy jungle was difficult to control because most of the time you could only see the soldier in front and back of you. We never had a control problem with the vee, wedge, or line formation in open terrain.

We required approximately eight to ten support troops in the rear supporting us in the field. Our normal resupply by helicopter was between three and five days. We strived to land the resupply Huey between 9:00–12:00 a.m. on resupply days to give us more time to move out of the area. I received the C ration request from my squad members and forwarded it to my platoon sergeant, who called it in to higher headquarters on a PRC 77 radio. We usually only ate two C ration meals a day; however, if a soldier wanted three meals a day, I ordered them. Other resupply items consisted of ammunition, smoke grenades, hand grenades, Claymores, trip flares, railroad flares, LAWs, and an occasional sundries box. A sundries box consisted of shaving cream, razor, razorblades, toothbrush, toothpaste, writing paper, envelopes, cigarettes, cigars, and candy. I don't remember receiving very many sundries boxes in the field. For some reason, they remained in the rear. In addition, we received four to five sets of new or used jungle fatigues. We simply took the dirty jungle fatigues off and put the new ones on over our dirty and stinky bodies. We sent the dirty fatigues back on the chopper or burned them. No one in my squad wore underwear, tee shirts, or socks. We never needed any new jungle boots because they were resilient, durable, and did not wear out. I can't remember a resupply that we did not receive mail. Mail was delivered to us in a large red or orange mailbag on the resupply chopper. Most of our incoming letters contained a packet of Kool-Aid or instant tea to mask and kill the taste of iodine tablets in our canteens. We wrote our letters when we could—during breaks, eating Cs, and in the evening after we had established our night defense positions. Outgoing mail was given to any helicopter crew member, to be mailed in the rear or to anyone going to the rear for any reason. We were directed to take a daily malaria pill, and every Monday, a large malaria pill called the Monday Monday pill. Most everyone in my squad blew these pills off because they were as useless as our insect repellent. By the way, the national bird of South Vietnam is the mosquito.

We moved out to our objective around 8:00 a.m. daily. We took short breaks depending upon the weather and the distance we humped. Between 11:00 a.m. and 1:00 p.m., we would stop if it was really hot, go into a perimeter defense, eat our C rations, and/or rest. Most of us just rested and did not eat anything at noon. We never stopped for our breaks or for our noon C rations at the same time during the day. We always used different break and feeding times to confuse the enemy because he watched us 24-7. After our noon break, which didn't last too long, we continued humping. Around 2:00 p.m., we would sometimes stop and sit up in a perimeter defense in the shade because of the heat. Later we continued our mission into the early evening. During this time, we always looked for our night defense position (NDP) or rest overnight (RON). We had two methods to select our NDP or RON. If we passed a good defensive NDP or RON in the early evening, we would continue humping a short distance and set up pseudo positions. Just prior to darkness, we would pick up and move back to this NDP or RON. This was called a button hook technique. The other method we used didn't have a name. We would stop a few hundred meters short of our prospective NDP or RON, conduct a visual reconnaissance, wait, and, prior to darkness, moved into our NDP or RON. Once in our NDP or RON, we established a perimeter defense using the clock technique or prominent terrain features. In the clock technique, the starting point was from twelve o'clock. The direction of movement could be twelve o'clock, or magnetic north could be twelve o'clock. We always knew which technique to use before we entered our NDP or RON site. In both scenarios, one squad had security from twelve to four, one squad had security from four to eight, and one squad had security from eight to twelve. In the prominent terrain method, the platoon leader would tell each squad leader that he had security from this tree to that tree or from this rock to that rock. These orders were repeated for the other two squads. Tactfully the platoon leader was supposed to direct his squads into position. However, after moving into several NDPs and RPN sites, we usually knew where to deploy, and the squad leaders automatically moved their squads into position on the perimeter. If the platoon leader or a squad leader saw an area not covered, we would coordinate and make adjustments to the perimeter. As the squad leaders formed the perimeter, the platoon leader or the artillery forward observer (FO) called in and registered artillery target reference points near our NDP or RON site. These target reference points facilitated and saved time if the platoon leader or FO had to call artillery during the night. I carried a small four-by-six-inch American flag. If time permitted, I hung it on a tree or bush in our squad position. The flag was symbolic and reminded us that our squad sector was solemn US territory.

After our platoon perimeter was established, we began our evening activities before darkness. I established two- to three-man security positions first depending on the strength of the squad. I had a full eleven soldiers in my squad when I departed the ship at Cam Rhan Bay, South Vietnam, in 1967. Later, my average squad strength was around eight soldiers. Shortages were due to wounded in action, malaria, and a lack of replacements. I always filled in and helped the two-man positions so we could all get some sleep and rest. I ensured each squad position placed a Claymore with trip flare to their front. The terrain dictated how far out we place the Claymores to our front. We didn't always place the Claymore the full distance of the electrical detonating cord. We placed them far enough out that the back blast wouldn't hit us and not so far that we could not see them. The soldier that placed the Claymore also placed the trip flare to the front of the Claymore. If a soldier on guard had his trip flare ignited anytime during his guard duty, he automatically fired his Claymore. We probably killed several monkeys from trip flares igniting. After we placed our Claymores and trip flares, the men would eat their C rations, talk, relax, read a love letter over and over, look at pictures, or conduct a short visit with a buddy across the perimeter. Just prior to darkness, it became quiet, and we fantasized about returning to the world, our future, girlfriend(s) or wife and family. During this brief personal quiet time, we felt we were in Utopia because everything was very still, serene, and we had solace and inner peace. As darkness settled in, we adhered to noise and light discipline, broke out our bedrolls, and crashed.

Each position established their guard roster and guard times. Normally the guard tour was one hour. My concern was that the soldiers on guard would go to sleep or move the guard wristwatch up ten to twenty minutes. Several times I would wake up and go check the guards in my squad only to find some asleep. It was always difficult to remain awake while on guard duty. I never chewed their ass when I found them asleep; I just talked to them quietly and recommended some techniques for staying awake.

In the morning, we got up early, rolled up our bed-rolls, and ate our C rations. The last task we did prior to moving was to retrieve our Claymores and trip flares. After we ate, we received our mission for the day; usually it was to continue to search and destroy.

Our platoon point squad was usually the first to see the enemy or to make contact with the enemy. These were usually chance contacts and resulted in brief but robust firefights. As we were laying down a base of fire, our platoon leader or artillery forward observer was calling for fire. This fire mission was sent to the nearest fire support base. Our fire support bases were normally on hills or mountaintops. Some firebases had both a battery of six 105-millimeter howitzers and six 155-millimeter howitzers. The fire request went to one of the firing batteries, and if the contact was heavy, both batteries would fire. The artillery always turned the tide; and the enemy either stood, fought, and died or withdrew.

If the firefight was longer than expected, or the enemy force was larger than estimated, we called higher headquarters for an air strike. Our higher headquarters would make a decision to launch a forward air control (FAC) aircraft. This aircraft was either the L-19 Birddog or the OV-10 Bronco. The FAC would fly over our position about three thousand to four thousand feet and contact us on our PRC 77 radio. We had to communicate with the FAC because we could not communicate directly with the jets using our PRC 77 radio. We told the FAC the enemy situation, estimated strength, enemy location, and our situation, our location, and the flight path for the jet's bombing runs. The FAC then fired a 2.75-millimeter rocket that landed on or near the enemy. This rocket was white phosphorus that marked the enemy position. The FAC would then communicate our data to the jets. Our aim was to always have the jets fly parallel to our position. We never wanted the jets to fly toward us or approach our position from the rear because the jets used drag bombs, and when dropped, a bomb may fall short or hang up and land on our position. The air strike serial usually consisted of two jets. Each jet made an average of three to four bombing runs then two to three mini–gun runs. The bombs were either five hundred–pound high explosive or napalm. The bombs always landed on the enemy. The FAC always moved to the rear of our unit and orbited until end of mission. If we needed more air strikes, and occasionally we did, we simply called the FAC and requested more air strikes.

Our platoon leaders commanded their platoons an average of four to six months in the field. They were then rotated to the rear to serve on staff at our large base camp in the rear. Our company commanders averaged six months in command in the field and then rotated to the rear to serve on staff at our base camp. Noncommissioned officers (NCO) and enlisted soldiers remained on line in the field for twelve months. In my unit, the NCOs and officers could not receive a rest and relaxation (R&R) slot. The R&R slots were reserved for enlisted soldiers. The NCOs and officers had to take a seven-day leave if they wanted relief and a break from the field. I did not take an R&R or leave during my first tour in South Vietnam.

Our battalion had a rigorous awards and decorations policy and standing operating procedures (SOP). According to our battalion commander, NCOs were only doing their duty if they performed a heroic deed and should not be recommended for an award. In contrast, if the enlisted soldiers came close to performing a heroic act, they should be recommended for an award. I saw soldiers recommended for valorous awards for simply providing supporting fire from a covered and concealed position.

My platoon conducted at least one ambush about every two weeks. These were either a day or night ambush. We selected our ambush site via a map reconnaissance, from orders received from higher headquarters, or from personal observation while patrolling or conducting a search-and-destroy operation. Higher headquarters occasionally selected these ambush sites from direct observation while flying in aircraft or from our battalion long-range patrols (LRPs). After an ambush site was selected, we moved just short of the site, stopped, and waited for evening. Just prior to darkness, we moved into our ambush site. We strived to be twenty to thirty meters from the kill zone. Occasionally we were closer and sometimes farther depending on the terrain. The ambush site and kill zone was usually a well-traveled trail or small dirt road. We deployed at least four two- to three-man positions facing the kill zone. Each of these positions had at least one Claymore facing the kill zone. If there were trees to our front, we put the back of our Claymores touching the front of these to increase the Claymore range and lethal effects. We never used trip flares in our kill zones. Sometimes we daisy-chained our Claymores. This technique ensured that a soldier with the clacker would fire all Claymores simultaneously into the kill zone. A clacker is the small handheld generator that when squeezed generated enough electricity to fire the Claymore. The majority of the time, each of the soldiers fired their Claymores individually. Although they were fired individually, all were fired very quickly and close together after the initial Claymore fired. After the Claymores fired, the positions facing the kill zone fired devastating small arms fire into the kill zone. We always had at least one M-60 machine gun that was positioned to fire into the kill zone for additional supporting fire. Every fifth round in our M-60 machine guns fired a red tracer. The enemy machines fired green tracers. The remainder of the platoon formed a perimeter for flank and rear security. This perimeter security element consisted of two- to three-man positions with Claymores and trip flares to their front. Occasionally, we conducted a day ambush, and we employed the same techniques that we used at night. We always had artillery registered at several reference points around the ambush site. We were successful and received the same results during both day and night ambushes.

We stayed in the field for weeks. Our first operation was code-named Operation Rose. During this operation, we stayed in the field for about two months before we returned to base camp. Staying clean and healthy in the field were constant challenges. Unwashed crotches and armpits often were raunchy and had a red rash that made walking, sitting, and being in the field difficult. Sweat and dirt made our scalps fertile ground for dandruff, rashes, scales, and sores. Some of our soldiers had trench foot. When we were near a stream, river, or bomb crater, we usually stopped to fill our canteens. If we felt secure, we would establish security and rotate soldiers to take a quick bath downstream. Sometimes we used soap, and sometimes we just rinsed off. We spent very little time at our base camp. When we were in base camp, it was only briefly, and we strived to get a short cold shower and a hot meal.

Tactical Lessons Learned

1. Always establish a perimeter (wagon wheel) defense for security during breaks and for night defense positions (NDP)
2. Always carry extra ammunition and rations
3. Always establish a personal hygiene plan
4. Clean every weapon and radio daily and after every firefight
5. Vary movement direction frequently
6. Ensure radio handsets are covered with a plastic bag
7. Wear gloves on all operations. Practice shooting with gloves on
8. Accurate night firing is absolutely critical
9. Never separate the M-60 gunner and assistant gunner
10. Platoon leaders and commanders should not ride in the first two helicopters
11. Use night observation devices as much as possible
12. Short cloverleaf patrols in the morning prior to movement is essential and very productive
13. Automatic ambush techniques in dead space(s) in an NDP worked and increased the security of units
14. Every soldier must carry a first aid kit prepared by the battalion medical platoon and treat himself when he gets a scratch or cut
15. If a grenadier or M-60 gunner is evacuated from the field, the weapon remains in the field
16. Always use iodine tablets to purify water obtained in the field
17. Change point man frequently
18. Use scout dogs in morning when it is cool
19. Don't move in the heat of the day
20. Soldiers must drink water frequently
21. Leaders must talk to their soldiers daily
22. A mirror is better for signaling helicopters than smoke or panels

23. Units must know how to make a flaming arrow to show friendly pilots the direction of the enemy at night
24. Leaders must continue to conduct professional development classes and train soldiers in the field
25. Let the soldiers lead whenever possible
26. Everyone in the unit must know how to request an artillery fire mission and request a MEDEVAC
27. Everyone in unit must take their turn and carry the M-60 machine gun
28. Every goodie box should be shared within the unit
29. Leaders must assist and help pull guard duty, especially at night
30. Don't stop at the same time daily for chow, breaks, or planning
31. Put medical doctors on MEDEVAC helicopters. Some patients require immediate doctor care, and they can begin to receive this immediate care if a doctor is aboard the MEDEVAC

Tet

General Westmoreland requested more troops in 1967 for combat operations. President Johnson denied this request. Although denied additional troops and caught by surprise, General Westmoreland directed counterattacks, and US and allied forces defeated the enemy and won overwhelmingly. Tet was a tremendous victory for the US Army and allies. The Tet victory brought dramatic changes for MACV and the US Army. These changes were the following:

1. Westmoreland was replaced by General Creighton Abrams.
2. US policy shifted from seeking military victory to shifting the majority of military combat operations to the South Vietnamese military.
3. General Abrams changed the tactics of search and destroy to clear and hold.

4. Shifted emphasis from body count to population security.
5. Increased emphasis on pacification and improving and modernizing the RVN military.
6. General Abrams closed Khe Sanh a key marine base.
7. Increased security to reduce Saigon mortar and rocket attacks.
8. Large multi-battalion operations ceased and replaced with thousands of small patrols by day and ambushes by night.
9. General Abrams had to personally approve any bombing or heavy artillery against any inhibited villages.

The day before Tet, we were conducting a search-and-destroy combat operation about five miles west of Phan Thiet. That night we received a radio message from higher headquarters directing us to go on 100 percent alert because of Tet. Everyone in my platoon was awakened and pulled guard duty in our fighting positions. We never heard of Tet and did not know what to expect from the enemy. Prior to daylight, we received additional radio messages explaining Tet and that the enemy had attacked and captured the city of Phan Thiet. At first light we were ordered to shoot an azimuth to Phan Thiet and to move out immediately. After we walked about two miles, a resupply Huey landed and resupplied us with ammunition. We were really loaded to the hilt with M-16 ammunition and extra LAWs. After we stuffed our ammunition in our rucksacks, we continued humping toward Phan Thiet. We moved about two klicks when we made contact with the enemy in a small village on the outskirts of Phan Thiet. The fight was on, and it was the biggest firefight of my twenty-year military career! Although outnumbered four to one, my battalion—3rd Battalion, 506th Airborne Infantry (Currahees)—pursued, engaged, fought, and defeated the enemy 24-7 from January 31 to February 25, 1968. My battalion was awarded the Valorous Unit Citation for extraordinary heroism. The official US Army citation is written below.

The 3rd Battalion (Airmobile), 506th Infantry,
101st Airborne Division distinguished itself by

extraordinary heroism against hostile enemy forces in the vicinity of the city of Phan Thiet, Binh Thuan Province, Republic of Vietnam, between 31 January 1968 and 25 February 1968. Operating as a separate battalion task force under the operational control of I field Force Vietnam, the 3rd Battalion (Airmobile) 506th Infantry combined with the territorial defense forces of Binh Thuan Province in a coordinated effort in the Tet counter-offensive on the city of Phan Thiet. Beginning at 1018 hours 31 January 1968 and throughout the offensive the Currahees almost continuously engaged determined enemy forces in intense and bitter fighting. Despite costly casualties, fatigue and the difficult obstacles of house to house combat the relentless Currahees, through twenty-six days of vicious street fighting and twenty-six nights of sustained flare-lit battles, succeeded in fixing and finally destroying the entrenched enemy pockets of resistance within the city and driving their decimated units from the populated hamlets of Phan Thiet. Fleeing the advancing Currahees, the estimated four reinforced enemy battalions left four hundred and eighty-six dead, by count, as the direct result of engagements with the paratroopers. Twenty Currahees had fallen in action and one hundred and forty-four of their comrades' sustained wounds. The fierce determined, devotion to duty, professionalism and extraordinary heroism demonstrated by the members of the 3rd Battalion (Airmobile) 506th Infantry, 101st Airborne Division, are in keeping with the highest traditions of the military service and reflect great credit upon themselves and the armed forces of the United States of America.

This citation was signed in the city of Washington on 20 April, 1968 by the Secretary of the Army, Stanley R. Reasor.

Steven E. Cook, Major, USA Retired
Elkins, West Virginia
Squad Leader, 3rd Platoon
Company B, 3rd Battalion, 506th Airborne Infantry

All friendly and enemy forces were supposed to be under a cease fire and truce during the 24th, 25th and 26th of December. On Christmas Eve 1967 the three maneuver platoons in our company came together and formed a company size perimeter. I was in the 3rd Platoon across the perimeter from SGT Cook and his 1st Platoon. Shortly after I assumed guard at 1100 I was looking through a starlight scope to my front. A starlight scope is a night seeing assistance device. Suddenly I saw a VC to my front through the starlight scope. Before I could alert my soldiers I saw a very big flash. An explosion went off beside me and blew shrapnel into my hand making me drop the starlight scope. I immediately fired my claymore and got my men into position for a ground attack. There was light contact and then the enemy withdrew. After the contact ended I turned on my flash light to notice much blood coming from my hand. We were supposed to be under a Christmas truce but that wasn't happening. The company went on 100 percent alert for the remainder of the night. No additional attacks were made on our company that night. On Christmas day a helicopter brought a hot turkey dinner to our position. Although the meal was only lukewarm it was a great morale boaster. About 1500 the company separated and each platoon went their separate ways.

Tom Croft
3rd Platoon
Company B, 3rd Battalion,
506th Airborne Infantry

DON'T CRY FOR US, SAIGON

The night before TET my platoon was resting in base camp overnight because we had been pulling perimeter guard and conducting local patrols. Al Woods was in my squad and I sit with him a few hours sharing war stories and talking about our girl friends back in the states. Although it was late at night we continued to talk. We were whipped because of an all-day patrol in the hot sun. We finally agreed to crash because we were so tired. The platoon leader woke us about 0100 and told us about a large enemy attack in the town of Phan Thiet while the South Vietnamese were celebrating TET. The platoon leader told us to get some sleep because tomorrow we would be in this large battle. We were up early next morning, ate our Cs, rolled our bed rolls up and received an extra-large supply of ammunition. My platoon was loaded up on several trucks and moved a short distance where we off loaded and made final preparations for battle. We started moving toward town and almost immediately begin receiving small arms fire and RPGs. The squad leader split our squad. Al Woods went one way and I went another. The small arms fire was really heavy that day. The platoon leader was calling artillery and the Air Force was in close air support. The crap went on all day and it was ugly. I was hearing about our platoon KIAs and the next thing I heard was that my squad member and friend Al Woods took an RPG to his head. His death really pissed me off. I decided that in the future I would no longer get into friendly talks, discussions or get close with anyone. I just couldn't face another close personal loss again. My logic was if I didn't know them very well their dying wouldn't hurt me as bad. I never thought about dying just everyone else. That is the way I handled it and it helped.

Tom Croft
3rd Platoon
Company B, 3rd Battalion,
506th Airborne Infantry

About a week after TET we received intelligence that an attack on our rear base camp was going to take place. Our company received the mission to move outside of our base camp and form a wide perimeter to provide additional security for our base camp. Our company sector was in the middle of a large Vietnamese cemetery. My squad and platoon were on one side of the perimeter and Sergeant Cook and his squad and platoon was on the opposite side of the company perimeter. Our company positions were stretched very thin because we had a large area to cover. Most Vietnamese cemeteries had shallow graves and mounds of dirt on top of these graves about three feet high. These mounds made it easy for the enemy to approach our positions fairly easy. To prevent the enemy from surprising us we placed extra claymores with trip flares to our front and ensured that the coverage overlapped. As the night progressed we went on 50% alert because we knew that the enemy would be probing us. About 0100 we detected an enemy soldier probing us. We waited patiently and finally he stuck his head up about two feet over a grave dirt mound. We were prepared and ready. We fired two claymores. We assumed that we got him because there wasn't any more enemy activity that night. At first light we got on line and moved forward to recon the area. We found a blood trail about 10 feet long and several intestines lying on the ground. There was two drag trails indicating that we killed two enemy soldiers that night. It was a good night for us.

Tom Croft
3rd Platoon
Company B, 3rd Battalion,
506th Airborne Infantry

I served in South Vietnam from November 1969-March 1970 in Company D, 3r Battalion 22n Infantry, 25th Infantry Division as an M-60 machine gunner. Our unit's area of operations was around the Tay Ninh area located in JJJ Corps. We conducted search and destroy operations and ambushes. We would conduct an air assault from our fire base into the field where we remained from 3–14 days before we returned to the fire base. Occasionally we would hump out of the fire base to conduct our missions. My unit would conduct several ambushes at night during our search and destroy mission.

On Christmas day 1969, Bob Hope came out to our fire base. Many of the senior soldiers that had 6 months or more time in country were allowed to go and see his show. The remainder of us with less time in country was sent out on a night ambush. I remember everyone remained awake while on that ambush. Rank had its privileges and time in country had its privileges.

I was wounded while setting up one of these ambushes on March 14th at 1745 hours. We were at the ambush site and preparing to put our Claymores out when an NVA soldier suddenly jumped up and tossed a hand grenade at me. The grenade exploded near me and resulted in a hairline fracture on my left leg, broke my right knee and put shrapnel in both legs, right arm, chest and neck. I knew it was 1745 because I looked at the medic's watch when he was bandaging me. A MEDEVAC flew me back to Tay Ninh to a US Army field hospital. A doctor told me that I was lucky because my dog tag chain had stopped a piece of shrapnel from severing a major artery in my neck. The shrapnel just stuck in my dog tag chain. I remember the doctor telling me that he just gave me some knock out drugs and for me to count backwards from 100. He said I would 't get past 98. I think I counted backwards to 82 before I went out.

I remained in Tay Ninh for two days and then they transported me to a military hospital on Ton Son Nhut Air Base outside Saigon. I remained there for two weeks. During these two weeks I strayed groggy and incoherent because of medical drugs. Finally, they put me on a plane and sent me to a military hospital in Japan. I stayed in Japan for 1 and a half months before they sent me to Walter Reed hospital in Washington, DC. After I healed up, the Army returned me to duty and I was reassigned to Fort Reilly, Kansas. I served my remaining time in the Army and was discharged in 1971.

Mike Chenoweth
Elkins, West Virginia

I served in South Vietnam during 1968-70 as a Ranger Patrol/Team leader in Company K, 75th Rangers. We supported the 4th Infantry Division. Our Area (AO) of Operations was with in a 50 mile radius of Pleiku and westward to the Cambodian border. Our AOs were always free kill zones. We operated in 5-7 man teams. We carried either AK-47s or CAR-15s. Our equipment consisted of the US Army issue Jungle Ruck and web gear. We carried a combination of 6 quarts of water. Usually this was two, two quarts canteens and two, two quart canteens. Each team member had about 25 magazines, a Claymore several hand and smoke grenades. We ate Long Range Patrol rations in the field. My patrol number, name and radio call sign was 33. My patrol consisted of three round eyes (Americans) and three Montagnards. Our patrol lasted 3-4 days depending on the mission.

We prepared 2-3 days in the rear for our mission. The first day in the rear we rested. The second day we received our mission and conducted an over flight of the AO if possible. I looked for LZs, PZs, RON sites, enemy positions and Blue lines for a water source. Upon return from the over flight we finalized our plan. On day four we infiltrated our AO. We inserted and exfiled our AO as early in the morning as possible. Emergency exfils was any time we had to leave the AO quickly.

Our shortest patrol was a day. We were inserted in the middle of a large punji stakes field and could not move.

There were additional booby traps also. I estimated the situation and decided we could not proceed with the mission and I called for immediate exfiltration. Our longest mission was 7 days. There was no contact and no bad flying weather. One of the division battalions was in heavy contact and all helicopters were committed to support the battalion in contact. We just hunkered down and went into a hide site for a few days until a bird became available. My company and team had two missions. One mission was sneak and peak and the other mission was offensive operations. On sneak and peak missions we moved very slowly and were seeking intelligence on enemy cache/logistics sites, base camps, infiltration routs, commo sites and enemy troop movements. We used cameras and field sketching to assist us in recording this intelligence. Our offensive operations consisted of ambushes, sniper operations, attacking and destroying small base camps, commo and cache sites. We used artillery, gunships and fast movers to assist us in destroying these targets.

My most significant sneak and peak mission was in the Ia Drang valley. On day two after infiltration we were in an observation site on a hill top observing a small road in the valley below. Around noon 5 Soviet Armor vehicles with tanks appeared on the road moving east. These vehicles had about 15 NVA soldiers walking on both sides pulling flank security. We reported the incident, called for Artillery and exited the area because the enemy knew Americans were in the AO.

My most significant hunter killer mission was also in the Ia Drang valley. We had just landed back at base camp and were putting away our gear when we had an emergency mission. A new team had been inserted and discovered vast cache sites and mass graves. They requested help and assistance. The only immediate team available was us. We quickly drew new rations and headed to the heli pad. Our platoon sergeant went with us because of the large cache and large grave yard. Once on the ground we divided into two man buddy teams to observe the area better. My platoon sergeant and I sit back-to-back. Soon we observed a large enemy force exiting the tree line. The enemy had a 6 man point element about 50 yards in front of the main body. I told the platoon sergeant that I will take the first three and he could take the second three. We opened fire on my command then the patrol consolidated and exited the area.

My most memorable event in South Vietnam did not involve combat. I received an in country R & R and flew from Pleiku to Saigon and waited for two days for a plane ride to Vung Tau. Vung Tau was the in country R & R site for US military personnel. I was tired of waiting for a plane and decided to take a Vietnamese taxi. It is approximately 100 miles from Saigon to Vung Tau. About half way there we came to a bridge that was out. You could walk across but could not drive across. I paid the taxi driver and walked across the bridge. I was lucky because on the other side was a Vietnamese businessman wanting a ride to Saigon. We simply swapped taxies and I continued on to Vung Tau. I had a very nice R & R and returned to my unit. I later found out that I had driven thru some of the worst and heavy enemy controlled and occupied territory in South Vietnam.

Ranger Doug Ashby
Team Leader, Company K, 75th Rangers
Belington, WV

I served proudly in South Vietnam for 25 months and a day from April 1968 to May 1970 as an Artillery battalion communications platoon wireman in the 41st Field Artillery and later as the assistant communications platoon chief and then as chief in the 7th battalion, 13th Artillery. Because I was in communications my radio call sign was Smoke Signal. Sometimes they just called me "DA Smoke." Both units were assigned to 1st Field Force. I

112

was attached to infantry units stationed forward on the following Landing Zones (LZ) and Fire Bases; Action, Uplift, English and Camps Fedel, Radcliff and Hong Kong mountain communications site. Initially I was assigned an M-79 Grenade Launcher and later an M-60 Machine Gun. While attached to these infantry units my primary job and duties were to ensure that all infantry units and supporting attachments in the field, LZs and Fire Bases had continuous communications. This involved me leaving the LZs and going to the field and inspecting the infantry company's communications. Occasionally I had to remain with the infantry company in a night defensive position (NDP) because the infantry unit would not request a helicopter in the evening because a helicopter landing would identify their position. Sometimes while I was in these NPDs the infantry unit would receive mortar and rocket fire followed by probing and/or a ground attack. During these attacks the infantry unit would call in artillery and air strikes.

On the LZs and Fire Bases I was assigned a bunker and pulled guard duty with the infantry. Because of personnel shortages I occasionally pulled guard duty outside the wire on a small listening post manned by three or four soldiers. I placed claymore mines and trip flares on and outside of the perimeters. Frequently the LZ and Fire Bases received mortar and rocket attacks. We received sniper fire occasionally. Probing and ground attacks were almost nightly events. During these ground attacks I was engaged in direct combat with the enemy. I saw my closest friend and several other soldiers wounded or killed in action. I always assisted in providing first aid and putting them on the medical evacuation helicopter (MEDAVAC). I was always scared!

Once a week I would leave the LZs and Fire Bases with a 4 man detachment and drive or walk the roads to lay or inspect communications wire to our main base camp in the rear. We were alone, acted as infantry and provided our own security. During these missions we incurred road and personnel mines, ambushes, sniper fire and mortar and rockets attacks. My biggest fear was being captured and never seeing my family again. Sometimes we moved with convoys to other base camps. Occasionally these convoys would go through the An Khe pass. We were always ambushed or received sniper fire when we went through this pass. My communications unit and the gun jeeps always returned fire. Our convoy frequently passed many dead and mutilated bodies on or beside the road. I still see and think about those bodies!

I always think about my combat days in South Vietnam. I think about the good and bad days and best of all my buddies. Thanks to Steve Cook for letting me tell my story. God bless America.

Clayton L. Ankney
Commo Chief
AKA "DA SMOKE"
Elkins, West Virginia

I served my second tour in South Vietnam from Dec 1967 to June 1968 in Company A, 3r Battalion, 1st Infantry, 11th Light Infantry Brigade. I was the platoon sergeant of the second platoon. We conducted search and destroy operations and ambushes around the Duc Pho area, LZ Bronco area and LZ Dottie area. Our best day was during TET when we pushed the NVA out of Quang Ngai city. We really kicked their ass. Our worst day was February 23, 1968 when my company had 2 soldiers KIA and 35 wounded fighting the NVA at the village of My Lai 4.

Jake "DA Snake" Roberts
Elkins, High School 1963
Elkins, West Virginia

The Vietnam War will not end until the last Vietnam War veteran has died!

Example of a U.S. Army Infantry Division in the Vietnam War

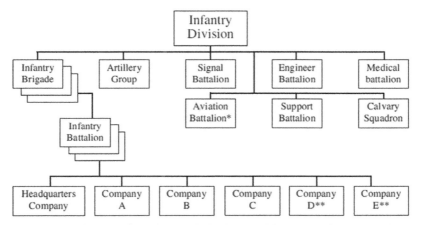

* 1st Calvary division and 101st Airborne Division had an aviation group with several assault and cargo lift battalions and companies.

** Company D and E added in 1969.

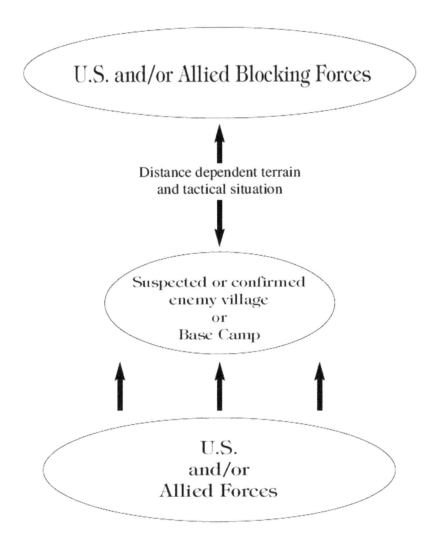

Attack of a suspected or confirmed enemy village or base camp

+
TRP1

Example of a Platoon Ambush Site

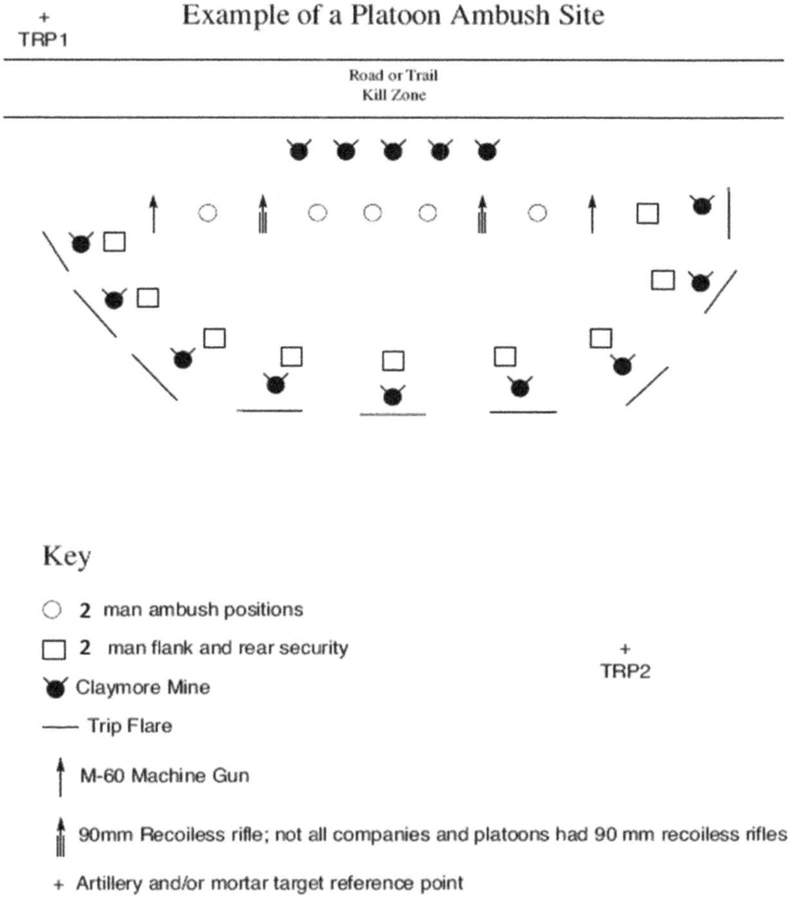

Road or Trail
Kill Zone

Key

○ **2** man ambush positions

□ **2** man flank and rear security

🌑 Claymore Mine

—— Trip Flare

↑ M-60 Machine Gun

💥 90mm Recoiless rifle; not all companies and platoons had 90 mm recoiless rifles

+ Artillery and/or mortar target reference point

+
TRP2

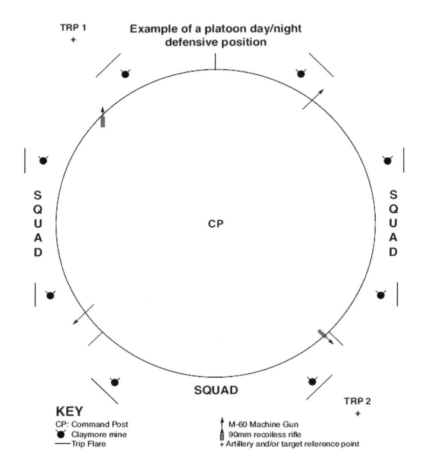

TRP 1
+

Example of a platoon day/night defensive position

SQUAD

SQUAD

CP

SQUAD

TRP 2
+

KEY
CP: Command Post
Claymore mine
——Trip Flare

M-60 Machine Gun
90mm recoiless rifle
+ Artillery and/or target reference point

Questions for Reflection

1. What was the primary US military offensive tactic used against the enemy?
2. What are search-and-destroy operations?
3. What military term replaced *search and destroy* after the 1968 Tet Offensive?
4. Why is the turnaround time important in an air assault?
5. Describe the dynamics of establishing an NDP.
6. Describe the mission and duties of an FAC.

Sgt. Cook, squad leader, 3rd Platoon, Company B, 3rd
Battalion, 506th Airborne Infantry on a search-and-destroy
operation showing the things we carried on our rucksack.

The author preparing for a daytime ambush in December 1967.

Sgt. Cook on Christmas Day 1967 preparing for a search-
and-destroy operation. Just another day in paradise!

Company B during the first Tet Offensive
in the town of Phan Thiet.

Sgt. Cook, squad leader, taking his turn
carrying the M-60 machine gun.

Sgt. Doug Ashby of Belington, West Virginia, and his Company
K, 75th Ranger LRRP team back at base camp Oasis.

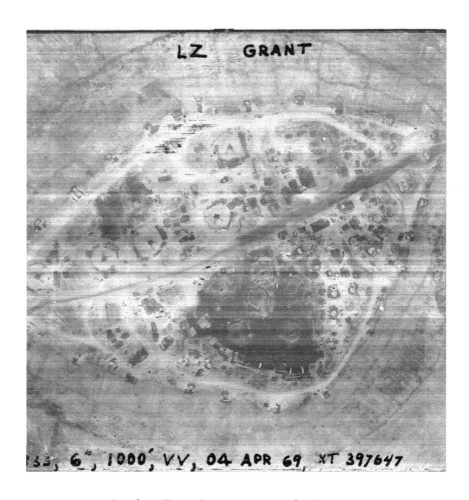

Landing Zone Grant, a 1st Cavalry Division
firebase near Tay Ninh in III Corps in 1969.

Example of a rice cache discovered by the 1st Cavalry
Division during the spring invasion of Cambodia in 1970.

CHAPTER 9

Pathfinder Operations

First in, last out.

The modern US Army Pathfinders are an elite force making up less than 1 percent of the total Army. Their primary mission is to infiltrate denied and hostile areas by air, land, and water to establish and set up parachute drop zones (DZ) and helicopter landing zones (LZ) for airborne and air assault missions. The Pathfinder's distinctive winged torch symbol comes from ancient Greece where runners opened up the Olympic Games, bearing the Olympic torch. The Pathfinder torch signifies the Pathfinder's primary mission: to light the way for airborne and air assault forces. The original red backing worn on the original Pathfinder Badge was changed to black in 1964 to signify night operations.

Modern US Army Pathfinders trace their illustrious lineage and history back to 1943. The 509th Parachute Infantry Battalion conducted a combat parachute jump in North Africa in 1942. The battalion was widely dispersed due to electronic and pilot navigational problems. Later the allies invaded Sicily in July 1943. Part of the invasion was a parachute assault. Again, the American and British airborne forces were widely dispersed. Some paratroopers were dropped more than seven miles from their assigned drop zones due to high winds, navigation errors, and no command and control of the parachute inbound troop carrier aircraft. In addition, darkness and inclement weather made it extremely difficult for aircraft to find the drop zone. The US airborne forces began working on an idea they had learned from the British. A small elite force would parachute in prior to the main assault with visual and electronic signaling devices to guide aircraft to the drop zones and gliders to their landing zones. This small elite force was later called Pathfinders, a name the American Airborne borrowed from the British.

The post-combat jump after-action report showed an immediate need for specially trained and equipped parachute elements that could enter an objective ahead of the main airborne force to

a. locate and mark parachute drop zones (DZ) and glider landing zones (LZ), and

b. provide positive control of the troop carrier aircraft during day and night parachute operations.

These elite groups would precede the airborne force aircraft and glider troops with visual and electronic signaling devices to guide aircraft to the designated DZs and LZs.

Captain John Norton organized and trained the first US Army Pathfinder teams in the 82nd Airborne Division in Sicily with assistance from the British airborne units. On September 13, 1943, these newly formed teams performed superbly during the highly successful night airborne reinforcement of the Salerno beachhead in Italy. On September 14, the 505th Parachute Infantry Regiment's Pathfinders led the way for that unit's successful night parachute assault.

Joint airborne and Pathfinder training continued in England with the British. On D-day, Pathfinders led the Normandy invasion (Operation OVERLORD). Pathfinders later spearheaded the large airborne operations in Holland (Operation MARKET GARDEN). During the Battle of the Bulge, Pathfinders were parachuted in to mark and control the critical airborne resupply of the surrounded American Forces. Pathfinders were also used twice in the Pacific theater with the 11th Airborne Division during the liberation of the Philippines. The Korean War saw limited use of the Pathfinders by the 187th Airborne Regimental Combat Team during two combat jumps and operations.

Pathfinder duties and operations expanded during the Vietnam War when the Army began to increasingly use helicopters to move troops and equipment around the battlefield. The LZ replaced the DZ in Vietnam as the Pathfinder's area of interest. The Vietnam War saw the largest use of Pathfinders due to the developments of helicopter and air assault tactics, techniques, and procedures. These air assault tactics, techniques, and procedures were pioneered by the 11th Air Assault Division (Test). The 11th Air Assault Division (Test) later was redesignated as the 1st Cavalry Division. These proven air assault tactics proved the need for Pathfinders. The 11th Pathfinder Company (Provisional) was the first and largest Pathfinder unit to serve in Vietnam, and a 1st Cavalry Pathfinder team was among the last Army units to leave Vietnam in 1972. The 11th Pathfinder Company was used extensively and successfully throughout South Vietnam and led the way for the 1970 spring Cambodia invasion. Nearly every US Army aviation battalion in the Vietnam War had a Pathfinder Detachment. Frequently, Pathfinders established helicopter landing zones, ground guided MEDAVACs, manned resupply points, and conducted sling loads missions in day and night in full view of the enemy and occasionally under enemy fire. Pathfinders also provided artillery and tactical air support to supported units in the field. Occasionally, Pathfinders were attached to accompany allied forces in the field. During these operations, Pathfinders provided adviser, infantry, and air assault assistance as required. The most successful missions were those when Pathfinders were in control; however, due to the small size of their units, and command arrangements, very little recognition was given to the Pathfinders.

After the Vietnam War, Pathfinders were assigned to the major airborne units and various combat aviation battalions/groups. In the late 1980s through 1990, there wasn't a pressing need or mission for Pathfinders. Subsequently, the Army began disbanding its Pathfinder units. The 101st Airborne Division (Air Assault), which had retained a Pathfinder unit during and after the Vietnam War, expanded its existing company and activated a second in 2005 by converting its long-range surveillance detachment (LRSD) into another Pathfinder company, giving each of its two aviation brigades a Pathfinder company. One of these two Pathfinder companies was deactivated in 2013.

Today's Pathfinder units continue to build upon the outstanding legacy of their pioneer units. The Pathfinder units today still live by the motto of "First in, last out" and proudly wear the Pathfinder torch. The Pathfinder mission remains to provide navigational assistance to unit commanders as required.

Pathfinders are trained at the US Army Pathfinder School at Fort Benning, Georgia. The mission of the United States Army Pathfinder School is to train personnel in the US Army and its sister services in a three-week course, during which the Pathfinder candidate learns how to navigate dismounted, establish and operate a day/night helicopter landing zone, establish and operate day/night parachute drop zones (DZs), including computed air release system (CARP) DZs, ground marked release system (GMRS) DZs, and Army verbally initiated release system (VIRS) DZs, conduct sling load operations, provide air traffic control (ATC) and navigational assistance to rotary wing (RW) and fixed wing (FW) airborne operations. All training and airborne operations will be conducted in accordance with FM 3-21.220 (Static Line Parachuting Techniques and Training) and FM 3-21.38 (Pathfinder Operations).

The US Army Pathfinder School is operated under the auspices of the 1st Battalion (Airborne), 507th Infantry Regiment. The 1-507th also oversees the doctrine and operation of the US Army Basic Airborne Course and the US Army Jumpmaster School.

Vietnam War and Era: US Army Pathfinder Units

The following US Army Pathfinder Units served in Vietnam:

1st Air Cavalry Division 1965–1972 Pathfinder Detachments and Teams

227th Pathfinder Detachment: 227th Assault Helicopter Battalion: In 1968, the 227th Pathfinder Detachment was renamed Team 1, 11th Pathfinder Company and attached to the 1st Brigade, 1st Cavalry Division

228th Pathfinder Detachment: 228th Assault Helicopter Battalion: In 1968, the 228th Pathfinder Detachment was renamed Team 2, 11th Pathfinder Company and attached to the 2nd Brigade, 1st Cavalry Division

229th Pathfinder Detachment: 229th Assault Helicopter Battalion: In 1968, the 229th Pathfinder Detachment was renamed Team 3, 11th Pathfinder Company and attached to the 3rd Brigade, 1st Cavalry Division

101st Airborne Division (Airmobile) 1965–72, Pathfinder Platoons and Detachments
    Pathfinder Detachment / 101st Aviation Battalion / 101st Airborne Division
    Pathfinder Detachment / 158th Aviation Battalion / 101st Airborne Division
    Pathfinder Detachment / 159th Aviation Battalion / 101st Airborne Division
    (159th Aviation Battalion formed from 308th Aviation Battalion / 12th Aviation Group / 1st Aviation Brigade)
    Headquarters, 101st Aviation Group (formed from Headquarters, 160th Aviation Group / 1st Aviation Brigade)
    101st Pathfinder Co / 101st Aviation Group / 101st Airborne Division

1st Aviation Brigade Pathfinder Company and Detachments
11th Aviation Group (transferred from 1st Cavalry Division in 1971)
11th Pathfinder Company / 11th Aviation Group / 1st Aviation Brigade (1971–73)
12th Aviation Group
    Pathfinder Detachment / Headquarters, 12th Aviation Group
    Pathfinder Detachment / 11th Aviation Battalion / 12th Aviation Group
    Pathfinder Detachment / 145th Aviation Battalion / 12th Aviation Group

Pathfinder Detachment / 210th Aviation Battalion / 12th Aviation Group

Pathfinder Detachment / 222nd Aviation Battalion / 12th Aviation Group

Pathfinder Detachment / 269th Aviation Battalion / 12th Aviation Group

Pathfinder Detachment / 308th Aviation Battalion / 12th Aviation Group

(308th Aviation Battalion used to form 159th Aviation Battalion, 101st ABN DIV)

16th Aviation Group

Pathfinder Detachment / HQ, 16th Aviation Group

Pathfinder Detachment / 14th Aviation Battalion / 16th Aviation Group

Pathfinder Detachment / 212th Aviation Battalion / 16th Aviation Group

17th Aviation Group

Pathfinder Detachment / 17th Aviation Group

Pathfinder Detachment / 10th Aviation Battalion / 17th Aviation Group

Pathfinder Detachment / 52nd Aviation Battalion / 17th Aviation Group

Pathfinder Detachment / 223rd Aviation Battalion / 17th Aviation Group

Pathfinder Detachment / 268th Aviation Battalion / 17th Aviation Group

Pathfinder Detachment / 160th Aviation Group (merged into 101st Pathfinder Company)

164th Aviation Group

Pathfinder Detachment / HQ, 164th Aviation Group

Pathfinder Detachment / 13th Aviation Battalion, 164th Aviation Group

Pathfinder Detachment / 214th Aviation Battalion, 164th Aviation Group

Pathfinder Detachment / 307th Aviation Battalion

165th Aviation Group (Air Traffic Control) (no Pathfinders)

Infantry Division / Separate Brigade Pathfinder Detachments / Platoons

Pathfinder Detachment / 1st Aviation Battalion / 1st Infantry Division

Pathfinder Detachment / 4th Aviation Battalion / 4th Infantry Division

Pathfinder Detachment / 9th Aviation Battalion / 9th Infantry Division

Pathfinder Detachment / 23rd Aviation Battalion / 23rd Infantry Division (Americal Division)

Pathfinder Detachment / 25th Aviation Battalion / 25th Infantry Division

Pathfinder Detachment / Troop F (Air) / 8th Cavalry / 196th Infantry Brigade (Separate)

Pathfinder Platoon / Headquarters and Headquarters Company / 3rd Brigade / 82nd Airborne Division

Pathfinder Platoon / Headquarters and Headquarters Company / 173rd Airborne Brigade (Separate)

Special Forces Group Pathfinder Platoon

1st Special Forces Pathfinder Platoon

Pathfinder Units Based in CONUS and Alaska during the Vietnam Era (1961–1975):

11th Pathfinder Company, 11th Aviation Group, 11th Air Assault Division (Test), Fort Benning, Georgia (1963–65)

Company E (Pathfinder), 227th Aviation Battalion, 1st Cavalry Division (TRICAP), Fort Hood, Texas (1971–1975)

Pathfinder Section, Headquarters and Headquarters Company, 6th Air Cavalry Combat Brigade (ACCB), III Corps, Fort Hood, Texas (1975–1989)

5th Pathfinder Detachment / 53rd Aviation Battalion, US Army Aviation School, Fort Rucker, Alabama

187th Pathfinder Detachment / Airborne Department, US Army Infantry School, Fort Benning, Georgia

Pathfinder Detachment / 82nd Aviation Battalion / 82nd Airborne Division, Fort Bragg, North Carolina

Pathfinder Detachment / 19th Aviation Battalion / US Army Alaska (USARAL), Fort Wainwright, Alaska (1961–1973)

Pathfinder Detachment / 222nd Aviation Battalion / US Army Alaska (USARAL), Fort Wainwright, Alaska (1973–1986)

In 2017, the US Army deactivated all Pathfinder units due to budget cuts. The 82nd Pathfinder Company was the last active duty Pathfinder unit to be deactivated. The National Pathfinder Association (NPA), which was formed in 2009, keeps the history and legacy alive of these incredible soldiers. While there are no current US Pathfinder units in the US Army today, the NPA helps keep the torch lit and shining brightly. The US Army still runs a Pathfinder School at Fort Benning, Georgia. The Pathfinder Badge is a coveted badge that few earn.

The thirteenth of September is National Pathfinder Day.

Vignettes

I served in the 145th Pathfinder Detachment of the 145th Combat Aviation Battalion (CAB) from November 1968 through May 1969. The battalion was located on the eastside of the runway at Bien Hoa Air Force base. While I was assigned to the unit, the battalion organization consisted of Headquarters and Headquarters Company (HHC), 68th Assault Helicopter Company (AHC), 118th AHC, and the 190th AHC. HHC consisted of battalion staff, personnel section, intelligence section, operations, supply, air traffic control, medical section, security platoon, and a Pathfinder Detachment. The 68th AHC consisted of two assault lift platoons called the Top Tigers and a gunship platoon called the Mustangs. The 118th AHC consisted of two assault lift platoons called the Thunderbirds and a gunship platoon called the Bandits. The 190th AHC consisted of two assault lift platoons and a gunship platoon called the Gladiators.

The 145th CAB provided and conducted helicopter general support operations to US and allied forces in III and IV CORPS almost daily. Pathfinders were always with the helicopters and provided a variety of Pathfinder support as needed by flight lead and the ground commander. Flight lead was normally the lead aircraft leading the mission and was usually flown by the company commander or a platoon leader. The flight consisted of 5–9 UH-1H helicopters. I always had one or two Pathfinders with me. We always picked the troops up as early as possible. The enemy situation on the pickup zone (PZ) determined if we flew with flight lead or we flew in different aircraft. If there wasn't a substantial enemy force in the US or allied area, flight lead would put us in on the PZ. In this scenario, the aircraft would land in a close trail formation on a road if available and either shut down or go to flight idle. This gave us time to organize and brief the ground forces, put the troops in pickup formation, brief on possible landing formations, gunship support, turnaround time, and radio call signs. After the five- to ten-minute briefing, we moved the troops to their respective aircraft and loaded them. If we knew the LZ was hot or we expected enemy activity, the Pathfinders flew on separate aircraft. No Pathfinder in my unit flew with flight lead if we expected enemy contact on the LZ because flight lead was always the first aircraft to take fire or get shot down. I usually flew on number three aircraft, and my teammate was two or three aircraft back.

The flight to our LZ was about five to ten minutes. I always looked at the beautiful scenery below and paid attention to the other aircraft. Although we used the trail formation for pickup, we usually flew in a staggered left or right formation until one minute out from the LZ. At one minute from landing, the gunships would prep the suspected enemy sites around the LZ with rockets and mini guns. Simultaneously, the aircraft would move into their landing formation. The landing formations were either a staggered left or staggered right formation. Just prior to landing the aircraft, door gunners would open up with their M-60 machine guns on suspected enemy positions. The gunships would cease firing and go into an orbit for fire support if needed. The lift aircraft almost always landed on target. Some had to move a few feet either direction to not hit a rock, stump, or land on a rice paddy. Allied troops were always slow in exiting the aircraft. Our smoke ship usually smoked the most danger-ous side of the LZ where we suspected the enemy to be waiting. This smoke shield concealed the aircraft landing and troops exiting. After exit, the troops begin seeking cover and concealment. I always moved with the ground force commander for coordination and notified him of the turnaround time. Our average turnaround time was twenty minutes. Turnaround time was very critical especially if enemy con-tact was made. We could normally put fifty to sixty allies on the ground with one lift but only forty to fifty US troops because of the weight differential. Our US troops were bigger, weighed more, and carried heavier rucksacks. That reduced the ACL to seven to eight for US troops.

I had smoke for the ensuing lifts landing on the LZ. I used Goofy Grape (Purple) and Banana (Yellow). The smoke was primar-ily for wind direction and not for finding the LZ. I carried a few Red smokes for emergencies. There are sixteen smoke grenades in a case. I carried a minimum of two cases per mission. After the subse-quent lifts landed and the ground commander had all his forces, they moved out for a search-and-destroy mission or to a prior designated objective. I always stayed near the ground commander and provided him artillery, gunship, MEDEVAC, and tactical air strikes if needed. We provided light infantry adviser duties also. Allied missions only lasted a day, and we extracted them just prior to dark. All I had to do was tell the South Vietnamese the aircraft are on the way, and they ran to get into pickup formation. US missions lasted several days. We stayed with the US as long as they needed us.

In another scenario if there were enemy contact or substantial enemy activity on or around the friendly PZ, one of the lift aircraft would insert us. Flight lead and the other lift aircraft would orbit away from the enemy activity for safety while we conducted our Pathfinder briefing to the ground commander. This briefing was the same plan and coordination as above for a friendly PZ.

Occasionally, a US or allied unit would call for a night emer-gency extraction. These were the missions we hated. We would get the call during the night that a friendly unit was experiencing great enemy pressure, which meant they were in trouble and needed to be extracted immediately. Our gear was always packed for just these situations. We grabbed our gear and ran to the flight line. During the pilots briefing, we learned the name of the unit, grid coordinates, and size of the PZ. We did not want to hear extreme enemy pressure on the friendly unit. Flight lead or one of the lift ships would insert us. Sometimes we landed very near the unit, and sometimes we had to move to the unit after we landed. While I was contacting the friendly unit on the ground, flight lead and the lift ships would orbit nearby. My first task when I contacted the unit was to determine who was in charge, assess both the friendly and enemy situation and how many soldiers had to be extracted. Sometimes there wasn't an officer or anyone in a position of authority, and I had to take charge of the friendly unit. This was very difficult if it was an allied unit. After I assessed the situation, I called flight lead and gave him the situation. Usually when we conducted emergency extractions, the PZ was either a one- or two-ship PZ. I never saw any PZs any larger for emergency extractions. I used the MX-290 beam bag lights at night to land the lift ships. To expedite leaving the PZ in an emergency, I always tied my beam bag lights together with 550 parachute cord. If I had to run to the aircraft after the last aircraft landed and loaded, I could pull the lights up and secure them in the aircraft while the aircraft was taking off and climbing to altitude. I always had one Pathfinder lead and escort the friendlies out in a file and put them on the aircraft. It always took longer extracting these units using a one- or two-ship PZ. When the last friendly element was loading, my Pathfinder would tell me "all friendlies are loaded," and we climb on board with them. During these emergency extractions, we had two great fears. Our first fear was that we would leave a friendly(s) behind, and they would be captured. We used the friendly chain of command and a head count to ensure that did not happen. I am proud to say we never left a friendly dead or alive on the battlefield. Sometimes it was difficult because we had to slug it out with the enemy with just our organic weapons. I did not call artillery or use our gunships because the situation was nebulous. I did not know exactly where the enemy was located, and I also did not want any fratricide. The enemy was always very close during these emergency extractions, and I did not want any friendlies shooting each other.

Our second fear was the last friendlies loading would not notify us, and we would be alone on PZ with the enemy. Usually flight lead or one of the lift ships would land quickly and extract us immediately upon request. During the Pathfinder extraction, I strived to have the gunships shoot harassing and interdiction fires on the suspected enemy locations for additional security and because I really enjoyed working the gunships!

Other Pathfinder Detachment missions included pulling observation duty outside the main gate at Bien Hoa Air Base. If an enemy ground attack was suspected on the air base, the command put several Pathfinders on top of a water tower about seventy-five feet high as observers. This sucked! The tower was about a block outside the main gate of the air base. We could see up and down the main road and any enemy vehicle or ground force moving toward the air base. If the enemy attacked the air base, we would be caught in a cross fire and isolated on top of a water tower. It was an excellent observation site to work the gunships. I usually drew the short straw for this mission because of my infantry expertise. The others were volunteers. The command would not send two corporals together on this mission.

Occasionally, we would deploy to assist in recovering a downed helicopter. We took one or two aircraft mechanics with us to assess the downed helicopter. Sometimes the mechanics could fix the problem; and pilots, with assistance from the aircraft mechanics, would fly the aircraft back to Bien Hoa for additional mechanical analysis and test flights. If the aircraft could not be repaired in the field, we would assist the mechanics to rig the helicopter with nylon straps for an air extraction. We would remain with the aircraft until a Hook (CH-47) medium lift would arrive on station and lift the downed aircraft back to the base camp at Bien Hoa Air Base.

Twice we deployed to search for the ninety-degree gearbox (tail rotor) that blew off the new Cobra gunships while they were conducting combat operations. The tail rotors on the new Cobras had some flaws initially, and they blew off occasionally. We usually deployed all Pathfinders on these search operations. We never found any tail rotors, and although we saw some NVA occasionally, we laid low, never made contact, called artillery on the enemy, and were extracted later in the evening.

> Steve Cook, Major, USA Retired
> Sergeant, 145th Pathfinder Detachment, 1st Aviation Brigade
> South Vietnam
> 1968–69

In March, I extended again for the 11th Pathfinder Company, 1st Cavalry Division. I served in the 11th Pathfinder Company from May 1969-June 1970. I arrived at the company headquarters located at Phuoc Vinh in early May and processed in. The company top sergeant was SFC Rondon. SFC Rondon was my platoon sergeant in the 101st Reconnaissance Company at Fort Campbell, Kentucky. He was very instrumental in recruiting me for the 11th Pathfinder Company. SFC Rondon assigned me to Team 1 located at Tay Ninh. I was programed to be the team sergeant later. I had to wait about four months until the current team sergeant reached his DEROS and returned to the states. During the interim, I went to the field and worked LZ White, Ike, Grant and Jamie. In the 1st Cavalry Division an LZ is the same as a Battalion Firebase. I was on the initial infantry air assault that opened LZ Becky. In August, I was reassigned to the rear to assist the team sergeant and to learn the team administration and tactical SOP. In September, the team sergeant departed for the world and I officially became the team sergeant. I was promoted to Staff Sergeant in November 1970.

As team sergeant, I kept two Pathfinders on each battalion size LZ in the 1st Brigade AO. Their missions included providing landing instructions for various helicopters and fixed wing landing on or near the LZ. If the infantry unit occupying the LZ conducted an air assault or moved via air to open a new LZ, a Pathfinder would accompany the assault force. Additional missions on the LZ included providing weather reports for the 11th Pathfinder Company Headquarters at Phuoc Vinh; MEDEVAC and gunship support and serve as a redundant communications site if the LZ tactical operations center communications were negated. Occasionally, a Pathfinder was part of daily LZ security patrols. This arrangement allowed me to keep several Pathfinders in the rear for LZ rotation, R&R and to provide Pathfinders for separate air assaults and additional missions. Some of our additional missions in the rear involved rigging equipment for external air movement by Hook or Sky Crane, administrative parachute jumps and providing Pathfinder support for very important persons and top brass. One of my special missions as team sergeant was to provide valuable input and detail in planning and preparing selected Team 1 Pathfinders for a combat jump in 1970. This jump was cancelled later due to an increase of enemy elements on the proposed Drop Zone.

*****

In January 1970 I received a warning order to provide Pathfinder support to the ARVN Airborne Division and selected Special Forces A and B camps. Team 1 was attached to the 7th

8th and 9th ARVN Airborne Infantry Battalions. Our mission was to provide Pathfinder support. This new mission required three new Allied LZ's manned with Pathfinders. In addition, Team 1 was attached to Special Forces Operational Detachments B-32 Tay Ninh East, A-334 Tong Le Chon, A-332 Katum and A-323 Thien Ngon to provide Pathfinder support. Pathfinder support was provided to these Special Forces units and the ARVN Airborne Infantry Battalions to prepare them for the Cambodian invasion in the spring of 1970. Team 1 was only resourced for three LZ's but had requirements for 10 LZ size missions. These critical personnel shortages required me to personally led several Pathfinder missions and air assaults into new LZ's. As team sergeant, I led two artillery raids into Cambodia. An artillery raid consisted of three Chinooks helicopters each filled with 25–30 South Vietnam Airborne Division soldiers and a 105 howitzer sling loaded beneath the Chinook. The Chinooks would land in Cambodia about one hour before dark and the 105's would fire all night. The Chinooks would return at day light and pick up troops and the 105's. Occasionally, I was the only American on the ground during these raids and provided Infantry Adviser duties to these allied soldiers in Cambodia. Later, I accompanied a South Vietnam Airborne Battalion on the initial air assault into the Fish Hook area of Cambodia during the spring invasion. One of our LZ's that we established in Cambodia was named LZ Chop. For several days, I was the senior enlisted infantry adviser in several of the Airborne Infantry companies and provided artillery, gunship, air strikes, MEDEVAC and other support as needed. However, I was elated that we finally were conducting combat operations in Cambodia. We did not complete the mission because President Nixon ordered us to withdraw. In June 1970, I returned to the states and entered OCS at Fort Benning, Georgia.

During this tour with the 11th Pathfinder Company in 1969, I lost four superb Pathfinders. The team leader of team 1 was First Lieutenant John F. Bradman when I arrived. He served several months as the team leader and decided he should go and be an infantry platoon leader. It is almost mandatory for an infantry lieutenant to serve at least 6 months as an infantry platoon leader for professional development and promotion to captain. We had a small going away party for him and he departed for one of the infantry battalions in the 1st Brigade area of operations. First Lieutenant Bradman was only an infantry platoon leader for a short while when he was KIA. His platoon was conducting a combat search and destroy operation north of Tay Ninh and received an emergency change of mission to recover bodies from a downed helicopter. I can't recall if the helicopter was shot down or crashed because of mechanical problems. As Lieutenant Bradman was assisting pulling KIA infantry soldiers from the crashed helicopter a friendly hand grenade accidently fell to the ground and exploded, killing Lieutenant Bradman almost immediately. Although he was not an assigned Pathfinder at the time of his death, the team and I still considered him a teammate and Pathfinder brother.

Corporal Jerry Bryant was KIA on September 5, 1969. Jerry was one of two Pathfinders on LZ

Ike north of Tay Ninh. During the night, LZ Ike received a mortar and rocket attack. Several US soldiers were wounded. The battalion operations called the rear headquarters for a MEDEVAC. Corporal Bryant volunteered to go outside of the wire and set up his landing lights to assist in landing the MEDEVAC. The LZ was receiving sporadic small arms fire and RPG's. As Jerry was ground guiding the MEDEVAC with his batons an RPG landed at his feet, exploded and severely wounded him. He was placed on a MEDEVAC and flown to the mobile surgical hospital at Tay Ninh. Corporal Bryant died a few hours later. Around mid-morning the next day, I went over to the hospital and identified his body.

Corporal James Hensley died on September 22, 1969. I selected James to participate in a combat jump. This drop zone for this combat jump was near the Cambodian border. On September 22, Corporal Hensley and several other Pathfinders were conducting pre-mission training in preparation for this combat jump. As part of this pre-mission training, a practice jump at night with full Pathfinder mission equipment and gear was conducted north of Tay Ninh. The Pathfinders were jumping the MC1 steerable parachute. After the parachute opened, the jumper pulled a fork in the rear riser to assist in steering the parachute. Despite jumping these steerable parachutes, high winds gusts suddenly blew the parachutes off the drop zone. All jumpers landed okay except Corporal Hensley. Corporal Hensley was blown off the drop zone and landed in a large ditch filled with water and drown. The combat jump was scrubbed temporarily.

After several weeks the 11th Pathfinder Company was ordered to continue pre-mission training to conduct this combat jump. I selected Corporal James Willoughby for this combat jump. Another night practice jump with full Pathfinder mission equipment and gear was conducted north of Tay Ninh near an old French fort. The Pathfinder team was jumping the steerable parachute. All Pathfinders landed okay except Corporal Willoughby. Corporal Willoughby landed on a mine, in an abandoned French mine field that surrounded an old French Fort and was killed in action immediately.

We mourned them and I had the 1st Brigade chaplain conduct a very short memorial service in the team hooch after each casualty. Usually, only the chaplain, the team leader and I were in attendance. I could not extract my Pathfinders from the field for the memorial because of critical combat missions. Sometimes a few of the Flying Circus pilots would attend. The Flying Circus was the 1st Brigade Flight Platoon. They flew Huey's and LOC's (OH-58 helicopter). They were called the Flying Circus because each pilot had an animal name as a radio call sign.

Steve Cook, Major, USA Retired
Staff Sergeant, Team Sergeant
Team 1, 11th Pathfinder Company, 1st Cavalry Division
South Vietnam, 1969–1970

I served as a Pathfinder on team 228 in the 11th Pathfinder Company from September 1967 to June 1969. I served on LZ Uplift, Gordon, Peanuts, and several I Corps LZs near the DMZ and a few LZ's around Tay Ninh when the 1st Cavalry Division moved into III Corps in 1968. I remember the good times we had when some of us would come back to base camp, conduct a parachute jump and drink beer. We had much camaraderie with our sister 227 and 229 Pathfinder teams. I have no really bad memories of Vietnam. War is difficult and I took and accepted the good with the bad. I learned to be flexible and roll with the punches. Most LZs were okay and some were crappy. I was accepted by the occupying force and felt like a part of the team. Vietnam was very beautiful, people were friendly and sometimes they were angry. We never know who or where the enemy was. One night we caught some folks in the wire and fired them up. We discovered later that they were supposed to be friendlies from a local village.

I attended my third Pathfinder reunion in September 2015. I was reluctant to attend at first. The camaraderie was stronger than apprehension and I finally attended with my good friend and brother Pathfinder Dan Gustafson who lives in my state. It was very emotional seeing old Pathfinders that I served with many moons ago. In thirty seconds the anxiety was gone and we were drinking beer together again and talking about old times. These Pathfinder reunions are therapeutic, soothing and helps to forget.

Joel Wellman
Pathfinder, Team 228, 1967–
1969, 11th Pathfinder Company
Elk River, Minnesota

I was a sergeant and served as a Pathfinder in the 11th Pathfinder Company of the 1st Cavalry Division in South Vietnam during the Vietnam War. I began my tour as a Pathfinder and acted as the assistant detachment sergeant. Later, in my tour I was promoted to staff sergeant and assumed duties as the detachment sergeant. I preferred to remain in the field as much as possible. I remember only returning to base camp twice during my tour.

In South Vietnam I served at Pleiku, Kon Tum, Bong Song, Phan Thiet and Tuy Hoa. I supported and worked with the 1st Brigade, 101st Airborne Division, Special Forces, a unit of the 25th Infantry Division and the ARVN Airborne Division. The 11th Pathfinder Company earned 2 Presidential Unit Citations during my tour.

Operation Paul Revere II was conducted on August 1–25, 1966. I was the senior Pathfinder on this operation and I had one additional Pathfinder to assist me. About August 4 we conducted an air assault on top of Chu Pong Mountain and cleared it down to the valley floor. This mountain was half in Cambodia and half in South Vietnam. Later, my assistant and I air assaulted in on the banks of the Ia Drang River and 30 minutes later landed several battalions of the ARVN Airborne Division by helicopters. We stayed with them all day and then returned to the 1st Battalion 7th Cavalry.

After returning to the 1st Battalion 7th Cavalry, we were attached to Company A. For several days light contact with the enemy was made and we killed three-five NVA each time. Every time the company made contact they got into a hurry and chased the enemy. We set a pattern and several days later we walked into a horseshoe ambush. It appeared to me that this company violated security and sound tactics.

Prior to this ambush I was assisting the company commander with tactics and navigation. On August 8, I very strongly advised him not to cross a clearing to our front without reconnoitering. The company commander told me he didn't have to time to reconnoiter the other side. I advised him to fire some artillery into the tree line on the other side of the clearing and he declined. Company A entered and began moving across the cleared field.

My assistant and I were following the lead platoon when they walked into an enemy horseshoe ambush at approximately 1200 hours. The battalion Sergeant Major was moving with Company A and moved forward when the firing began. I yelled at 1Lt White the company executive officer and asked him where he wanted us. Lt White told me to move back up the trail about 50 yards and block it. After moving back approximately 50 yards I saw a termite mound and took cover behind it. We were digging small holes and firing at the enemy simultaneously. Our position became part of the company defensive position. The enemy attacked the company from all directions. Platoon Sergeant Floyd was near my position directing his platoon when he was KIA. He landed near me and I reached across his body and felt bone splinters protruding from his right shoulder. I continued firing because the NVA was directly to our front and close. After 15 minutes I checked on the Sergeant Floyd again. I lifted his head and the ants had already eaten some of his eyes and were in his mouth. The Sergeant Major was near my position when he was hit with at least once with a 50 caliber machine gun in the forehead at the inside of his right eye brow. His left leg was blown off at the top of his boot. I think he had several small arms wounds also. The Sergeant Major died immediately.

My Pathfinder assistant and I helped repel repeated NVA ground attacks. The NVA had at least three heavy machine guns and hundreds of AK-47 assault rifles, several light machine guns, mortars and Rifle Propelled Grenades. All of the 12 soldiers around me was killed or wounded. My Pathfinder assistant and I fired approximately 100 magazines as we helped to repel the repeated NVA ground attacks. The company commander was wounded and the executive officer assumed command. We called in several airstrikes of A1E Skyraiders and F4 Phantoms. The artillery fired approximately 2200 rounds in support. In addition, many helicopter gunships provided continuous fire support during the battle.

The first relief unit to land and assist us was company B, 1st Battalion, 7th Cavalry. The relief force began to land at approximately 1600 hours. I made my way over and briefed the relief company commander, Captain Livingston. I told Captain Livingston that the Pathfinders will establish a LZ in a clearing about 200 meters away. The enemy broke contact with company A and began with-drawing. Although the LZ was unsecured I continued landing reinforcements and evacuating the wounded. I ordered my assistant to depart the combat area and catch the next helicopter. Company A had to be withdrawn from combat and be reconstituted back at base camp. Evacuation of Company A continued early the next morning. Many of the friendly KIA were placed close to the LZ and remained there until late the next day due to rain and other challenges. We were unable to cover them with ponchos because the landing choppers blew them off. They were very exposed to the rain and elements. For example, I recall one soldier lying on his face with the back of his head missing and his skull was empty. This hole in his head was full of rain. Friendly casualties were 26 US soldiers KIA and 86 wounded. Enemy casualties were 106 KIA, numerous wounded and 8 prisoners of war.

I remained on the ground and provided Pathfinder support to Company B as required and needed. The next day Major General John Norton the Commanding General of the 1st Cavalry Division arrives and gets a briefing on the combat operation.

We learned later that Company A ran into a base camp that consisted of an NVA antiaircraft battalion. That battalion was armed with US 50 caliber machine guns and explains the intense enemy fire. The only thing that saved us was that the antiaircraft machine guns could not deflect their barrels below horizontal.

I still see the eyes, tongues, protruding bones, missing limbs, soldiers screaming in pain and the vile and retched smell of this battle.

Tommy Shook
345 Hoof Beat Trail
Kerrville, TX 78028-8714

Questions for Reflection

1. What is the mission of US Army Pathfinders?
2. Describe the term *flight lead*.
3. What was the mission of the smoke ship during Pathfinders operations?
4. Define the term ACL.
5. Describe an artillery raid.

Staff Sergeant Cook, Team 1 team sergeant, 11th Pathfinder Company, extracting members of the 2nd Battalion, 8th Cavalry, 1st Cavalry Division near the Cambodian border, January 1970.

Staff Sergeant Cook in front of Team 1 hooch, January 1970.

Sergeant Cook, 145th Pathfinder Detachment
landing nine UH-1Hs near the Seven Mountains
area in IV Corps, December 1968.

Sergeant Cook landing UH-1Hs in the Delta area,
February 1969. Note the shotgun on the webgear.

Sergeant Cook infiltrating by boat to conduct a Pathfinder mission in the Delta, February 1969. Maybe the first water infiltration for any Pathfinder mission.

Four members of the 145th Pathfinder Detachment returning from a Pathfinder mission in the Delta, February 1969. From left to right: Resor, Gordon, Rosie, and Sergeant Cook with a hatchet in his hand.

Staff Sergeant Cook, 11th Pathfinder Company landing at Special
Forces Camp A-323, Thien Ngon, near the Cambodian border.

A 145th Aviation Battalion smoke ship laying down
a smoke screen to conceal helicopters landing. Five
helicopters are landing just to the left of the smoke.

Sergeant Cook returning from a Pathfinder
mission in the Delta, March 1969.

CHAPTER 10

US Army Special Forces Operations

A hundred men we will test today but only
three will win the Green Beret.

The United States Army Special Forces (USSF), also referred to as the legendary Green Berets, are an elite, multipurpose force for high-priority targets of strategic criticality. The USSF make up a unique unconventional, combat arms organization. They are highly trained and seasoned professionals and combat proven as the most versatile Special Forces (SF) warriors in the world.

USSF lineage dates back to more than two hundred years of unconventional warfare in United States history. Special Forces evolved from US Army elite units of World War II and the Office of Strategic Services (OSS). During World War II, the OSS was formed to collect intelligence and conduct unconventional warfare (UW) behind enemy lines to support resistance groups in Europe and the Far East. After the war, several UW officers and principals used their empirical UW expertise to develop UW tactics, techniques, and procedures (TTP). UW later became a primary mission for Special Forces.

In 1952, the 10th Special Forces Group was activated and established at Fort Bragg, North Carolina, with Colonel Aaron Bank as the first commander. Colonel Bank and a small cadre conducted the first Special Forces training for the new units. This training consisted of advanced UW TTPs. The unit's mission was to infiltrate by air, land, or sea behind enemy lines, establish contact with the resistance, and organize the resistance to conduct UW against the enemy.

Many senior Army officers did not care or support Special Forces in the early days of development. However, President Kennedy and his senior adviser General Maxwell Taylor were strong supporters and advocates for Special Forces and their strategic capability.

It would be impossible to give a comprehensive description of Special Forces missions, roles, duties, and functions in the Vietnam War. Most Special Forces that served in Vietnam will say they were different and they belonged to the United States Special Forces and not the US Army. Special Forces wore their distinctive green berets, which set them apart from other military. Special Forces thought conventional military forces in Vietnam were too rigid, spit-and-polish, Mickey Mouse, and in some cases too combat restrictive. Special Forces in Vietnam kept their mission first and often used adaptive ad hoc tactics, techniques, and procedures to ensure mission success. Occasionally, a lack of conformity is exactly what made the Special Forces soldier effective in Vietnam. Special Forces were well suited for the war or conflict in South Vietnam because the war was unconventional by definition and within their warrior skill set. Special Forces were the premier military force well trained to play a lead role in not only the training and development of the indigenous soldier but also in fighting in a guerrilla warfare environment. Special Forces were not only soldiers, teachers, and diplomats; they were a dynamic military fighting force that set the standard for all other military forces in Vietnam.

Special Forces units arrived in Vietnam in 1957 and left in 1973. The 1st Special Forces Group on Okinawa deployed operational A-teams to South Vietnam in 1957. These Special Forces A-teams trained a small group of approximately fifty-eight South Vietnamese in Special Forces tactics, techniques, and procedures. This small group would form the nucleus of the South Vietnamese Special Forces. The South Vietnamese Special Forces were called Luc Luong Dac Biet (LLDB). According to Colonel Francis J. Kelly, this development of paramilitary groups would be a primary focus and one of the missions of the Special Forces operations in Vietnam. In 1961, the 1st and 5th Special Forces Groups deployed A-teams to South Vietnam to assist with the training of the LLDB and Montagnards of the Central Highlands in unconventional warfare, counterinsurgency, and basic infantry tactics.

In addition, these Special Forces teams began training ethnic minorities in South Vietnam and organized them into the Civilian Irregular Defense Group (CIDG). The majority of the CIDG were Rhade and Jarai Montagnards.[10] The Montagnards were indigenous tribes of the South Vietnam Central Highlands. The CIDG also included a few Cambodians, Laosians, Chinese Nungs, and Vietnamese. The Central Intelligence Agency paid the CIDG. By 1965, more than eighty CIDG camps had been built and fortified. Some camps were approximately two klicks from the Cambodian and Laos borders. The CIDG program peaked at forty-five thousand men. USSF trained and organized the CIDG into an effective fighting and combat force. Some CIDG missions were interdiction of NVA infiltration routes, destroying communications sites, logistics storage areas, enemy base camps, and border surveillance.[11] Additional missions included direct action against NVS sanctuaries and command and control centers. Mobile strike force units were formed from the CIDG.

The ARVN LLDB placed officers in each CIDG camp to serve as command and staff. A USSF A-team were assigned to these camps and served as advisers. Each camp was authorized 530 CIDG personnel and consisted of three companies of 132 each, 3 recon platoons, and several mortars and/or 105 howitzers. An A-Camp Special Forces soldier would find himself not only training, advising, and fighting with the indigenous population but also providing medical care, education, agricultural and construction assistance to the Vietnamese troops, CIDG, their families, and the local villagers. They were self-sufficient and able to support the camp's population over a sustained period or during a prolonged siege. And regardless

---

[10.] Francis J. Kelley, *The Green Berets in Vietnam, 1961–71* (1973), 20–25.
[11.] Ibid., 33–36, 46.

of rank, they would work side by side with everyone to ensure the success of the mission.

USSF were trained to conduct UW in foreign lands behind enemy lines. However, in Vietnam, they now found themselves fighting guerrilla warfare not in enemy territory, but in "friendly" territory. Many of the USSF A-teams arriving in South Vietnam were short-handed and had minimal Special Forces expertise. The hard and difficult SF communications and medical skills became critical because of these personnel shortages. Duty tours for USSF increased from six months to a year in South Vietnam. Individual replacements arrived via a new team replacing an old team. This replacement system had a detrimental effect on team military operations. The majority of A-camps were in very remote areas of South Vietnam, out of friendly artillery fire, and were left to defend for themselves. The ARVN and LLDB command failed in many instances to support these A-camps with logistics, personnel, fire support, and administration resulting in many A-camps with poor defenses. These A-camps were usually attacked by hard-core professional soldiers of the NVA with support from traitors on the inside of the camp. Occasionally, these traitors were numerous and wreaked havoc on the remaining defenders.

From 1964–1966, USSF trained and fielded three long-range reconnaissance projects in South Vietnam. These projects were called Project DELTA, Project SIGMA, and Project OMEGA.[12] Project DELTA consisted of USSF A-detachments, CIDG, and LLDB that formed small combined teams to conduct long-range reconnaissance and intelligence collection missions within South Vietnam. These small teams varied from six to ten personnel. Project DELTA's organization varied and was never an official unit formed by official documents. The reconnaissance teams were usually deployed and inserted at dusk or at night by helicopter. They egressed from their areas of operation after a few days via helicopter at dusk or at night. Occasionally, some teams infiltrated over land by foot. These teams had the mission of intelligence collection, directing air strikes,

---

12. Ibid., 97.

capturing prisoners, and leading reaction forces to targets. Project DELTA was deactivated in 1971.

Because of Project DELTA's success, General Westmoreland authorized and organized Project SIGMA and OMEGA. These two projects were created to give the US military I and II Field Forces in South Vietnam a long-range reconnaissance capability. Project SIGMA and OMEGA were similarly organized. The reconnaissance elements consisted of eight Roadrunner teams and eight reconnaissance teams. Roadrunner teams consisted of up to four indigenous personnel. They wore PAVN uniforms and carried PAVN weapons and had appropriate documentation. They conducted long-range reconnaissance of NVA and VC trail networks and systems. The reconnaissance teams consisted of two USSF and four indigenous personnel. They conducted aggressive patrolling collecting comprehensive intelligence on PAVN and VC trails, base camps and performed detailed terrain analysis.

The Mike Force was a company size force of 150 CIDG personnel and 25 USSF officers and men. Each of the four tactical CORPs had a Mike Force. The Mike Force backed up Project SIGMA and OMEGA reconnaissance teams. In addition, they reinforced A-camp security, defenses, and A-camps under siege.

Project GAMMA was another highly classified intelligence collection unit. They were also known as Detachment 57. Project GAMMA conducted LRRP missions into Cambodia.

Mobile Strike Force commands were USSF-organized indigenous companies that could project combat power throughout South Vietnam. Each CORP's tactical zone had a company-size Mobile Strike Force. They were used for CIDG camp defense missions and search-and-destroy operations. They received the name *Mike Force* because the letter *M* for *mobile* is expressed as *mike* in the phonetic alphabet. In 1968, the Mike Forces and the Mobile Guerilla Forces combined into a new unit called the Mobile Strike Force Command.[13]

In August 1969, General Abrams ordered the demobilization and phaseout of the CIDG program because of major fraud and cor-

---

[13.] Ibid., 114–119.

ruption. The US and South Vietnamese military leaders and governments agreed to convert the CIDG camps into ARVN Ranger camps. The last CIDG camp was converted in January 1971. In March 1971, the 5th Special Forces Group halted all operations and departed for the US

The Special Forces in Vietnam had unwavering support from the top military commanders. Even with their distaste for conformity to Army rules and regulations, the Green Berets proved time and time again that their methods were effective. Special Forces team members are adroit, work closely together, and rely on each other for long periods of time. In South Vietnam, their ability to function in remote areas, under adverse conditions, with little to no additional support system, and in unconventional warfare would be the standard for the Special Forces of today. The Special Forces men earned on the battlefield their rightful place in the United States Army. Tough, resourceful, dedicated, and efficient, the men of the Special Forces stood and fought as well and as bravely as those of any fighting unit in our country's history. They are firmly committed to their official motto of "Free the Oppressed."

> On April 9, 1987, the Secretary of the Army and I approved the establishment of Special Forces as a separate branch of the Army. This event marks a significant milestone in the Army's efforts to enhance its warfighting capabilities across the full spectrum of conflict.

> General Wickham, Chief of Staff, US Army
> April 12, 1987

Army Special Forces today are responsible for conducting unconventional warfare, special reconnaissance, foreign internal defense, direct action, and counterterrorism missions throughout the world.

I served my first tour in South Vietnam from April 1966-Mar 1967 in the 5th Special Forces Group. I was a Corporal and assigned as the junior Engineer Sergeant on A-Team 246 or 248 located in I Corps. I can't remember the exact team number. As an A-Team member I pulled guard on the perimeter, checked security at night and conducted patrols and ambushes with the indigenous forces around the A Camp.

After 7 months on an A-Team I volunteered for MACV-SOG. I was accepted and assigned to Recon Team West Virginia. We had 5 US Special Forces on the team; no indigenous personnel. My team members were DD Rohrbaugh, Eddie Spears AKA Dog, Al Sarti and Big Bob Ramsey. Rohrbaugh was the 10 team leader. I was the 11 and assistant team leader. Dog and Al were security. Big Bob was drag, rear security.

We were assigned to Command and Control North in I Corps. We launched our recon missions into Laos from a Special Forces camp at Kham Duc. If the weather was bad we moved to Phu Bai and launched from there. We usually were inserted and extracted by helicopter. Occasionally, we had to walk into and out of Laos because the enemy improved and increased his observations of Landing Zones (LZ) and flight routes into and out of Laos. The enemy also added dedicated infantry forces and tracking teams around the LZs.

Our missions lasted 3-4 days. If we made contact with the enemy we broke contact using the Australian Peel. The Australian Peel is basically laying down a base of fire and every man leap frogging one at a time to the rear for a specified time, then you run. It was a great breaking contact technique. After we were a safe distance from the enemy we moved to a Pickup Zone (PZ) and called for extraction. Our missions included reconnaissance of the Ho Chi Minh trail, enemy base camps, enemy training sites, command and control sites and logistics sites.

Jake "DA Snake" Roberts
Green Beret
Elkins, High School 1963
Elkins, West Virginia

160

Special Forces Vietnam A-camp radio operators had different experiences based on the strategic situation for each camp. I served in camp A-102 adjacent to Tien Phuoc, a small village located in our Guerrilla Warfare Operational Area (GWOA). The village consisted of mud huts that were scattered several kilometers along a dirt road that ran north and south and had a friendly paramilitary contingent called a Regional Force Popular Force that provided a small degree of security. We designated the village a Safe Area. Anything outside of the Safe Area in our GWOA was "No Man's Land," a free fire zone. In addition to Air Force tactical air support, various howitzer batteries from regular army units rotated in to provide us with artillery support.

The camp contained the normal Special Forces twelve-man A-team, our Vietnamese Special Forces counterparts (Luc Luong Dac Biet, or LLDB), and Civilian Irregular Defense Group (CIDG) guerilla fighters. We conducted aggressive tactical operations commonly referred to as patrols outside of the populated area in No Man's Land, including reconnaissance patrols, raids on hostile VC villages, and ambushes. For many Special Forces camps, there was no Safe Area. No Man's Land started at the camp's edge. Patrols consisted of two American Special Forces, two LLDB counterparts, an interpreter, and a number of CIDG guerrilla fighters. The number of CIDG guerrillas depended on the particular mission of the patrol. Everyone, regardless of his primary job, took turns going on patrols into the jungle to look for and destroy the enemy. The only exception was that, for obvious reasons, at least one radio operator and one medic had to remain inside the camp at all times.

The two camp radio operators were generally responsible for communications inside the camp, within their GWOA, and between the camp and next higher headquarters, and adjacent other military organizations. The next higher headquarters in the case of A-102 was the C-team Company Headquarters in Da Nang. Some camps also communicated with B-teams and all camps had access to 5th Special Forces Group Headquarters in Nha Trang. Radio operators also served as advisors to their Vietnamese radio operator counterparts in camp and to the Vietnamese guerrilla fighters when on tactical operations.

Radio operators were responsible for anything that had electrons running through it. My specific responsibilities included maintaining internal field telephone communications between bunkers and other structures within the camp, providing very high frequency (VHF) short-range voice radio communications between the camp and tactical operations in the field, and high frequency (HF) long-range voice and encrypted Morse code radio communications between the camp and company headquarters. I also maintained the camp's engine generators and power distribution systems.

Other than patrols, which were never typical, a typical day for me would start about first light with a trip to the commo (communications) bunker to make a radio check with company headquarters on the HF radio to determine if there were any messages waiting to be received, then off to coffee and breakfast. After chow, I returned to the commo bunker to send a weather report (important to the aviation units), followed a little later with a SITREP. Throughout the day, I serviced generators; checked periodically for incoming messages from other stations; encrypted

162

and transmitted intelligence reports, supply requests, B52 bombing request, etc. over HF radio; drove the duce-and-a-half (2.5-ton cargo truck) to our dirt runway near camp to pick up whatever was being delivered by fixed wing aircraft; popped smoke for incoming helicopters to give them wind direction and approximate speed; alerted the camp to the approach of high ranking visitors arriving via helicopter (Run to your bunker, take off your shorts and flip flops and put on a uniform and boots.) I performed other mundane tasks necessary to do my part to ensure our camp ran smoothly, like trapping and killing rats in the storage building. In the evening, I sent a report to company HQ providing the coordinates where H and I (harassment and interdiction) artillery fire would be directed on known or suspected enemy locations. Of course, I provided contact with higher headquarters when the camp came under rocket, mortar and/or ground attack in the middle of night.

Because I was the only contact with the outside world, I served as the news reporter for the rest of the team members. During evening chow, I informed team members of significant events, including enemy attacks on other camps, wounded or killed Special Forces brothers, information relayed from other camp members traveling on other missions around Vietnam, scheduled visits from high-ranking visitors, expected severe weather, schedules for next day's incoming cargo aircraft and supplies, etc. . I recall one team member mentioning that he was to meet an SF brother, his good friend, in Da Nang in a few days and sadly having to inform him that I had just received a message that his friend was KIA.

For entertainment, we mostly played penny ante poker in the evening, sometimes with decks of cards so worn that we recognized each card from its marred back. We once had a cache of 2.75 inch air to ground rockets. Several of us cut the ends of the rocket container tubes out and made launchers of them. We used a tactical radio battery to fire them at a distant mountain several miles away, competing to see who could get the closest to a designated target. We decided that might not be such fun when one of the tubes fell over just as it launched. The rocket, with a high explosive warhead attached, bounced across the camp and exploded harmlessly at the perimeter. That caused quite a stir with the more mature members of the team. Then there was the time I put a block of TNT under a small bolder and blew it out of a hole that the CIDG were digging. The blast lifted the rock out of the hole, much to the delight of the CIDG, but one piece went flying toward Mamasan's kitchen, landing on the ground and rolling into the door. She wasn't amused. We also played with captured chicom (Chinese Communist) grenades taped to rocks to fish in the river that bordered the southern edge of camp. I won't tell you what we did with the rats.

Life in a Special Forces camp was not all bad, even if some times were more than a bit rough.

Johnny Jacks
05B (18E) Radio Operator
Staff Sergeant
Special

Questions for Reflection

1. Describe the lineage of USSF.
2. What was a primary mission of USSF when they were activated in 1952?
3. Compare and contrast the LLDB to the CIDG.

4. Describe strategic goals and missions of Project DELTA, SIGMA, OMEGA, and GAMMA.
5. Explain the missions of the Mike Force.

CHAPTER 11

Classified Operations

If I tell ya, I have to kill ya!

United States Central Intelligence Agency

The United States established the Central Intelligence Agency (CIA) in 1947 to direct and manage all foreign intelligence operations. In 1954, the CIA assigned Lieutenant Colonel Edward Lansdale to Saigon, South Vietnam, as CIA station chief. One of his early successes was his Black PSYOP campaign against North Vietnam. This PSYOP campaign yielded a mass migration of nine hundred thousand North Vietnamese to South Vietnam. The majority of these migrants were Catholic. Later, the CIA rebelled against President Diem. In 1963, following a massive Buddhist uprising, many senior ARVN officers and generals conspired in a major coup against President Diem. The CIA notified the ARVN generals that they unofficially had US support for the coup against President Diem. In November 1963, President Diem was assassinated in a military coup. After the coup, CIA station chief William Colby sought to foster a guerilla war in the North with CIA-trained South Vietnamese infiltrators.

The CIA supported the USSF in South Vietnam in conducting unconventional warfare by providing PSYOP, recruiting weapons, equipment, and fiscal supporting programs. The establishment of paramilitary units, primarily with Montagnards, was very successful. In addition, the CIA supported eighty-plus USSF base camps to monitor and attack enemy border areas and supply lines. One of the CIA's major missions in South Vietnam was to gather intelligence. To accomplish this arduous task, the CIA recruited and established a massive network of four hundred indigenous agents and intelligence officials. Washington depended upon the CIA in Saigon for daily intelligence to assist in military and political decisions. These reports included a mix of good and bad intelligence. The CIA scripted the Saigon political chaos and corruption and did not present a favorable impression of the South Vietnamese military. Throughout the 1960s, the CIA sought to destroy VC cadres and infrastructure with pacification operations.

Beginning in 1966, the CIA conducted a secret war in Laos. The CIA trained, armed, and equipped, primarily, the Hmong tribe to fight the communist Pathet Lao and to monitor and sever the Ho Chi Minh trail. This secret Army of forty thousand was commanded by General Vang Pao in Laos. The CIA had and used a clandestine air service called Air America, and its mission was to supply General Pao's Army with food, supplies, Army, ammunition, and soldiers.

As early as 1965, the CIA concluded that the Vietnam War was stalemated and that the United States could not win.

In 1970, the CIA in South Vietnam came under close scrutiny and tremendous pressure from the US Congress. This criticism stemmed from revelations concerning several CIA-sponsored programs that included the Phoenix Program, wiretapping and spying on American critics of the war. In addition, the CIA was accused of involvement in drug operations in Southeast Asia that supported and increased the heroin market in the US. These allegations and abuses led Congress to amend the Foreign Assistance Act in 1974 that mandated the CIA to only conduct intelligence missions and operations abroad.

When the South Vietnamese government surrendered in 1975, the CIA conducted a frantic evaluation of US and allied personnel. Among the evacuees was President Thieu with several large containers of gold. The CIA flew President Thieu with several suitcases full of gold to Taiwan. Many CIA employees, operatives, and agents could not be evacuated and were later captured along with key documents by the North Vietnamese.[14]

Air America

General Claire L. Chenault and Whiting Willower started the civil air transport (CAT) in China after World War II. In 1950, the CIA purchased these air assets. The civil air transport continued to fly commercial routes and flew for US secret intelligence operations in Southeast Asia. In 1959, the CIA changed the name from CAT to Air America. As the US role in Southeast Asia increased, Air America increased their air intelligence support operations. The majority of these operations were conducted in Laos supporting the Royal Lao government.

In 1961, Air America expanded in Laos. The majority of these air support operations supported the Hmong tribesmen.[15] The Hmong tribesmen were scattered throughout the Plain of Jars, usually on isolated mountainous terrain. There was a communications void between the Hmong paramilitary units and the CIA. To negate this void, Air America, following a CIA directive, developed several aircraft for short-takeoff-and-landing (STOL) capability. This new STOL capability included new fixed wing aircraft. In 1961, the US government transferred 14 UH-34 helicopters from US assets to Air America. This new fleet of modern aircraft enabled Air America access to primitive airfields in the jungles of Laos. Air America immediately began to resupply the Hmong units with Army ammunition, food, equipment, and replacements.

In 1962, the Declaration of the Neutrality of Laos reduced Air America operations temporarily. In 1964, full-scale military operations resumed when North Vietnam military forces invaded the Plain of Jars and attacked government positions. The Plain of Jars was not the primary objective of the North Vietnamese. The North

---

[14.] All data came from declassified top-secret documents and open sources.
[15.] Christopher Robbins, *Air America* (1979).

Vietnamese only wanted to protect their supply lines on the Ho Chi Minh trail from North Vietnam to South Vietnam.

During the next four years, guerrilla warfare supported by the CIA and Air America was prevalent in Laos. Because of their expansion, the US Air Force began to fly combat close air support missions in Laos. Air America provided search-and-rescue missions for these Air Force combat air missions.

During the late '60s, North Vietnam military forces continued to grow in Laos and increased Air America hazards and impeded operations.

In February 1974, a cease-fire agreement led to a coalition government for Laos. In June, Air America transferred operations and missions from Laos to Thailand. Air America lost ninety-seven crew members in the Laos campaign due to enemy action and aircraft operational accidents. Air America continued to fly in South Vietnam conducting a variety of missions. In 1972, the CIA determined that Air America and related companies were no longer required or needed. Air America had a major role in evacuating Saigon in April 1975. In 1976, Air America ceased all operations, transferred or sold assets, and returned approximately twenty million dollars to the US treasury.

Continental Air Services

Continental Air Services (CAS) was a subsidiary of Continental Airlines that began flight operations in Southeast Asia in September 1965. Robert Six was president of the company. CAS primarily flew for the Agency for International Development. They also supported CIA guerilla forces in Laos. Several staff members of Air America flight operations also served in key CAS positions. The De Havilland Twin Otters and Pilatus Porters were the primary aircraft of CAS. CAS aircraft flew ammunition, food, supplies, and personnel throughout Southeast Asia. CAS's fleet consisted of fifty aircraft. Air America and CAS conducted parallel missions and identical tasks to support CIA operations in Laos and Southeast Asia.[16] Both air organizations operated under very difficult conditions. As the war wound down, CAS missions declined. In December 1975, CAS and all assets were terminated.

Bird and Sons Aviation

Bird and Sons was an air carrier owned by William H. Bird that operated in Southeast Asia during the periods 1960–1965 and 1970–1975. Bird owned and operated a construction company in Southeast Asia. Because of the US escalating paramilitary operations in Laos, Bird established an air section in his company. These aircraft were primarily short-takeoff-and-landing airplanes. Bird and his aircraft were under contract to the US Agency for International Development. Bird and Sons also flew for the CIA. The CIA preferred Bird and Sons aircraft over Air America because they responded quicker and had better aviation and piloting skills.[17] Bird sold his air section and air assets to Continental Air Services in September 1965 for $4.2 million.

Operations Plan 34A

In November 1963, President Kennedy approved Operations Plan 34A (OPLAN 34A). Operations Plan 34A was a US-backed and -supported covert intelligence gathering and harassment operation conducted along the North Vietnam coastline and islands. South Vietnam commandos and mercenaries raided North Vietnam supply dumps, radar sites, military positions, and kidnapped selected enemy personnel identified as very important persons.

United States Navy and Marines conducted covert intelligence, electronic monitoring, and identified coastal radar sites north of the 17th parallel. These were called De Soto missions. The first De Soto mission against North Vietnam was conducted in 1962. Additional De Soto missions included intercepting and searching ships bringing supplies, arms, and ammunition to enemy forces in South Vietnam.

[16.] R. E. G. Davies, *Continental Airlines: The First Fifty Years* (1985).
[17.] Sterling Seagrave, *Soldiers of Fortune* (1981).

Commando teams from South Vietnam routinely sailed and landed on the North Vietnam coastline. The commandos used US boats called Swifts. They were slow and replaced with Norwegian boats called Nasties. Nasties were armed with .50-caliber machine guns and 81MM mortars. Nasties had a six-man US crew, an officer and five enlisted men.

On August 2 and 4, De Soto missions resulted in the Gulf of Tonkin incident when USS naval destroyers *Maddox* and *Turner Joy* reacted to North Vietnamese PT boat attacks against them. This incident was a pivotal point of De Soto missions and led to the Gulf of Tonkin Resolution.

Military Assistance Command Vietnam– Studies and Observation Group

The United States Military Assistance Command Vietnam-Studies and Observation Group (MACV-SOG) was a US Special Operations unit that was activated in January 1964 as a subordinate Military Assistance Command Vietnam command and unit. MACV-SOG was the first and truly joint combat operations headquarters and unit before any present special operations headquarters was formed. Although the majority of personnel were Special Forces, the unit was not a Special Forces unit. MACV-SOG was a joint US Army, Navy, Air Force, and Marine command. They were under the direction of special activities of the Joint Chiefs of Staff in the Pentagon. The unit consisted of two thousand US personnel. MACV-SOG area of operations included North and South Vietnam, Cambodia, Laos, and the Chinese provinces of Kwang Tung, Yen Nan, Kwargsi, and Hainan Island. MACV-SOG was a highly classified Joint Special Operations Force that conducted covert and clandestine special sensitive missions in Southeast Asia prior to and during the Vietnam War. These inclusive sensitive missions included the following:

- Cross-border operations
- Reconnaissance and intelligence gathering
- Strategic reconnaissance

- Rescuing downed pilots
- Friendly and enemy prisoner snatches
- Raids and ambushes
- Naval operations
- Air operations
- Border and Ho Chi Minh trail surveillance
- Propaganda
- Agent processing and infiltration
- Direct action
- Inserting rigged and booby trapped ordinance in enemy arms caches

Colonel Clyde Russel was MACV-SOG's first commander. Initially, MACV-SOG adopted the Special Forces mission of unconventional warfare behind enemy lines.[18] Soon MACV-SOG added additional classified and sensitive missions. One of these sensitive missions was to parachute trained agents into North Vietnam.[19] Most were captured quickly after their insertions.

Prior to operation Shining Brass, the only cross-border effort was conducted by all South Vietnamese recon teams. This operation was called Operation Leaping Lena and was a failure. In September 1965, the Pentagon authorized MACV-SOG to begin cross-border operations into Laos. This cross-border operation was called Operation Shining Brass.[20] This operation would insert US reconnaissance teams on the ground to observe and report on the Ho Chi Minh trail and other logistical sites in Laos. In November, MACV-SOG launched and inserted its first American-led mission across the Laos border against ALPHA-1. ALPHA-1 was an enemy truck motor pool, truck stop and transfer area. This was a successful mission providing valuable intelligence. William H. Sullivan was the US ambassador to Laos. Ambassador Sullivan was determined that he would control and decide which US operations would be conducted

---

18. Richard H. Shultz Jr., *The Secret War against Hanoi* (1999).
19. Ibid.
20. Ibid., 212–214.

inside Laos. He limited MACV-SOGs operations, targets, depth of operations, and length of operations. MACV-SOG nicknamed Ambassador Sullivan the Field Marshal. MACV-SOG operations continued to grow and expand until 1972.

A command and control element was established at Da Nang, South Vietnam, to command and control operations in Laos. These US recon teams consisted of three Americans and up to twelve indigenous mercenaries. The three launch sites were called forwarding operating bases (FOB) and located near the border. Initially, these FOBs were located at Kham Duc, Kontum, and Khe Sanh. Kham Duc also served as a training base for new US recon team personnel. A recon team was selected, given a target or mission briefing, and began in-depth planning and training. When the team was ready, they were helilifted over the border by US Marine Corps or South Vietnamese H-34 helicopters. The team would infiltrate the area of operations, gather intelligence, and attempt to remain undetected. These recon teams could not communicate directly with their headquarters. They communicated with a forward air controller (FAC). The FAC was the team's lifeline. The FAC coordinated for air strikes and extraction as needed.

In April 1967, MACV-SOG commenced Operation Daniel Boone. Operation Daniel Boone was a cross-border recon mission into Cambodia.[21] MACV-SOG and the 5th Special Forces Group were clairvoyant because both were preparing for this mission. The Pentagon ruled in favor of MACV-SOG. Two 5th Special Forces Group projects SIGMA and OMEGA were transferred to MACV-SOG to support Operation Daniel Boone. Operation Daniel Boone missions had more restrictions than Operation Shining Brass operations and missions in Laos. Some of these restrictions were as follows:

- Initially no infiltration aircraft; recon teams had to walk across the border
- No tactical air support for air strikes
- No FAC for contingencies
- Recon teams were smaller

[21.] Ibid., 50.

In 1966–67, North Vietnam began unloading ships in the port of Sihanoukville and trucking the supplies to base areas near the South Vietnam border. Operation Daniel Boone was a cross-border recon mission into Cambodia to gather intelligence on these enemy logistics sites and systems.

In 1966, MACV-SOG organized and fielded the Joint Personnel Recovery Center (JPRC). The JPRC had the following missions:

- Collect and coordinate POW escapes and evades data
- Rescue US and allied POWs
- Conduct POW search-and-rescue missions as directed

Operation Bright Light was a MACV-SOG initiative in 1970 to launch POW rescue missions throughout Southeast Asia almost immediately.

MACV-SOG had the organic ability to support recon team contingencies. This support consisted of company- and platoon-size Hatchet Forces. The commanders, officers, and noncommissioned officers of these Hatchet Forces were US Special Forces. The Hatchet Force mission was to reinforce, extract, and/or rescue recon teams that required assistance.

In 1967, MACV-SOG supported the new Muscle Shoals mission. Muscle Shoals was a section of the electronic and physical barrier system along the demilitarized zone (DMZ) between North and South Vietnam in I Corps. MACV-SOG recon teams conducted reconnaissance and emplaced electronic sensors in the Western DMZ and in Southeastern Laos.[22]

The US news media mentioned Operation Shining Brass in a newspaper article. Concerned of a mission compromise, MACV-SOG changed and designated new cover names for all operational elements. Shining Brass was renamed Prairie Fire and assigned to the new ground studies group. Footboy was the new cover name for all operations conducted against the North Vietnamese.

[22.] Ibid., 233.

MACV-SOG long-term agent operations in North Vietnam were mediocre at best. Because of this posture, MACV-SOG initiated a new agent program. New agent teams deployed into North Vietnam would be smaller, of shorter duration, and the operational area would be closer to South Vietnam. This new MACV-SOG initiative was called STRATA. STRATA was an all-Vietnamese short-term road watch and target acquisition team.

MACV-SOG had an operational transition year in 1968. Operations in North Vietnam almost ceased because of Tet. Tet was the largest North Vietnamese offensive to date. Tet was a major victory for the US. Soon the American people and government began to turn negative against the US commitment to South Vietnam. Many of MACV-SOG's missions shifted to South Vietnam and supported the US and allied military. President Johnson ceased all US operations north of the 20th parallel. Johnson's order effectively ended MACV-SOG operations in North Vietnam. MACV-SOG had several internal problems.

1. Communist spies had penetrated MACV-SOG at various levels. This fact can be substantiated by many former MACV-SOG members. General Singrub, one of the commanders of MACV-SOG, discovered through vetting that his jeep driver was a North Vietnamese spy. These spies notified the North of MACV-SOG infiltrating agent teams into North Vietnam. Once captured, the enemy were experts at converting the team radio operator to work for the North. The team radio operator would request supplies and maybe personnel. Upon infiltration, these assets were quickly captured.[23]

2. MACV-SOG followed the CIA failed mission profile for three years.

3. Washington didn't actively pursue the formation of a resistance movement in the North. Washington's goal was a free South Vietnam. The major concern was if the US toppled

---

[23.] Ibid., 50.

MAJOR (RETIRED) STEVEN E COOK

the Hanoi regime, it would lead to open rebellion similar to the Hungarian uprising of 1956. In this scenario, Washington's concern was the Soviet Union would intervene and crush the uprising.

4. The North Vietnamese intelligence and counterintelligence were better than the CIA's intelligence programs. The North Vietnamese had learned security and intelligence from years of French conducting unconventional and covert operations in the North. The CIA was reluctant to conduct intelligence operations in the North because similar intelligence operations in the Soviet Union and Eastern Europe had been failures. The CIA considered the North a tough nut to crack and more difficult to penetrate.

5. In 1969, MACV-SOG recon teams and forces were prohibited in Cambodia. These forces and recon teams were relegated to security operations in South Vietnam.

6. The bombing halt in the North freed the North Vietnamese to displace and move their antiaircraft defenses closer to the Ho Chi Minh trail. These additional antiaircraft defenses took its toll on aircraft, and losses rose proportionately.

7. In 1969, the North Vietnamese improved their tactics, techniques, and procedures for negating MACV-SOG recon teams. The North Vietnamese developed early warning systems in depth. Air watch units were formed and placed between the recon team launch sites and suspected landing zones (LZ). North Vietnam placed these observation teams near suspected LZs to alert security forces when a helicopter landed. MACV-SOG recon missions became more dangerous, and the time on ground was shortened. Compromising, mauling, capture, or total destruction of recon teams became more frequent.[24]

8. The US Cooper-Amendment passed by Congress prohibited US ground forces from entering Cambodia or Laos for any future operation or mission.

[24.] Ibid., 255–256.

MACV-SOG was disbanded in May 1973. MACV-SOG operations were kept secret until the early 1990s when many of the operations, missions, and documents were declassified.

Project Phoenix

In 1968, William Colby, chief of the CIA's Far East Division, negotiated a decree signed by President Thieu of South Vietnam formally establishing the Phoenix Program. Project Phoenix was a top secret program that identified and eliminated the Viet Cong infrastructure (VCI) in South Vietnam. The VCI supported the Viet Cong with logistics, minor terrorist attacks, new members, and direct terrorist attacks and activities against the US and allied forces in South Vietnam. The South Vietnamese military system proved inadequate in gathering intelligence against the VCI.

Phoenix was a very effective US and allied program that collected enemy intelligence, arrested and neutralized selected enemy personnel. Project Phoenix selected their enemy targets from South Vietnamese governmental and police circulated blacklists known as operatives of the VCI. Phoenix field and operational forces consisted of South Vietnamese police forces, provincial reconnaissance units, and US Navy air and sea assets. If the enemy was not killed, they were captured and sent to higher headquarters for interrogation.

The drawdown of US personnel and Vietnamization hampered the Phoenix Program, and operations suffered and were scaled back. In the spring of 1972, the South Vietnamese national police assumed responsibility for the Phoenix Program. In December 1972, the US ended the Phoenix Program. Overall, the Phoenix Program was a success.[25]

Provincial Reconnaissance Units

The Provincial Reconnaissance Units (PRU) were established and organized in South Vietnam during April 1969. The PRU was

---

[25.] Dale Andrade, *Ashes to Ashes: The Phoenix Program and the Vietnam War* (1990).

an addition to the South Vietnamese National police force. The PRU were part of the Phoenix Program and were detached in platoon-size units assigned to provincial headquarters. The PRU special missions were the following:

1. Capturing or killing Viet Cong political cadre, intelligence agents, tax collectors, and other principals
2. Encouraging the population to support the South Vietnamese government
3. Destabilizing the Viet Cong influence and control over and among the civil population
4. Capturing or killing political enemies of the South Vietnamese government

The PRU were under the operational control and direction of the CIA. The CIA provided training, logistics, and foreign weapons to the PRU for clandestine operations. PRUs had approximately one hundred US advisers assigned. The PRU were commanded by US and ARVN officers. Many PRU soldiers were ARVN defectors, criminals, thugs, and anyone who had a grudge against the Viet Cong, North Vietnamese Army, or any communist. US advisers had little control of PRU operational techniques, especially enemy torture techniques. The PRU wore a mix of uniforms. The most common and popular uniforms were the tiger-stripe uniform and black pajamas. The black pajamas were the peasant and rural uniform throughout South Vietnam.[26]

In 1970, General Abrams withdrew support for PRU operations and ordered US PRU advisers to stand down. Soon MACV began to consolidate and streamline the ARVN forces. The PRU were not part of the South Vietnam military and continued to operate until South Vietnam lost the war in 1975.

[26.] Jeffery J. Clarke, *Advice and Support: The Final Years 1965–1973* (1988).

Questions for Reflection

1. What was an early CIA campaign against North Vietnam, and why was the program successful?
2. Describe the Air America operation/mission in Southeast Asia.
3. Which US agency did Continental Air Services primarily support in Southeast Asia?
4. Why did the CIA prefer Bird and Sons Aviation over Air America?
5. Which US president approved OPLAN 34A?
6. What was OPLAN 34A's primary mission?
7. List three missions conducted by MACV-SOG.
8. List four MACV-SOG internal issues and problems.
9. Why did Project Phoenix target the Viet Cong infrastructure?
10. List the two special missions of the Provincial Reconnaissance Units.

CHAPTER 12

Da Smokin' Sixties

Meanwhile, back in the USA.

The civil rights movement, antiwar movement, and the Free Speech movement was the genesis that thrust the countercultural environment on America. The antiwar movement and major dissent gained national standing in 1965 and peaked in 1968 as the US escalated and continued the Vietnam War. The Vietnam War divided and polarized America. Social strife crossed many churches, businesses, colleges, families, and neighbors. The Civil Rights campaigns of the 1960s, the peace and antiwar movement, formed one of the most divisive coalitions in the twentieth century. Each group had separate goals and objectives. The only issue that united the dissenting groups was their combined and joint opposition to the Vietnam War. The Hawks on the other hand were largely right wing and conservative Republicans and Democrats. The Hawks supported the Vietnam War and viewed it as absolutely necessary to check global communism. The majority of antiwar protesters were viewed as treasonous or traitors. College students comprised the shock troops of the peace and antiwar movement. These shock troops were mobile, very vocal, and confronted the police and National Guard forces with rocks, bricks, sticks, eggs, tomatoes, and various incendiary devices. The first American antiwar protests took place in 1963. At the beginning of 1965, the antiwar movement on campuses needed a major event or catalyst to catapult their cause and justify their protests to

America. President Johnson provided this catalyst in February 1965 when he ordered the US to bomb North Vietnam. After that, most college students willingly protested the Vietnam War.[27]

The major goals and objectives of the peace and antiwar movements were the following:

1. Mass protests across the US to protest the Vietnam War
2. Lower US military morale
3. Disrupt and end the US draft
4. Discredit the domino theory
5. Influence US African American civil rights
6. Influence US women liberation
7. Influence US and world news media
8. Influence American values and attitudes
9. Influence and dictate US domestic and foreign policy

As the war escalated, so did the antiwar and peace movement. Protesting was popular. Protesters stated that antiwar demonstrations were the best places for college students to "get laid, get high, listen to rock music and to party." The dissenters used a social unrest cocktail of booze, drugs, and pop music to prep for the antiwar protests. The protesters used diverse tactics of violent and nonviolent demonstrations, grassroots organization and mobilization, congressional lobbying, voting challenges, civil disobedience, professional draft dodging, teach-ins, and political violence.[28] Underground presses became a productive means and source of disseminating operation orders, intelligence, antiwar rhetoric, information, recruiting and dissent, and dove propaganda. Doves were the diverse antiwar people and consisted of college students, peaceniks, liberals, and anti-draft citizens. Initially, this unconventional lobbying had some influence on the US population and government. By 1967, the doves and the peace movement reduced American support for the Vietnam War impressively.

[27.] Joseph A. Amter, *Vietnam Verdict* (1982), 124–125.
[28.] Ibid., 124–125.

The American peace and antiwar movement of the 1960s was the most fruitful and effective antiwar movement in US history. This peace movement was a significant force in limiting the Vietnam War in the late 1960s. The following is a microcosm of some results of this prolific antiwar movement:

1. Expedited US troop withdrawal from Southeast Asia
2. Reduced US troop morale in South Vietnam
3. Contributed to a lack of discipline of US troops in Vietnam
4. Spearheaded legislation that reduced and eventually stopped US war funding
5. Contributed to an increase of drug abuse by US troops in South Vietnam
6. Contributed and agitated racial strife among US troops in South Vietnam
7. Contributed to US troops refusing combat orders
8. Encouraged US troops to murder and/or frag senior US noncommissioned officers and commissioned officers
9. Reduced US combat operations in Southeast Asia
10. Polarized America
11. Created massive civil disobedience in America
12. Made a mockery of the US draft system that led to ending the draft

The majority of artists, writers, and musicians openly opposed the Vietnam War and exploited their discipline to blatantly support their cause. The Students for a Democratic Society (SDS) was one of the initial protest groups of the early 1960s.[29] They served as the collegiate unit of the Old Left institution of the League for Industrial Democracy. Key members and activists included Jack London, Upton Sinclair, Michael Harrington, and intense radicals Al Haber and Tom Hayden. Some prominent writers and poets that opposed the Vietnam War were Denise Levertov, Robert Bly, Allen Ginsberg, Robert Duncan, Peter Saul, Nancy Spero, and Ronald Haeberle.

[29.] Ibid., 124, 125, 127, and 136.

They used military weapons and aircraft in their works and US government officials to dramatize their work. Pete Seeger, Joan Baez, Gail Kubik, John Downey, Joni Mitchell, Lou Harrison, William Mayer, Phil Ochs, Bob Dylan, Robert Fink, Richard Wernick, John Lennon, and Yoko Ono were musicians that incorporated music in their protests. Rock and roll and folk music were the theme most often used to support the peace movement. One of the earliest musical protests against the Vietnam War was P. F. Sloan's folk song "Eve of Destruction." Jimi Hendrix was not an official protestor; however, he did protest the violence that was conducted on both friendly and enemy sides of the war. His number one protest song was "Machine Gun." The number one protest song of the 1960s was "The Fish," sang by Country Joe and the Fish. This song was almost always sung at all protests and later performed at Woodstock by Country Joe. The peace movement and antiwar protesters viewed rock and roll and folk music as absolutely necessary in assisting and supporting the dissent movement. Joan Baez and Bob Dylan performed protest music that spanned the gap between young and old. "The music promoted and enhanced a feeling of solidarity among all the antiwar protesters."

Women were a large part of the peace and antiwar movement in America. Male leaders of the peace movement sometimes relegated females in the antiwar movement to second-class status. Some peace movement male leaders viewed females as sex objects and just plain secretaries or telephone operators. Females in the peace movement were not considered critical thinkers who could develop solutions for the peace movement. Mothers and older ladies participated in demonstrations as advocates for peace. Women joined the peace movement for various reasons:

1. Women disliked the idealization of the violence of war and the antiwar movement.
2. Sexism played a major role that caused many women to break ranks from the antiwar movement and create separate female peace groups or join existing groups.
3. To oppose the draft of America's youth. Several of these female dissent groups established free counseling centers

to apprise young Americans of draft age legal and illegal methods to oppose the draft.

4. Many American women sympathized with Vietnamese civilians affected by the atrocities of war. They opposed the US and allied use of napalm.

5. Women wanted to establish the true equality of the sexes.

Some of the most proficient and active female protest groups were the following:

1. *Women Strike for Peace (WSP).* This group used a moderate approach to effectively transmit the antiwar message to mainstream Americans. Bella Abzug was an active member who was elected to the US House of Representatives in 1970.

2. *Another Mother for Peace (AMP).* Firm and persistently opposed the draft.

3. *Women's Liberation Movement.* Protested to establish true equality of sexes and equality for all American women in all aspects of life and society.[30]

America's largest religious antiwar organization was the Clergy and Laymen Concerned about Vietnam (CALCAV). This antiwar organization was founded in October 1965 by New York religious leaders, including Rabbi Abraham Heschel, Father Daniel Berrigan, and Reverend Richard Neuhaus. The executive director of CALCAV was Richard Fernandez. Fernandez strengthened CALCAV and established local chapters to protest the Vietnam War. The two major goals of CALCAV were to end the US bombing of North Vietnam and a negotiated settlement to the Vietnam War. They protested at the 1968 Democratic Party National Convention in Chicago. As clergy, they avoided the stigma of radical antiwar protesters. The most prominent member of CALCAV was Dr. Martin Luther King

---

[30.] Charles DeBenedetti, *An American Ordeal* (1990), 54–56, 95, and 123.

Jr. Dr. King gave many speeches to support the antiwar protesters. His speeches were not racial but sought to end the Vietnam War.

The clergy were often a forgotten group of protesters. They did play a major role in protesting. Most clergy had their own view of the war and how to protest it. The clergy did not believe in the Vietnam War and sought to end it.

The 1968 Tet Offensive in South Vietnam was significant in shifting public opinion from supporting to opposing the war. During Tet, the NVA and Viet Cong conducted massive offensive attacks against more than one hundred urban centers and US and allied military bases in the South. Some enemy attacks only yielded temporary success. US and allied military counterattacks basically wiped out the Viet Cong, and they ceased to be a significant threat. Although the US won a great military victory, the American media and notable news reporters such as Walter Cronkite misinterpreted the events of Tet as a US military weakness. The brilliant US counterattack that almost immediately recaptured every NVA- and VC-occupied town, city, and terrain was overshadowed and obscured by the ferocity and traumatic reality of war broadcast into virtually every television screen in America and the world. Tet was a great offensive political victory for the communists because it broke the will of US leadership and Americans to continue the war in Southeast Asia. The increased casualty lists of Tet aided and abetted the news media propaganda machine. During Tet, an NLF officer suspected of participating in the Hue massacre was executed in Saigon by General Loan, a South Vietnamese National Police Chief. This summary execution was filmed and photographed by the media and provided a conspicuous image that helped sway US public opinion against the war. The media also exploited the My Lai massacre as another example of poor US military leadership and resolve during the Vietnam War. The massacre occurred on March 16, 1968, when an estimated five hundred civilians were massacred in and near the hamlet of My Lai in South Vietnam by elements of the US Americal Division's 11th Infantry Brigade. Later the museum of My Lai claimed the 504 civilians, mostly women and children, had been indiscriminately shot and killed. Tet and the My Lai massacre gave new impetus to the antiwar movement. On October 15, 1969, as a token of solidarity, hundreds of thousands of people conducted massive antiwar demonstrations across America as a national moratorium against the war. Many Americans missed work or took a sick day to participate in these demonstrations. A second moratorium was conducted on November 15 but was small and had no significant results.

Conscientious objectors was a US classification for active-duty military or individuals that were draft eligible who opposed war or refused to participate in military combat because of religious or moral reasons. Conscientious objector status was not automatic and not always awarded based on beliefs. Historic pacifists such as Quakers and Jehovah's Witnesses were usually granted conscientious objector status. As the war in South Vietnam escalated, large numbers of American men faced increasing odds of being drafted and sent to South Vietnam. There were numerous draft deferments available. Conscientious objector quickly became a popular possibility to avoid the draft. Local draft boards varied in granting conscientious objector status. Some draft boards granted conscientious objector status, and some denied all conscientious objector applications. The Selective Service System had three conscientious objector categories.

1. Category I-A-O: Conscientious objector eligible for draft and available for noncombat military duty such as cooks, transportation, and supply duties.
2. Category I-O: Conscientious objector available for civilian work that contributed to US national health or safety.
3. Category I-W: Conscientious objector serving two years of public service such as hospital orderlies or other low-paying public service jobs.

Legal and accepted conscientious objectors endured isolation, scorn, and were assigned to perform very difficult duties. Unofficially, conscientious objectors faced and endured harsh punishments, and several were sent to prison.[31]

[31.] Ibid., 165–167.

Opposition to the draft was one of several reasons for demonstrations and antiwar protests. Protests to bring attention to the draft began in 1965 when student protesters from the University of California, Berkeley, conducted the first public draft card burning in America. During ensuing demonstrations, student activists continued to burn their draft cards. These draft card–burning rallies were protesting the Vietnam War and not the overall draft system.

The Selective Service System contained four thousand local draft boards in the 1960s. The majority of these draft boards were staffed with unpaid volunteers, usually veterans of World War I and/or II and largely white middle-class males. In 1967, females were finally authorized to serve on draft boards. During World War II, the average age of a draftee was twenty-six. During the Vietnam War, the average draft age was nineteen. During the Vietnam War, approximately 26.8 million male baby boomers were drafted. In 1968, at the height of the Vietnam War, 60 percent of US casualties were a nineteen- to twenty-year-old draftee.

Discrimination and favoritism were the norms for numerous draft deferments and exceptions. Safe havens such as the National Guard and reserve slots were very difficult to procure. The majority of these slots were rewarded to sons of prominent citizens. Often it was the underprivileged without connections who were drafted. These inequities caused draft card turn-ins and a minor exodus to Canada, Sweden, and Mexico to avoid the draft. This exodus prompted personnel turbulence in the workplace, separated family members, and polarized Americans. Some Americans refused to pay a portion of their taxes that was destined for the war effort.

The draft board biases contributed to the Vietnam War's unpopularity. In January 1973, a day after the Paris Peace Accords were signed, President Nixon ended the draft and instituted the all-volunteer military.

As the antiwar movement and demonstrations spread beyond college campuses, only a small portion of US government officials sided with and had sympathy for the doves. Widespread opposition to the Vietnam War within the government began to appear in 1968, immediately after the Tet Offensive. Opposition and dissent lead to violence. The Tet Offensive and massive civil unrest shifted public opinion dramatically and contributed to President Johnson not seeking reelection. On October 31, 1968, President Johnson halted Operation Rolling Thunder, the failed bombing campaign of North Vietnam.

The 1968 Democratic Party National Convention was held in Chicago on August 26–29. "This convention was afflicted with civil unrest, protests, controversy, heated exchanges and debates on the convention floor. Proceedings were controlled by a loyal Democratic political force, personally directed by Mayor Daley with support of the Illinois National Guard." On March 25, President Johnson learned that his closest advisers now opposed the war. Six days later, Johnson withdrew from the presidential race.

The outside of the convention hall looked like a prisoner-of-war camp. The convention hall was surrounded with barbed wire, armed National Guardsmen, and gun jeeps. Thousands of antiwar protestors converged, protested, sang songs, waved flags and banners, and lobbied in support of antiwar candidate Senator George McGovern. Several violent confrontations and clashes were recorded and documented by the media. These skirmishes were almost immediately watched on home television by stunned Americans. Approximately seven hundred demonstrators were arrested, and an unspecified number were injured.

Antiwar protestors, activists, and the peace movement used the following chants and slogans during their demonstrations, protests, rallies, and sit-ins. These chants and slogans built morale and unified and motivated the dissenters.

1. "Hell no, we won't go" was a popular antiwar and draft chant.
2. "End the nuclear race, not the human race," used by Women Strike for Peace (WSP) in antinuclear demonstrations and later by antiwar protestors.
3. "Stop the war, feed the poor" was a popular slogan used by minority antiwar dissenters.

4. "Hey, hey, LBJ, how many kids did you kill today?" was a popular chant used by students that were in opposition to President Johnson.
5. "Thou shall not kill" was a popular chant used by students to protest chemical companies that made napalm and herbicides.
6. "Making money burning babies," same as number 5 above.
7. "Not my son, not your son, not their sons" was an antiwar and anti-draft slogan used by the Women Strike for Peace (WSP).
8. "War is not healthy for children and other living things" was a popular slogan of Another Mother for Peace. The slogan was popular on posters and leaflets.
9. "Ho, Ho, Ho, Chi Minh, the Viet Cong are gonna win" was a very popular and common antiwar chant during antiwar marches and rallies in the 1960s.
10. "Girls say yes to men who say no" was an anti-draft slogan used by the Students for Democratic Society (SDS) and other peace organizations.

Despite the increasing depressing news of the Vietnam War, the majority of Americans continued to support President Johnson's Vietnam goals and objectives. There was a feeling that the goal of preventing a communist takeover of a pro-Western government in South Vietnam was a noble endeavor. Many Americans wanted America to disengage from the Vietnam War with honor. As the Vietnam War gradually declined in 1970–71, the successful antiwar and peace movement of the 1960s began to dismantle and greatly reduced protests and operations.

Several reasons affected the unraveling of the antiwar movement.

1. Many demonstrators questioned the efficiency of the antiwar movement and demonstrations.
2. Large defections and dropouts hindered and reduced antiwar operations.

3. Internal dissension over antiwar strategies and tactics increased among the antiwar protestors.
4. Bitter infighting continued to sap energy, alienate activists, and hamper antiwar planning.
5. This discord was internally generated and fanned by the US government.

Some of the conspicuous and noticeable antiwar, peace organizations, movements, methods, actions, and activities are listed below:

1. American Society of Friends (Quakers): The core peace movement always existed in Quaker society and ramped up during the Vietnam War.
2. National Committee for a Sane Nuclear Policy (SANE): SANE was a middle-class organization that practiced liberal peace activism. Their major goal was a reduction in nuclear weapons.
3. Student Peace Union (SPU): The SPU was formed in 1959 on college campuses. Similar to other peace organizations, the SPU was more liberal than radical. SPU's goal was to restructure American society. The SPU dissolved in 1964, and its mission was assumed by a more active movement, Students for a Democratic Society.
4. Students for a Democratic Society (SDS): The SDS was formed on college campuses in 1960. The SDS focused on domestic concerns, civil rights, and the military industrial complex during the early years of existence. The SDS supported President Johnson and his Great Society programs. As the Vietnam War escalated, the SDS became more active and antiwar.
5. Teach-ins: Organized on March 24 at the University of Michigan. Teach-ins were similar to civil rights seminars. Teach-ins quickly spread to college campuses across America, and their goal was to recruit faculty members for the antiwar cause.

6. Underground Press Syndicate: Organized in 1966 by college campus editors and became an effective method to share protest methods.

7. Liberation News Service: Formed in 1967; was an active method to disseminate intelligence and protest methods.

8. Pentagon march: A two-day march on the Pentagon conducted in October 1967 attracted national news attention and coverage. March leaders called on young men to turn in their draft cards.

9. Fort Hood Three: In 1966, three young soldiers from Fort Hood refused to serve in South Vietnam. This refusal was applauded among dissenters of the war.

10. Underground Railroads: Underground railroads were formed across America to funnel draft evaders to Canada or to Sweden. Specified US churches provided sanctuary for draft evaders also.

11. Civil rights leaders: The antiwar movement and protestors gained an ally in 1965 when the majority of civil rights leaders became active frontrunners for peace in South Vietnam. The civil rights leaders supported the antiwar movement because of moral reasons.

12. Eugene McCarthy, Robert Kennedy, and George McGovern: These were democrats and peace candidates who ran for president in 1968.

13. Draft board raids: Draft boards in major cities were raided. The protestors burned and shredded draft files.

14. Chemical companies: Several major chemical companies were targeted for sabotage because they produced and manufactured napalm.

15. Washington march: In 1969, five hundred thousand protestors marched on Washington demonstrating against the Vietnam War.

16. Free Speech Movement (FSM): The FSM linked the civil rights movement and the antiwar crusades.

17. National organization of draft resisters: Formed in March 1967.

18. Committee for a Sane Nuclear Policy (SANE): A liberal international organization with a goal of halting atmospheric nuclear testing.
19. Committee for Non-Violent Action (CNVA): A radical pacifist organization that used civil disobedience in direct action against military action.
20. American Writers and Artists against the War in Vietnam
21. Americans for Democratic Action
22. Student Nonviolent Coordinating Committee
23. The League of Women Voters: This antiwar group called for an end to US involvement in Vietnam.
24. Vietnam Veterans against the War
25. National Black Anti-Draft Union (NBAWADU)
26. National Black Draft Counselors (NBDC): An organization developed to assist and help young black men avoid being drafted.
27. Black Women Enraged: Organized in Harlem and was an antiwar movement.
28. Women's International League for Peace and Freedom (WILPF): An early peace movement and organization founded in 1919. This organization provided women an early opportunity to join the antiwar movement.
29. Sisters of Notre Dame de Namur: This group used and popularized the use of kneel-ins and prayer to stop the Vietnam War.
30. Student Peace Union
31. The Student Libertarian Movement: Opposed the Vietnam War and the draft. Occasionally supported the civil rights movement.
32. Clergy and Laymen Concerned about Vietnam (CALCAV)
33. Furman University Corps of Kazoos (FUCK): Organized at Furman University in South Carolina to make fun of the military and ROTC programs. This group spread to several other campuses in America.
34. Workshop in Nonviolence (WIN): Liberal authors who wrote antiwar and peace articles for major newspapers.

35. Fxxk the Army (FTA): A group that used the initials that stood for Fxxk the Army. This group was led by Jane Fonda and Donald Sutherland.
36. Traditional peace groups like Fellowship of Reconciliation, the War Resisters League, Catholic Workers Movement, and the American Friends Service Committee, although small, were active participants in the peace movement.
37. Various committees, movements, and campaigns were organized for peace in Vietnam including Campaign to end the Air War, Catholic Peace Fellowship, Campaign for Disarmament, Campaign to Stop Funding the War, and the Central Committee for Conscientious Objectors.
38. Vietnam Day Committee

Timeline of Major Peace Demonstrations, Opposition, and Antiwar Activities Conducted during the 1960s

1964

May 12: A dozen young men publicly burned their draft cards in New York City.
December: Joan Baez led a large antiwar demonstration in San Francisco.

1965

March 16: Alice Herz set herself on fire in the first known self-immolation to protest the Vietnam War. She was an eighty-two-year-old pacifist.
March 24: Teach-in protest organized and led by professors was conducted at the University of Michigan. This teach-in escalated to thirty-five campuses across America.
April 17: The first of several large antiwar marches were conducted in Washington DC. The march was led by the Students for a Democratic Society (SDS) and the Student Nonviolent Coordinating Committee (SNCC).

May: The Vietnam Day Committee organized large-scale draft card burning at the University of California, Berkeley. Additional antiwar activities included a teach-in and a burning in effigy of President Johnson.

May: The first overseas anti–Vietnam War demonstration was conducted in London near the US Embassy.

June: Large protests were conducted on the steps of the Pentagon.

August: Activists attempted to stop and/or impede the movement of troop trains in California.

October: The antiwar movement and protests significantly expanded in America and overseas. Some protests numbered one hundred thousand and were held simultaneously in many cities including New York, San Francisco, Paris, Rome, and London.

October 15: Approximately forty people staged a sit-in at the Ann Arbor, Michigan, draft board. They were arrested, prosecuted, and sentenced to ten to fifteen days in jail. Additional protests were held in forty US cities.

November 2: A thirty-one-year-old pacifist, Norman Morrison set himself on fire below the window of Secretary of Defense Robert McNamara at the Pentagon.

November 27: Three prominent protestors—Coretta Scott King, SDS President Carl Oglesby, and Doctor Benjamin Spock—spoke at an antiwar rally in Washington DC. Other large-scale rallies occurred simultaneously across America.

1966

January 29: More than six hundred artists gathered for Angry Arts Week. Angry Arts Week was a series of dance, art, film, poetry, and music that served as a catalyst to increase the antiwar movement among artists.

February: Approximately one hundred Vietnam War veterans attempted to return their military awards and decorations to a White House guard. They were refused and turned away.

March 26: Antiwar demonstrations and protests were held in many cities across America and the world.

May 15: A large antiwar demonstration and protest took place outside the White House and near the Washington Monument.

June: American students with others in England formed the Stop It Committee. This prominent protest group participated in every English antiwar demonstration.

July 3: A group of four thousand to five thousand antiwar protesters demonstrated outside the American Embassy in London. The protesters scuffled with police, and several were arrested.

July: Joan Baez and A. J. Muste organized several protests conducted over several days in an antiwar tax protest. This protest encouraged citizens to refuse to pay their taxes, especially the amount designated for funding the Vietnam War.

July: Antiwar protests, demonstrations, teach-ins, and sit-ins continued at many college campuses.

1967

January 14: Approximately thirty thousand demonstrators stage a Human Be-In in San Francisco's Golden Park.

February: Members of Women Strike for Peace (WSP) marched to the Pentagon, conducted a peaceful demonstration, but were refused a meeting with Secretary of Defense Robert McNamara.

February 8: American Christian groups stage a nationwide Fast for Peace.

March 12: A three-page antiwar ad appeared in the *New York Times*. This ad contained approximately seven thousand signatures of teachers and professors.

March 17: Another group of antiwar demonstrators march to the Pentagon and protest the Vietnam War.

March 25: Dr. Martin Luther King Jr. led a large march of five thousand protestors against the Vietnam War in Chicago.

April: Muhammad Ali was drafted but refused induction. He was stripped of his heavyweight title and found guilty of violating the Selective Service Act. In June, the Supreme Court overturned his conviction.

MAJOR (RETIRED) STEVEN E COOK

April 4: Dr. Martin Luther King Jr. gave an antiwar speech in New York City.

April 15: The Spring Mobilization Committee to End the War in Vietnam organized four hundred thousand antiwar demonstrators and marched from Central Park to the United Nations building in New York City. Later, Coretta Scott King along with twenty thousand antiwar demonstrators marched in San Francisco near the city hall.

April 24: A small group of antiwar protestors led by Abbie Hoffman interrupted the New York Stock Exchange with verbal antiwar chants and slogans.

May 2: A mock trial was conducted in Stockholm alleging that the US had committed war crimes in South Vietnam.

May 22: A fashionable department store in Brussels burnt down. Speculation pointed to the Belgian Maoists against the Vietnam War.

May 30: Several Vietnam War veterans attended a peace demonstration in Washington DC, and the next day, they formed the Vietnam Veterans against the War.

June 23: A coalition of more than eighty antiwar groups conducted a massive war protest in Los Angeles.

July: Antiwar protests and demonstrations continued across America.

August 28: Several US congressmen made antiwar speeches before Congress.

September 20: Over one thousand members of Women Strike for Peace (WSP) rally at the White House. Some minor scuffling with the police tarnished the nonviolent reputation of the WSP.

October: Antiwar demonstrations were conducted in The Hague, Netherlands. Stop the Draft Week in America resulted in major clashes at the Oakland, California, military induction center. Over one thousand draft cards were returned to local draft boards.

October 20: Over three hundred students at the University of Wisconsin attempted to prevent Dow Chemical Company from holding job fairs on campus.

October 21: The National Mobilization Committee to End the War in Vietnam organized one hundred thousand antiwar protesters at the Lincoln Memorial in Washington DC; later, thirty thousand marched to the Pentagon. There were several clashes with police and soldiers.

1968

January 15: The first all-female antiwar protest was conducted in Washington DC. Over five thousand women rallied with the goal to get Congress to withdraw troops from the Vietnam War.

January 18: During a conference in the White House about juvenile delinquency, black singer Eartha Kitt yelled at Mrs. Johnson about many young men dying in South Vietnam.

January 30: The Tet Offensive resulted in higher US casualties and increased heavy criticism against the Pentagon and American foreign policy.

February: Small antiwar protests continued.

March 12: Antiwar candidate Eugene McCarthy received more votes than expected in the New Hampshire primary.

March 16: Robert Kennedy joined the presidential race as an antiwar candidate.

March 17: Over ten thousand rallied peacefully outside the US embassy in London. The rally later turned into a riot.

April 17: An antiwar riot in Berkley was filmed by the news media and broadcast overseas, igniting reactions and small demonstrations.

April 26: In a show of unity, a million college and high school students boycotted class to support the antiwar movement.

April 27: Police in Chicago beat antiwar protesters for marching.

August 26–29: During the Democratic National Convention held in Chicago, antiwar marchers demonstrated throughout the city. Tensions between the protesters and police quickly intensified and terminated in a police riot.

October: US public opinion on war shifted from support for the war to opposition.

1969

March: Students at SUNY in Buffalo destroyed a Themis construction site to protest the Vietnam War. Women Strike for Peace picketed Washington DC in the first large antiwar demonstration since Nixon's inauguration.

April 6: Several spontaneous antiwar protests and rallies in New York City's Central Park were recorded by the media.

May 22: The Canadian government announced that immigration officials had lessened and reduced constraints on US draft evaders attempting to cross the Canadian border for permanent residence.

July 16: Activist David Harris was arrested for refusing the draft. He was sentenced and served fifteen months in prison.

July: Many small antiwar demonstrations continued.

August 15–18: The Woodstock Festival was held on a farm in Bethel, New York. This was a pivotal music event and a large antiwar gathering.

October 15: Millions of Americans took the day off from work and school to participate in a Moratorium to End the War in Vietnam.

October: A Gallup poll reflected that 60 percent of respondents stated that the Vietnam War was a mistake.

November: Several corporate offices and military installations in and around New York City were bombed by antiwar organizations.

November 15: The New Mobilization Committee to End the War in Vietnam (New Mobe) organized and conducted a large antiwar demonstration of up to five hundred thousand protesters in Washington DC. A similar demonstration was conducted in San Francisco, simultaneous with the New York City demonstration

December: The And Babies poster is published. This poster by Ronald Haeberle was a color photo of the My Lai massacre. The poster vented the antiwar sentiment that so many Americans felt about the Vietnam War.

Questions for Reflection

1. Name and describe four major goals of the peace and anti-war movement.
2. Name and describe four results of the peace and antiwar movement.
3. Name and describe three reasons for women to join the peace and antiwar movement.
4. Describe the 1968 Democratic National Convention and how the convention affected the Vietnam War.
5. Name and describe four antiwar chants and/or slogans.
6. Why did the peace and antiwar movement decline?
7. Name three antiwar and peace organizations and describe their goal, mission, or objective.

Moratorium Day, November 15, 1969.
At the Washington Monument.

Antiwar demonstrators marching.

Chapter 13

Nixon's Asian Abyss

Peace with honor? Should I stay, or should I go?

President Nixon frequently wrote or stated that ending the Vietnam War was his first priority. Although President Nixon initially escalated America's involvement in the Vietnam War, he subsequently ended US involvement by 1973. Nixon's intent and goal was to bring the Vietnam War to an honorable end. He brought death, destruction, and disgrace instead.

At the end of 1967, Nixon told his family he planned to run for president a second time. Nixon believed that with the Democrats torn over the issue of the Vietnam War, a Republican had a good chance of winning, although he expected the election to be as close as in 1960.

After doing poorly in the New Hampshire primary, President Johnson withdrew unexpectedly as a presidential candidate. Nixon secured the nomination on the first ballot at the Republican convention. Nixon selected Maryland governor Spiro Agnew as his running mate for vice president. This logic would unite the party, appealing to both northern moderates and southerners disaffected with the Democrats.

Vice President Hubert Humphrey was Nixon's Democratic opponent in the general election. Humphrey was nominated at a tumultuous convention marked by violent protests. Throughout the campaign, Nixon portrayed himself as a figure of stability during a period of national unrest and upheaval. He appealed to what he later called the "silent majority" of socially conservative Americans who disliked the hippie counterculture and the antiwar demonstrators. Agnew became an increasingly vocal critic of these groups, solidifying Nixon's position with the right.

Nixon waged a prominent, professional, and better television advertising campaign than Humphrey. Nixon used the meet and greet technique with supporters in front of cameras and promised "peace with honor" in the Vietnam War. This "peace with honor" was a concept and election promise that did not define any specifics of how he hoped to end the war. Nixon would only promise that he had a "secret plan" to end the war, a plan that never existed, as he later admitted to an interviewer.

President Johnson's negotiators began peace talks in March 1968 with a goal to reach a truce in Vietnam prior to the election. Nixon received astute analysis on the peace talks from Henry Kissinger and advice from Anna Chennault. She advised South Vietnamese president Thieu not to go to Paris to join the talks, to wait out the storm, and suggested that Nixon would give him a better deal if elected. Johnson was well aware of the situation and had both Chennault and the South Vietnamese ambassador to Washington bugged. Johnson was furious and blamed Nixon for these shenanigans and for trying to undermine US foreign policy.

On October 31, with no agreement, Johnson announced a unilateral halt to the bombing; and those peace negotiations would start in Paris on November 6. On November 2, after speaking with Chennault again, Thieu stated he would not go to Paris. Johnson telephoned Nixon, who denied any involvement; the president did not believe him. Johnson felt he could not publicly mention Chennault's involvement, which had been obtained by wiretapping.

In a three-way race between Nixon, Humphrey, and independent candidate Alabama governor George Wallace, Nixon defeated Humphrey by nearly five hundred thousand votes. In his victory speech, Nixon pledged that his administration would try to bring the divided nation together. Nixon said, "I have received a very gracious message from the Vice President, congratulating me for winning the election. I congratulated him for his gallant and courageous fight against great odds."

Nixon was inaugurated as president on January 20, 1969. His inauguration did not end the war, and the war escalated in Southeast Asia.[32] America was losing three hundred soldiers weekly in South Vietnam when Nixon took office. The war was broadly unpopular in the United States, with violent protests against the war ongoing. The Johnson administration had agreed to suspend bombing in exchange for negotiations without preconditions, but this agreement never fully took force. According to Walter Isaacson, a noted author, soon after taking office, Nixon had concluded that the Vietnam War could not be won, and he was determined to end the war quickly. Nixon sincerely believed he could intimidate North Vietnam through the madman theory. The madman theory was Nixon projecting power through the perceived use of atomic bombs and weapons.

Later, Nixon approved a secret bombing campaign of North Vietnamese and allied Khmer Rouge positions in Cambodia in March 1969 (code-named Operation Menu), a policy begun under Johnson.[33] These operations resulted in heavy bombing of Cambodia; by one measurement, more bombs were dropped over Cambodia under Johnson and Nixon than the Allies dropped during World War II. In mid-1969, Nixon began efforts to negotiate peace with the North Vietnamese, sending a personal letter to North Vietnamese leaders and conducting peace talks in Paris. Initial talks, however, did not result in an agreement. In May 1969, Nixon publicly proposed to withdraw all American troops from South Vietnam provided North Vietnam also did so, and for South Vietnam to hold internationally supervised elections with Viet Cong participation.

In July 1969, Nixon visited South Vietnam, where he met with his US military commanders and President Nguyen Van Thieu. Amid protests at home demanding an immediate pullout, he implemented a strategy of replacing American troops with Vietnamese troops, known as Vietnamization. He soon instituted phased US

[32.] Richard Nixon, *In the Arena* (1990), 342.

[33.] *The Memoirs of Richard Nixon* (1978), 381.

troop withdrawals but authorized incursions into Laos, in part to interrupt the Ho Chi Minh trail, used to supply North Vietnamese forces that passed through Laos and Cambodia. In July, US troop withdrawal began. The gradual withdraw of US military from South Vietnam was a critical and necessary component of Nixon's plan to end the war. Nixon announced the ground invasion of Cambodia to the American public on April 30, 1970.[34] The Cambodian incursion proved little except that the Army of the Republic of Vietnam was not ready to fight and conduct military operations on its own. His responses to protesters included an impromptu early-morning meeting with them at the Lincoln Memorial on May 9, 1970. Documents uncovered from the Soviet archives after 1991 reveal that the North Vietnamese attempt to overrun Cambodia in 1970 was launched at the explicit request of the Khmer Rouge and negotiated by Pol Pot's then second-in-command, Nuon Chea. Nixon's campaign promise to curb the war contrasted with the escalated bombing and led to claims that Nixon had a "credibility gap" on the issue.

In 1971, excerpts from the *Pentagon Papers*, which had been leaked by Daniel Ellsberg, were published by the *New York Times* and the *Washington Post*.[35] When news of the leak first appeared, Nixon was inclined to do nothing; the *Papers*, a history of United States' involvement in Vietnam, mostly concerned the lies of prior administrations and contained few real revelations. He was persuaded by Kissinger that the papers were more harmful than they appeared, so the president tried to prevent publication. The Supreme Court eventually ruled for the newspapers.

Operation Linebacker I

During March through September 1972, the North Vietnamese launched the Eastertide Offensive as two hundred thousand North Vietnamese soldiers under the command of General Giap waged an all-out military assault to conquer South Vietnam. Giap's immediate

---

[34.] Ibid., 449.
[35.] Ibid., 508.

objective is conquering the major cities of Quang Tri in the North, Kontum in the Central Highlands, and An Loc in the South. Nixon declared, "The bastards have never been bombed like they're going to be bombed this time." Nixon commenced Operation Linebacker I on May 10, 1972. The operation was a massive air bombing of North Vietnam. Operation Linebacker I was a classic conventional air interdiction operation that stopped a conventional invasion by 14 NVA divisions. Operation Linebacker I had three strategic objectives:

1. Destroy enemy supplies inside North Vietnam
2. Isolate North Vietnam from receiving external logistics
3. Interdict and destroy the infiltration of logistics and troops into the battle sites of South Vietnam

For the first time, US planners and commanders had more latitude to select critical targets. Smart precision-guided munitions and advanced navigational bombing systems minimized collateral damage. Highways, railroads, bridges, warehouses, petroleum sites, military sites, and power-producing facilities were bombed. By September, it was apparent that Linebacker I was having a major impact in the North. On September 23, Nixon ordered a bombing halt, but Hanoi balked at the peace terms. Linebacker I ended on October 23, 1972.

Operation Linebacker II: The Air Force's Eleven-Day War

On December 13, the Paris peace talks stalled and broke down. President Nixon immediately issued an ultimatum to Hanoi.[36] Nixon told Hanoi, "Return to the conference table within 72 hours or else." To demonstrate his seriousness to Thieu, Nixon ordered the heavy Operation Linebacker II bombings of North Vietnam in December 1972. Because of winter weather, the Air Force was forced to use the B-52 and the F-111 fighter-bombers and the Navy's A-6 Intruders. These were the only US aircraft with all-weather bombing capability.

[36.] Ibid., 734–741.

The majority of the missions were conducted by B-52s. The target lists were virtually identical to Linebacker I. Mines were also dropped by aircraft into Hai Phong harbor. Over the next several nights, massive B-52 strikes continued to pound North Vietnam. These strikes contained from thirty to one hundred B-52s in each air bombing mission. Linebacker II ended on December 29 as the most intensive bombing campaign of the entire war, with over one hundred thousand bombs dropped on Hanoi and Haiphong. Although Linebacker II ended, the bombing did not. B-52s continued to bomb NVA strategic targets in North Vietnam's southern panhandle.

Linebacker I was an interdiction campaign to compel the North to negotiate seriously. Linebacker II was a strategic bombing campaign aimed at the will of the Hanoi leadership to come to a quick agreement on a cease-fire. Peace talks between Kissinger and Le Duc Tho resumed in January. Fifteen B-52s were shot down during Linebacker II.

As US troop withdrawals continued, the draft was reduced and, in 1973, ended; the Armed Forces became all-volunteer. After years of fighting, the Paris Peace Accords were signed at the beginning of 1973. The agreement implemented a cease-fire and allowed for the withdrawal of remaining American troops; however, it did not require the 160,000 North Vietnam Army regulars located in the South to withdraw. The North Vietnamese agreed to an immediate cease-fire and the release of all American prisoners of war. Vietnam is still divided. Once American combat support ended in 1973, there was a brief truce, before fighting broke out again, this time without American combat involvement. North Vietnam invaded and conquered South Vietnam in 1975.

Nixon Doctrine

The Nixon Doctrine is made public. It advocates US military and economic assistance to nations around the world struggling against communism, but no more Vietnam-style wars involving American troops.[37]

When Richard Nixon became the president of the United States in 1969, US combat troop involvement in the Vietnam War had been continuing for almost four years. It had so far resulted in a sacrifice of more than thirty thousand Americans and countless Vietnamese civilians and soldiers. Because Nixon campaigned for "peace with honor" regarding Vietnam in 1968, peace with Vietnam became an important plan for Nixon. During a stopover at Guam in the middle of an international tour, President Richard Nixon issued the Nixon Doctrine, also known as the Guam Doctrine, during a "Silent Majority" speech in a press conference on July 25, 1969. According to Gregg Brazinsky, Nixon stated that "the United States would assist in the defense and developments of allies and friends," but would not "undertake all the defense of the free nations of the world." This doctrine meant that each ally nation was in charge of its own security in general, but the United States would act as a nuclear umbrella when requested. The Doctrine argued for the pursuit of peace through a partnership with American allies. The Nixon Doctrine implied the intentions of Richard Nixon shifting the direction on international policies in Asia, especially aiming for "Vietnamization of the Vietnam War." Many interpreted the Nixon Doctrine as meaning that Nixon planned to abandon South Vietnam once US troops had withdrawn.

President Nixon, in an Address to the Nation on the war in Vietnam (November 3, 1969), stated,

1. "First, the United States will keep all of its treaty commitments."
2. "Second, we shall provide a shield if a nuclear power threatens the freedom of a nation allied with us or of a nation whose survival we consider vital to our security."
3. Third, in cases involving other types of aggression, we shall furnish military and economic assistance when requested in accordance with our treaty commitments. But we shall

---

[37.] Ibid., 394–395.

look to the nation directly threatened to assume the primary responsibility of providing the manpower for its defense."

The Doctrine was also applied by the Nixon administration to other Asian countries such as the Philippines, Thailand, South Korea, and others that might be threatened by communist aggression.

While Nixon was president, a resolution of the Vietnam War was essentially mandatory due to growing public opinion in favor of withdrawal. A Gallup poll in May 1970 showed 56 percent of the public believed sending troops to Vietnam was a mistake. Of those over fifty years old, 61 percent expressed that belief, (compared to 49 percent of those between twenty-one and twenty-nine years old), even if tacit abandonment of the SEATO Treaty was ultimately required, resulting in a complete communist takeover of South Vietnam.

Vietnamization

President Richard Nixon developed and implemented Vietnamization in 1969 to end the US involvement in the Vietnam War by combining a policy of South Vietnamese self-reliance with a policy of détente with the Soviet Union and China. Nixon hoped that the communist powers would pressure the North into ending the war. Many elements were essential if Vietnamization were to be successful. Major US goals were to expand, equip, and train South Vietnam's forces and assign to them an ever-increasing combat role, at the same time steadily reducing the number of US combat troops. Other major tasks included pacification of rural areas, providing essential services to all citizens, security for the populace, and improving the economy. Subsidiary objectives included land reform, local hamlet and village elections, increasing the rice harvest, and eliminating the Viet Cong.[38]

Initiated by the Viet Cong's Tet Offensive, the policy referred to US combat troops specifically in the ground combat role, but did

---

[38.] Ibid., 274, 392, 400–401, 448–453.

not reject combat by the US Air Force, as well as the support to South Vietnam, consistent with the policies of US foreign military assistance organizations. US citizens' mistrust of their government began after the Tet Offensive worsened and with the release of news about US soldiers massacring civilians at My Lai (1968), the invasion of Cambodia (1970), and the leaking of the *Pentagon Papers* (1971).

The name *Vietnamization* came about accidentally. At a January 28, 1969, meeting of the National Security Council, General Andrew Goodpaster, deputy to General Creighton Abrams and commander of the Military Assistance Command, Vietnam, stated that the Army of the Republic of Vietnam (ARVN) had been steadily improving, and the point at which the war could be "de-Americanized" was close. Secretary of Defense Melvin Laird agreed with the point, but not with the language: "What we need is a term like 'Vietnamizing' to put the emphasis on the right issues." Nixon immediately liked Laird's word.

Vietnamization fit into the broader détente policy of the Nixon administration, in which the United States no longer regarded its fundamental strategy as the containment of communism but as a cooperative world order, in which Nixon and his chief adviser Henry Kissinger were focused on the broader constellation of forces and the bigger world powers. Nixon had ordered Kissinger to negotiate diplomatic policies with Soviet statesman Anatoly Dobrynin. Nixon also opened high-level contact with China. US relations with the Soviet Union and China were of higher priority than South Vietnam.

Nixon said Vietnamization had two components. The first was "strengthening the armed forces of the South Vietnamese in numbers, equipment, leadership and combat skills." The second was "the extension of the pacification program (i.e. military aid to civilians) in South Vietnam." To achieve the first goal, US helicopters would fly in support; however, helicopter operations frequently required ground operations and involvement of US military personnel. Thus, ARVN candidates were enrolled in US helicopter schools to take over the air operations. As observed by Lieutenant Dave Palmer, to qualify an ARVN candidate for US helicopter school, he first needed to learn English; this, in addition to the months-long training and practice in the field, made adding new capabilities to the ARVN take at least two years. I had six South Vietnamese Army Officer Candidates in my Infantry Officer Candidate class in 1970 at Fort Benning, Georgia. Their English was mediocre at best, and their performance was worse. Palmer did not disagree that the first component, given time and resources, was achievable. However, "pacification, the second component, presented the real challenge . . . it was benevolent government action in areas where the government should always have been benevolently active . . . doing both was necessary if Vietnamization were to work."

Under the Nixon administration, Henry Kissinger, Nixon's chief adviser, asked the Rand Corporation to provide a list of policy options, prepared by Daniel Ellsberg. On receiving the report, Kissinger and Schelling asked Ellsberg about the apparent absence of a victory option; Ellsberg said, "I don't believe there is a win option in Vietnam." While Ellsberg eventually did send a withdrawal option, Kissinger would not circulate something that could be perceived as defeat.

Nixon directed the Joint Chiefs of Staff to prepare a six-step withdrawal plan. The commandant of the Marine Corps General Leonard F. Chapman remembered, "I felt, and I think that most Marines felt, that the time had come to get out of Vietnam." Marine redeployments started in mid-1969, and by the end of the year, the entire 3rd Marine Division had departed from South Vietnam. General Abrams stated that "Vietnamization was a South Vietnam slow surrender." General Abrams also objected and opposed the accelerated timetable of American troop withdrawal in 1971.

In the aftermath of the Tet Offensive, ARVN units were able to take control of areas held by the Viet Cong. General Tran Van Tra of the Viet Cong forces in the South stated, "We suffered large sacrifices and losses with regard to manpower and materiel, especially cadres at the various echelons, which clearly weakened us. Afterward, we were not only unable to retain the gains we had made but had to overcome a myriad of difficulties in 1969 and 1970." Some ARVN units, especially that had been operating closely with US troops or using US facilities, could quickly move into a dominant role in their areas.

Other ARVN units faced more of a challenge. For example, the ARVN 5th Division was directed to move from its existing base camp, Phu Cuong, to that of the US 1st Infantry Division in Lai Khê, while the US division moved southeast to Dĩ An. The ARVN unit had to retain its previous operational responsibility, while replacing a division that was far better equipped with helicopters than a standard US division. At Phu Cong, Major General Nguyen Van Hieu, the 5th Division commander, was able to use a local Popular Force battalion for base security. The Popular Force battalions, however, did not move away from the area in which they were formed.

Soon after the last US military forces departed, the South Vietnamese were required to prosecute the war without major military, economic, and financial aid and assistance from the US and from their former allies. In the spring of 1975, the North invaded and attacked the South. After the initial victories, the North accelerated their offensive. On April 30, the last Marines departed from the American Embassy in the early morning, ending the US presence in South Vietnam. At noon, the North Vietnamese Army steamrolled into Saigon and occupied the presidential palace. The swift retribution that Nixon promised after the North violated the peace agreement never materialized. The war was over.

Why Vietnamization Failed

Vietnamization was not the Marshall Plan and was a catastrophic miscalculated blunder by Nixon. In 1969, Nixon abdicated his prosecution of the war to the South Vietnamese government through Vietnamization. He was captivated and enamored with Vietnamization. Nixon's misconceived Vietnamization pipe dream had military, economic and fiscal problems. Nixon was combining the war, Vietnamization, troop withdrawal, and peace negotiations, hoping that Hanoi would realize that a peace deal would yield a better position and settlement for the North. The US troop withdrawals only emboldened the North. With US troops departing South Vietnam, the North stepped up attacks against the South. All Hanoi had to do was wait out the US troop withdrawals. Gradual withdrawal placated US public opinion and added time for Nixon to implement Vietnamization.

Vietnamization imposed severe hardships and constraints on the South Vietnamese Army that could not be overcome and solved. The US transferred massive amounts of equipment, weapons, and materiel to the ARVNs; however, Congress reduced funding that limited the combat operations of the South to fight the high-technology war, which they had been trained. The ARVNs never achieved the leadership and direction required in an effective military. Pervasive corruption was the ARVN's most debilitating deficiency. The massive ARVN corruption ruined their will to fight and weakened and handicapped their chain of command. Senior officers operated their logistics and technical services for their own personal financial benefit. The ARVNs were underpaid, and most had to buy their own rations. Combat operations were curtailed, and many conducted ineffective pseudo deployments that never engaged the NVA. The ARVNs had sufficient numbers in their ground forces but had very few jets in their Air Force to support and sustain any ARVN ground military operation.

Vietnamization limited and phased out US military operations. There were no large-scale reconnaissance-in-force missions. Small unit operations, patrolling, and no major battles were the order. These scaled-back operations encouraged and strengthened the NVA and gave them time to plan and conduct battalion-size and larger operations against US and allied firebases and military installations. American artillery and air strike requests had to have the initials of the chief of province included. Occasionally, this took several additional minutes to get his initials.

Nixon failed to honor his promise that the US would keep all its treaty agreements, including military and economic aid if requested. In 1973, Nixon began to experience political turbulence and troubles at home, apathy was rabid in the US Congress, and war weariness was increasing among Americans. Congress severely cut the foreign aid to South Vietnam from $2.3 million to $1 million for 1974. South Vietnam had to cut military operations as much as 50 percent because the US could not replace and resupply ARVN equipment as permitted by the Paris peace treaty. After Congress discovered the illegal bombing in Cambodia on May 10, 1973, they cut off all funding for further US air operations in Southeast Asia. Congress continued to constrain and keep Nixon in check. In June, the US Congress passed the Case-Church Amendment, which mandated no further military actions in Southeast Asia. This amendment was a carte blanche menu for Hanoi to wage another invasion and unrestricted military operations in the South without fear of US bombing or reprisal. On November 6, 1973, Congress approved the War Powers Act in spite of Nixon's veto. The Watergate scandal forced Nixon to resign in August 1974. Gerald Ford assumed the presidency.

On January 7, 1975, the NVA attacked and captured the provincial capital of Phuoc Binh. The US failed to respond, and Hanoi knew that most Americas had lost interest in South Vietnam. Capturing Phuoc Binh delighted Hanoi, and the North politburo knew that the NVA could attack and capture key towns in the Central Highlands. The final military phase and operation had begun. Although the US Congress approved a token humanitarian package, they refused to approve having American military reenter the war.

The Southeast Asia Treaty Organization (SEATO) failed. This organization was an international organization for collective defense in Southeast Asia created by the Southeast Asia Collective Defense Treaty, or Manila Pact, signed in September 1954 in Manila, Philippines. The formal institution of SEATO was established on February 19, 1955, at a meeting of treaty partners in Bangkok, Thailand. The organization's headquarters was also in Bangkok. Eight members joined the organization.

SEATO was intended to be a Southeast Asian version of the North Atlantic Treaty Organization (NATO), in which the military forces of each member would be coordinated to provide for the collective defense of the members' country. Organizationally, SEATO was headed by the secretary-general, whose office was created in 1957 at a meeting in Canberra, with a council of representatives from member nations and an international staff. Also present were committees for economics, security, and information.

Unlike the NATO alliance, SEATO had no joint commands with standing forces to support South Vietnam. Without permanent military, members were to confer in case of aggression against a signatory or protocol state. In addition, SEATO's response protocol in the event of communism presenting a "common danger" to the member nations was vague and ineffective, though membership in the SEATO alliance did provide a rationale for a large-scale US military intervention in the region during the Vietnam War (1955–1975). Despite its name, SEATO mostly included countries located outside of the region but with an interest either in the region or the organization itself. They were Australia, France, New Zealand, Pakistan (including East Pakistan, now Bangladesh), the Philippines, Thailand, the United Kingdom, and the United States.

Vietnam, Cambodia, and Laos were prevented from taking part in any international military alliance as a result of the Geneva Agreements signed July 20 of the same year, concluding the end of the First Indochina War. However, with the lingering threat coming from communist North Vietnam and the possibility of the domino theory with Indochina turning into a communist frontier, SEATO got these countries under its protection—an act that would be considered to be one of the main justifications for the US involvement in the Vietnam War. Cambodia however rejected the protection in 1956.

Primarily created to block further communist gains in Southeast Asia, SEATO is generally considered a failure because internal conflict and dispute hindered general use of the SEATO military; however, SEATO-funded cultural and educational programs left long-standing effects in Southeast Asia. SEATO was dissolved on June 30, 1977, after many members lost interest and withdrew.

The Paris Peace Accords

After Hanoi's final victory in 1975, North Vietnamese General Tran Van Tra stated in the Communist Party organ *Nhan Dan* that by late 1972, his troops were on the verge of defeat. Had the war continued some months further, the South, with continued US support, could have emerged victorious by evicting all enemy forces from South Vietnam. Faced with defeat, Hanoi offered substantial concessions sought by Henry Kissinger in previous negotiations. Kissinger took the bait. The ensuing process brought South Vietnamese military operations to a halt and prevented a military victory for the South. The US then dragooned the South Vietnamese into accepting the ill-conceived 1973 Paris Peace Accords.[39]

The Paris Peace Accords of 1973 was a sham, a travesty, and not ratified by the US Senate. This renegade ad hoc document was a mere diplomat backroom drug deal to fast-track the end of the war for the US. Although it ended the US involvement, the war continued for the South Vietnamese against the North. There was no quid pro quo in the accords. The remaining objectives of the Paris Peace Accords were not achieved; no national council was created for reconciliation, no political settlement was reached, and no elections were conducted. Two years after the accords were signed, the agreement faded away and was forgotten.

The document began with the statement that "the United States and all other countries respect the independence, sovereignty, unity, and territorial integrity of Vietnam" as recognized by the 1954 Geneva Agreements on Vietnam." The inclusion of this provision was a victory for the communist side of the negotiations by allowing that the war was not a foreign aggression against South Vietnam. The main military and political provisions of the agreement were as follows:

> Beginning on January 27, 1973 at midnight, Greenwich Mean Time—in Saigon time, 8 A. M. on January 28—there would be an in-place cease-fire. North and South Vietnamese forces were to hold their locations. Both North and South tried to seize more territory before the truce. The North were fighting more aggressively before the truce began and penetrated more than 400 towns

---

[39.] Ibid., 322–329, 445, 446, 583–590, 888, 889, and 977.

and hamlets and cut all major highways. Kissinger capitulated, compromised and permitted Hanoi to maintain approximately 160,000 NVA soldiers in the South. Approximately 50 percent of these soldiers were infused into major Viet Cong leadership positions. This proxy force was held in escrow until a major offensive by the North. Both sides were permitted to resupply military materials to the extent necessary to replace items consumed in the course of the truce.

There would be no negotiations or elections as scripted in the accords between the two South Vietnamese parties—Saigon and the Viet Cong—toward a political settlement that would allow the South Vietnamese people to "decide themselves the political future of South Vietnam through genuinely free and democratic general elections under international supervision.

The war continued as before, preventing the reunification of Vietnam, which was to be "carried out step by step through peaceful means," as specified in the accords. The Paris Peace Accords did not extinguish the North's determination to fight on. After the NVA captured the province capital of Phuoc Binh, the Soviet Armed Forces chief general Viktor Kulikov flew to Hanoi and offered an increase of 400 percent in military aid to continue military operations in the South. General Kulikov stated, "The 400 percent increase in military aid is to destroy the South Vietnamese Army." China immediately followed and provided critical military aid. This was in violation of chapter I, article 3 of the Paris Peace Accords.

Hanoi trumped and played the US. For five months, the negotiations stalled as North Vietnam demanded that all bombing of North Vietnam be stopped, while the US side demanded that North Vietnam agree to a reciprocal de-escalation in South Vietnam; it was not until October 31 that Johnson agreed to end the air strikes and serious negotiations could begin.

One of the largest hurdles to effective negotiation was the fact that North Vietnam and its ally in South Vietnam, the National Front for the Liberation of South Vietnam (NLF, or Viet Cong), refused to recognize the government of South Vietnam; with equal persistence, the government in Saigon refused to acknowledge the legitimacy of the NLF. W. Averell Harriman was a veteran diplomat and Johnson's personal representative initially for the peace talks. Harriman resolved this dispute by developing a system by which North Vietnam and the US would be the named parties; NLF officials could join the North Vietnamese team without being recognized by South Vietnam, while Saigon's representatives joined their US allies.

Another juvenile debate concerned the table to be used at the conference. The North favored a circular table, in which all parties, including NLF representatives, would appear to be "equal" in importance. The South Vietnamese argued that only a rectangular table was acceptable, for only a rectangle could show two distinct sides to the conflict. Eventually a compromise was reached, in which representatives of the northern and southern governments would sit at a circular table, with members representing all other parties sitting on individual square tables around them.

In 1969, Richard Nixon succeeded to the US presidency and replaced Harriman with Henry Cabot Lodge Jr., who was later replaced by David Bruce. Also that year, the NLF set up a Provisional Revolutionary Government (PRG), to gain government status at the talks. However, the primary negotiations that led to the agreement did not occur at the peace conference main table at all. Kissinger may have been exceeding his charter and developing US foreign policy in secret backroom negotiations. These secret backroom negotiations were carried out during secret meetings between Kissinger and Le Duc Tho, which began on August 4, 1969. Why weren't these backroom secret negotiations transparent?

The major breakthrough came on October 8, 1972. North Vietnam had been disappointed by the results of its Nguyen Hue Offensive (known in the West as the Easter Offensive) and feared increased isolation if Nixon's efforts at détente significantly improved US relations with the chief communist powers, the Soviet Union, and the People's Republic of China, who were backing the North Vietnamese military effort. In a meeting with Kissinger, Tho significantly modified his bargaining line, allowing that the Saigon government could remain in power and that negotiations between the two South Vietnamese parties could develop a final settlement. Within ten days, the secret talks drew up a final draft. Kissinger held a press conference in Washington during which he announced that "peace is at hand."

When Thieu, who had not been informed of the secret negotiations, was presented with the draft of the new agreement, he was furious with Kissinger and Nixon (who were perfectly aware of South Vietnam's negotiating position) and refused to accept it without significant changes. He then made several public radio addresses, claiming that the proposed agreement was worse than it actually was. Hanoi was astonished, believing that it had been duped into a propaganda ploy by Kissinger. On October 26, Radio Hanoi broadcast key details of the draft agreement.

However, as US casualties mounted throughout the conflict, American domestic support for the war had deteriorated, and by 1973, there was major pressure on the Nixon administration to withdraw. Consequently, the US brought great diplomatic pressure upon their South Vietnamese ally to sign the peace treaty even if the concessions Thieu wanted could not be achieved. Nixon pledged continued substantial aid to South Vietnam, and given his recent landslide victory in the presidential election, it seemed possible that he would be able to follow through on that pledge. With the US committed to disengagement (and after threats from Nixon that South Vietnam would be abandoned if he did not agree), Thieu had little choice but to accede.

On January 15, 1973, Nixon announced a suspension of offensive actions against North Vietnam. Kissinger and Tho met again on January 23 and signed off on a treaty that was basically identical to the draft of three months earlier. The agreement was signed by the leaders of the official delegations on January 27 at the Majestic Hotel in Paris.

Nixon gave the South to the North and united the countries, as stipulated in the Paris Peace Accords. Chapter V, Article 15, Paragraph A states, "The military demarcation line between the two zones at the 17th parallel is only provisional and not a political or territorial boundary as provided for in paragraph 6 of the Final Declaration of the 1954 Geneva Conference." This paragraph negated the North/South boundary at the 17th parallel and in essence reunited the two countries before the war was over and which had long been Hanoi's objective.

Chapter V, Article 15 also countermands and nullifies Chapter I, Article 1, which states, "The United States and all other countries respect the independence, sovereignty, unity, and territorial integrity of Vietnam as recognized by the 1954 Geneva Agreements on Vietnam." The 160,000 NVA troops that were permitted to remain in the South post peace treaty were more than occupational troops. They were the advance guard for future Hanoi military offensives in the South.

The Paris Peace Accords had little practical effect on the conflict, and was routinely flouted, mainly by the North Vietnamese, as well as the Saigon government, which enlarged the area under its control in 1973. The Peace Treaty was flawed and not enforceable. North Vietnamese military forces blatantly moved through the southern provinces and, two years later, were in position to capture Saigon.

Nixon had secretly promised Thieu that he would use airpower to support the Saigon government should it be necessary. During his confirmation hearings in June 1973, Secretary of Defense James Schlesinger was sharply criticized by some senators after he stated that he would recommend resumption of US bombing in North Vietnam if North Vietnam launched a major offensive against South Vietnam. However, Nixon was driven from office due to the Watergate scandal in 1974, and when the North Vietnamese did begin their final offensive early in 1975, the United States Congress (controlled by the Democratic Party) refused to appropriate the funds needed by the South Vietnamese, who collapsed completely.

Thieu resigned, accusing the US of betrayal, in a TV and radio address: "At the time of the peace agreement the United States agreed to replace equipment on a one-by-one basis. But the United States did not keep its word. Is an American's word reliable these days? The United States did not keep its promise to help us fight for freedom and it was in the same fight that the United States lost 50,000 of its young men." The swift retaliation from the US never came.

The insidious Paris Peace Accords was Nixon's akin to commit legal treason and genocide against the South Vietnamese government and people. One could also argue that Nixon committed international treason against the Saigon government and aided and abetted the enemy via the Paris Peace Accords.

The North Vietnamese entered Saigon on April 30. Schlesinger had announced early in the morning of April 29, 1975, the evacuation from Saigon by helicopter of the last US diplomatic, military, and civilian personnel. The South Vietnamese government had lost the war. The only successful Vietnamization program was in the North. The Second Indochina War was over, and the Third Indochina War began almost immediately.

Questions for Reflection

1. Why was ending the Vietnam War Nixon's first priority?
2. Why did Nixon begin a gradual withdrawal before the Paris Peace Accords was signed?
3. Define the madman theory.
4. Define Operation Linebacker I and II.
5. Define the Nixon Doctrine.
6. Define and compare Vietnamization to the Marshall Plan.
7. Why did the South Vietnamese military fail?
8. Define the 1973 War Powers Act.
9. Why did SEATO fail?
10. Why was the Paris Peace Accords secretive and not more transparent?
11. Why didn't Nixon enforce the Paris Peace Accords?
12. Was Kissinger Hanoi's Trojan horse at the Paris Peace Accords?

CHAPTER 14

The Good Guys

There are no noble wars, just noble warriors.

The United States (US) began deploying military combat troops to South Vietnam in 1965. The majority of troops that fought in the Vietnam War were US Army soldiers. In September 1950, the Military Assistance Advisory Group (MAAG) was formed in Vietnam. The primary mission of the MAAG was to provide advisers, service support, and realistic combat training to the Republic of Vietnam military. In 1962, the Military Assistance Command Vietnam (MACV) was activated and assumed all duties of the MAAG. MACV was a joint command and coordinated all US military activities in South Vietnam. All MACV commanders and the majority of personnel on the joint staff were from the US Army. MACV was the sole commanding headquarters of all US military forces in South Vietnam. Subordinate commands were the following:

1. US Army Vietnam (USARV)
2. US Seventh Air Force
3. US III Marine Amphibious Force
4. US Navy units in South Vietnam
5. 5th Special Forces Group
6. IV Corps Advisory Group

The South Vietnam military divided the country into four corps tactical zones (CTZs). The US divided South Vietnam into two command and control regions called field forces: I Field Force commanded, planned, conducted, and controlled all land combat operations in the north; II Field Force commanded, planned, conducted, and controlled all land combat operations in the South. Later, III Field Force was activated to command, plan, conduct, and control land combat operations near the demilitarized zone.

Prior to 1965, America's support to South Vietnam consisted primarily of financial, logistical, economic, and military advisers. On February 7, 1965, the Viet Cong conducted a major attack against US military barracks at Camp Holloway near Pleiku and a nearby helicopter base, killing nine Americans and destroying several aircraft. In response, President Johnson ordered retaliatory air strikes against the North. Additional air assets were sent to South Vietnam that required an increase in combat forces. In March 1965, President Johnson ordered the deployment of 3,500 Marines and the Army's 173 Airborne Brigade to South Vietnam to assist in protecting US Air Force airfields. The Marine's mission was to guard the air base at Da Nang. Within a month, President Johnson secretly authorized the Marines to move out and engage the enemy in combat. Later in 1965, US military strength in South Vietnam began to increase dramatically. On July 28, President Johnson announced that he had ordered the addition of fifty thousand more troops for deployment to South Vietnam. The MACV commander General Westmoreland immediately submitted requests for more military forces. In 1966, General Westmoreland asked to raise the US troop ceiling in South Vietnam to 429,000. In 1967, General Westmoreland perpetually requested more troops beyond the authorized cap. The rigorous steady increase of US military troop levels is depicted below.

Total U.S. Military Personnel in South Vietnam

Date	Army	Navy	Marine Corps	Air Force	Coast Guard	Total
Jan 1, 1961	800	15	2	68	0	About 900
Jan 1, 1962	2,100	100	5	1,000	0	3,205
Jan 1, 1963	7,900	500	500	2,400	0	11,300
Jan 1, 1964	10,100	800	800	4,600	0	16,300
Jan 1, 1965	14,700	1,100	900	6,600	0	23,300
Jan 1, 1966	116,800	8,400	38,200	20,600	300	184,300
Jan 1, 1967	239,400	23,300	69,200	52,900	500	385,300
Jan 1, 1968	319,500	31,700	78,000	55,900	500	485,600
Jan 1, 1969	359,800	36,100	81,400	58,400	400	536,100
Apr 1969	*363,300*	*36,500*	*81,800*	*61,400*	*400*	*543,400**
Jan 1, 1970	331,100	30,200	55,100	58,400	400	475,200
Jan 1, 1971	249,600	16,700	25,100	43,100	100	334,600
Jan 1, 1972	119,700	7,600	600	28,800	100	156,800
Jan 1, 1973	13,800	1,500	1,200	7,600	100	24,200

*Peak Military Strength

MACV Major Operations
1964

Barrel Roll, Dec 14–Mar 29
Pierce Arrow, Aug 5

1965

Harvest Moon, Dec 8–20
Game Warden, 1965–1970
Flaming Dart, Feb
Market Time, 1965–1972
Steel Tiger, Apr 1965–Dec 1968
Tiger Hound, 1965–1973
Piranha, Sep

1966

Masher, Jan 24–Mar 6
Ala Morna, Dec 1, 1966–May 15, 1967

Hawthorne, June 2–20
Paul Revere I and II, May–Dec
Sea Dragon, Oct 1966–Oct 1968
Utah, Mar 4–7
Fairfax, Jul
White Wing, Jan 24–Mar 6
Abilene, Mar 30–Apr 15
Lexington III, Apr 17–June 9
Prairie, Aug 3, 1966–Mar 18, 1967
Texas, Mar 20–24
Attleboro, Nov 5–25
Irving, Oct 1–24
Crazy Horse, May 16–June 5

1967

King Fisher, July 16–Oct 31
Cedar Falls, Jan 8–26
Malheur I and II, May–Aug
Yellowstone, Dec 8, 1967–Feb 24, 1968
Wheeler, Nov 1967–Nov 1968
Macarthur, Oct 31, 1967–Jan 31, 1969
Lejeune, Apr 7–22
Junction City, Feb 22–May 14
Union I and II, Apr 21–June 5
Uniontown, Dec 1967–Mar 1968
Pershing, Feb 1967–Feb 1968
Scotland, Nov 1967–Mar 1968

1968

Pegasus/Lam Son 207A, April 1–15
Delaware, Apr 19–May 17
Niagara, Jan–Mar
Somerset Plain, Aug
Nevada Eagle, May 1968–Feb 1969

1969

Massachusetts Striker, Mar 1–May 8
Bold Mariner, Jan–Jul
Atlas Wedge, Mar 18–Apr 2
Apache Snow, May 10–June 7
Menue, Mar 18, 1969–May 26, 1970
Defiant Stand, Sep 7

1970

Jefferson Glenn, Sep 1970–Oct 1971
Binh Tay, May–June
Texas Star, Apr 1–Sep 5

1971

Lam Son 719, Feb 8–Mar 24

1972

Thunder Head, May 29–June 19

Major Battles, Raids, and Incursions

Ap Bac, Jan 2, 1963
Nam Dong, July 6, 1964
Binh Gia, Dec 28, 1964–Jan 1, 1965
Dong Xoai, June 9–12, 1965
Ia Drang, Oct 19–Nov 26, 1965
Khe Sanh, Apr–Oct 1967
Con Thien, Sep–Oct 1967
Song Be, Oct 27, 1967
Dac To, Nov 1967
Hue, Jan–Feb 1968
Khe Sanh, Jan–Mar 1968

Dong Ha, Apr 29–May 15, 1968
Kham Duc, May 11–12, 1968
Hamburger Hill, May 11–20, 1969
Cambodian Incursion, May–Jun 1970
Son Tay (Raid), Nov 20–21, 1970
Quang Tri, Mar–Apr 1972
An Loc, Apr 1972
Hue, Mar 1975
Ban Me Thuot, Mar 1975
Xuan Loc, Apr 9–23, 1975

MACV Military Campaigns

1. Advisory	Mar 15, 1962–Mar 7, 1965
2. Defense	Mar 8, 1965–Dec 24, 1965
3. Counteroffensive	Dec 25, 1965–June 30, 1966
4. Counteroffensive, Phase II	Jul 1, 1966–May 31, 1967
5. Counteroffensive, Phase III	Jun 1, 1967–Jan 29, 1968
6. Tet Counteroffensive	Jan 30, 1968–Apr 1, 1968
7. Counteroffensive, Phase IV	Apr 2, 1968–June 30, 1968
8. Counteroffensive, Phase V	Jul 1, 1968–Nov 1, 1968
9. Counteroffensive, Phase VI	Nov 2, 1968–Feb 22, 1969
10. Tet 69 / Counteroffensive	Feb 23, 1969–Jun 8, 1969
11. Summer/Fall 1969	Jun 9, 1969–Oct 31, 1969
12. Winter/Spring 1970	Nov 1, 1969–Apr 30, 1970
13. Sanctuary Counteroffensive	May 1, 1970–Jun 30, 1970
14. Counteroffensive, Phase VII	Jul 1, 1970–Jun 30, 1971
15. Consolidation I	July 1, 1971–Nov 30, 1971
16. Consolidation II	Dec 1, 1971–Mar 29, 1972
17. Cease-Fire	Mar 30, 1972–Jan 28, 1973

From March to December 1965, the MACV mission in South Vietnam was to delay the enemy while gaining time to build base camps. During this period, MACV attempted to consolidate its ground operations more efficiently. Based on this initiative, MACV organized the US Army Vietnam (USARV). This resolution assigned the Marine Corps to I Corps tactical zone to plan and conduct combat operations. The US Army was to operate primarily in II and III Corps tactical zones. The ARVNs, with US military advisers, had primary responsibility for the Delta area in IV Corps tactical zone.

US Army

At the height of the Vietnam War, seven of the Army's nineteen divisions were in South Vietnam. The seven divisions were 1st Infantry Division, 1st Cavalry Division, 4th Infantry Division, 9th Infantry Division, 25th Infantry Division, American Infantry Division (23rd Infantry Division), and the 101st Airborne Division. An armored Cavalry regiment and a few separate infantry brigades were assigned to South Vietnam also. A separate aviation brigade, engineer command, communications command, and various logistical units provided combat support and combat service support as needed. Generally, the divisions and separate units had specified areas of operation. The 1st Cavalry Division and 101st Airborne Division changed areas of operation occasionally.

The Army's primary mission in South Vietnam was to seek out and kill the enemy, destroy enemy base camps, cache sites, communications sites, and impede or stop enemy infiltration. General Westmoreland, the MACV commander, mounted large multi-battalion search-and-destroy operations to find the enemy and force him to fight. Westmoreland conceived the strategy of attrition. He envisioned that we could kill more enemy faster than could be replaced. Mission success or failure depended on enemy body count. The first major US Army engagement in the Vietnam War occurred in the Ia Drang Valley in November 1965. The 1st battalion of the 7th Cavalry Regiment, 1st Cavalry Division conducted an air assault by helicopter into LZ Xray and almost immediately engaged elements and units of three NVA Regiments. An estimated 3,561 of the enemy was killed. This battle proved the helicopters' value in war.

Army divisions had large base camps throughout South Vietnam. The division brigades and maneuver infantry battalions had forward firebases. Some units called firebases LZs. The mission of these firebases was to provide logistics, artillery support, and command and control for the maneuvering infantry companies conducting combat operations in the field. Usually, a maneuvering infantry company took its turn and pulled firebase security. A 105-artillery battery was assigned to each firebase for fire support. Occasionally, a 155-artillery battery was assigned also. In this scenario, a battery was assigned a position on one end of the firebase, and the other battery covered the other end. The firebase had a berm of dirt as its inner perimeter. This berm prevented the enemy from direct observation and direct fire into the firebase. Outside firebase security consisted of several perimeters of concertina wire, tangle foot, Claymore mines, and foo gas. A three- to four-man observation/listing post was placed about one hundred meters outside the outer wire at night for security. Most firebases were within the artillery fan of other firebases and could provide mutual fire support.

The Vietnam War was a small unit war and actions. The majority of firefights were conducted by companies, platoons, and squads. After Tet, 7,040 National Guardsman were called up, and about half served in the Vietnam War. In 1969, redeployments began; and 25,000 were sent home. Redeployments continued at a steady rate. In 1970, President Nixon redeployed 150,000 troops. By the end of November 1971, another 100,000 had redeployed. The 1972 Easter Offensive conducted by the enemy was the last major battle for the US Army. In 1972, General Abrams departed South Vietnam and was replaced by General Fred Weyand. After the Paris peace agreement was approved and signed the Americans were virtually out of the war. Only a small attaché office and the US embassy remained.

Subtle issues and problems for the US Army in South Vietnam were the following:

1. Lack of professionals among the officer corps. Ticket punching seemed to be the theme of the officer corps. Most infantry officers only spent three to four months in

the field then rotated back to a firebase or rear base camp for a staff or support job.

2. Enlisted soldiers spent their entire twelve months in the field. Many enlisted soldiers developed a lack of confidence and respect in officers because of their reduced field time.

3. The replacement system was mediocre at best. Because of DEROS, KIAs, WOIAs, first sergeant details in the rear, extensions, reenlistments for other units, and compassionate reassignment, replacements were slow to arrive in the field.

4. Returning soldiers faced the anger and frustration of the antiwar movement when they returned to America.

US Navy

The United States Navy 7th Fleet was largely oriented for nuclear war during the early 1960s. The majority of their support ships were of World War II vintage with outdated equipment. After the Gulf of Tonkin incident in 1964, the Navy immediately began to redress these shortcomings. Gunnery skills were updated, the battleship *New Jersey* was reactivated, and aircraft were modified to carry conventional bombs and munitions vice nuclear weapons. US Navy aircraft carriers played a major role in the Vietnam War. During the course of the war, nineteen aircraft carriers served separate combat deployments in the South China Sea, serving in both Dixie and Yankee stations. The carriers rotated in and out of the operational areas. Some carriers deployed nine times to the combat zone. The list of carriers includes the following:

-*America* CVA 66
-*Constellation* CVA 64
-*Enterprise* CVAN 65
-*Franklin D. Roosevelt* CVA 42
-*Hornet* CVS 12
-*Intrepid* CVS 11
-*Midway* CVA 41
-*Ranger* CVA 61

-*Bon Homme Richard* CVA 31
-*Coral Sea* CVA 43
-*Forrestal* CVA 59
-*Hancock* CVA 19
-*Independence* CVA 62
-*Kitty Hawk* CVA 63
-*Oriskany* CVA 34
-*Saratoga* CVA 60

-Shangri-La CVS 38   *-Ticonderoga* CVA 14
-Yorktown CVS 10

There were seventy to one hundred aircraft on each carrier. The primary attack aircraft for the Navy was the F-4 Phantom. The Phantom received pod-mounted cannons to increase and enhance its dogfighting capability and skills. Carrier missions took on additional missions of engaging the enemy in North and South Vietnam, Laos, Cambodia, and against the 1,200-mile South Vietnamese coastline. Additional 7th Fleet missions included the following:

1.   Providing direct naval fire support to US and allied forces in South Vietnam
2.   Harassment and interdiction fire on land targets in North and South Vietnam
3.   Interdict, stop, and halt enemy maritime vessels carrying personnel, logistics, supplies, arms, and ammunition. These maritime interdiction vessels consisted of aircraft carriers, swift boats, cutters, destroyers, minesweepers, and patrol gunboats.
4.   Coastal surveillance

In 1965, the operational command transferred from the 7th Fleet to Naval Advisory Group (NAG). In April 1966, NAG became the newly created Naval Forces Vietnam (NAVFORV). NAVFORV developed and used a three-zone patrol system. This plan consisted of outer and inner ship barriers, and the farthest zone was the air barrier. The outer ship barrier operated within forty miles of the South Vietnamese coast stretching from the DMZ to the Cambodian border in the Gulf of Thailand. Their mission was to stop, interdict, and seize enemy infiltrating resupply vessels. Approximately fifty enemy infiltrating resupply vessels were seized.

The inner ship barrier operated in shallow waters along the South Vietnamese coast to interdict and stop enemy wooden junks and trawlers. This was an arduous mission because the enemy junks would be infused with thousands of civilian noncombatant junks and sampans. In 1968, the US Navy began to conduct inland river patrols and operations in South Vietnam predominately in the Mekong Delta.

The air barrier was the farthest out barrier. Using the following aircraft, the Navy conducted air surveillance to identify suspicious vessels, photograph them, and report the situation to coastal surveillance centers along the South Vietnamese coast for disposition. The air barrier aircraft included the A-1 Skyraiders, P-2 Neptunes, P-3 Orions, and the P-5 Marlins. These aircraft operated from Dixie Station carriers; and airfields include Cam Ranh Bay, Tan Son Nhut, U-Tapao in Thailand, and Sangley Point in the Philippines. Dixie Station was a fixed point off the East coast of South Vietnam in the South China Sea. The majority of Dixie Station carrier operations were air strikes conducted in South Vietnam, Cambodia, and Laos. Yankee Station was a fixed point east of the coast of North Vietnam in the South China Sea. Yankee Station was a crucial staging and launching area for the 7th Fleet to conduct air strikes against North Vietnam. These air strikes supported operation Rolling Thunder, Pierce Arrow, Barrel Roll, and Flaming Dart.

I served two tours on an US aircraft carrier off the coast of North Vietnam at Yankee Station. During my first tour I was a Lieutenant and a US Navy aviator aboard the USS Forrestal during 1965–66. I flew F-4s and conducted bombing missions in North and South Vietnam. We usually flew two planes on a mission. My jet carried 8, 250 pounds drag bombs. The majority of my missions were in the north but occasionally we were diverted to conduct an emergency bombing mission in the south. My greatest concern while flying in the north was the flying telephone poles. A flying telephone pole is a North Vietnamese Surface to Air Missile (SAM). My greatest concern while flying in the south was the Anti-Aircraft Artillery (AAA). I flew XX combat missions.

My second tour was during 1967–68 aboard the USS Bon Homme Richard, CVA-31. Her nick name was "Bonnie Dick" and that is what everyone called her. The Bonnie Dick was the most prestigious and decorated US aircraft carrier in the South China Sea. Her awards, decorations and accolades include:

- Awarded the Presidential Unit Citation in 1967.
- Awarded the Navy Unit Citation in 1968.
- Awarded the Meritorious Unit Citation with two stars in 1969–70.
- Air crews shot down 9 MIGs in air combat which was more than the other carriers combined on all deployments up till 1968.
- Air crews introduced the Walleye Missile in combat.
- No air wing accidents on board.
- Made more ALPHA strikes than any other carrier during the Vietnam War. ALPHA strikes are 20 or more aircraft attacking a single target on the ground.
- Had first air wing assigned that was authorized to conduct combat missions down town Hanoi.
- Never lost a fighter in air to air combat with the enemy.

I served as the aircraft handling officer and the assistant air boss on the Bonnie Dick. As the aircraft handling officer my duties involved moving all aircraft on ship anytime to launch, park after landing and ensuring all aircraft on missions were recovered safely back aboard. My additional duties included crash and salvage recoveries, fueling of aircraft, arming of aircraft, all catapult operations and recovery operations. My biggest issue was the commanders of the aircraft units always wanted me to launch their aircraft first. I could not violate the *flight launch schedule. Sometimes I did accommodate the good commanders and launch his aircraft them first.*

We worked 12 hour shifts, 24/7 in various weather conditions day and night. The 12 hours began at the time of the first launch. The daily average aircraft launched on the Bonnie Dick was 150 using two catapults. I am very proud to state that on one occasion I launched 173 aircraft with only one catapult. The other catapult was down for repairs.

About 3 months prior to DEROS, I was transferred up-stairs and made the assistant air boss. The air boss and assistant are only on duty when the aircraft are flying and conducting combat operations. While on duty I remained close to the air boss. The air boss was responsible for all flight operations on deck, in the air and air traffic control around the carrier. My one bad experience involved an F-18C returning from a bombing mission. The aircraft was shot up badly but we did land and recover the aircraft. On another occasion I had two aircraft shot up and I decided it was too dangerous to land them because they may crash or explode on landing. I ordered both crews to eject over the ocean near the carrier and both crews were recovered by helicopter quickly and safely returned to the ship.

John Thaubald
Captain, USN Retired
Elkins High School, 1950
Elkins, West Virginia

US Navy SEALs

United States Navy SEALs (Sea, Air, and Land) conducted operations up to twenty miles inland in South Vietnam. SEALs used a variety of infiltration techniques. They launched from submerged submarines and swam or used small boats or a combination. These small boats included the following:

- river patrol boats (PBRs)
- fast patrol craft (PCF)
- SEAL Team Assault Boats (STABs)
- landing craft mechanized (LCM)
- light SEAL support craft (LSSC)
- medium SEAL support craft (MSSC)

The US Navy submarines *Perch*, *Tunny*, and *Grayback* were remodeled to house and carry SEAL teams on various operations. During the Vietnam War, a squadron of UH-1 helicopter gunships and a squadron of OV-10 Broncos were dedicated as direct support for SEAL teams. These two SEAL air support squadrons operated primarily in the Mekong River Delta.

In 1963, SEAL teams supported and conducted combat missions into North Vietnam with South Vietnamese naval commandos. These missions included raiding and destroying power plants, harbor facilities, and railroads. Additional missions included collecting intelligence, coastal mapping, and beach landing site reconnaissance.

In 1965, SEALs were ordered to infiltrate the Rung Sat Special Zone and conduct combat operations. The Rung Sat is a thick mangrove swamp seven miles south of Saigon (Ho Chi Minh City). The thick terrain made it very difficult to maneuver and conduct any combat operation. SEALs formed small three- to seven-man hunter-killer teams that assaulted enemy-controlled villages, conducted ambushes, and collected intelligence. Combat operations were so effective that after eighteen months of operations, the Rung Sat was declared liberated and no longer was an enemy safe base area.

In 1967, MACV-SOG ordered SEALs to increase combat operations in the Mekong Delta. One of these missions was to conduct reconnaissance and provide intelligence to the combined US Army and Navy Mobile Riverine Force. From 1968–70, SEALs conducted classified operations along the entire South Vietnamese coast. SEALs worked with US Special Forces to assist and train the ARVN Provincial

Reconnaissance Units (PRUs). In 1970–72, SEALs had many successes rescuing numerous ARVN POWs in the Mekong Delta. No US POWs were found or rescued. During 1970–72, SEALs advised and trained South Vietnamese Navy commandos. The last SEAL platoons were withdrawn from South Vietnam in 1972.

US Coast Guard

In April 1965, President Johnson authorized and ordered selected US Coast Guard (USCG) units to deploy to South Vietnam to help the Navy conduct combat operations. The USCG missions were as follows:

1. Preventing enemy weapons, ammunition, logistics, and personnel from entering South Vietnam via maritime sea and inland waterways
2. Patrolling the Cambodian border, the South Vietnam Gulf, and the South Vietnamese coast
3. Stopping, boarding, and searching enemy junks and sampans
4. Support US and allies with patrol boats, fire support, and illumination for night operations
5. Interdicting and destroying enemy supply vessels
6. Support the US Navy as required
7. Training South Vietnamese stevedores in loading and unloading equipment, explosives, and safety
8. Inspecting US and allied port facilities
9. Training US and allied boat crews
10. Assisting and advising US and allies on port security
11. Assisting US Navy Military Sea Transportation service in resolving problems on three hundred merchant ships supporting US and allies
12. Deploying buoy tenders and fixed navigational aids in ports and along the South Vietnamese coast
13. Rescuing US pilots downed behind enemy lines using USCG helicopters. These were the HH-3E and HH-53C

helicopters. The helicopters were stationed at Da Nang, South Vietnam

14. Constructing electronic navigation systems that provided precision guidance for US Air Force aircraft

This USCG Task Force consisted of several USCG cutters. USCG Squadron 1 contained seventeen 82-foot patrol boats (WPBs). Each cutter maintained a crew of two officers and nine enlisted men. Armament consisted of five .50-caliber machine guns and an 81 mm mortar. These cutters were powered by diesel engines, had a speed of 17 knots, and had a shallow draft of 6.5 feet.

Squadron 1 was divided into two divisions. Division 11 patrolled and conducted combat operations from the Cambodian border to the Gulf Coast of South Vietnam. Division 12 patrolled and conducted combat operations from the DMZ to Saigon. Subsequently, the mission required additional resources. Division 13 was deployed to South Vietnam in 1966 and patrolled the Mekong Delta region. These three USCG divisions were very busy and patrolled 70 percent of the time.

In 1967, USCG Squadron 3 was activated at Subic Bay in the Philippines. Squadron 3 maintained three cutters on patrol to assist the US Navy. In 1969, the US Navy destroyers were withdrawn from Yankee and Dixie Station. USCG cutters assumed the Navy mission and continued combat missions in the outer barrier.

The South Vietnamese stevedores benefited from USCG Explosive Loading Detachments (ELDs) training. The stevedores became more efficient, and docked ships unloading times were cut in half. During the Vietnam War, the ELDs ensured that there was never a major explosive incident in any port where USCG ELDs were stationed. From 1965–1973, eight thousand US Coast Guardsmen served in South Vietnam and maritime operational areas.

US Navy Seabees

Several Seabees were deployed to South Vietnam in June 1954. In January 1963, two 13-man Seabee Technical Assistance teams deployed to South Vietnam to assist US Special Forces in building Special Forces base camps, support the Civilian Irregular Defense Group, and conduct civic action support. In 1965, the first Seabee full Naval Mobile Construction Battalion deployed to South Vietnam to support and build airfields for the US Marines.

Seabee deployments increased rapidly each year and peaked in 1969. Seabee battalions in South Vietnam were commanded and controlled by two Naval Construction Regiments. Seabees fought alongside their Marine and Army counterparts as needed. During Tet, the Seabees organized their own organic combat forces for security and fought in direct support of their Marine and Army units.

Seabee construction projects in South Vietnam included the following:

-Building new roads   -Paving existing roads
-Building new barracks   -Constructing new bridges
-Building new civilian schools   -Building new civilian housing
-Building civilian orphanages   -Constructing military airfields
-Building new military coastal -Constructing large bunkers for
  facilities   base camps
-Building new civilian hospitals -Building new civilian wells
-Constructing new civilian utility -Constructing new civilian irriga-
  facilities   tion systems
-Training Vietnamese civilian in new construction skills

Most major Seabee construction projects were completed by 1968, and they began to redeploy. The last Seabee departed South Vietnam in November 1971. A small contingent remained for contingencies and redeployed in 1972.

US Riverine Forces

Riverine warfare was another new paradigm for the US and allied military. Riverine warfare was a daily tedious battle and river operations to control the Mekong River, its tributaries, and the Mekong Delta. After the Mekong River crosses from Cambodia into South Vietnam, it divides into four branches—the My Tho, Ham Luong, Co Chien, and Hau Giang. These branches feed the Mekong Delta south of Saigon. The Mekong Delta was of great strategic importance to the US and allies. The delta contained about half the population of South Vietnam and virtually covered the entire IV Corps tactical zone. Highway 4 was a major north south highway and was the only paved road in the Delta. A large abundance of travel, commerce, and South Vietnamese depended on the Delta's rivers and canals. The Mekong Delta was the ideal environment for riverine warfare and operations because it included 2,400 kilometers of natural waterways, and most were interconnected by four thousand kilometers of man-made canals.

The Mekong Delta was a major Viet Cong (VC) stronghold. In 1966, US intelligence estimated that approximately eighty-two thousand VC operated in the Delta. The enemy units were composed of the 9th VC Division and up to twenty-seven separate VC battalions and seventy solo companies. In 1965, the US Navy began to build a substantial river force. The United States military formed a provisional Mobile Riverine Task Force (TF) in the Delta as a result of joint Navy and Army combat operations in the Rung Sat special zone. The Maritime Riverine Force became fully operational in June 1967. This TF consisted of these:

-US Navy TF 15	-US Navy TF 116
-US Navy TF 117	-US Navy Helicopter Attack Squadron
-US Navy SEAL Teams	-US Army 2nd Brigade, 9th Infantry Division
-ARVN 7th Division	-ARVN 9th Division
-ARVN 21st Division	-RVN 6 River Assault Groups
-RVN 11 Coastal Groups	

This force increased and expanded to 250 Mark 1 and Mark 2 patrol boats. Although the patrol boats were lightly armed, they were robust; and surprise was their biggest asset. The patrol boats operated from mother ships, usually converted Landing Ship Tanks.

Mark 1 Patrol Boat
    Crew: Four: captain, seaman, gunner's mate, and engineman
    Weight: 7.4 tons
    Length: 31 feet
    Beam: 10 feet, 7 inches
    Draft: 1 foot 10 and ½ inches
    Speed: 25–30 knots
    Fuel capacity: 160 gallons
    Armament: Forward – One twin .50-caliber machine gun mounted in a rotating tub
        Engine cover – One M60 machine gun, one Mark 18 40 mm grenade launcher
        Stern – One .50-caliber machine gun, one 40 mm Mark 18 grenade launcher
Mark 2 Patrol Boat
    Crew: Four: captain, seaman, gunner's mate, and engineman
    Weight: 8 tons
    Length: 32 feet
    Beam: 11 feet and 7 ½ inches
    Draft: 2 feet
    Speed: 25–30 knots
    Fuel capacity: 160 gallons
    Armament: Forward – One twin .50-caliber machine gun mounted in a rotating tub
        Engine cover – Two M60 machine guns, one Mark 19 40 mm grenade launcher
        Stern – One .50-caliber machine gun

This Maritime River Force (MRF) was not a true task force with a single commander. The MRF Army units were under the command and control of the commanding general of II Field Force. He delegated his operational control to the commanding general of the 9th Infantry Division in the Delta. The US Navy units came under the command and control of the commander of US Navy Forces in South Vietnam. The Military Assistance Command Vietnam (MACV) planning directive 12–66 dated December 10, 1966, stipulated that the relation between the Navy and Army TF units would be of cooperation and coordination with the Navy providing close support to the Army. The Navy connotation was that close support implied that they commanded, controlled, and directed the Army units. This created friction and interservice rivalry between the Army and Navy commanders.

Riverine operations usually consisted of airmobile, ground search-and-destroy, and riverine attacks. When contact was made with the enemy, all commanders maneuvered forces to attack and moved into blocking positions to cut off possible escape routes. Artillery fire, helicopter, gunship attacks and air strikes assisted ground troops to destroy and attrite the enemy. In the early years, riverine operations were successful and usually caught the enemy by surprise. Eventually, the enemy changed tactics, techniques, and procedures. The enemy placed large command detonated mines in the waterways and ambushed the riverine forces on boats with recoilless rifles, RPGs, and B-40 rockets along the shore. The enemy also employed floating mines, swimmer saboteurs, and suicide attack boats. The riverine force adapted quickly and changed tactics and developed countermeasures and defenses to negate these enemy threats.

The area of operations and mission was normally selected by the 2nd Brigade commander of the 9th Infantry Division. After coordination with TF 117, the joint staff used the reverse planning process to develop task organization, scheme of maneuver, objectives, movement plan, fire plan, and loading plan. The final operations order was briefed to both Army and Navy commanders. A joint tactical operations center on a flagship controlled all troop movements. The 2nd Brigade executive officer supervised the Army element. The brigade commander and his battle staff exercised command and control from a forward firebase located on land. Occasionally, the brigade commander and the brigade operations officer usually flew overhead in a command and control helicopter during daylight, especially if contact was established by the enemy. The battalion commanders moved their command post aboard the command ship of the river assault squadron during combat operations.

By 1968, the Navy component of the MRF had grown to its full strength of four river assault squadrons. Simultaneously, the MRF reorganized into two Mobile Riverine Groups (MRG). In July 1968, the 9th Infantry Division moved its division headquarters from Bearcat to Dong Tam. The remaining two brigades moved to several base camps in the Delta. With the entire 9th Infantry Division in the Delta, the 2nd Brigade mission changed to pacification of Kien Hoa province. Mobile Riverine Group ALPHA continued to support the 2nd Brigade of the 9th Infantry Division. MRG BRAVO shifted operations to the southern Delta and maneuvered with selected units of the South Vietnamese Marine Corp. In February 1969, the MRF was reduced and operations were scaled back. River Assault Division 91 turned twenty-five river assault craft over to the RVN Navy. Later in 1969, the MRF River Flotilla 1 and the 2nd Brigade of the 9th Infantry Division were deactivated and withdrawn from South Vietnam.

The MRF was very successful at tactical and operational levels. Some successes and victories were the following:

1. Highway 4 in the Delta was opened and secured.
2. Farming, agricultural products and people moved freely on Highway 4.
3. The northern Delta was pacified and secured.
4. The US Navy transferred the majority of its river patrol boats to the RVN Navy.
5. The US Navy trained the RVN Navy in maritime riverine operations.

Conducting combat operations in the Mekong Delta had special challenges and issues. Some of these challenges were as follows:

1. Saltwater corroded weapons, radios, ammunition, and equipment.
2. Tides, water depth, river obstructions, and low bridges often constrained, impeded, or stopped combat operations.

3.   Many river and canal banks were not suitable or impossible for landing sites.
4.   Immersion foot and other lower-leg problems increased when the troops conducted land operations for more than two consecutive days.
5.   Detailed maps were lacking and outdated.
6.   Armored forward turrets made the boats too bow heavy.
7.   The rules of engagement were too restrictive. Patrol boats had to wait to be shot at before returning fire.
8.   The MRF did not have ample patrol boats to conduct operation in the Delta.
9.   The water-jet pumps on the river patrol boats were prone to fouling with dirt and/or mud from the waterways.
10. US Navy brass considered carrier operations more important than riverine operations.
11. The MRF did not have dedicated helicopters to move troops quickly.
12. The 2nd Brigade of the 9th Infantry Division was substituted for maritime-trained US Marines. The Marines should have been designated as the maritime land combat force.

US Air Force

The United States Air Force (USAF) provided diverse contributions to the Vietnam War as advisers to the MAAG in the 1950s and ending with large strategic bombing campaigns in 1972. In November 1961, President Kennedy ordered the USAF 4400th Combat Crew Training Squadron air commandos to South Vietnam. The air commando's missions were the following:

1.   Train the South Vietnamese Air Force pilots and crews.
2.   Provide close air support for the ARVN and US advisers.
3.   Provide close air support to the US Special Forces.
4.   Profess and prove the USAF could provide better and quicker close air support than the newly developed Army helicopter gunships.

After the Gulf of Tonkin incident in 1964, President Johnson escalated the air, sea, and land war. During 1965, the USAF was given more flexibility and increased its war efforts. One of President Johnson's escalation initiatives was to order Operation Rolling Thunder. Operation Rolling Thunder was a prolonged US bombing campaign conducted from March 2, 1965, to October 31, 1968, targeting specified targets in North Vietnam. The majority of bombing missions were conducted by the USAF. US Navy and Marine aircraft assisted in the bombing effort. Operation Rolling Thunder had two objectives.

1. Destroy the North Vietnamese defense systems, industrial base, and logistics networks.
2. Impede or stop the North Vietnamese support infiltrating into South Vietnam.

Most of the bombing missions were in the North Vietnam panhandle. Operation Rolling Thunder failed to achieve its goals and objectives and remains as a classic airpower failure. When Operation Rolling Thunder stopped bombing in North Vietnam, the bombing missions shifted to infiltration routes, choke points, rest stops, truck parks, vehicles, and logistics on and along the Ho Chi Minh trail. It is estimated that six thousand enemy trucks and vehicles on the trail were destroyed by AC-47 and AC-130 gunships.

The USAF provided air support to US and allied forces in South Vietnam. The air support mission aircraft consisted of the following:

*F-4 Phantom	*AC-47 "Spooky" Gunships
*F-100s	*AC-130 Gunships
*A-1 Skyraiders	*B-52 Heavy Bombers

The majority of USAF bombing occurred in South Vietnam. From 1962–1972, four million tons of bombs were dropped in South Vietnam against the enemy. The majority of the bombing tonnage was from B-52 Arc Light missions. Arc Light missions were flown against known or suspected enemy base camps and/or troop concentrations. Airpower was key and a deciding factor in the following major battles and sieges:

1. Tet
2. Khe Sanh
3. Hamburger Hill

4. Loc Ninh
5. The NVA Easter Offensive
6. Con Thien

As a result of the NVA Easter Offensive in South Vietnam, President Nixon ordered Operation Linebacker I. Linebacker I began on May 9, 1972, with the aerial mining of Hai Phong harbor. Enemy infiltration routes in the southern panhandle of North Vietnam were bombed. The USAF played a major role in Linebacker I; however, several Navy and Marine aircraft assisted in the bombing campaign. Only fighter-bombers were used during Linebacker I; no B-52s were used. Linebacker I saw the introduction of smart bombs by US air assets. These smart bombs were laser and electronic optically guided precision munitions. Linebacker I was successful and ended on October 23, 1972, when the NVA halted their offensive. The success of Linebacker I was superb, catastrophic, and compelled the North Vietnamese leadership to reenter serious peace discussions. South Vietnamese leadership refused to participate in these peace negotiations. The negotiation resumed briefly in November but quickly stalled. Because of the North Vietnam politburo stubbornness and refusal to negotiate further, President Nixon ordered Operation Linebacker II.

Operation Linebacker II began on December 18, 1972, and was initially intended as a three-day comprehensive bombing mission by USAF B-52s. This three-day bombing campaign continued for eleven days until the North Vietnamese politburo was forced to resume peace talks with the United States. The bombing continued until the North Vietnamese and US principals could agree on an agenda. Linebacker II officially ended on December 29, 1972. Linebacker II was the largest major bombing campaign of the Vietnam War. The bombing intensity was unlimited, unrestricted, and very lethal. For example, one bombing mission involved 125 B-52s hitting ten separate targets in fifteen minutes. The USAF lost 15 B-52s during

Linebacker II. Although Linebacker II B-52 bombing raids stopped, fighter-bombers continued to hit military and strategic targets in North Vietnam.

The difference between Linebacker I and II were the bombing intensity and strategic objectives. Linebacker I compelled the North Vietnamese to negotiate seriously. Linebacker II was psychological and broke the will of the North to continue resistance, fighting, and forced them to agree to a quick return to the negotiation table in Paris where a peace agreement was reached soon.

At the conclusion of the Vietnam War, the USAF had dropped 8 million tons of bombs on Southeast Asia. The USAF lost 2,257 aircraft, mostly by antiaircraft fire over South Vietnam. Very few were lost due to accidents.

Major USAF air bases in Southeast Asia were as follows:

-Da Nang, South Vietnam	-Udorn, Thailand
-Chu Lai, South Vietnam	-Korat, Thailand
-Phu Cat, South Vietnam	-Utapao, Thailand
-Qui Nhon, South Vietnam	-Ubon, Thailand
-Tuy Hoa, South Vietnam	-Nakhon Phanom, Thailand
-Cam Ranh Bay, South Vietnam	-Don Muang, Thailand
-Dong Ha, South Vietnam	-Takhli, Thailand

US Marines

In 1962, President Kennedy deployed the US Marine Corps (USMC) H-21 Shawnee helicopter units to South Vietnam to support the Republic of Vietnam Military (RVN). The support mission consisted of transporting the ARVN with US advisers throughout the Mekong Delta. On March 8, 1965, the first US ground combat troops of the 9th Marine Expeditionary Brigade deployed to Da Nang, South Vietnam. As the war escalated, the Marine force of ground and aviation units increased, and the 9th Marine Expeditionary Brigade became the III Marine Amphibious Force. The increase of Marine units increased their missions. They continued to defend Da Nang air base and deployed to the five northern provinces in South

Vietnam to conduct combat missions and operations. Initially, the Marines formed civic action platoons and emphasized pacification in the southern I Corps. After several months of limited success with pacification, the Marines began to conduct regimental search-and-destroy operations.

In July 1966, MACV intelligence determined that an NVA division had crossed the DMZ and moved into northern I Corps. This new enemy threat deployed the Marines north, and they constructed a series of fire and combat bases south of the DMZ. In 1967, the Marines fought many battles with the NVA at locations such as the Rockpile, Gio Linh, Khe Shah, Con Thien, and Cam Lo. During 1967, the 1st Marine Division continued counterinsurgency in southern I Corps against the VC, and the 3rd Marine Division fought a conventional war against the NVA in northern I Corps.

In 1967, MACV ordered US Army units into southern I Corps, freeing up more Marines to deploy north. January 1968 produced two major attacks against the Marines at Khe Sanh and during Tet. The Marines adopted high-mobility techniques from the US Army. By mid-1969, the US Army and ARVN assumed responsibility of the majority of I Corps. The 3rd Marine Division redeployed to America.

In 1970, the Marine area of operations shrank to Quang Nam province and its defense of Da Nang. Most of the old Marine bases were destroyed or turned over to the US Army or ARVN. In April 1971, the III Marine Amphibious Force was withdrawn from South Vietnam and redeployed to Okinawa.

Several F-4 Phantom jets provided tactical air support for the South Vietnamese military during the NVA Easter Offensive of 1972. No Marine ground combat troops were engaged in this NVA offensive. The USMC had 12,926 Marines killed in action and another 88,542 wounded in action in the Vietnam War. These casualties were more than the Marines suffered in World War II.

The Republic of Vietnam Army (RVN)

(Caveat: I used various sources for facts and accuracy researching the RVN military. Troop strength, aircraft, maritime vessels,
weapons, logistics, and materiel varied between sources. Some data
may be subject to confirmation.)

In 1949, Vietnamese emperor Bao Dai and the French developed a concept to establish a Vietnamese National Army to fight
the Viet Minh. The RVN Army grew from an initial strength of
150,000 to nearly one million soldiers when it collapsed in 1975.
Several problems plagued the initial slow recruitment and training
of the Vietnamese Army. Most Vietnamese were ambivalent toward
Bao Dai's authority and government. Many thought Bao was a puppet of the French. The majority of combat operations were led by
French officers and sergeants. Weapons and equipment were obsolete, archaic, and not in good condition.

The Americans took over after the French left. The Americans
immediately demanded more combat initiative and a more aggressive
attitude and posture for the Army. An increase in fire support and
newer modern weapons and an improved logistics system were new
ingenuities implemented by the Americans. The majority of the RVN
did not have the M-16 rifle until mid-1968. Old French officer and
NCO Corps schools and training centers were upgraded and mod-
eled after US Army professional and tactical development schools.
From 1965–1975, the US strengthened and stepped up all training
programs and concentrated on junior officer and NCO training and
leadership. Newer equipment, better American military training,
increased helicopter support, and a vast improvement in logistics
and technical services exacerbated rifts in the RVN officer corps and
caused the RVN Army to become dependent upon US support.

At its peak in 1975, the RVN regular Army had 450,000 troops
organized into thirteen divisions, seven Ranger groups, and several
separate battalions and regiments. The RVN Army Regional forces
totaled 475,000 troops. The popular forces were relegated to guard-
ing and providing security for villages and cities. The popular forces

were called Ruff Puffs by the Americans and totaled around 400,000 troops. The RVN regular forces consisted of the following:

1st Infantry Division	1st Ranger Group	3rd Armored Cavalry Squadron
2nd Infantry Division	2nd Ranger Group	
3rd Infantry Division	3rd Ranger Group	
5th Infantry Division	4th Ranger Group	
7th Infantry Division	5th Ranger Group	
9th Infantry Division	6th Ranger Group	
18th Infantry Division	7th Ranger Group	
21st Infantry Division	41st Ranger Border Defense Group	
22nd Infantry Division	42nd Ranger Border Defense Group	
23rd Infantry Division	81st Ranger Border Defense Group	
25th Infantry Division		
Airborne Division		

The following were issues and problems of the RVN Army:

1. Lack of mobility, command, and control to employ troops and equipment effectively
2. Officer promotions were based on social position and loyalty to the regime rather than leadership, combat ability, and integrity
3. The majority of the RVN Army were Buddhists, led mostly by Catholic senior officers
4. Widespread corruption at all levels
5. Commanders inflated unit strengths and kept the surplus pay
6. Lack of consistent leadership

During the 1975 NVA invasion, almost seven RVN Army divisions eroded away because of a lack of South Vietnamese airpower, overloaded road systems, desertions, and a lack of unit cohesion. Elite Airborne and Ranger units held their ground. Despite critical maneuvering and last-minute rallying, South Vietnam could not be saved. The RVN Army suffered 254,256 deaths between 1960 and 1975.

RVN Air Force (VNAF)

In 1955, the VNAF was a small Air Force that consisted of twenty-eight F-28F fighter-bombers, thirty-five C-47 cargo aircraft, and around sixty L-19 reconnaissance aircraft. Later, America replaced the F-8F with a combat version of the T-28 trainer. By the end of 1962, the VNAF had expanded and had a squadron of AD-65 fighter-bombers and three squadrons of L-19s. The VNAF supported the RVN military with tactical missions that included reconnaissance, close air support, airlift operations, artillery spotting, and MEDEVAC. Prior to 1965, the VNAF performance was mediocre at best. Some flying issues were the following:

1. Lack of fully qualified flight leaders and warriors.
2. Morale was low, and the pilots were not motivated.
3. Most pilots did not like to fly at night.
4. Pilots' command and control and chain of command for missions was lethargic and slow to approve bombing missions.
5. There were too many commanders that had to approve the bombing mission.
6. The ground commanders did not understand and appreciate the firepower of the VNAF.
7. Logistics, maintenance, and support could not keep up with the aircraft maintenance.

During 1965, the VNAF increased its size and missions. The always durable A-1 Skyhawk replaced the T-28 and became the backbone of the VNAF. By 1968, the VNAF had expanded to sixteen thousand men and had about four hundred aircraft. These new aircraft included the A-37 Dragonfly, C-130 cargo aircraft, and a squadron of F-5 Freedom Fighter jets.

The VNAF participated in Operation Rolling Thunder and continued to make significant contributions to the air and land campaigns. Operation Rolling Thunder missions were reduced because of the growing demand for air strikes in the South. By mid-1968, the VNAF flew 25 percent of the air strikes in the South. Problems continued to plague the VNAF. Because of these problems, the VNAF flew very few air support missions during Tet. Some problems were the following:

1. Very few English-speaking pilots in the VNAF
2. High accident rate
3. Maintenance problems were staggering
4. No VNAF supply system. Most of the VNAF supplies and logistics came from the RVN Army
5. Did not receive a fair share of new helicopters and aircraft from the US

When the US withdrew in 1972, the VNAF had grown to almost fifty thousand personnel and around forty-four squadrons of diverse aircraft. By June 1974, the VNAF was the fourth largest Air Force in the world that included two thousand aircraft and approximately sixty-three thousand personnel. The 1975 North Vietnamese offensive virtually destroyed the VNAF. There are four reasons for the VNAF demise.

1. The VNAF logistics and supply system remained broken and unreliable.
2. The US Congress eliminated funding for fuel, spare parts, and bombs.
3. The NVA had handheld SA-7 surface-to-air missiles that reduced the VNAF missions and make the flying missions more hazardous.
4. The US typically gave the VNAF low-performance aircraft. The aircraft fire, avionics, flying and support systems were scaled down and subpar. Normally, the majority of VNAF aircraft did not have modern electronics, navigational aids, and fire control systems.

RVN Marine Corps (VNMC)

The VNMC was established in 1954 by a special decree signed by President Diem. Shortly after the VNMC was activated, US Marine Corps advisers were attached and trained the VNMC in combat operations, supply, and logistics. Over time the VNMC expanded to nine infantry battalions, three artillery battalions, and several support battalions. Under USMC tutelage, the VNMC quickly became a fierce fighting force. The VNMC were one of Saigon's strategic reserve units that were deployed to reinforce the RVN military during heavy and tough fighting in all four combat tactical zones.

The VNMC participated in the 1970 invasion of Cambodia and provided valuable combat assistance during the recapture of Hue during the 1968 Tet Offensive. Although vastly outnumbered, the VNMC were key in defeating the NVA during the 1972 Easter Offensive. The VNMC suffered 20 percent casualties during this heavy fighting.

In 1973, all USMC advisers were redeployed to the US military bases in America. As the RVN government began to unravel in 1975, the VNMC took up defensive positions near Saigon and Da Nang. As the war ended, the VNMC faded away. Around two hundred escaped to the US after the war.

RVN Navy (VNN)

The VNN was formed and chartered in 1952 with the ships and materiel from the French Navy. After 1955, the VNN was supplied from the US and, at its peak, was the largest Navy in Southeast Asia. The US assisted in building the VNN to 42,000 personnel, 672 various maritime ships and vessels, 450 patrol craft, and 245 junks. In 1956, the VNN formed the coastal junk force to patrol the waters around the DMZ to impede or halt the North Vietnamese from infiltrating men, weapons, and logistics in South Vietnam. Additional VNN missions included conducting sea and maritime combat operations at sea, along the South Vietnamese coast and in the Mekong Delta. The VNN intercepted thousands of enemy maritime craft ferrying munitions and personnel along the coast and in the Mekong Delta.

In 1959, the VNN, with assistance from the US, upgraded their ships and training. Training sites were located in Saigon, Nha Trang, and Cam Ranh Bay. From 1962–64, the VNN rapidly expanded training and repair bases and organization, administration procedures, and communications were improved. Ships and craft supplied by the US Navy to the VNN to conduct maritime combat operations included the following:

-Patrol rescue escorts   -Motor boats
-Large support landing ships   -Large infantry landing ships
-Tank landing ship   -Medium landing ships
-Mine sweepers

In 1968, plans for the transfer of US Navy assets to the VNN had been formulated. In 1969, President Nixon announced and adopted the policy of Vietnamization. Vietnamization involved a phased transfer to the VNN of US river, coastal, and sea maritime ships, vessels, and crafts. By mid-1969, the US Mobile Riverine Force stood down, and the VNN assumed sole responsibility for river operations. The Mobile Riverine Force transferred sixty-four riverine assault craft to the VNN. At the end of 1970, the US Navy ceased all operations in South Vietnam and redeployed to US bases. They transferred 293 river patrol boats and 224 riverine assault craft to the VNN. During 1970, the US transferred control of coastal and sea operations to the VNN. The US Navy transferred four Coast Guard cutters and a variety of additional sea vessels. In 1972, the VNN took command of the last sixteen US coastal radar sites.

As a result of the Paris Peace Accords, the US drastically cut financial aid to the RVN military, including the VNN. Because of a lack of US funding, the VNN was compelled to reduce all operations by 50 percent. Over six hundred river craft and twenty-two ships were moored. In 1974, four VNN ships fought a sea battle with the Chinese Navy over the Paracel Islands two hundred nautical miles east of Da Nang. One VNN ship was sunk, and the remaining sustained light to heavy damage.

Prior to Saigon falling on April 30, 1975, a contingent of VNN officers secretly organized a VNN thirty-ship flotilla of thirty thousand sailors, their families, and other civilians. This flotilla linked up with the US 7th Fleet and sailed with them to Subic Bay, Philippines. Most of the VNN flotilla ships were infused into the Philippine Navy.

Problems and issues for the VNN:

1. Careerism and political activity of many naval officers weakened military operations
2. VNN participation in the 1963 coup against President Diem damaged officers' and sailors' morale and hampered the war effort
3. The majority of sailors were not trained in technical skills required for their jobs
4. Low pay
5. Austere living conditions aboard the ships, vessels, and craft
6. Desertions
7. Low recruitment rate
8. Rapid deterioration of legacy ships and craft
9. Lack of spare parts, supplies, and fuel
10. Maintenance could not keep pace with high-tempo combat operations

Allied Forces, Participation, and Support

The Republic of Vietnam appealed for military, economic, technical, and humanitarian foreign aid in July 1964. Over forty international nations provided aid and assistance. This aid and assistance included the following:

-Civilian doctors and nurses   -Combat troops
-Economic aid   -Financial aid
-Military medical teams   -Political advisers

-Military civil affairs teams   -Military training advisers
-Civilian construction teams   -Civilian refugee support teams

The following countries provided military troops, aid, and assistance. The strength peaked in 1969.

-Australia   7,672 combat troops
-South Korea   50,003 combat troops
-Thailand   11,586 combat troops
-New Zealand   552 artillery and civic action troops
-Philippines   2,061 psychological operations troops
-Republic of China   31 pilots, civic action and admin troops
-Spain   13 medical troops

The following countries provided nonmilitary aid and assistance:

-   Argentina: 5,000 tons of wheat and vaccines
-   Belgium: medical supplies
-   Brazil: 5,000 sacks of coffee and medical supplies
-   Cambodia: $93 million in government development; built a tuberculosis clinic and provided doctors to teach at hospitals
-   Costa Rica: several ambulances
-   Denmark: medical supplies and trained South Vietnamese nurses in Denmark
-   Ecuador: medical supplies
-   Federal Republic of Germany: economic and humanitarian aid totaling 7.5 million annually, and they provided 200 medical personnel. In 1966, Germany provided the SS *Helgoland* to provide the South Vietnamese civilians medical assistance. In addition, Germany provided 47 refugee support teams
-   France: $155 million for cultural activities
-   Greece: $15,000 for medical supplies
-   Guatemala: 15,000 units of typhoid-paratyphoid serum
-   Honduras: medicine and clothing

- Iran: petroleum products and civilian doctors
- Ireland: $2,800 to the South Vietnamese Red Cross equivalent
- Israel: pharmaceutical supplies
- Italy: a 10-person surgical team
- Japan: $55 million of economic aid
- Laos: $10,000 for South Vietnamese refugees
- Liberia: $50,000 for medical supplies
- Luxembourg: blood transfusion equipment
- Malaysia: military training to South Vietnam military officers; officers were sent to Malaysia for training
- Morocco: 10,000 cans of sardines
- Norway: funding for flood and Tet refugees
- Pakistan: financial assistance and clothing for South Vietnamese flood victims
- South Africa: medical supplies
- Spain: several small medical teams
- Switzerland: medical teams and equipment
- The Netherlands: scholarships for South Vietnamese doctors; constructed tuberculosis centers and expanded several current hospitals
- Turkey: medicine, vaccines, and cement
- Tunisia: scholarships for South Vietnamese students
- United Kingdom: lab equipment for Saigon University and X-ray equipment and printing presses for the South Vietnamese government
- Uruguay: food and medicine
- Venezuela: two civilian doctors and 500 tons of rice

Questions for Reflection

1. When was the MAAG established in the Republic of Vietnam (RVN)?
2. Name two subordinate commands of MACV.
3. How many corps tactical zones were in South Vietnam?

4. What were the date and peak strengths of US military in South Vietnam?
5. Name six MACV campaigns.
6. How many US Army divisions were in South Vietnam?
7. Describe the mission of a firebase.
8. Identify three issues and problems of the US Army in South Vietnam.
9. Describe two US Navy 7th Fleet missions during the Second Indochina War.
10. Identify and discuss Yankee and Dixie Station.
11. What is the Rung Sat?
12. Identify two US Navy SEAL missions.
13. Identify six US Coast Guard missions in South Vietnam.
14. How did the US Navy Seabees support the US Special Forces in 1963?
15. Name six construction projects conducted by the US Navy Seabees in South Vietnam.
16. Briefly locate and describe the Mekong Delta.
17. Name the major US and allied units assigned to the Maritime Riverine Force in South Vietnam.
18. Name the US Air Force commando missions in South Vietnam.
19. Define and contrast Operation Linebacker I to Operation Linebacker II.
20. When did the first US ground combat troops of the 9th Marine Expeditionary Brigade deploy to South Vietnam?
21. Where were the majority of US Marines deployed in South Vietnam?
22. The RVN Army was organized into how many divisions?
23. What was the mission of the RVN Popular Forces?
24. Name two issues and problems of the RVN Army.
25. Name two issues and problems of the South Vietnam Air Force.
26. Name two reasons for the South Vietnam Air Force's demise.

27. Name four issues and problems of the South Vietnam Navy.
28. How many international nations provided aid and assistance to South Vietnam?
29. Name the international nations that provided military troops and aid to South Vietnam.
30. Name five international nations that provided nonmilitary aid to South Vietnam.

Chapter 15

The Bad Guys

We will bomb them back to the Stone Age!
—General Curtis E. LeMay

The North Vietnamese Army and the Viet Cong

The People's Army of Vietnam (PAVN) was known to America and the US military as the North Vietnamese Army (NVA). "Determined to Fight American Aggression," the North Vietnamese Army was a formidable fighting force. Both the Viet Cong (VC) in the South and the regulars in the North were part of the NVA. Although separate, the VC and the NVA ultimately were commanded and controlled under the same command structure. The terms National Liberation Front, Viet Cong, North Vietnamese Army, and People's Army of Vietnam are used interchangeably.

After the Diem Bien Phu victory, the NVA rapidly consolidated, reorganized, and improved the military. During the late 1950s, the North Vietnamese received vast war materiel from China and the Union of Soviet Socialist Republic. This new military aid led to the activation of new artillery and armor units. A small Air Force was also created. Until 1965, the NVA used the VC in the South to conduct guerilla warfare against the Republic of Vietnam (RVN). After the US committed combat troops in 1965, the NVA was needed to augment the VC in the South with regular combat forces from the North.

Hanoi preferred to rely on volunteers, but as commitments and demands increased in the South, the communist government in the North began to recruit all medically fit males between ages eighteen and twenty-five. The North declared partial mobilization in July 1966. Later, as the war casualties increased, the draft eligibility age was modified to everyone between ages sixteen and forty-five.

Tet was a military disaster for the NVA and VC in 1968. The VC were virtually eliminated and rendered combat ineffective for the remainder of the war. It is estimated the VC lost 250,000 to 300,000 between 1962 and 1975. After Tet in 1968, the NVA took on the main responsibility for the war in South Vietnam. Tet curtailed NVA and VC operations in the South. The US and allies detected deterioration in the fighting ability of the NVA and VC for the remainder of 1968. The NVA reorganized as conventional infantry after Tet and began conducting larger and increased combat missions in the South. The 1972 Easter Spring Offensive was repelled by elite ARVN forces and with aid of substantial US air strikes. The ensuing three years yielded massive troop, equipment, arms, ammunition, and materiel buildups preparing the NVA for the final offensive and attack on Saigon in April 1975.

In the North, up to two million local forces and civilian militia provided security for Hanoi, major cities, and coastal defense. Hanoi had one of the largest air defense systems. The North had a small Navy that consisted of only a few dozen small boats, and its primary mission was coastal security. The NVA air branch was small and provided a limited defense for Hanoi and was never a major threat for the US Air Force.

NVA tactics were diverse. They ranged from guerilla warfare to large-scale multi-infantry division conventional offensives and attacks. Organized and equipped as a regular Army, the NVA were extremely well motivated, tenacious, and merciless when on the attack. They were very elusive on the defense and avoided all contact with US and allied forces. The NVA believed that getting in close and grabbing the belts of US and allied forces during ground attacks would give them an advantage and prevent the US and allies from using artillery for fear of fratricide. This tactic was a misconception, did not work against the US forces, and only had a mixed success against ARVN forces. If the NVA had a single battlefield weakness, it was similar to many communist armies; they had an inflexible attitude to the changing tactical situation. The consequence of this was extremely high rates of attrition. The VC had specified operational areas of operations; the NVA did not and were not confined and restricted to a certain area of operations.

During 1975, as the war was ending, the NVA were close to a million soldiers in strength. The VC were deactivated or infused into the NVA. Most significantly, the North Vietnamese military and political strategies were synchronized. The North Vietnamese diplomatic missions, activities, and military operations were mutually supporting. Worldwide communist support systems always provided labor, military intelligence, and food.

For US and allied forces, fighting against the NVA was a totally different situation than confronting the VC. The NVA had integral weapons platoons for additional fire support and occasionally-reasonable artillery supporting fire.

Organization of an NVA Infantry Company

1 Company Headquarters (HQ) Section
3 X Rifle Platoon (each 1 X Rifle Platoon HQ Section, 4 X Rifle Squads)
1 Weapon Platoon (1 Weapons Platoon HQ Section, 1 Mortar Squad, 1 Heavy Machine Gun Squad, 1 Recoilless Rifle Squad)
1 Recce (Recon) Squad

Company HQ Section
1 Captain, 1 Senior Sergeant, 1 RTO, and 1 Runner

Rifle Platoon HQ Section
1 2nd Lieutenant, 1 Senior Sergeant, and 1 Runner

Rifle Squad
1 Sergeant, 1 Rifle Propelled Grenade (RPG), 1 RPD Light Machine Gun (LMG), and 6 Riflemen

Weapons Platoon HQ Section
1 2nd Lieutenant, 1 Senior Sergeant, and 1 Runner

Mortar Squad
1 Sergeant, 2 Corporals, 6 Riflemen, and 3 82 mm Mortar (3 crew/ Mortar)

Heavy Machine Gun (HMG) Squad
1 Sergeant, 2 Corporals, 6 Riflemen, and 3 12.7 mm HMGs

Recoilless Rifle Squad
1 Sergeant, 1 Corporal, 6 Riflemen, and 3 75 mm Recoilless Rifle

Recce (Recon) Squad
1 Senior Sergeant, 1 Sergeant, and 10 Riflemen

The RTO in an NVA company HQ section was employed differently than in US and allied forces. The NVA company HQ communications was with its battalion only and very infrequently— usually involving a single situation report on a daily basis. The radio was not used as a means of communication between the company HQ and its organic maneuver platoons. Most communications were generally done by using a runner, signal rockets, whistles, smoke, and bugles.

Viet Cong (VC) Local Guerillas

These VC were the archetypal "farmers by day, soldiers by night," comprising those either too old or too young to fight in the regular VC units or the NVA. These locals were usually dressed as local peasant farmers. Their missions consisted of intelligence gathering, sniping, and emplacing booby traps. Acting as porters, scouts, and guides, the locals supported VC Regional and Main Force units. The local force size was dependent on the size of the local village or hamlet and ranged from a single three-man cell to a platoon of three to four squads.

VC Main Force Regional Guerillas

The Main Force Regional units of the Viet Cong usually operated as independent companies and frequently operated in platoons, squads, and cells. The Main Force guerillas were permanent full-timers and were better equipped and trained than the local guerrillas. These guerillas were mostly locals and remained close to their home areas. They wore pith helmets, were known as "hard hats," and were organized along NVC military units.

Organization of a Viet Cong Infantry Company

1 Company Headquarters (HQ) Section
3 X Rifle Platoons (each 1 X Platoon HQ Section, 4 X Rifle Squad)
Combat Support Elements (Attached)

Company HQ Section
1 Captain, 1 Lieutenant, 1 RTO, and 2 Runners

Rifle Platoon HQ Section
1 Lieutenant, 1 Senior Sergeant, and 1 Runner

Rifle Squad
1 Sergeant, 1 Corporal, 1 RPD 7.62 mm MG, and 6 Riflemen

Combat Support
1 Sergeant, 2 Corporals, 1 .30-cal MG (3 crew), 1 60 mm Mortar (3 crew), 1 57 mm Recoilless Rifle (RR) (3 crew), and 3 Riflemen

Based on several sources, the NVA and VC Order of Battle (OB) for the four corps tactical zones are depicted below for 1967–68. This may not be conclusive or static because units occasionally moved from corps to corps.

I Corps

Unit and Strengths (All corps strengths are based on 1967–68 US military intelligence estimates)
2nd NVA Division 6,450
>1st VC Infantry Regiment (40th, 60th, 70th, and 80th Battalions) – 2,000
>3rd NVA Infantry Regiment (1st, 2nd, and 3rd Battalions) – 1,300
>21st NVA Infantry Regiment (1st, 2nd, and 3rd Battalions) – 1,500
>2nd VC Infantry Regiment (1st, 2nd, and 3rd Battalions) – 1,650

324B NVA Division 7,800
>803rd NVA Infantry Regiment (1st, 2nd, and 3rd Battalions) – 2,600
>812th NVA Infantry Regiment (4th, 5th, and 6th Battalions) – 2,600
>90th NVA Infantry Regiment (7th, 8th, and 9th Battalions) – 2,600

325th NVA Division 7,790
>101 D NVA Infantry Regiment (1st, 2nd, and 3rd Battalions) – 1,800
>95C NVA Infantry Regiment (4th, 5th, and 6th Battalions) – 1,550
>18C NVA Infantry Regiment (7th, 8th, and 9th Battalions) – 1,650
>5th NVA Infantry Regiment (814th Sapper Battalion and 416th Battalion) – 1,390
>6th NVA Infantry Regiment (800th, 806th NVA Battalion, and 802nd VC Battalion) – 1,400

Nondivisional Units 3,200
    1st NVA Battalion, 31st Infantry Regiment, 341st NVA Division
    2nd NVA Battalion, 31st Infantry Regiment, 341st NVA Division
    402nd VC Sapper Battalion
    120th VC Montagnard Infantry Battalion
    409th VC Sapper Battalion
    804th VC Infantry Battalion
    808th VC Infantry Battalion
    810th VC Infantry Battalion

II Corps

Unit and Strengths
1st NVA Division 9,525
    32nd NVA Infantry Regiment (334th, 635th, and 966th Battalions) – 1,760
    66th NVA Infantry Regiment (7th, 8th, and 9th Battalions) – 1,700
    88th NVA Infantry Regiment (K4, K5, and K6 Battalions) – 1,880
    24th NVA Infantry Regiments (4th, 5th, and 6th Battalions) – 1,500
    33rd NVA Infantry Regiments (K1 and K3 Battalions) – 860
    95B NVA Infantry Regiment (4th, 5th, and 6th Battalions) – 1,825
3rd NVA Infantry Division 2,870
    18th NVA Infantry Regiment (7th, 8th, and 9th Battalions) – 1,170
    22nd NVA Infantry Regiment (7th, 8th, and 9th Battalions) – 1,700
5th NVA Infantry Division 3,620
    95th NVA Infantry Regiment (4th, 5th, and 6th Battalions) – 1,700

18th NVA Infantry Regiment (7th, 8th, and 9th Battalions) – 1,920

Nondivisional Units 2,290

30th VC Infantry Battalion 95th NVA Artillery Battalion
145th VC Artillery Battalion   186th VC Infantry Battalion
407th VC Sapper Battalion 840th VC Infantry Battalion

III Corps

Unit and Strengths

5th VC Infantry Division 3,300

27th VC Infantry Regiment (1st, 2nd, and 3rd Battalions) – 1,650 Phuoc Tuy

275th VC Inf. Regiment (1st, 2nd, and 3rd Battalions) – 1,650 Phuoc Tuy

7th NVA Infantry Division 5,250

141st NVA Infantry Regiment (1st, 2nd, and 3rd Battalions) – 1,800 Tay Ninh

165th NVA Infantry Regiment (1st, 2nd, and 3rd Battalions) – 1,950 Tay Ninh

52nd NVA Infantry Regiment (3 unidentified battalions) – 1,500 Tay Ninh

9th VC Infantry Division 10,260

271st VC Infantry Regiment (1st, 2nd, and 3rd Battalions) – 1,300

272nd VC Infantry Regiment (1st, 2nd, and 3rd Battalions) – 1,070

273rd VC Infantry Regiment (1st, 2nd, and 3rd Battalions) – 1,100

2nd VC Infantry Regiment (267th and 269th Battalions) – 1,200

69th VC Artillery Regiment (52nd and 58th Arty, and 56th Air Defense Battalions) – 1,700

70th VC Infantry Regiment (D1, D2, and D3 Battalions) – 1,450

84th NVA Artillery Regiment (1st, 2nd, and 3rd Rocket Battalions) – 1,200
101st NVA Infantry Regiment (1st, 2nd, and 3rd Battalions) – 1,240

Nondivisional Units 2,380

C10 VC Sapper Battalion	Dong Nai VC Infantry Battalion
1st VC Infantry Battalion	8th VC Artillery Battalion
46th VC Recon Battalion	725th NVA Sapper Battalion

IV Corps

Unit

D 509th VC Infantry Battalion	D 857th VC Infantry Battalion
D 7164th VC Infantry Battalion	Tay Do VC Infantry Battalion
U Minh 2nd VC Infantry Battalion	U Minh 10th VC Infantry Battalion
501st VC Infantry Battalion	503rd VC Infantry Battalion
504th VC Infantry Battalion	512th VC Infantry Battalion
514th VC Infantry Battalion	516th VC Infantry Battalion

Weapons and Aircraft of the NVA and VC

The NVA and the Southern communist guerrillas National Liberation Front (NLF) or VC, as they were commonly referred to during the war, largely used standard Warsaw Pact weapons. Weapons used by the North Vietnamese also included Chinese communist variants, which were referred to as CHICOMs by the US military. The NVA and VC used a mix of weapons that included Warsaw Pact, US, and CHICOM. The Viet Cong were not always able to be supplied by the ARVN. Sometimes they took weapons from US soldiers after an attack or raided US or South Vietnamese weapon stockpiles. This increased the number of weapons available to the NVA and VC and gave balance against the US arsenal.

The NVA artillery included the following:

-ZU-23 twin 23 mm antiaircraft -M1939 37 mm antiaircraft gun
gun

-S-60 57 mm antiaircraft gun   -85 mm air defense gun M1939
                                  (52-K)

-100 mm air defense gun KS-19 -KS-1982 mm, 107 mm, 120
                                  mm, and 160 mm mortars

-122 mm Katyusha rockets   -Type 63 multiple rocket launcher

-BM-21 Grad   -BM-25 (MRL) limited numbers

-122 mm gun M1931/37 (A-19) -122 mm howitzer M1938
                                  (M-30)

-D-74 122 mm Field Gun   -130 mm towed field gun M1954
                                  (M-46)

-152 mm howitzer M1943 (D-1) -152 mm towed gun-howitzer
                                  M1955 (D-20)

The North Vietnamese military air section included the following aircraft:

-MiG-21 jet fighter   -MiG-19 jet fighter; used in lim-
                                  ited numbers

-MiG-17 jet fighter   -MiG-15 jet fighter; used in lim-
                                  ited numbers

-Shenyang J-6 jet fighter   -Shenyang J-5 jet fighter
-An-2 aircraft   -Mi-4 helicopter
-Mi-1 helicopter   -Mi-2 helicopter
-Mi-8 helicopter

The Northern Air section aircraft weapons included the following:

-K-13 (missile)
-Gryazev-Shipunov GSh-23   -Nudelman-Rikhter NR-30
-Nudelman N-37   -Nudelman-Rikhter NR-23

The NVA and VC small arms included the following:

-Soviet AK-47   -PPSh-41
-SKS   -US M-16
-US M-14

NVA and VC handguns included the following:

-Tokarev TT-33   -Makarov PM
-P-64 Polish handgun   -Nagant M1895 revolver
-Type 14 8 mm Nambu Pistol   -Stechkin automatic pistol
-Walther P38   -Luger P08
-Mauser C96

NVA and VC automatic and semiautomatic rifles included the following:

- AK-47 and AKM (from the Soviet Union and Warsaw Pact)
- Type 56 assault rifle (from the People's Republic of China)
- Vz. 58 assault rifle (from Czechoslovakia)
- Type 63 assault rifle
- Sturmgewehr 44 assault rifle
- SVD-63 semiautomatic marksman rifle
- Gewehr 43 semiautomatic rifle
- M1 Carbine semi-automatic rifle (captured during the First Indochina War)
- MAS-49 rifle (captured French rifle from First Indochina War)
- SKS semiautomatic carbine
- SVT-40 semiautomatic rifle

NVA and VC bolt action rifles included the following:

- MAS-36 rifle – captured French rifle from First Indochina War

- Mosin-Nagant bolt-action rifles and carbines (Russian main World War II battle rifle)
- Mauser Kar 98k bolt-action rifle
- Type 38 Rifle (captured from the Japanese during World War II)
- Type 99 Rifle (captured from the Japanese during World War II)

NVA and VC submachine guns included the following:

- K-50M submachine gun (Vietnamese edition, based on Chinese version of Russian PPSh-41, under license)
- PPS-43 submachine gun
- PPSh-41 submachine gun (both Soviet and Chinese versions)
- PPD-34/38 submachine gun
- PPD-40 submachine gun
- MP-38/MP-40 (captured by the Soviets during World War II)
- Škorpion vz. 61 submachine gun
- MAT-49 submachine gun
- PM-63 submachine gun
- Type 100 submachine gun
- Thompson submachine gun

NVA and VC machine guns included the following:

-Type 99 LMG

-RPK light machine gun

-Degtyarev DP light machine gun

-MG-34 light machine gun

-Uk vz. 59 general-purpose MG

-DShK heavy machine gun

-RPD light machine gun

-PK light machine gun

-SG-43/SGM medium machine guns

-G-42 medium machine gun

-ZB-53 machine gun (from Czechoslovakia)

-PM M1910 heavy machine gun

NVA and VC Grenades and other explosives:

-F1 grenade
-Type 67 CHICOM stick grenade
-RG-42 grenade
-RGD-5 grenade
-9K32 Strela-2 antiaircraft weapon
-RPG-2 anti-tank weapon
-RPG-7 anti-tank weapon
-Type 69 RPG anti-tank weapon
-SPG-9 73 mm recoilless rifle
-B-10 recoilless rifle
-B-11 recoilless rifle

NVA and VC flamethrowers included the following:

-    -LPO-50 Flamethrower (limited use)

NVA and VC vehicles included the following:

-PT-76 amphibious tank
-Type 62 light tank
-Type 63 amphibious tank
-BTR-40 APC
-BTR-60 APC
-BTR-152 APC
-BRDM-1
-BRDM-2
-Type 63 Armored
Personnel Carrier
-Type 63 antiaircraft
self-propelled systems
-ZSU-57-2 antiaircraft self-pro-
pelled systems
-ZSU-23-4 antiair-
craft self-propelled
-T-34-85 medium tank,
used in limited numbers
-T-54/55 main battle tanks
-Type 59 main battle tanks
-IS-2/3/10 heavy tank
-SU-100 self-propelled guns
in limited numbers
-Bicycles

NVA and VC land mines included the following:

A wide variety of antipersonnel ordnance and booby traps were used in the Vietnam War, including punji stakes.

-    M14 Mine (used by US Forces until 1973)

- MBV-78A1 (Vietnamese variant of Russian POMZ AP mine)
- Type 58 and Type 59 (Chinese copy of Russian POMZ-2 and POMZ-2M AP mines)
- OZM series of Russian bounding mines

NVA and VC uniforms varied. Although the NVA were issued the standard khaki uniform with pith helmet, they wore a mix of NVA, US, and allied uniforms. The NVA uniforms included khaki, US and allied olive drab jungle fatigues, tiger stripes, camouflaged fatigues, and civilian attire. The majority of VC wore uniform they could beg, borrow, or steal. Whenever we engaged the VC, we always saw a mix of uniforms worn by the enemy. The VC usually wore civilian shorts and tee shirts. The NVA and VC wore a mix of NVA and US military web gear. Footwear for the NVA and VC consisted of flip-flops, Batta Boots, Ho Chi Minh sandals, and US jungle boots. I never saw any NVA of VC wear any type of helmet in combat. They wore soft boonie hats.

Logistics

Logistics played a major role for the NVA in determining the outcome of the Second Indochina War. Infiltration of troops, weapons, ammunition, and materiel into South Vietnam from the North was necessary and critical for a northern victory. Logistics was the most important aspect of the North's early involvement strategy.

United States and allied forces' logistics in South Vietnam were superior to the North's logistical system of equipping, supplying, and transporting troops during combat operations in the South. Although the enemy logistic systems and methods were rudimentary, they were effective because of the following:

1. The enemy utilized guerilla tactics that protracted the war without American domestic support.
2. The enemy set the operational tempo by tailoring combat operations to their existing resources and logistics.

3. The rugged environment, triple canopy, subtropical climate, and several monsoon seasons annually reduced, curtailed, and hampered friendly combat operations.

4. Many roads in South Vietnam were not negotiable for friendly vehicle resupply because of deep ruts, mud quagmires in wet weather, destroyed bridges, landslides, and the threat of enemy ambushes.

5. The proximity of large logistical caches in Cambodia, Laos, and resupply by China played a crucial role in supplying war materiel and supplies to the enemy in the South.

6. Although North Vietnam and China were foes, China's opposition to America prompted them to provide the North with combat weapons, ammunition, and combat materiel.

7. The USSR almost immediately began to supply North Vietnam to offset Chinese influence.

8. The enemy in South Vietnam learned very quickly that US and allied helicopters were vulnerable to ground fire.

9. Friendly, secure logistical installations were normally non-existent in the South. The majority of combat resupply missions originated and launched from isolated base camps and firebases.

10. During Vietnamization, major enemy units were recalled from the South, reequipped, rearmed, retrained, and returned to their former locations in the South.

The North Vietnamese knew that timely logistics were the key to enemy success in the South. The majority of NVA in the South were combat infantry with few logistic or support personnel. Northern logistical doctrine mandated and directed that war supplies and materiel were to be dispersed in hidden caches through likely operational areas in the South. Combat supplies were to be stockpiled near objectives prior to attacks or offensives. Local labor in the South was used as porters to transport supplies to these forward staging and assembly areas. Large underground storage facilities were constructed in Laos and Cambodia for future combat contingencies in the South.

Logistical support infiltration routes included the Ho Chi Minh trail, Sihanouk trail and sea routes. The Sihanouk trail began at Sihanoukville on the coast of Cambodia. Large cargo ships flying neutral flags docked and unloaded a variety of massive combat supplies with no resistance. The majority of these supplies and war materiel were transported by truck to Phnom Penh and were pushed down to large NVA base camp areas in the safety of Cambodia. The US had difficulty stopping, impeding, and limiting these supply ships from docking at Sihanoukville. The Cambodian government was purposefully oblivious to these shipments to appease Hanoi. A substantial quantity of supplies were sent to the seven mountains area in IV Corps of South Vietnam and to sanctuaries inside Cambodia close to the border for contingencies.

In 1959, the North Vietnamese government created Group 559 to infiltrate NVA, weapons, ammunition, and combat materiel south on the Ho Chi Minh trail. The Ho Chi Minh trail was a complex network of foot and animal paths, and roads from North Vietnam through eastern Laos to South Vietnam. Construction of the Ho Chi Minh trail began in 1955. Early roads were mere trails that gradually were widened. The first transport system was elephants. The US Central Intelligence Agency destroyed most of the elephants. Ponies and bicycles were substituted for the elephants. The bicycles were reinforced with metal, floor boards, and modified handlebars to facilitate movement for porters. Ultimately, thousands of porters were used on the trail. Up to five hundred pounds could be transported on these modified bicycles. The NVA soldier averaged fifteen to twenty miles per day on the trail. Truck convoys averaged fifty to seventy-five miles at night on the trail. The north needed sixty tons of supplies daily to supply the southern fighting forces. Twenty truckloads daily fulfilled this requirement. The trail system stretched for approximately six hundred miles of well-concealed roads. Infiltrators on the trail included NVA soldiers and regroupees. Regroupees were South Vietnamese trained in the North and returned to the South to serve as cadre or military officers in the VC. All infiltrators received special political and military training in the North prior to heading south. After training was completed in training camps, the infiltrators were transported by truck, bus, and rail to Dong Hoi. Dong Hoi was the southernmost secure city in the North and was the final stop in the North prior to heading south on the trail. Infiltrators walked and pushed bicycles down the trail to the DMZ. Once they arrived at the DMZ, they entered the Ho Chi Minh trail and headed south. Initially, the trip south could take up to six months. In 1969, the trail matured, and travel time was reduced to six to eight weeks. NVA and regroupees carried about two pounds of rice per day along with an eighty-pound rucksack, gear, weapon, and venomous snakebite antidote. The marching unit on the trail was usually a platoon of thirty soldiers. The marching units remained on trails to save the dirt roads for the supply convoys at night. Each platoon had a guide and a political cadre. The majority of guides had their own personal routes between relay stations and camps. Success depended on march discipline and camouflage.

In 1965, construction of rest facilities and barracks began on the trail. Eventually, two fuel pipelines were constructed along the trail to support vehicles, cargo trucks, and tanks. By 1971, the Ho Chi Minh trail had fourteen major relay stations. Each station was a complex of combat support systems. By 1973, the majority of enemy logistics entered South Vietnam via the Ho Chi Minh trail.

The Ho Chi Minh trail had many dynamics, perils, horrors, and terrors. Ten to twenty percent of the infiltrators failed to complete the trip south. Some reasons for not completing the long march were the following:

1. The trail was perpetually bombed by numerous air strikes daily. The marchers constantly heard the noise of bombers and reconnaissance planes overhead. This threat slowed the marchers and forced them to seek cover frequently.
2. Long rainy seasons caused catastrophic floods that washed away many man-made trails and turned streams into large non-navigable rivers.

3. Amoebic dysentery and malaria were a main scourge and prevalent on the trail. Cemeteries were established throughout the trail to bury the dead.
4. Wild animals such as bear, tigers, and venomous snakes attacking or biting the marchers
5. Repairing bridges took time. All vehicle and footbridges were very vulnerable to air attack.

The north had teams for every contingency and function on the trail. Some of the teams were as follows:

- Path and road repair teams
- Vehicle and footbridge repair teams
- Communication teams
- Petroleum, oil, and lubricant teams
- Security units of up to sixty soldiers at each truck park or camp
- Relay teams. Truck crews worked in relay teams driving back and forth on a trail section. No trucks drove the entire route
- Antiair teams were added in the late '60s to increase security
- Special teams were organized in the late '60s and deployed to observe and serve as early warning for US helicopters infiltrating Special Forces teams and units on or near the trail

Despite the massive US bombing campaign against the North, Hanoi managed to keep the Ho Chi Minh trail open, functional, and productive.

Group 759 was organized to supply the South via the South China Sea. Resupplying combat materiel and combat personnel via the South China Sea to South Vietnam was not as successful as using the Ho Chi Minh and Sihanouk trails. Most supply operations were conducted by small northern sea vessels close to the South Vietnamese coast. They resembled small smuggling operations rather than major supply shipments. Up until 1975, the US and allied forces practically stopped all northern sea resupply shipments to the South.

Guerrilla Environment and Society

Intelligence now substantiates the North was fundamentally not affected by the US and allied air war. United States and allied airpower in the North was never lethal and decisive as planned and intended until Operation Linebacker II. The bombing campaign in the North failed to achieve US major military and political objectives. The relentless bombing campaign was supposed to resolve and end the war within six months. The air war only produced awesome bombing statistics. These astounding statistics are 350,000 bombing missions flown, 655,000 tons of bombs dropped in the North, 918 US aircraft lost, and 818 US pilots killed.

The North Vietnamese were very tenacious, innovative, Spartan, flexible, selfless, and adaptive. Patriotism was stressed over arts, books, radio, and other social events. Industries and storage facilities were removed from urban centers and dispersed across the farmland and countryside. These factories, storage facilities, living areas, and workers were covered and camouflaged. Some major factories were dispersed into as many as fifty locations for continuity. Workers with their families moved to or near these factory locations to shorten commute time and for added security. Many government schools and government agencies moved into the suburbs or a short distance from town for bombing protection and security.

When the planes came to bomb, the North had a slogan: Combat and Construct. Their first action was to try and shoot a US or allied fighter or bomber down. Initially, the North used small arms and automatic weapons against the planes. Half of the home and local self-defense units were women skilled in rifle marksmanship, automatic weapons, and basic tactics, techniques, and procedures. Later, they had shoulder-fired surface-to-air missiles and large surface-to-air missiles mounted on transport trucks. After the planes departed the area, the construction crews of the mobile "shock brigade" appeared and cleaned up and repaired the bombing damage.

Approximately two million civilians were formed into mobile "shock brigades" in North Vietnam to work full-time traveling to repair roads, bridges, and railroads. Gravel, pioneer tools, and rails were cached and stored along major roads and railroads, enabling workers to rapidly repair damage.

Major bridges of cement and steel were replaced with temporary makeshift bamboo stocks. Some bridges were repaired below the water to prevent detection from the air. Floating bridges of sampans linked together, and ferries kept the cargo trucks moving. One boat was placed on one side of the river, and another boat was moored and camouflaged on the opposite side of the river. At night, the workers simply pulled the two boats together, forming a pontoon bridge. No bridge or crossing site was out of commission or action for more than a few hours. Logistics trucks traveled at night without headlights. All trucks were covered with foliage and camouflage nets.

Camouflage was a way of life in the North. It was mandatory for kids to wear camouflage while attending school. School children moved from building to building via trench complexes. Classrooms had shoulder-high reinforced mud walls. Student school desks were a makeshift bunker and protection from bombing.

In major cities, a common one-person concrete cylinder kept civilian casualties relative low. They were placed every few feet in every street in major cities. These concrete cylinders were also placed in homes, work sites, and along commuter roads. Covers were made of concrete, which the user pulled over the cylinder top for added protection. Several cities were linked by tunnels. Families lived in these tunnels and continued to farm and work in factories at night. Families sometimes dug small catacombs with dirt floors, canvas walls, and used oil lamps for warmth and light.

During 1970, the countryside and environment in the North was quickly changing, recovering, and favoring the government. The northern military generals and political leaders learned from their mistakes and modified their tactics to negate and minimize exposure to US airpower. The guerrilla environment in the North was a way of life that outlasted US high technology and airpower. During these trying times, the northern military, political, diplomatic programs, activities, and actions were synchronized and mutually supporting. The Soviet Union and China continued to provide substantial food, materiel, military arms, ammunition, and labor that sustained the North during the bombing campaign and air strikes.

Ho Chi Minh's successor was Le Duan. Le Duan stated, "The strategic guidelines are to fight a protracted war, gaining strength as one fights. In those times our people showed unimaginable strength. We were one mind and united. And, we will forever remain a nation."

North Vietnamese prime minister Phan Van Dong stated, "We Vietnamese continued to live, work and fight. Our collective leadership remained the same throughout the last few decades and symbolizes the unity of the entire population."

Tunnel Systems and Complexes

The communists Viet Minh began digging tunnel systems and complexes in the 1940s in the South in order to conduct combat operations more efficiently against the French. Initially, these tunnels were small, short, and temporary. During the early 1960s, when the US began to increasingly escalate military operations in South Vietnam, the Viet Minh expanded and improved their tunnels.

The enemy dug thousands of miles of tunnels in South Vietnam. The enemy underground facilities were well-developed underground complexes and systems consisting of bunkers, sleeping areas, classrooms, caches, observation points, sniper-firing positions, kitchen and dining areas, rest and relaxation areas, training areas, and medical facilities—all connected by tunnels. Several complexes and systems had ordinance factories, theaters, and music halls. Some tunnel systems and complexes housed complete villages underground. The majority of tunnels had booby traps consisting of boxes of scorpions and/or venomous snakes that would overturn on any intruder when a trip wire was tripped. When these boxes overturned, they would drop the scorpions and/or venomous snakes on the heads of US tunnel rats. All tunnels were carefully designed. Many turns were incorporated so that enemy grenades and gunfire were less effective.

MAJOR (RETIRED) STEVEN E COOK

Airtight trapdoors allowed occupants to move from one section to another to avoid tear gas or smoke.

The Cu Chi tunnels were famous. They were constructed in hard laterite clay, which was ideal for tunneling. Cu Chi was the end of the line for more than two hundred kilometers of underground tunnels. These tunnels were the most complex part of a network of tunnels that linked enemy support bases from the Saigon outskirts all the way to the Cambodian border. The Cu Chi tunnels also served as a base for the 1968 Tet attack on Saigon and surrounding US bases.

Large scale B-52 bombing raids aimed to destroy the tunnels were unsuccessful and failed. Enemy after-action reports revealed that the average underground system and complex only lost about 50 yards of tunnel space from B-52 bombing raids. Massive search and destroy missions also failed to detect and destroy the Cu Chi tunnel systems and complexes. When US and allied ground forces conducted these multi-battalion search and destroy operations, the enemy simply vanished underground and waited until the military forces on the surface departed the area before resurfacing. An estimated 50,000 enemy died defending the Cu Chi tunnels. Today, the Cu Chi tunnels are a major tourist attraction.

Tunnel Rats were the only known threat to enemy tunnel systems and complexes in the South. Only the 25th Infantry Division and the 1st Infantry Division of the US Army trained and maintained formal Tunnel Rat units. The Tunnel Rats' minimum gear was a pistol and flashlight. Some Tunnel Rats carried additional gear such as radios, rifle, hand grenades and explosives. After a Tunnel Rat completed his mission, engineers were usually called in to destroy the tunnels with explosives. In other US units, Tunnel Rats were volunteers or detailed for ad hoc tunnel missions. My unit seldom found a tunnel. When we did find a tunnel, we normally only explored a short distance inside, and then we called the engineers in to blow the tunnel.

Perhaps the most famous and notable Tunnel Rat was Sergeant Robert Batten. He was called Batman by his fellow Rats. He was small, a loner, fearless, and had a sixth sense. Batman served three tours in South Vietnam as a soldier in the Big Red One Infantry

Division. During his tours and exploring enemy tunnels, his eight-man team accounted for more than one hundred enemy dead and many more captured. Although Batman was wounded four times, he survived and returned home.

Enemy Mines and Booby Traps

The enemy used a variety of US, Soviet, and Chinese mines and booby traps including punji stakes. These were another economy of force and efficient option for the enemy to employ to kill or maim many US and allied military in the field, cities, and towns and villages. They were used primarily in the field to stop or impede friendly movement and mobility. Booby traps amounted to 11 percent of the fatalities and 17 percent of US wounded. Intelligence estimated that 70 percent of US armor losses in South Vietnam were attributed to mines.

The enemy concentrated booby traps on routes commonly traveled by friendly military. Larger antivehicle and tank booby traps and mines were employed primarily on well-traveled roads, bridges, and choke points on rivers. Some common mines and booby traps were the following:

- Various hand grenades
- Jettisoned aircraft fuel tanks filled with explosives
- Punji stakes made from wood, bamboo, and metal rods
- Punji pits
- Crossbows
- Various personnel and anti-tank mines including the Bouncing Betty mine
- Various mortars and artillery shells bound together
- Bicycles filled with explosives and placed in cities and towns (very popular)
- Boxes filled with scorpions and/or venomous snakes

The majority of booby traps were prepared in small underground booby trap and mine factories. Enemy mines and booby traps were constructed from artillery, mortar shells, pipes, and virtually anything that would hold explosives. Soviet and Chinese military mines were also used. Mines and booby traps were detonated by trip wires, direct pressure, pressure release, and command detonated. The most popular booby trap was a trip wire across a trail connected to a hand grenade.

North Vietnamese Allies
Union of Soviet Socialist Republics

In 1946, the Vietnamese struggle with the French was a low priority for the Kremlin. The Soviet leader Joseph Stalin was always suspect of Ho Chi Minh because of his unorthodox view of Marxist-Leninist doctrine. In 1946, Viet Minh hostilities with the French increased. Because the French were militarily superior to the Viet Minh, Hanoi requested military aid from Moscow. After the French were defeated at Dien Bien Phu, Hanoi concentrated and escalated its war efforts in the South. Nikita Khrushchev, the premier of the Soviet Union, wanted Hanoi to maintain a peaceful coexistence with America and the world. As the Vietnam War intensified, Khrushchev and the Soviets became more cautious. Khrushchev characterized the war as too dangerous and did not trust the North Vietnamese government. Post–Khrushchev Soviet leaders took greater interest in the North's war with the South. After Khrushchev was overthrown, the new Soviet premier Alexei Kosygin visited Hanoi in February 1965 and supported Hanoi's struggle for national liberation and their goal of uniting North and South Vietnam. During this visit to Hanoi, Kosygin promised that Soviet aid would increase and signed several treaties for full, diverse support for the North Vietnamese effort. The Soviets believed initially these large military and economic support packages would gain and win an ideological advantage over China. Soviet aid was primarily advanced weapons, surface-to-air missiles, and jet fighter aircraft. Future losses in military equipment, vehicles, and raw materials were quickly offset and replaced by increased aid from the Soviets.

The Soviets could not ignore the US escalation in South Vietnam and Southeast Asia. Soviet and North Vietnamese relations were mediocre and cursory until the US escalated the war. During the war, the Soviets fully supported the increased combat role of the North Vietnamese and provided enormous military and economic aid.

The Soviets were seeking ways and methods to wean North Vietnamese support and dependency on China. Soviet leadership seized opportunity from the expanding war to undermine US prestige; bog down the US in a quagmire war; test and rate its own weapons, tactics, and procedures under combat conditions; and analyze US combat tactics, weapons, and materiel.

The Soviets provided military and civilian advisers, surface-to-air missiles (SAMs), tanks, fighter jets, and three thousand technicians. Many Soviet technicians were directly involved in the combat effort by manning SAM sites, antiaircraft artillery sites, and radar sites. In 1968, North Vietnamese air defenses included Soviet 152 fighter aircraft, 8,000 antiaircraft artillery (AAA), and 40 SA-2 surface-to-air missile battalions. Several North Vietnamese air bases housed these Soviet fighter aircraft. President Johnson prohibited any US aircraft from attacking any air base in the North that housed Soviet aircraft. Approximately 100 of these fighter aircraft were maintained in a safe sanctuary in Southern China for contingencies. North Vietnamese AAA was responsible for 80 percent of US aircraft losses over Southeast Asia.

Soviet aid to North Vietnam increased dramatically as the war intensified. Prior to Tet, Soviet aid amounted to 80 percent of all support received by North Vietnam. After Tet, Soviet military and economic aid began to decrease, and the Soviets supported the Paris peace talks. During a major peace talk deadlock, the Soviets pressured the North Vietnamese to accept a compromise.

The 1972 Easter Offensive into South Vietnam was spearheaded by Soviet tanks. In 1972, the Soviets continued to provide massive economic and military aid to North Vietnam. Without Soviet aid, the North Vietnamese could not have continued to conduct combat operations in the South. After the war, the Soviets continued to support the Socialist Republic of Vietnam with food and fuel. In 1979, the Soviets obtained use of naval and air bases in the South. The majority of these bases were former US bases. Soviets and the Socialist Republic of Vietnam relations remained close into the mid-1980s. The Soviets considered Vietnam a Soviet client state.

China

The communist victory in China led to a substantial increase of Chinese aid to the Viet Minh. The Chinese provided sanctuaries and large shipments of arms to the Viet Minh regulars and guerillas. General Giap, in early 1950, was encouraged by the Chinese support and began comprehensive offensive operations against the French. In 1951, China provided advisers that trained the Viet Minh and assisted in planning major military operations. The Chinese communists supported the Viet Minh guerillas against France. Chinese aid was vital to the Viet Minh and was a major factor that was critical in defeating the French at Dien Bien Phu. Chinese artillery generals developed the fire support plan for the Viet Minh at Dien Bien Phu.

After the Gulf of Tonkin incident, China deployed a squadron of MIG-15s and MIG-176 jets to help North Vietnam continue in the fight. In 1964 and '65, China provided 320,000 engineer and artillery troops to North Vietnam for construction of new radar, railroads, and logistics to facilitate movement of supplies from southern China. Chinese artillery troops built, manned, and operated AAA sites to defend against US air attacks. China also provided huge quantities of arms, ammunition, vehicles, uniforms, foot gear, rice, and sports equipment to the NVA. Chinese aid to the NV was greater in quantity than the Soviets. Chinese aid was low tech and averaged over $200 million annually at the war's peak. Over 300,000 support personnel were sent to North Vietnam to provide assistance in engineering, road and railroad construction, and air defense. United States intelligence estimated that China provided three quarters of all military aid given to North Vietnam during the war. However, China refused to deploy fighter pilots to North Vietnam.

China's main goal was to prevent the Second Indochina War from escalating. The Chinese did not want a direct military confrontation with the US. China was the first communist state to recognize the National Liberation Front in South Vietnam. In 1971, the Chinese government endorsed the peace plan ending the war. Several military clashes occurred between China and Vietnam during the late 1970s. During the '90s, tensions eased between the two countries; and presently, excellent relations exist between the two countries.

Cuba

Cuba was very involved in the Vietnam War. Cuba provided an engineering battalion called the Giron Brigade. Their mission was to maintain route 9, a major North Vietnamese supply road into Southern Vietnam. Cuba provided guards and management of a POW camp and operated a field hospital just north of the DMZ. Professional Cuban interrogators worked in Hanoi at a prison called the Zoo. Many of these PIW interrogators were brutal operators and used extreme torture techniques. Seventeen US military personnel were taken to Cuba for experiments that improved Cuban POW interrogation and torture techniques.

Questions for Reflection

1. When were the first US combat troops deployed to South Vietnam?
2. Why was Tet a military disaster for the North Vietnamese government?
3. Contrast the Viet Cong local guerillas to the Viet Cong main force regional forces.
4. Why was the enemy's rudimentary logistic system effective?
5. Describe the trip from North Vietnam into South Vietnam on the Ho Chi Minh trail.
6. Describe the guerrilla society and environment in North Vietnam.

7. How did the enemy tunnel systems aid in their military operations?
8. What was a Tunnel Rat?
9. What was the primary use of enemy mines and booby traps?
10. Contrast Soviet premier Nikita Khrushchev's support to North Vietnam to his successor premier Alexei Kosygin.
11. Describe Cuba's involvement in the Vietnam War.

Viet Cong soldier.

NVA antiaircraft rocket section.

Rudimentary transportation system on the Ho Chi Minh trail during the early part of the war.

Truck convoy on the Ho Chi Minh trail, c. 1970.

Bicycles modified to carry up to five hundred
pounds on the Ho Chi Minh trail.

Example of an enemy tunnel complex, used
by both NVA and Viet Cong.

CHAPTER 16

Agent Orange and Other Herbicides Used in Southeast Asia

Those who do not remember history are destined to repeat it.
—Author unknown

Agent Orange or Herbicide Orange (HO) is one of the herbicides and defoliants used by the US military as part of its herbicidal warfare program, Operation Ranch Hand, during the Vietnam War from 1961 to 1971. Agent Orange is a catchphrase that refers to several herbicides that were used in Southeast Asia. The Vietnamese government estimates four hundred thousand people were killed or maimed and five hundred thousand children were born with birth defects as a result of the use of contaminated batches of the compound.

The two herbicides that compose Agent Orange are 2, 4-D, and 2, 4, 5-T. The latter is considered to be less biodegradable. A 50:50 mixture of 2, 4, 5-T and 2, 4-D was manufactured for the US Department of Defense primarily by Monsanto Corporation and Dow Chemical. The 2, 4, 5-T used to produce Agent Orange was contaminated with 2, 3, 7, 8-tetrachlorodibenzodioxin (TCDD), an extremely toxic dioxin compound. It was given its name from the color of the orange-striped 55 US gallon barrels in which it was shipped, and was by far the most widely used of the so-called rainbow herbicides.

During the Vietnam War, between 1962 and 1971, the United States military sprayed nearly 20 million US gallons of material containing chemical herbicides and defoliants mixed with jet fuel in Vietnam, eastern Laos, and parts of Cambodia, as part of Operation Ranch Hand. The program's goal was to defoliate forested and rural land, depriving guerrillas of cover and crops. Another goal was to destroy the ability of peasants to support themselves in the countryside and forcing them to flee to the US-dominated cities, thus depriving the guerrillas of their rural support and food supply.

The US began to target food crops in October 1962, primarily using Agent Blue. In 1965, 42 percent of all herbicide spraying was dedicated to food crops. Rural-to-urban migration rates dramatically increased in South Vietnam, as peasants escaped the war and famine in the countryside by fleeing to the US-dominated cities.

United States Air Force records show that at least 6,542 spraying missions took place over the course of Operation Ranch Hand. By 1971, 12 percent of the total area of South Vietnam had been sprayed with defoliating chemicals, at an average concentration of thirteen times the recommended United States Drug Administration (USDA) application rate for domestic use. In South Vietnam alone, an estimated 10 million hectares (25 million acres, 39,000 square miles) of agricultural land was ultimately destroyed. In some areas, TCDD concentrations in soil and water were hundreds of times greater than the levels considered safe by the US Environmental Protection Agency. Overall, more than 20 percent of South Vietnam's forests were sprayed at least once over a nine-year period.

In 1969, it was revealed to the public that the 2, 4, 5-T was contaminated with a dioxin, 2, 3, 7, 8-tetrachlorodibenzodioxin (TCDD), and that the TCDD was causing many of the previously unexplained adverse health effects, which were correlated with Agent Orange exposure. TCDD has been described as "perhaps the most toxic molecule ever synthesized by man." Internal memoranda revealed that Monsanto (a major manufacturer of 2, 4, 5-T) had informed the US government in 1952 that its 2, 4, 5-T was contaminated. In the manufacture of 2, 4, 5-T, accidental overheating of the reaction mixture easily causes the product to condense into the toxic self-condensation product TCDD. At the time, precautions were not taken against this unintended side reaction, which also caused the Seveso disaster in Italy in 1976.

While degradation of 2, 4, 5-T with a half-life on a scale of days can be achieved by adding bacteria of a special strain, "no substantial degradation" was observed in the same soil without addition of bacteria. The half-life of dioxins in soil is more than ten years, and that of TCDD in human fat tissue is about seven years.

A 1969 report authored by K. Diane Courtney and others found 2, 4, 5-T could cause birth defects and stillbirths in mice. Several studies have shown an increased rate of cancer mortality for workers exposed to 2, 4, 5-T. In one such study, from Hamburg, Germany, the risk of cancer mortality increased by 170 percent after working for ten years at the 2, 4, 5-T–producing section of a Hamburg manufacturing plant. Three studies have suggested prior exposure to Agent Orange poses an increased risk of acute myelogenous leukemia in the children of Vietnam veterans.

Spraying was usually done either from helicopters or from low-flying C-123 Provider aircraft, fitted with sprayers and MC-1 Hourglass pumping systems, and one thousand US gallon chemical tanks. Spray runs were also conducted from trucks, boats, and backpack sprayers.

In 1965, members of the US Congress were told "crop destruction is understood to be the more important purpose . . . but the emphasis is usually given to the jungle defoliation in public mention of the program." Soldiers were told they were destroying crops because they were going to be used to feed guerrillas. They later discovered nearly all the food they had been destroying was not being produced for guerrillas; it was, in reality, only being grown to support the local civilian population. For example, in Quang Ngai province, 85 percent of the croplands were scheduled to be destroyed in 1970 alone. This contributed to widespread famine, leaving hundreds of thousands of people malnourished or starving.

The US military began targeting food crops in October 1962, primarily using Agent Blue; the American public was not made aware of the crop destruction programs until 1965 (and it was then believed that crop spraying had begun that spring). In 1965, 42 percent of all herbicide spraying was dedicated to food crops.

Extensive testing for dioxin contamination has been conducted at the former US air bases in Da Nang, Phu Cat, and Bien Hoa. Some of the soil and sediment on the bases have extremely high levels of dioxin requiring remediation. The Da Nang Air Base has dioxin contamination up to 350 times higher than international recommendations for action. The contaminated soil and sediment continue to affect the citizens of Vietnam, poisoning their food chain and causing illnesses, serious skin diseases, and a variety of cancers in the lungs, larynx, and prostate.

Dioxins from Agent Orange have persisted in the Vietnamese environment since the war, settling in the soil and sediment and entering into the food chain through the animals and fish that feed in the contaminated areas. Movement of dioxins through the food web has resulted in bioconcentration and biomagnification. The areas most heavily contaminated with dioxins are the sites of former US air bases.

Studies have shown that veterans who served in the South during the war have increased rates of cancer, and nerve, digestive, skin, and respiratory disorders. Veterans from the South had higher rates of throat cancer, acute/chronic leukemia, Hodgkin's lymphoma, and non-Hodgkin's lymphoma, prostate cancer, lung cancer, colon cancer, soft tissue sarcoma, and liver cancer. With the exception of liver cancer, these are the same conditions the US Veterans Administration has determined may be associated with exposure to Agent Orange/dioxin, and are on the list of conditions eligible for compensation and treatment.

Military personnel who loaded airplanes and helicopters used in Operation Ranch Hand probably sustained some of the heaviest exposures. Others with potentially heavy exposures included members of US Army Special Forces units who defoliated remote campsites and members of US Navy river units who cleared base perimeters.

While in Vietnam, the veterans were told not to worry and were persuaded the chemical was harmless. After returning home,

Vietnam veterans began to suspect their ill health or the instances of their wives having miscarriages or children born with birth defects might be related to Agent Orange and the other toxic herbicides to which they were exposed in Vietnam. Veterans began to file claims in 1977 to the Department of Veterans Affairs for disability payments for health care for conditions they believed were associated with exposure to Agent Orange, or more specifically, dioxin, but their claims were denied unless they could prove the condition began when they were in the service or within one year of their discharge.

By April 1993, the Department of Veterans Affairs had only compensated 486 victims, although it had received disability claims from 39,419 soldiers who had been exposed to Agent Orange while serving in Vietnam. Since 1978, several lawsuits have been filed against the companies that produced Agent Orange, among them Dow Chemical, Monsanto, and Diamond Shamrock.

The chemical companies involved denied that there was a link between Agent Orange and the veterans' medical problems. However, on May 7, 1984, seven chemical companies settled the class-action suit out of court just hours before jury selection was to begin. The companies agreed to pay $180 million as compensation if the veterans dropped all claims against them. Slightly over 45 percent of the sum was ordered to be paid by Monsanto alone. Many veterans who were victims of Agent Orange exposure were outraged that the case had been settled instead of going to court and felt they had been betrayed by the lawyers. "Fairness hearings" were held in five major American cities, where veterans and their families discussed their reactions to the settlement and condemned the actions of the lawyers and courts, demanding the case be heard before a jury of their peers. Federal Judge Julius Weinstein refused the appeals, claiming the settlement was "fair and just." By 1989, the veterans' fears were confirmed when it was decided how the money from the settlement would be paid out. A totally disabled Vietnam veteran would receive a maximum of $12,000 spread out over the course of ten years. Furthermore, by accepting the settlement payments, disabled veterans would become ineligible for many state benefits that provided far more monetary support than the settlement, such as food stamps, public assistance, and government pensions. A widow of a Vietnam veteran who died of Agent Orange exposure would only receive $3,700.

In 1980, New Jersey created the New Jersey Agent Orange Commission, the first state commission created to study its effects. The commission's research project in association with Rutgers University was called the Pointman Project. It was disbanded by Governor Christine Todd Whitman in 1996. During Pointman I, commission researchers devised ways to determine small dioxin levels in blood. Prior to this, such levels could only be found in the adipose (fat) tissue. The project studied dioxin (TCDD) levels in blood as well as in adipose tissue in a small group of Vietnam veterans who had been exposed to Agent Orange and compared them to those of a matched control group; the levels were found to be higher in the former group.

The second phase of the project continued to examine and compare dioxin levels in various groups of Vietnam veterans, including Army, Marines, and brown-water riverboat Navy personnel.

In 1991, the US Congress enacted the Agent Orange Act, giving the Department of Veterans Affairs the authority to declare certain conditions "presumptive" to exposure to Agent Orange/dioxin, making these veterans who served in Vietnam eligible to receive treatment and compensation for these conditions. Through this process, the list of "presumptive" conditions has grown since 1991, and currently the US Department of Veterans Affairs has listed prostate cancer, respiratory cancers, multiple myeloma, type II diabetes, Hodgkin's disease, non-Hodgkin's lymphoma, soft tissue sarcoma, chloracne, porphyria, porphyria cutanea tarda, peripheral neuropathy, chronic lymphocytic leukemia, and spina bifida in children of veterans exposed to Agent Orange as conditions associated with exposure to the herbicide. This list now includes B-cell leukemias such as hairy cell leukemia, Parkinson's disease, and ischemic heart disease (these last three having been added on August 31, 2010).

Starting in 2005, the US Environmental Protection Agency (EPA) began to work with the Vietnamese government to measure the level of dioxin at the Da Nang Air Base. Also in 2005, the Joint Advisory Committee on Agent Orange, made up of representatives of Vietnamese and US government agencies, was established. The committee has been meeting yearly to explore areas of scientific cooperation, technical assistance, and environmental remediation of dioxin.

A breakthrough in the diplomatic stalemate on this issue occurred as a result of United States President George W. Bush's state visit to Vietnam in November 2006. In the joint statement, President Bush and President Triet agreed "further joint efforts to address the environmental contamination near former dioxin storage sites would make a valuable contribution to the continued development of their bilateral relationship."

In late May 2007, President Bush signed into law a supplemental spending bill for the war in Iraq and Afghanistan that included an earmark of $3 million specifically for funding the programs for the remediation of dioxin "hotspots" on former US military bases and for public health programs for the surrounding communities; some authors consider this to be completely inadequate, pointing out that the US air base in Da Nang, alone, will cost $14 million to clean up and that three others are estimated to require $60 million for cleanup.

Secretary of State Hillary Clinton stated during a visit to Hanoi in October 2010 that the "US government would begin work on the clean-up of dioxin contamination at the Da Nang air base." In June 2011, a ceremony was held at Da Nang airport to mark the start of US-funded decontamination of dioxin hotspots in Vietnam. Congress has allocated $32 million so far to fund the program.

On January 31, 2004, a victim's rights group, the Vietnam Association for Victims of Agent Orange/dioxin (VAVA), filed a lawsuit in the United States District Court for the Eastern District of New York in Brooklyn, against several US companies for liability in causing personal injury by developing and producing the chemical, and claimed that the use of Agent Orange violated the 1907 Hague Convention on Land Warfare, 1925 Geneva Protocol, and the 1949 Geneva Conventions. On March 10, 2005, Judge Jack B. Weinstein of the Eastern District, who had presided over the 1984 US Veterans class-action lawsuit, dismissed the lawsuit, ruling there was no legal basis for the plaintiffs' claims.

He concluded Agent Orange was not considered a poison under international law at the time of its use by the US, the US was not prohibited from using it as an herbicide, and the companies that produced the substance were not liable for the method of its use by the government. The US government was not a party in the lawsuit, due to sovereign immunity, and the court ruled the chemical companies, as contractors of the US government, shared the same immunity. The case was appealed and heard by the Second Circuit Court of Appeals on June 18, 2007. The Court of Appeals upheld the dismissal of the case, stating the herbicides used during the war were not intended to be used to poison humans and therefore did not violate international law. The US Supreme Court declined to consider the case. Three judges on the Second Circuit Court of Appeals in Manhattan heard the appeal on June 18, 2007. They upheld Weinstein's ruling to dismiss the case. They ruled that, though the herbicides contained a dioxin (a known poison), they were not intended to be used as a poison on humans. Therefore, they were not considered a chemical weapon and thus not a violation of international law.

To assist those who have been affected by Agent Orange/dioxin, the Vietnamese have established "peace villages," which each host between fifty and one hundred victims, giving them medical and psychological help. As of 2006, there were eleven such villages, thus granting some social protection to fewer than a thousand victims. United States veterans of the war in Vietnam and individuals who are aware and sympathetic to the impacts of Agent Orange have supported these programs in Vietnam. The Vietnamese government provides small monthly stipends to more than two hundred thousand Vietnamese believed to be affected by the herbicides; this totaled $40.8 million in 2008 alone. The Vietnam Red Cross has raised more than $22 million to assist the ill or disabled, and several US foundations, United Nations agencies, European governments and nongovernmental organizations have given a total of about $23 million for site cleanup, reforestation, health care, and other services to those in need.

The Air Force operation to remove Herbicide Orange from Vietnam in 1972 was named Operation Pacer IVY while the operation to destroy the Agent Orange stored at Johnston Atoll in 1977 was named Operation Pacer HO. Operation Pacer IVY (In Ventor Y) collected Agent Orange in South Vietnam and removed it in 1972 aboard the ship MV *Transpacific* for storage on Johnston Atoll. The Environmental Protection Agency (EPA) reports that 1,800,000 gallons of Herbicide Orange was stored at Johnson Island in the Pacific and 480,000 gallons at Gulfport, Mississippi.

Research and studies were initiated to find a safe method to destroy the materials, and it was discovered they could be incinerated safely under special conditions of temperature and dwell time. However, these herbicides were expensive, and the Air Force wanted to resell its surplus instead of dumping it at sea. Among many methods tested, one possibility of salvaging the herbicides was by reprocessing and filtering out the 2, 3, 7, 8-tetrachlorodibenzo-p-dioxin (TCDD) contaminant with carbonized (charcoaled) coconut fibers. This concept was then tested in 1976, and a pilot plant was constructed at Gulfport, Mississippi. From July to September 1977, during Operation Pacer HO (Herbicide Orange), the entire stock of Herbicide Orange from both storage sites at Gulfport, Mississippi, and Johnston Atoll was subsequently incinerated in four separate burns in the vicinity of Johnson Island aboard the Dutch-owned waste incineration ship MT *Vulcanus*.

A December 2006 Department of Defense report listed Agent Orange testing, storage, and disposal sites at thirty-two locations throughout the United States, as well as in Canada, Thailand, Puerto Rico, Korea, and in the Pacific Ocean. The Veteran Administration has also acknowledged that Agent Orange was used domestically by US forces in test sites throughout the US, with Eglin Air Force Base in Florida being one of the primary testing sites.

Other Rainbow Herbicides used in Southeast Asia were the following:

Agent Purple: A formulation of 2, 4-D and 2, 4, 5-T used between 1962 and 1964

Agent Green: Contained 2, 4, 5-T and was used between 1962 and 1964

Agent Pink: Contained 2, 4, 5-T and was used between 1962 and 1964

Agent White: A formulation of Picloram and 2, 4-D

Agent Blue: Contained Cacodylic acid

Agent Orange II: A formulation of 2, 4-D and 2, 4, 5-T used in 1968 and 1969; sometimes referred to as Super Orange

Agent Dinoxol: A formulation of 2, 4-D and 2, 4, 5-T. Small quantities were tested in South Vietnam between 1962 and 1964

Agent Trinoxol: Contained 2, 4, 5-T. Small quantities were tested in South Vietnam between 1962 and 1964

Agent Bromacil: Small quantities were tested in South Vietnam between 1962 and 1964

Agent Diquat: Small quantities were tested in South Vietnam between 1962 and 1964

Agent Tandex: Small quantities were tested in South Vietnam between 1962 and 1964

Agent Monuron: Small quantities were tested in South Vietnam between 1962 and 1964

Agent Diuron: Small quantities were tested in South Vietnam between 1962 and 1964

Agent Dalapon: Small quantities were tested in South Vietnam between 1962 and 1964

Vietnam War veterans may be eligible for disability compensation and health care benefits for the following diseases, which the Veterans Administration has recognized as associated with exposure to Agent Orange and other herbicides.

Al Amyloidosis: A rare disease caused when an abnormal protein, amyloid, enters tissues or organs

Chronic B-Cell Leukemia: A type of cancer that affects white blood cells

Chloracne: A skin condition that occurs soon after exposure to chemicals and looks like common forms of acne seen in teenagers

Diabetes Mellitus Type 2: A disease characterized by high blood sugar levels resulting from the body's inability to respond properly to the hormone insulin

Hodgkin's disease: A malignant lymphoma cancer characterized by progressive enlargement of the lymph nodes, liver, and spleen and by progressive anemia

Ischemic Heart Disease: A disease characterized by a reduced supply of blood to the heart that leads to chest pain

Multiple Myeloma: A cancer of plasma cells, a type of white blood cell in bone marrow

Non-Hodgkin's Lymphoma: A group of cancers that affect the lymph glands and other lymphatic tissue

Parkinson's disease: A progressive disorder of the nervous system that affects muscle movement

Peripheral Neuropathy, Acute and Subacute: A nervous system condition that causes numbness, tingling, and motor weakness

Porphyria Cutanea Tarda: A disorder characterized by liver dysfunction and by thinning and blistering of the skin in sun-exposed areas

Prostate Cancer: Cancer of the prostate; one of the most common cancers among Vietnam War male veterans

Respiratory Cancers: Cancers of the lung, larynx, trachea, and bronchus

Soft Tissue Sarcomas: A group of different types of cancers in body tissues such as muscle, fat, blood and lymph vessels, and connective tissues

A new disease presumed by the Veterans Administration to be caused by exposure to Agent Orange is essential thrombocythemia. Essential thrombocythemia is caused by bone marrow producing too many blood platelets. This can lead to abnormal bleeding or blood clots.

For additional details on Agent Orange and other herbicides, contact your local Veterans Administration hospital.

Questions for Reflection

1. Identify two reasons for using Rainbow Herbicides in Southeast Asia.
2. Describe Operation Ranch Hand.
3. Describe five serious human health effects as a result of exposure to Agent Orange.
4. Identify two civilian chemical companies that produced Agent Orange.
5. Identify five of the Rainbow Herbicides.

Four C-123s spray herbicides over South Vietnam.

Another example of herbicide use.

CHAPTER 17

Vietnam War Facts, Lies, Myths, Phonies, and Awards

It is time the American people learn that a surprisingly high number of people who claimed to have served in South Vietnam or in elite units, in fact, DID NOT!

Facts

-   West Virginia had the highest casualty rate per capita in the nation. There are 711 West Virginians on the Vietnam Memorial wall in Washington DC.
-   9,087,000 American military served on active duty during the official Vietnam era from August 5, 1965, to May 7, 1975.
-   3,403,100 Americans served in uniform in the Southeast Asia Theater, which included South Vietnam, Laos, Cambodia, Thailand, and sailors in adjacent South China Sea waters.
-   American Vietnam veterans represented 9.7 percent of their generation.
-   The first American to die in Vietnam was LTC Peter Dewey on September 26, 1945. He was gunned down on his way to the airport by the Viet Minh who apparently mistook him for a French officer. His body was never recovered.

- 58,270 US military were killed in action (KIA) in South Vietnam. Their names are now listed on the Vietnam War memorial in Washington DC. Their names are arranged in the order in which they were taken from us by date, and within each date, the names are alphabetized.
- 12 US soldiers on the wall were 17 years of age.
- 5 US soldiers on the wall were 16 years of age.
- PFC Dan Bullock was only 15 years old when he was KIA in South Vietnam.
- 997 US soldiers were killed on their first day in South Vietnam.
- 1,448 US soldiers were killed in action on their last day of duty prior to reporting to the processing station for shipment back to America.
- 31 sets of US brothers are on the wall.
- 54 US military KIA attended Thomas Edison High School in Philadelphia.
- 8 US military females are on the wall.
- 244 US Medals of Honor were awarded during the Vietnam War; 153 of them are on the wall.
- The most casualty deaths for a single day was on January 31, 1968; 245 KIAs were recorded.
- The most casualty deaths for a single month was May 1968; 2,415 KIAs were recorded.
- 75,000 US military were severely disabled.
- 23,214 US military were 100 percent disabled as of 1980.
- 5,283 US military lost limbs.
- 1,081 US military sustained multiple amputations.
- Of those KIA, 61 percent were younger than 21. 11,465 of those US military KIA were younger than 20 years old.
- Of those KIA, 17,539 were married.
- Average age of US military KIA was 23.1 years of age.
- Average age of US enlisted KIA was 22.37 years of age, not 19.
- Average age of US Officers KIA was 28.43 years of age.
- Average age of US Warrants KIA was 24.73 years of age.

- Average age of infantry soldiers KIA was 22.55 years of age.
- The oldest US military KIA was 62 years old.
- As of January 2017, there were about 1,600 American military still unaccounted for (missing in action) from the Vietnam War.
- 97 percent of US Vietnam veterans were honorably discharged.
- 91 percent of US Vietnam veterans say they are glad they served.
- 74 percent of US Vietnam veterans say they would serve again, even knowing the outcome.
- US Vietnam veterans have a lower unemployment rate than the same nonveteran age groups.
- US Vietnam veteran's personal income exceeds that of our nonveteran age group by more than 18 percent.
- 87 percent of Americans hold Vietnam veterans in high esteem.
- According to several Veterans Administration studies, there is no significant difference in drug usage between Vietnam veterans and non-Vietnam veterans of the same age group.
- US Vietnam veterans are less likely to be in prison; only one half of 1 percent of Vietnam veterans have been jailed for crimes.
- 85 percent of US Vietnam veterans made successful transitions to civilian life.
- The South Vietnamese military totaled about 850,000 at peak.
- The South Korean Army in South Vietnam totaled 50,000.
- The Australian military in South Vietnam totaled 7,672.
- The Thailand military in South Vietnam totaled 5,000.
- The Philippine military in South Vietnam totaled 5,500.
- The New Zealand military in South Vietnam totaled 550.
- The North Vietnamese Army totaled 461,000 and was located in both North and South Vietnam.
- The Chinese military in North Vietnam totaled 170,000.
- The Soviet Union had 3,000 military in North Vietnam.

- The North Korean military had 500 military in North Vietnam.
- The South Vietnam military had 195,000 KIA.
- South Vietnam had 430,000 civilians killed as a result of combat action.
- The South Korean Army had 5,099 KIA in South Vietnam.
- The Australian military had 500 KIA in South Vietnam.
- The New Zealand military had 37 KIA in South Vietnam.
- The Thailand military has 351 KIA in South Vietnam.
- The North Vietnamese Army had 65,000 KIA in South Vietnam.
- The Chinese military had 1,446 KIA in North Vietnam.
- The Soviet Union had 16 KIA in North Vietnam.

Rumors, Misinformation, Myths, and Lies

Falsehoods are oral or written statements that undermine the cohesive fabric of any organization, but especially a fraternal brotherhood of combat soldiers. When misinformation or lies about Vietnam veterans are allowed to fester or continue, especially when the information is derogatory, it can ruin a veteran's reputation. Please question or refute any misinformation or lies whenever you hear them. If you have doubts or questions, ask someone in a position to know the truth. If you don't question these lies, you condone the spreading of misinformation and perpetuate the rumors, falsehoods, and misinformation.

Myth: Common belief is that most Vietnam veterans were drafted.
Fact: Over 2/3 of the men who served in Vietnam were volunteers compared to 2/3 of the men who served in World War II being drafted. Approximately 70% of those killed in Vietnam were volunteers.
Myth: The news media has reported that total suicides among Vietnam veterans range from 50,000 to 100,000; 6 to 11 times the non-Vietnam veteran population.

Fact: Mortality studies show that 9,000 is a better estimate. The Center for Disease Control, Vietnam Experience Study Mortality Assessment showed that during the first 5 years after discharge, deaths from suicide were 1.7 times more likely among Vietnam veterans than non-Vietnam veterans. After that initial post-service period, Vietnam veterans were no more likely to die from suicide than non-Vietnam veterans. In fact, after the 5-year post-service period, the rate of suicides is less in the Vietnam veterans' group.

Myth: Common belief is that a disproportionate number of blacks were killed in the Vietnam War.

Fact: 86.3% of the men who died in Vietnam were Caucasians. 12.5% were black, 1.2% were other races. Sociologists Charles C. Moskos and John Sibley Butler, in their recently published book *All That We Can Be*, said they analyzed the claim that blacks were used like "cannon fodder during Vietnam" and can report definitely that this charge is untrue. Black fatalities amounted to 12.5 percent of all Americans killed in Southeast Asia, a figure proportional to the number of blacks in the US population at the time and slightly lower than the proportion of blacks in the Army at the close of the war.

Myth: Common belief is that the war was fought largely by the poor and uneducated.

Fact: Servicemen who went to Vietnam from well-to-do areas had a slightly elevated risk of dying because they were more likely to be pilots or infantry officers. Vietnam veterans were the best educated forces our nation had ever sent into combat. 79% had a high school education or better.

Myth: The common belief is the average age of an infantryman fighting in Vietnam was 19.

Fact: Assuming KIAs' accurately represented age groups serving in Vietnam, the average age of an infantryman serving in Vietnam to be 19 is a myth. The actual average age of the military serving in Vietnam was 22. The average age of military that fought in World War II was 26 years of age.

Myth: The common belief is that the domino theory was proved false.

Fact: The domino theory was accurate. The countries of the Association of Southeast Asian Nations, Philippines, Indonesia Malaysia, Singapore, and Thailand remained free of communism because of the US commitment to Vietnam. The Indonesians threw the Soviets out in 1966 because of America's commitment in Vietnam. Without that commitment, communism would have swept all the way to the Malacca Straits, which is south of Singapore and of great strategic importance to the free world. If you ask people who live in these countries, they have a different opinion from the American news media. The Vietnam War was the turning point for communism.

Myth: The common belief is the fighting in Vietnam was not as intense as in World War II.

Fact: The average infantryman in the South Pacific during World War II saw about 40 days of combat in four years. The average infantryman in Vietnam saw about 240 days of combat in one year thanks to the mobility of the helicopter. The average infantry soldier in the 101st Airborne Division in South Vietnam saw about 320 days of combat. One out of every 10 Americans who served in Vietnam was a casualty. The US military had 58,150 KIA, and 304,000 were wounded out of 2.7 million who served. Although the percent that died is similar to other wars, amputations or crippling wounds were 300% higher than in World War II. 75,000 Vietnam veterans are severely disabled. MEDEVAC helicopters flew nearly 500,000 missions. Over 900,000 patients were airlifted, of which one half were Americans.

Myth: Kim Phuc, the little 9-year-old Vietnamese girl running naked from the napalm strike near Trang Bang on June 8, 1972, was burned by Americans bombing Trang Bang. This was repeatedly reported as a fact by the news media.

Fact: No American had any involvement in this incident near Trang Bang that burned Phan Thi Kim Phuc. The planes doing the bombing near the village were Vietnamese Air Force and were being flown by Vietnamese pilots in support of South Vietnamese troops on the ground. The Vietnamese pilot who dropped the napalm in error is currently living in the United States. Even the Associated Press photographer, Nick Ut, who took the picture, was Vietnamese. The incident in the photo took place on the second day of a three-day battle between the North Vietnamese Army who occupied the village of Trang Bang and the ARVNs who were trying to force the NVA out of the village. Later reports in the news media that an American commander ordered the air strike that burned Kim Phuc are incorrect. There were no Americans involved in any capacity.

Myth: The United States lost the war in Vietnam.

Fact: The United States military did not lose the war in Vietnam. The South Vietnamese government and military lost the war. The American military was not defeated in Vietnam. The American military did not lose a battle of any consequence. From a military standpoint, it was almost an unprecedented performance. General Westmoreland, quoting Douglas Pike, a professor at the University of California at Berkeley, stated, "The Vietnam War was a major military defeat for the VC and NVA." The fall of Saigon happened on April 30, 1975, two years after the American military left Vietnam. The last US military departed South Vietnam on March 29, 1973.

How could we lose a war we had already stopped fighting? We fought to an agreed stalemate. The peace settlement was signed in Paris on January 27, 1973. It called for release of all US prisoners, withdrawal of US forces, limitation of both sides' forces inside South Vietnam, and a commitment to peaceful reunification. The 140,000 evacuees in April 1975 during the fall of Saigon consisted almost entirely of civilians and Vietnamese military, not American military running for their lives. There were almost twice as many casualties in Southeast Asia, primarily Cambodia, the first two years after the fall of Saigon in 1975, than there were during the ten years the US was involved in Vietnam. Credit for the perceived loss and the countless assassinations and torture forced upon the Vietnamese, Laotians, and

Cambodians goes mainly to the American media and their undying support-by-misrepresentation of the antiwar movement in the United States.

As with much of the Vietnam War, the news media misreported and misinterpreted the 1968 Tet Offensive. It was reported as an overwhelming success for the communist forces and a decided defeat for the US forces. Nothing could be further from the truth. Despite initial victories by the communist forces, the Tet Offensive resulted in a major defeat of those forces. General Vo Nguyen Giap, the designer of the Tet Offensive, is considered by some as ranking with Wellington, Grant, Lee, and MacArthur as a great commander. Still, militarily, the Tet Offensive was a total defeat of the communist forces on all fronts. It resulted in the death of some 45,000 NVA troops and the complete, if not total, destruction of the Viet Cong elements in South Vietnam. The organization of the Viet Cong units in the South never recovered. The Tet Offensive succeeded on only one front, and that was the news front and the political arena. This was another example in the Vietnam War of an inaccuracy becoming the perceived truth. However, even though it was inaccurately reported, the news media made the Tet Offensive famous.

Wannabees and Phonies

Phony war veterans, long a plague on society, have only become more emboldened with the recent wars in Iraq and Afghanistan. A federal law upheld by the Supreme Court was necessary and states, "It is unlawful for fakers to lie about being a hero for personal gain." Phonies and wannabees posed such a serious problem that the Stolen Valor Act was passed by Congress in 2006. This act made it unlawful to falsely claim verbally or in writing to have received any military medal. Congress amended this act with inaction in 2006. Because of increased public pressure and congressional lobbying, President Obama signed a new revised version of the original Stolen Valor Act into law on May 20, 2013. This revised bill included a fraud provision, making it a crime to lie about awards for personal gain. The impersonation of a veteran, forging any military document, impersonating an officer, wearing a military uniform or unauthorized military medals is a crime in violation of US Code Title 18 and the Stolen Valor Act. Recently, we have seen thousands claiming to be a military hero. Their stories and tears are showstoppers. These impostors steal our tax dollars, veteran benefits, and embarrass real veterans.

Odds are one will run into a phony or wannabee at some point. Unfortunately, many individuals deceitfully claim military decorations, which were not awarded to them. Wearing unauthorized awards is disrespectful to service personnel who have earned legitimate awards. Almost 14 million Americans and other nationalities have falsely claimed to have served in Vietnam. As of the Census taken during 2000, the surviving US Vietnam War population estimate is 1,002,511. This is difficult to believe, losing nearly 711,000, between 1995 and 2000. That's 390 per day. During the 2000 Census count, the number of Americans falsely claiming to have served in country is 13,853,027. By this census, four out of five who claim to be Vietnam veterans are not!

The wannabees' favorite military units in South Vietnam are the 101st Airborne Division, 1st Cavalry Division, or Special Forces. Some wannabees claim to have been a member of all three units. On any given night, especially Friday and Saturday, the number of customers at local bars and clubs claiming to be Special Forces or SEALs is phenomenal. Some wannabees and young veterans that claim to have been in South Vietnam are only in their forties; that is impossible! That would make them one to five years old when they were claiming to have served in South Vietnam.

Wannabees have various reasons for claiming to have served in South Vietnam. Some have low self-esteem, no confidence, or never achieved much in life. Some want to beef up their image with friends, employers, and various associations and organizations. But the number one reason is that they want to impress someone, usually a female. Wannabees come from all cultures, religions, races, nationalities, political parties, gender, social status, professions, and both white- and blue-collar jobs. They are very easy to identify. They are usually the ones at a club, bar, or restaurant doing the most talking and bragging about their heroic achievements in South Vietnam. It only takes one about three to five questions, and his credentials are disqualified. I have him nailed! Wannabees and phonies also weasel into military reunions, events, and funerals. Wannabees and phonies are very clever. Several have erased legitimate Veterans' names on military documents and substituted their name. With highly technological computers and copying machines, counterfeiting is easy. With these virtually realistic documents, they apply for jobs and state, federal, and Veterans Administration benefits.

Here are some options if one suspects someone is a phony. Don't be afraid to challenge the wannabee or phony. Real heroes won't mind if you ask them questions. Remember, impostors love to boast, and decorated veterans usually are modest and rarely draw attention to their heroic achievements.

Ask to see their military discharge (DD-214), military identification card, or their Veterans Administration card and any pictures. The military DD-214 is now the most falsified military document. Seek the assistance of known veterans. Tell them of the suspected phony and collectively ask for these documents. If the suspected wannabee states that they didn't go through normal training or they were in a classified unit and they can't talk about their service, chances are they are a phony. Everyone should have one combat picture that they can produce. Pictures don't lie! Chances are they won't have any of these documents on their person, especially if they are in a bar. Tell them you understand and that you will meet them back at the bar tomorrow at a prearranged time and that you expect them to bring something to substantiate their Veteran status. I suspect that you will never see them again. A true veteran should have one of the following cards: military identification card, Veterans Administration–issued card for health care, Veterans Administration identification card, and/or Veteran's designation on state driver's license or state identification card.

Surf the Internet for someone wearing the Medal of Honor. The Congressional Medal of Honor Society maintains a list of living Medal of Honor recipients at www.cmohs.org. Also, www.pownetwork.org maintains a list of phony veterans. The Web also has a consolidated list of everyone that has been awarded the Distinguished Service Cross.

Check the ribbons on their uniform. Wannabees and phonies occasionally wear their ribbons in the wrong order. Another method to check a wannabee's authenticity is to ask the suspect to identify his ribbons and how he won them.

Military personnel care about their physical appearance and stay in shape. Some veterans over the years will gain some weight. However, most impostors are overweight and have a slovenly appearance in uniform.

Don't accept the excuse that the military operation was top secret. All military receive an annual efficiency report. If the mission was top secret, the narrative and comment section will state CLASSIFIED; however, the personal data of name, rank, unit, and social security number will still be written in the admin section of the efficiency report.

General George Washington established the Badge of Military Merit in 1782. He recognized the potential for impostors and wrote: "Should any who are not entitled to these honors have the insolence to assume the badges of them, they shall be severely punished."

The good news is once again it is unlawful for fakers, phonies, and wannabees to lie about being a hero for personal gain that is not de minimis—relatively small.

Fraudulent and phony veterans charities have bilked people out of hundreds of millions of dollars. These professional con artists are slowly being caught and brought to justice. In March 2017, fifty-seven con artists were caught and charged with using a veterans charity to front illegal gambling, racketeering, and money laundering. Many phony veteran charities enlist nonsuspecting veterans, civilians, and occasionally convicted felons to solicit donations, raise money, and support their cause. These phony veterans charities are turning selected veterans into beggars. An excellent watchdog group is Charity Watch, founded by Army veteran Steve Udovich. Phony veterans organizations depend on people being ignorant of who they really are. Americans are patriotic but unsuspecting. If you suspect a veteran's charity is a con, contact Charity Watch.

The Vietnam War's Most Highly Decorated Servicemen

Name	Service	Branch	
1LT Robert L. Howard	Army	Special Forces	MOH, DSC, SS
COL George E. Day	Air Force	Fighter Pilot	MOH, AFC, SS
PO1st Class James Williams	Navy	River Patrol Boat	MOH, NC, SS
MAJ Patrick H. Brady	Army	MEDEVAC Pilot	MOH, DSC
RADM James Stockdale	Navy	Fighter Pilot	MOH, SS (4)
SSG Joe R. Hooper	Army	Infantry	MOH, SS (2)
MAJ Leo K. Thorsness	Air Force	Fighter Pilot	MOH, SS (2)
LTC Andre C. Lucas	Army	Infantry	MOH, SS (2)
MAJ Bernard F. Fisher	Air Force	Fighter Pilot	MOH, SS
CPT James P. Fleming	Air Force	Helicopter Pilot	MOH, SS
CPT Harold A. Fritz	Army	Infantry	MOH, SS
SSG John G. Gertsch	Army	Infantry	MOH, SS
SP/6 Lawrence Joel	Army	Medic	MOH, SS
CPT James E. Livingston	Marines	Infantry	MOH, SS
LT Thomas R. Norris	Navy	SEAL	MOH, SS
CPT Riley L. Pitts	Army	Infantry	MOH, SS
MAJ Stephen W. Pless	Marines	Helicopter Pilot	MOH, SS
MAJ Jay R. Vargas	Marines	Infantry	MOH, SS
LTC James H. Kasler	Air Force	Fighter Pilot	AFC (3), SS
COL David H. Hackworth	Army	Infantry	DSC (2), SS (7)
COL Thomas H. Tackaberry	Army	Infantry	DSC (2), SS (3)
CPT Barry R. McCaffrey	Army	Infantry	DSC (2), SS (2)
COL George S. Patten, IV	Army	Infantry	DSC (2), SS
SGT Adelbert F. Waldron	Army	Sniper	DSC (2), SS
1LT Joseph P. Donovan	Marines	MEDEVAC Pilot	NC (2), SS
COL John A. Dramesi	Air Force	Fighter Pilot	AFC (2), SS
CPT Lelan T. Kennedy	Air Force	Fighter Pilot	AFC (2), SS
BG James R. Risner	Air Force	Fighter Pilot	AFC (2), SS
BG John R. Deane Jr.	Army	Infantry	DSC (2)
COL Henry E. Emerson	Army	Infantry	DSC (2)
BG James F. Hollingsworth	Army	Infantry	DSC (2)
CPT Michael A. McDermott	Army	Infantry	DSC (2)
MAJ William W. Roush	Army	Infantry	DSC (2)

1LT Dennis C. Tomcik	Army	Infantry	DSC (2)
MSG Jack L. Williams	Army	Special Forces	DSC (2)
CPT Martin L. Brandtner	Marines	Infantry	NC (2)
MAJ Charles E. Getz	Army	Infantry	DSC, SS (6)
CMDR James B. Linder	Navy	Fighter Pilot	NC, SS (4)
CPT Jeffery S. Feinstein	Air Force	Fighter Pilot	AFC, SS (4)
CPT Richard S. Ritchie	Air Force	Fighter Pilot	AFC, SS (4)
COL Robert M. White	Air Force	Fighter Pilot	AFC, SS (4)
CPT Charles B. DeBellevue	Air Force	Fighter Pilot	AFC, SS (3)
LTC James E. McInerney Jr.	Air Force	Fighter Pilot	AFC, SS (3)
CPT Fred Shannon	Air Force	Fighter Pilot	AFC, SS (3)
LT Randall H. Cunningham	Navy	Fighter Pilot	NC, SS (2)
Lt William P. Driscoll	Navy	Fighter Pilot	NC, SS (2)
COL Robin Olds	Air Force	Fighter Pilot	AFC, SS (2)
CPT Dale E. Stovall	Air Force	Rescue Pilot	AFC, SS (2)
1LT Davis A. Christian	Army	Infantry	DSC, SS (2)

Key

MOH	Medal of Honor
DSC	Distinguished Service Cross
NC	Navy Cross
AFC	Air Force Cross
SS	Silver Star

CHAPTER 18

How to Honor and Thank Veterans of All Wars

Most Vietnam War veterans were let down. It is never too late to thank them for their combat service. If you see one, tell them that; I do.

President Trump signed a proclamation into law that officially designates March 29 an annual national day of recognition for veterans of the Vietnam War. March 29 recognizes the day in 1973 when the bulk of US troops left South Vietnam, and Hanoi released the remaining US POWs. The Department of Veteran Affairs estimates that America is losing as many as 382 Vietnam War veterans daily. It has become increasingly important that America act now to honor and thank them for their service. To coin a phrase from Nike, if a situation exists to thank a veteran, "just do it."

President Kennedy once said that "a nation reveals itself not only by the people it produces, but also by the people it honors, the people it remembers." Several folks have asked me how to honor veterans, especially on Veterans Day. These folks most of the time tell me that it is just so hard to say anything or that it is very difficult to approach Veterans, and when we do speak to them, we don't know what or how to say anything. Here are some suggestions and great ideas for thanking the veterans you may come across both on Veterans Day and beyond.

1. Volunteer at a veteran's organization. The American Legion, Paralyzed Veterans of America, Habitat for Humanity, Vietnam Veterans of America, Veterans of Foreign Wars, and the Home Depot Foundation are a few that will appreciate your help and support. These veteran organizations need volunteers to help with their veterans' outreach programs. Say thank-you by giving your time. These organizations are always in need of volunteers. Don't underestimate the power of personal interaction. Your kind words and a few moments of your time could make all the difference in the world. It is never too late, and no initiative is too small when it comes from the heart. Several of these veteran organizations are located in Elkins. A list of veterans organizations is listed at the end of this chapter.

2. Buy a meal for a homeless vet. We've all seen them—they stand by the side of the road holding signs asking for food, money, warmth, or all of the above. And while there's no way to make sure their veteran claim is legitimate, that shouldn't matter. Buy the gentleman a sandwich and thank him for his service. I recommend that you take the veteran to a food establishment and buy him a meal; eat with him and talk to him. Be careful after the meal; the veteran may want you to drive him someplace. If you feel uncomfortable driving the veteran, don't. Sometimes asking a friend to accompany you is the best decision. Use your discretion if the veteran asks you for money.

3. Fly the United States flag! I fly my US flag in front of our house daily. More and more neighbors in our neighborhood are beginning to exhibit some Americanism and fly the US flag. I also recommend that you put a US flag sticker on your vehicle and wear a flag pin on your lapel. Be a proud patriot and fly the US flag and/or wear your flag pin.

4. Visit your local military recruiter's office and thank them for their service. Recruiters work a tough job with long hours and little thanks. Give these recruiters a little cheer. I take the local Army recruiter out for lunch every few

months and visit him monthly and help brief the new recruits occasionally.

5. Ask a loved one, friend, or neighbor for stories about their time in service—and listen patiently. Don't take it personally if some may not want to talk about their war experience. Sometimes a veteran is just waiting for someone to ask him so he may vent. For other veterans, service was the best time of their lives. Take a few minutes to listen to stories of service from someone in your extended family.

6. Mail cards and letters to veterans. Nearly three million people serve in the United States military. Millions more have served in the recent past. You know a veteran even if you think you don't. Put on your thinking cap and send a thank-you card to everyone you know who has ever served in the military. What about your scout leader, little league coach, high school coach, pastor, or college professor? You may be surprised who was a veteran.

7. Ask your school, college, or organization to join the History Channel's Take a Veteran to School program. If you have a veteran at home or if you are a veteran, volunteer to help.

8. Change your Facebook page to feature a favorite veteran— even if your vet is your great-uncle Felix, who you never met, who served in WWI. Embellish it and run with it. Please ensure Uncle Felix is okay with Facebook first.

9. Just say "thank you." Take a moment to thank a veteran for his or her service. A little recognition goes a long way. If it is a Vietnam War veteran, I always say, "Thank you for your service, and welcome home!" You may want to embellish this thank-you with a handshake and/or a hug.

10. Understand your life was and is worth dying for. Vietnam War veterans fought for your freedom. Our current veterans stand ready to fight for your freedom—strive to be worthy of the sacrifice. The first article in the US military code of conduct says, "I am an American fighting man. I serve in the forces which guard my country and our way of life. I am prepared to give my life in their defense."

11. Visit and/or volunteer at the Veterans Hospital and Home in Clarksburg, West Virginia. Volunteer hours can be as short as an hour or a full eight-hour day. Talk to the veterans while you are there. They have diverse, meaningful, and respectful jobs for you. You won't have to clean bedpans. Volunteering is dignified and noble.

12. Visit and volunteer at veteran monuments and cemeteries. There is a veteran monument located in Elkins. One of the city's prominent flower shops maintains the site. The flower shop cuts the grass, plants flowers, and decorates the monument on specified holidays. This flower shop is always in need of volunteers. Almost every county seat in West Virginia has a veterans monument. The city of Grafton in Taylor County, West Virginia, has a National Veterans Cemetery. A visit or tour of Washington DC would not be complete without a visit to Arlington National Cemetery. According to the Washington DC park service, the Vietnam Wall is the most visited monument in the DC area.

13. Visit the Reserve Officer Training Corps (ROTC) at selected colleges. Davis and Elkins College (D & E) doesn't have an ROTC; however, D & E does have a Veterans Outreach program. The Veterans Outreach program can put you in touch with college veterans attending D & E.

14. If you see a veteran, ask him for advice and recommendations on how you may help, aid, assist, or honor veterans.

15. An excellent method to support veterans is to contact Team Red, White and Blue (RWB). Founded in 2010, Team RWB has approximately 100,000 members in over 177 communities in the United States and the world. They bring veterans, their families, and American citizens together through authentic social interaction, community physical fitness, and shared experiences. Team Red, White and Blue connects and supports veterans of all ages. They seek methods to partner with local veterans hospitals to use physical and social activity that will engage veterans to help themselves in transition. Team RWB emphasizes and

encourages veterans to help brother veterans. If the veteran has any limitations, an occupational therapist will be present to ensure the veteran performs within their capability. They give local communities a chance to interact with veterans, which is beneficial. Frequently, people say the military should do a better job of transitioning veterans from military service to civilian life. The military's job is to fight and win wars. Local veterans and their communities must partner to ensure a successful transition. You may make a donation or volunteer. The intent of the Team Red, White and Blue is to

a. raise awareness and enlist the public's aid for the needs of injured service members;

b. help injured service members aid and assist each other;

c. provide unique direct programs and services to meet the needs of injured service members; and/or

d. enrich the lives of America's veterans by connecting them to their community through physical and social activities. Team RWB is a registered 501C3 nonprofit organization. Their federal ID number for donations is 27-2196347.

Their contact information is as follows:

Team Red, White and Blue
1110 W. Platt St
Tampa, Florida 33606
TeamRWB.com

Call or e-mail them, and they will entertain your questions and provide advice on their dynamic programs to help, aid, and assist veterans and their families. They will also provide you with contact data for the local Team RWB in Fairmont, West Virginia.

16. Make it a habit of attending all future Veterans Day parades and/or ceremonies. Virtually every town in America has a parade or ceremony on Veterans Day. Several Veterans Day

ceremonies are conducted in local schools and at the local All Veterans Memorial.

Veterans Day is celebrated on November 11. Originally called Armistice Day, this holiday was established to honor Americans who had served in World War I. Veterans Day falls on November 11, the day when that war ended in 1918, but it now honors veterans of all wars in which the United States has fought.

Veterans Day is a celebration to honor America's veterans for their patriotism, love of country, and willingness to serve and sacrifice for the common good. Veterans' organizations hold parades and the President customarily places a wreath on the Tomb of the Unknowns at Arlington National Cemetery.

Veterans Day is set aside to thank and honor all who served honorably in the military in wartime or peacetime. In fact, Veterans Day is largely intended to thank living veterans for their service, to acknowledge that their contributions to our national security are appreciated, and to underscore the fact that all those who served, not only those who have lost their lives, have sacrificed and done their duty. Honoring our past and current veterans helps ensure we can maintain the strong heritage of service that Americans have always valued.

17. Buy a poppy or donate to the cause. The poppy has a rich history that began during World War II and was inspired by the poem "In Flanders Fields." Several veteran organizations sell poppies. The Poppy Program continues to be a source of income for veteran organizations and therapy for many disabled veterans. The Poppy Program is symbolic of veterans helping veterans.

18. Donate your car to a veterans organization.

19. Continue to show respect and gratitude to our current generation of warriors returning from Iraq and Afghanistan.

20. *Hire a veteran!* Veterans make excellent employees and superb supervisors.

Local Veteran Organizations

Veterans of Foreign Wars
536 N Randolph Avenue
Elkins, WV 26241
Phone 304-636-7360

American Legion
326 Railroad Avenue
Elkins, WV 26241
Phone 304-636-3930

Disabled American Veterans
Pringle Tree Chapter
Buckhannon, WV 26201
Phone 304-472-6611

Military Order of the Purple Heart
Clarksburg, WV 26301
Phone 304-623-4280

Marine Corp League
PO Box 852
Elkins, WV 26241
Phone 304-636-4365

Vietnam Veterans of America
PO Box 467
Elkins, WV 26241
304-823-1688
304-630-2288

Chapter 19

Rules, Regulations, and Conduct

Not *Robert's Rules of Order*

Nine Rules for Personnel of US Military
Assistance Command Vietnam

The majority of US military advisers assigned to South Vietnam
received a seventy-five-page handbook. The introduction of this
handbook set the stage for the nine rules. The introduction follows:

> The Vietnamese have paid a heavy price in suffer-
> ing for their long fight against the communists.
> We military men are in Vietnam now because
> their government has asked us to help its soldiers
> and people in winning their struggle. The Viet
> Cong will attempt to turn the Vietnamese people
> against you. You can defeat them at every turn by
> the strength, understanding and generosity you
> display with the people. Here are the nine simple
> rules listed in the hand book.
>
> > 1. Remember we are special guests here; we
> >   make no demands and seek no special
> >   treatment.

2. Join with the people! Understand their life, use phrases from their language and honor their customs and laws.
3. Treat women with politeness and respect.
4. Make personal friends among the soldiers and common people.
5. Always give the Vietnamese the right of way.
6. Be alert to security and ready to react with your military skill.
7. Don't attract attention by loud, rude or unusual behavior.
8. Avoid separating yourself from the people by a display of wealth or privilege.
9. Above all else you are members of the US military forces on a difficult mission, responsible for all your official and personal actions. Reflect honor upon yourself and the United States of America.

US Military Code of Conduct

The code of conduct below was used by the US military during the Cold War and the Second Indochina War. The code was developed in June 1958 by the Joint Chiefs of Staff. Every officer, warrant officer, noncommissioned officer, and enlisted personnel of the active-duty military, National Guard and Reserves received a copy of the code on a billfold-size card. Everyone in my unit had to memorize the code. The code of conduct consists of six imperatives from the military Graphic Training Aid Card 21–50, which are depicted below:

1. I am an American fighting man. I serve in the forces which guard my country and our way of life. I am prepared to give my life in their defense.

2. I will never surrender of my own free will. If in command I will never surrender my men while they still have the means to resist.

3. If I am captured I will continue to resist by all means available. I will make every effort to escape and aid others to escape. I will accept neither parole nor special favors from the enemy.

4. If I become a prisoner of war, I will keep faith with my fellow prisoners. I will give no information or take part in any action which might be harmful to my comrades. If I am senior, I will take command. If not, I will obey the lawful orders of those appointed over me and will back them up in every way.

5. When questioned, should I become a prisoner of war, I am bound to give only name, rank, service number, and date of birth. I will evade answering further questions to the utmost of my ability. I will make no oral or written statements disloyal to my country and its allies or harmful to their cause.

6. I will never forget that I am an American fighting man, responsible for my actions, and dedicated to the principles which make my country free. I will trust in my God and in the United States of America.

Rules of Engagement

Rules of engagement (ROE) in the Vietnam War were necessary to prevent losses and maintain the support of the population. Rules of engagement limited the destruction of civilian property, collateral damage, and prevented indiscriminate injury and deaths of noncombatants. The insurgency war in Vietnam did not have well-defined front lines, and occasionally the ROE were difficult to enforce. The US military Joint Chief of Staff was the proponent for the ROE in South Vietnam. ROE stipulated that B-52 strikes must be at least one kilometer from any noncombatant inhabited area in the South. The White House controlled the air targets in the North.

The MACV commander in South Vietnam issued 40 ROE directives. Commanders on search-and-destroy operations were ordered to use firepower in lieu of maneuvering troops to prevent friendly casualties. Harassment and interdiction fires were often criticized and under close scrutiny because they could not be observed. The ARVNs were not limited by ROE and only made a mediocre effort to abide by the MACV directives. Although US advisers advised the ARVNs to obey the ROE, they seldom complied.

CHAPTER 20

Prisoners of War, Missing in Action, and Killed in Action

> I am an American fighting man. I serve in the forces
> which guard my country and our way of life. I am
> prepared to give my life in their defense.
> —Article 1, US Military Code of Conduct

The Vietnam War prisoner of war (POW) and missing in action (MIA) issue concerns the fate of United States servicemen who were reported as prisoners or missing in action (MIA) during the Vietnam War and associated theaters of operation in Southeast Asia. The term has also referenced issues related to the treatment of affected family members by the governments involved in these conflicts. Following the Paris Peace Accords of 1973, 591 American prisoners of war (POWs) were returned during Operation Homecoming. The US listed about 1,350 Americans as prisoners of war or missing in action, and roughly 1,200 Americans reported killed in action and body not recovered. Many of these were airmen who were shot down over North Vietnam or Laos. The fate of those missing in action has always been one of the most troubling and unsettling consequences of any war. In this case, the issue has been a highly emotional one to those involved, and is often considered the last depressing, divisive aftereffect of the Vietnam War for the United States.

Following the Paris Peace Accords of January 1973, US prisoners of war were returned during Operation Homecoming during

February through April 1973. During this period, 591 POWs were released to US authorities; this included a few captured in Laos and released in North Vietnam. US president Richard Nixon announced that all US servicemen taken prisoner had been accounted for. At that time, the US listed about 1,350 Americans as prisoners of war or missing in action and sought the return of roughly 1,200 Americans reported killed in action and body not recovered. Investigation of the fate of all the missing service personnel would end up residing with the Defense Prisoner of War/Missing Personnel Office. The Joint POW/MIA Accounting Command also played a major role in subsequent investigations. In 1973, the Defense Department established the Central Identification Laboratory–Thailand to coordinate POW/MIA recovery efforts in Southeast Asia.

During the late 1970s and 1980s, the friends and relatives of unaccounted-for American personnel became politically active, requesting the United States government reveal what steps were taken to follow up on intelligence regarding last-known-alive MIAs and POWs. The National League of Families of American Prisoners and Missing in Southeast Asia created the POW/MIA flag in 1971 when the war was still in progress. This organization was created by Sybil Stockdale, Evelyn Grubb, and Mary Crowe as an originally small group of POW/MIA wives in Coronado, California, and Hampton Roads, Virginia, in 1967. Sybil Stockdale's husband, Navy commander James Stockdale, was shot down in 1965; and she was determined to make the American people aware of the mistreatment of US POWs. This publicity resulted in better treatment of US POWs from the fall of 1969 on. Later, it was led by Ann Mills Griffiths. Its stated mission was and is "to obtain the release of all prisoners, the fullest possible accounting for the missing and repatriation of all recoverable remains of those who died serving our nation during the Vietnam War in Southeast Asia." The league's most prominent symbol is its POW/MIA flag.

The National Alliance of Families mission was for the Return of America's Missing Servicemen was founded in 1990. Their goal was and remains to resolve the fates of any unreturned US prisoners of war or missing in action from all wars.

In the mid-1980s, the US and Vietnam increased the frequency of high-level policy and technical meetings to help resolve the POW/MIA issue. The US government viewed this work as a humanitarian obligation. The Vietnamese slowly began to return American remains that they had previously collected and stored. Eventually they permitted the US to excavate a few crash sites. The Lao government, with whom the US government maintained diplomatic relations, also agreed to several crash-site excavations in the mid-1980s.

Interest in the POW/MIA issue intensified in June 1992 when president of the Russian Federation Boris Yeltsin told NBC News in an interview that some Americans captured during the Vietnam War may have been transferred from Hanoi to the Soviet Union: "Our archives have shown that it is true, some of them were transferred to the territory of the former USS.R. and were kept in labor camps. We don't have complete data and can only surmise that some of them may still be alive."

Senator Bob Smith introduced a 1991 resolution to create a Senate Select POW/MIA Committee. Senator and fellow Vietnam War veteran John Kerry was the chair of the committee, and its third key member was Senator and former Vietnam War POW John McCain. Compared to earlier congressional investigations into the POW/MIA issue, this one had a mandate to be more skeptical and ask harder questions of government officials than before. Some of the most publicized testimony before the committee came in September 1992, when former Nixon Defense Secretaries Melvin Laird and James Schlesinger said that the US government had believed in 1973 that some American servicemen had not been returned from Laos, despite Nixon's public statements to the contrary. Schlesinger said, "As of now, I can come to no other conclusion. But that does not mean there are any alive today." Laird said in retrospect of Nixon's assurances that all POWs were coming home; I think it was unfortunate to be that positive.

The committee issued its unanimous findings on January 13, 1993. In response to the central question of whether any American POWs were still in captivity, it stated: "While the Committee has some evidence suggesting the possibility a POW may have survived to the present, and while some information remains yet to be investigated, there is, at this time, no compelling evidence that proves that any American remains alive in captivity in Southeast Asia."

With regard to the possibility that American POWs survived in Southeast Asia after Operation Homecoming, the committee said this: "We acknowledge that there is no proof that US POWs survived, but neither is there proof that all of those who did not return had died. There is evidence; moreover, that indicates the possibility of survival, at least for a small number, after Operation Homecoming."

Committee vice-chairman Smith seemed to back away from the committee's findings within months of their being issued, appearing in April 1993 on *Larry King Live* with POW/MIA activist Bill Hendon, stressing his partial dissent from the majority report and touting new evidence of North Vietnam having held back prisoners in 1973 and then, in the Senate in September 1993, saying he had "very compelling" new evidence of live prisoners.

When President Bill Clinton lifted the trade embargo on February 3, 1994, he stated, "I have made the judgment that the best way to ensure cooperation from Vietnam and to continue getting the information Americans want on POWs and MIA's is to end the trade embargo. I've also decided to establish a liaison office in Vietnam to provide services for Americans there and help us to pursue a human rights dialogue with the Vietnamese government. I want to be clear; these actions do not constitute a normalization of our relationships. Before that happens, we must have more progress, more cooperation and more answers. Toward that end, this spring I will send another high-level US delegation to Vietnam to continue the search for remains and for documents." In 1995, President Bill Clinton normalized diplomatic relations with the country of Vietnam. This establishment of diplomatic relations between the US and Vietnam in 1995 laid the groundwork for a cooperative and beneficial arrangement for both sides.

By the late 2000s, the remains of over seven hundred Americans killed in Southeast Asia had been returned and identified. Efforts continued to recover nearly 1,800 Americans who remained unaccounted for. Working jointly, American and Vietnamese experts focus on Last Known Alive cases, which involve missing Americans whom the US believed might have survived their initial loss incident. Outcomes of these investigations have helped resolve the live prisoners' questions. The US has identified 296 individuals as Last Known Alive cases in all of Southeast Asia, and following full investigations, the Defense Department has determined that more than 190 are deceased.

The MIA mission continues after forty years. The official document that ended America's military participation in the Vietnam War in 1973 contained a provision that supports many veteran organizations. Article 8 of the Agreement on Ending the War and Restoring Peace in Vietnam, also known as the Paris Peace Accords, stipulated that the former combatants would cooperate to facilitate the exhumation and repatriation of the remains of war dead. Immediately after the document was signed, the US created the Four-Party Joint Military Team (FPJMT) and the Joint Casualty Resolution Center (JCRC) to carry out Article 8. The FPJMT negotiated details of remains recovery while the JCRC carried out the actual fieldwork.

According to Paul D. Mather, author of *MIA: Accounting for the Missing in Southeast Asia*, the JCRC was a unique organization in the annals of military history. Activated on January 23, 1973, in Saigon, it consisted of 140 volunteers, mostly Green Berets commanded by Brigadier General Robert C. Kingston. During JCRC's original tenure, which ended with the fall of Saigon in April 1975, Army Captain Richard M. Rees became the only American killed by hostile action during an MIA remains recovery operation on December 15, 1973, at a helicopter crash site some twelve miles southwest of Saigon. After the Rees incident, the US trained South Vietnamese to conduct recovery operations. With South Vietnam's defeat, JCRC relocated its headquarters to Hawaii and moved its field teams to Bangkok, Hong Kong, the Philippines, Malaysia, and Singapore.

In 1992, the Joint Task Force-Full Accounting (JTF-FA) was established to focus specifically on Vietnam War cases and officially replace JCRC. On October 1, 2003, the Pentagon established the Joint POW/MIA Accounting Command (JPAC) at Joint Base Pearl Harbor-Hickman in Hawaii. Its motto: "Until They Are Home."

Many of the National Veteran Organizations maintain their quest to ensure that the US government keeps the POW/MIA issue elevated as a national priority.

According to the Defense Department's POW/MIA Accounting Agency (DPAA), 696 sets of American remains were recovered from Vietnam and positively identified as of May 2014. There remains 1,275 military personnel unaccounted for in Vietnam, 307 in Laos, and 53 in Cambodia. It is crucial that Vietnam War veterans share with DPAA any intelligence they may have regarding the whereabouts of missing comrades. The DPAA made 201 individual identifications of remains of US military troops in fiscal year 2017. This sets a new record. Family members of MIAs should submit DNA to help make identification easier. Go to www.dpaa.mil to learn more about what you can do to help.

Staff Sergeant Gail M. Kerns, Local Hero and Prisoner of War

Staff Sergeant Gail M. Kerns was born February 24, 1947, in Valley Bend, West Virginia (WV). He graduated from Tygart Valley High School in 1965. Gail was the yearbook editor and a member of the National Honor Society. After graduation, Gail attended WV Tech, majoring in electrical engineering.

In September 1967, Gail was inducted into the US Army. After completing basic and advanced individual training, Gail was assigned to Fort Benning, Georgia, to attend the twenty-two-week Noncommissioned Officer Leadership course.

In September 1968, Gail was sent to South Vietnam. He spent several days at Cam Ranh Bay in processing. Later, he was shipped to his base camp in Pleiku. He processed in and was finally assigned to Company A, 3rd Battalion, 12th Infantry, 4th Infantry Division as a squad leader. The days and nights were long, hot, dry, and muggy. He often thought of the date that he would be eligible for seven-day rest and recreation (R&R) in Hawaii. Finally, he was awarded his R&R. After the much needed R&R in Hawaii, Sergeant Kerns returned to his base camp at Pleiku and was sent immediately back into the field.

On the morning of March 27, 1969, Sergeant Kerns and his platoon were on a reconnaissance-in-force mission to locate and report on enemy activity northwest of Pleiku near the Cambodian border. His platoon suddenly came under intense hostile fire from well-entrenched and well-concealed North Vietnamese Army (NVA) soldiers. According to several surviving platoon members, the platoon sustained heavy casualties and was forced to withdraw. Sergeant Kerns was among the initial wounded in the firefight. There were eight US soldiers listed as tentatively missing in action (MIA).

Several attempts were made to reenter and search the battle area in the afternoon. All rescue attempts were stopped and repelled by well-armed dug-in NVA. To prevent further casualties, Company A withdrew to covered and concealed positions and called in air strikes and artillery for several days. On March 30, Company A again attacked the entrenched NVA fortifications with no avail. Company A withdrew and called in air strikes and artillery for one week. Upon completion of the bombardment, several long-range reconnaissance patrols (LRRPs) were sent into the area for a reconnaissance and a bomb damage assessment. During the reconnaissance, the LRRPs discovered five of the eight missing bodies. Those five bodies recovered were sent to the US mortuary and identified. The LRRPs did not find SP/4 Clarence Latimer, Sergeant Raymond Czerwiec, or Sergeant Gail Kerns. Soon the search-and-recovery effort terminated, and all three soldiers were officially listed as missing in action.

Sergeant Kerns was shot in the left side of his head. When he regained consciousness, he was a prisoner of war. The NVA imprisoned Sergeant Kerns in a camp located in the mountains close to the Cambodian border. He was kept in isolation. Other American military prisoners tried to give Sergeant Kerns part of their food ration but were refused and rejected by the NVA guards. Sergeant Kerns lapsed in and out of consciousness for days. The other American POWs asked the camp commander to allow Sergeant Kerns to be moved in with them so they could help give him physical therapy needed to restore the use of his left arm. This privilege was also denied. Sergeant Kerns lost the use of his left arm and about 50 percent use of his right leg. As a result of his wounds, Sergeant Kerns developed epilepsy. The

NVA guards provided very little medical assistance. His diet consisted of rice, bread, and tea. Occasionally, he received bananas. Sergeant Kerns was in a ten-by-twenty-five-foot cage, which he shared with three other prisoners. After several months, Sergeant Kerns regained some of his body motions and was allowed to go outside and stretch his legs and body. There were twelve American prisoners in his camp. Sergeant Kerns spent two years in this camp in Cambodia.

In March and April 1971, the Vietnamese decided to move all the prisoners to Hanoi. The move was difficult because of the condition of his body. He walked part of the day and was carried on a bamboo stretcher part of the day. Walking up the hills was the hardest. He slid down the hills on his rear end. He had to suck it up and continue or risk being shot. One of his fellow prisoners fell behind and was shot. Halfway to Hanoi, the march stopped, and they were put on trucks.

After arriving in Hanoi, Sergeant Kerns was secured in the famous Hanoi Hilton. The majority of prisoners in the Hanoi Hilton were pilots. At night, he could hear the American bombers conducting bombing over Hanoi.

During his confinement in the Hanoi Hilton, Sergeant Kerns continued having seizures at irregular times ranging from small seizures to grand mal seizures. He kept his faith in God, and God became a very big factor in his life. He also continued his faith in the United States and that his country was doing all it could to get him and the other prisoners home.

In January of 1973, things began to change for Sergeant Kerns and the other prisoners. All prisoners were given more to eat, extra time out of their cells, and more cigarettes. They did not realize that they were being prepared for their long trip home.

On January 27, 1973, in Paris, France, the Paris Peace Agreement was signed, and the Vietnam War was officially over. It was decided that the prisoners would be divided into groups and released at two-week intervals beginning with those who were the most severely hurt and those who had been held for the longest. His family was finally informed that he was alive and that he would be in the second group to be released. His family was not told of his injuries.

A week prior to his release, he was given a new shirt, pants, socks, and a lightweight jacket. The North Vietnamese government let him bring home his prison uniform. On March 5, 1973, Sergeant Kerns was placed on a US Air Force C-141 plane and headed for Clark Air Force Base in the Philippines. As he came down the ramp of the plane at Clark Air Force Base, he walked with great difficulty supported by a nurse. There was a discussion as to whether he should go down in a wheelchair, but he insisted on walking. When he stepped on American soil at Andrews Air Force Base outside of Washington DC, he dropped to his knees and kissed the ground to symbolize his gratefulness in returning home.

After receiving medical attention at Valley Forge Military Hospital in Pennsylvania, Sergeant Kerns returned home to Valley Bend, West Virginia, with his wife, Rebecca, and to a new home.

Sergeant Kerns was medically retired in September 1973 as a staff sergeant. His military awards include the Purple Heart, Bronze Star with First Oak Leaf Cluster, National Defense Service Medal, Vietnam Service Medal, Vietnam Campaign Medal, Civil Action Medal, Good Conduct Medal, Combat Infantry Badge, Vietnam Gallantry Cross, nine overseas bars, and the M-16 Expert Badge.

Staff Sergeant Kern's ceaseless efforts to conduct himself strictly in accordance with the code of conduct and policies of the prisoner organization in the difficult conditions of a communist prison clearly demonstrated his loyalty, love of country, and professionalism. By his unselfish dedication to duty, he reflected great credit upon himself and the United States Army.

Military from the Local Area Who Died in the Vietnam War

No one has greater love than this, to lay
down one's life for one's friends.

—John 15:13

Tygart Valley, Chapter 812, Vietnam Veterans of America (VVA) is located in Elkins, West Virginia. The chapter jurisdiction encompasses Randolph, Barbour, Tucker, Grant, Hardy, Pendleton, Pocahontas, Webster, and Upshur counties. In 2007, Steven E. Cook, Chapter 812 president, recommended that the following veterans that resided in Chapter 812s jurisdiction be approved as honorary members. On December 7, 2008, these heroic veterans who died in the Vietnam War were approved by the chapter and designated as honorary members of Tygart Valley Chapter 812, VVA. These veterans died in Southeast Asia or in stateside hospitals after being evacuated as a result of wounds, injuries, or illness in the combat zone.

Honorary Member Appointment Order 001; Dated Dec 7, 2008; Tygart Valley Chapter 812, Vietnam Veterans of America, Elkins, West Virginia

James Vincent Antolini/SGT US Army/May 9, 1968/Norton, WV/ Vietnam Veterans Memorial Panel 57E-Line 18

Randall Arbogast/SP4 US Army/May 31, 1967/Valley Head WV/ Vietnam Veterans Memorial Panel 21E-Line 20

Charles Fredrick Armentrout/SGT US Army/May 22, 1970/Kline, WV/Vietnam Veterans Memorial Panel 10W-Line 78

Stanley William Armentrout/SSG US Army/July 23, 1968/ Pocahontas County, WV/Vietnam Veterans Memorial Panel 39W-Line 72

Kenneth Ray Barkley/SP6 US Army/Mar 23, 1969/Elkins, WV/ Vietnam Veterans Memorial Panel 28W-Line 16

Rex Allan Bowyer/SP4 US Army/Feb 1, 1968/Philippi, WV/Vietnam Veterans Memorial Panel 36E-Line 46

Garry Lee Burgess/SP4 US Army/June 19, 1966/Pickens, WV/ Vietnam Veterans Memorial Panel 08E-Line 62

Roger Lee Carpenter/PFC US Army/Apr 14, 1968/Barbour County, WV/Vietnam Veterans Memorial Panel 49E-Line 51

William Lee Carr Jr./LCPL USMC/Jul 19, 1968/Flemington, WV/ Vietnam Veterans Memorial Panel 51W-Line 10

John Andrew Charnoplosky/SGT US Army/Nov 15, 1971/Philippi, WV/Vietnam Veterans Memorial Panel 02W-Line 67

Lloyd Allen Chess/CPL US Army/Nov 26, 1968/Cowen, WV/ Vietnam Veterans Memorial Panel 38W-Line 64

Everette Austin Currence/PFC USMC/Jul 25, 1966/Rock Cave, WV/Vietnam Veterans Memorial Panel 09E-Line 73

George Washington Darnell Jr./SP4 US, Army/May 9, 1968/ Marlinton, WV/Vietnam Veterans Memorial Panel 57E-Line 18

James Oliver Daugherty Jr./CPL US Army/Apr 4, 1969/Pocahontas County, WV/Vietnam Veterans Memorial Panel 27W-Line 9

Ronald Philip Dean/PFC USMC/Apr 21, 1968/Buckhannon, WV/ Vietnam Veterans Memorial Panel 51E-Line 19

William Dely/CPL USMC/June 13, 1966/Selbyville, WV/Vietnam Veterans Memorial Panel 08E-Line 44

James Elliott Ryan Dewey/CPL US Army/Apr 4, 1967/Pendleton County, West Virginia/Vietnam Veterans Memorial Panel 17E-Line 98

Ronald Lee Fenstermacher/PFC USMC/ Jul 24, 1968/Buckhannon, WV/Vietnam Veterans Memorial Panel 09E-Line 67

Luster Clark Friel/PFC US Army/Apr 15, 1966/ Marlinton, WV/ Vietnam Veterans Memorial Panel 06E-Line 114

Roger Dale Griffith/PFC US Army/Jan 5, 1968/Elkins, WV/ Vietnam Veterans Memorial Panel 33E-Line 36

Lowell Roger Groves/PFC US Army/Mar 6, 1969/Upshur County, WV/Vietnam Memorial Panel 30W-Line 54

Robert Hugh Gumm Jr/SGT US Army/Nov 13, 1970/Cowen, WV/ Vietnam Memorial Panel 06W-Line 56

Thomas G. Hess/SGT US Army/May 3, 1970/Elkins, WV/Vietnam Memorial Panel 11W-Line 91

James Rush Hickman/SP/4 US Army/Dec 31, 1965/Philippi, WV/ Vietnam Memorial Panel 04E-Line 46

Isaac Paul Huffman/PFC US Army/Oct 11, 1967/Volga, WV/ Vietnam Memorial Panel 27E-Line 90

Thomas Alan Johnson/SSG US Army/Feb 14, 1968/Albert, WV/ Vietnam Memorial Panel 39E-Line 33

Bernard Francis Jones/CPT US Army/ Oct 16, 1967/Coalton, WV/ Vietnam Veterans Memorial Panel 28E-Line 15

Fred Michael Kerns/LCPL USMC/Jul 29, 1969/Elkins, WV/ Vietnam Veterans Memorial Panel 20W-Line 71

Raymon Dale Kesling/SSG US Army/Feb 24, 1967/Buckhannon, WV/Vietnam Veterans Memorial Panel 15E-Line 85

Ronald Lee Kesling/CPL USMC/Dec 27, 1967/Buckhannon, WV/ Vietnam Veterans Memorial Panel 32E-Line 75

Cecil Wilbert Kittle Jr./SGT US Army/Nov 17, 1965/Huttonsville, WV/Vietnam Veterans Memorial Panel 03E-Line 82

Charles Wesley Lantz/MSG US Army/Mar 17, 1967/Bayard, WV/ Vietnam Veterans Memorial Panel 16E-Line 102

Larry Joseph Lowther/SP5 US Army/Jun 20, 1970/Volga, WV/ Vietnam Veterans Memorial Panel 09W-Line 73

Victor Allen Mazitis Jr./PFC US Army/Dec 8, 1967/Tucker County, WV/Vietnam Veterans Memorial Panel 31E-Line 65

Douglas Wayne McCarty/SGT US Army/April 11, 1968/Pocahontas County, WV/Vietnam Veterans Memorial Panel 49E-Line 23

Johnny Ellis McLe/CPL US Army/Jul 4, 1969/Webster Springs, WV/Vietnam Veterans Memorial Panel 21W-Line 62

Fairley Wain Mills/SP4 US Army/May 4, 1966, Camden-On-Gully, WV/Vietnam Veterans Memorial Panel 07E-Line 26

Steve Paul Mollohan/SSG US Army/Feb 6, 1966/Pickens, WV/ Vietnam Veterans Memorial Panel 05E-Line 7

Thomas Wayne Moore Jr./SSG US Army/Mar 2, 1967/Webster Springs, WV/Vietnam Veterans Memorial Panel 16E-Line 2

James Michael Nesselrotte/PFC US Army/Jun 19, 1969/Webster County, WV/Vietnam Veterans Memorial Panel 22W-Line 92

Garland Andrew Newhouse/SP4 US Army/Mar 21, 1967/Upper Glade, WV/Vietnam Veterans Memorial Panel 17E-Line 10

Hubert Jackson Payne/PFC US Army/Nov 17, 1967/Webster County, WV/Vietnam Veterans Memorial Panel 30E-Line 11

Ronald Keith Pennington/LCPL USMC/April 27, 1967/Hambleton, WV/Vietnam Veterans Memorial Panel 18E-Line 104

Dennis Stover Pitsenbarger/A1C USAF/June 29, 1965/Pendleton County, WV Vietnam Veterans Memorial Panel 02E-Line 24

Billy Wayne Rapp/SGT US Army/Mar 21, 1969/Gorby, WV/ Vietnam Veterans Memorial Panel 28W-Line 2

Dallas Ratliff/SGT USMC/Sep 11, 1967/Webster Springs, WV/ Vietnam Veterans Memorial Panel 26E-Line 57

Sylvester William Redman/TSGT USAF/Oct 8, 1969/Petersburg, WV/Vietnam Veterans Memorial Panel 17W-Line 52

Leslie Wayne Reed/SSG US Army/Nov 19, 1967/Buckhannon, WV/ Vietnam Veterans Memorial Panel 30E-Line 31

William Lewis Reger/SP/4 US Army/Nov 8, 1969/Buckhannon, WV/Vietnam Veterans Memorial Panel 16W-Line 46

Jack Lee Rexrode/SP4 US Army/Mar 19, 1969/Bartow, WV/ Vietnam Veterans Memorial Panel 29W-Line 83

Samuel Dewey Rider Jr./SGT US Army/Mar 3, 1968/Marlinton, WV/Vietnam Veterans Memorial Panel 42E-Line 56

Robert James Salisbury/SFC US Army/Nov 10, 1969/Cowen, WV/ Vietnam Veterans Memorial Panel 16W-Line 54

Donald Francis Schnably/CPT US Army/Dec 1, 1969/Philippi, WV/Vietnam Veterans Memorial Panel 15W-Line 14

Gary Monzel Shannon/SP5 US Army/June 30, 1970/Mabie, WV/ Vietnam Veterans Memorial Panel 09W-Line 107

David Henry Shiflett/PFC US Army/May 11, 1969/Montrose, WV/ Vietnam Veterans Memorial Panel 25W-Line 55

Robert Lee Simmons/CW2 US Army/Jun 9, 1971/Elkins, WV/ Vietnam Veterans Memorial Panel 03W-Line 71

Roger Lee Simpson/SGT US Army/Jun 26, 1969/Belington, WV/ Vietnam Veterans Memorial Panel 21W-Line 20

Lee Roy David Sprouse/CPL US Army/June 25, 1968/Dunmore, WV/Vietnam Veterans Memorial Panel 55W-Line 39

Eugene Edward Stout/MSG USMC/Dec 28, 1966/Webster Springs, WV/Vietnam Veterans Memorial Panel 13E-Line 94

Samuel Reed Summerfield/PFC US Army/Sep 16, 1968/Elkins, WV/Vietnam Veterans Memorial Panel 43W-Line 10

Russell Allen Taylor/CPL US Army/Aug 26, 1969/Elkins, WV/ Vietnam Veterans Memorial Panel 19W-Line 123

Robert Dewey Thompson/SGT US Army/May 23, 1967/Wymer, WV/Vietnam Veterans Memorial Panel 20E-Line 92

Watson L. Underwood Jr./SGT US Army/Apr 2, 1968/Huntersville, WV/Vietnam Veterans Memorial Panel 47E-Line 44

Jacob Harold Van Meter Jr/SGT US Army/Oct 7, 1967/Slatyfork, WV/Vietnam Veterans Memorial Panel 27E-Line 67

Cecil Young Ware/SSG US Army/Feb 24, 1966/French Creek, WV/ Vietnam Veterans Memorial Panel 05E-Line 75

John Ray Williams/SGT US Army/Nov 29, 1968/Marlinton, WV/ Vietnam Veterans Memorial Panel 37W-Line 9

Lewis Dixon Wilmoth/SP4 US Army/Jul 25, 1967/Frank, WV/ Vietnam Veterans Memorial Panel 24E-Line 1

Marshall David Wolford/CPL US Army/Aug 7, 1968/Pocahontas County, WV/Vietnam Veterans Memorial Panel 49W-Line 28

Roger Duane Young/SP4 US Army/Mar 26, 1969/Bolair, WV/ Vietnam Veterans Memorial Panel 28W-Line 56

Every Veterans Day, ceremonies and memorials are special. John Roberts, a proud Vietnam War veteran, created the Idaho Field of Heroes Memorial in Pocatello, Idaho. At the 2014 Memorial Day ceremony, John Roberts said, "It's not enough to know how many people died, it's not enough to try and remember once a year that a lot of people have given that last full measure of devotion, it's more important to know who they are."

An American POW being paraded in Hanoi, North Vietnam.

Another American POW being paraded in Hanoi.

After his release, an American POW's reunion with his family.

Appendix A

The Terminology Gap

Say what?

Numbers, Words, Key Terms, Glossary, Lexicon, and Acronyms Used in the Vietnam War

A1E: A propeller-driven bomber. The A1E was a great bomber that could stay on station and provide fire support for a few hours.

A-Team: A twelve-man Special Forces team.

AA or ALPHA-ALPHA: Automatic Ambush, a combination of Claymore mines configured to detonate simultaneously when triggered by a trip wire / battery mechanism.

AAA: Antiaircraft artillery, also known as Triple A.

AAR: After-Action Reports.

ABCCC: Airborne Battlefield Command and Control Center.

AC: Aircraft Commander.

AC of S: Assistant Chief of Staff.

ACAV: Armored cavalry assault vehicle.

ACE: A fighter pilot who has shot down five enemy aircraft is called an ACE.

ACL: Allowable cargo load; the number of soldiers that can fly in an aircraft safely.

ACR: Armored Cavalry Regiment.

AE: Advisory Element.

AF: Air Force.

AFB: Air Force base.

AFN: Armed Forces Network radio stationed in Saigon.

AFRTS: Armed Forces Radio and Television service stationed.

AG: Adjutant General; responsible for personnel actions, assignments, awards, and administration.

Age of Aquarius: Denotes the hippy and drug culture of the 1960s and 1970s.

Agent Orange: A defoliant and herbicide containing trace amounts of the toxic contaminant dioxin that was used during the Vietnam War to destroy enemy food sources and defoliate areas of jungle growth.

AHC: Assault Helicopter Company.

AID: Agency for International Development.

Air Assault: See *air mobility* below.

Air Cav: Air Cavalry and airmobile; helicopter-borne infantry.

Air Mobility: Air mobility: Air mobility warfare was new battlefield tactical doctrine developed during the early 1960s. This new type of warfare was an advantageous tactical use of helicopters because it increased combat power through greater mobility. Air mobility doctrine entailed the use of helicopters to conduct reconnaissance by air, find the enemy, move and position artillery, supplies, and troops rapidly on the battlefield. Air mobility operations are fast-paced actions, flexible, and provided a quick and sometimes an immediate response to any enemy action. The advent of the helicopter gunship provided an extra dimension of firepower for ground troops. Initially the gunships were armed with only the 7.62 machine gun, grenade launcher, and 2.75 mm rockets. Later anti-tank missiles were added. These armed anti-tank gunships helped turn the tide for the allies during the 1972 Easter Offensive. Gunships provided fire support for troops on the ground occasionally beyond the normal range of conventional artillery. Air mobility warfare in South Vietnam paved the way for new and modern helicopter utility, cargo, and gunships. New air mobility/assault terms emerged from the Vietnam War.

	Old Term	New Term
1.	Troop Lift	Combat Assault
2.	Pickup	Extraction
3.	Drop-Off	Insertion
4.	Flying in trees	Nap of earth (NOE)

Airborne: Personnel trained to parachute from aircraft.

Airburst: Explosion of a munition in the air.

AIROPS: Air Operations.

AIT: Military Advanced Individual Training.

AK-47: The Russian Kalashnikov rifle used by the VC/NVA; weighed 11.3 pounds loaded.

Alpha Boat: Assault Support Patrol Boat (ASPB). A light, fast shallow draft boat designed specifically to provide close support to riverine infantry. Armament consisted of machine guns (M-60 and .50 caliber), plus whatever the boat crew could scrounge. M-79s and LAWs were common.

AMB: Ambassador.

Americal: The US 23rd Infantry Division.

AMF: A military slang saying that literally means "Adios, Motherf——."

AMMO: Ammunition.

ANG: Air National Guard.

Annamite Mountains: The North/South mountain range traversing South Vietnam.

Anti-Malaria Pills: Ingested on a daily basis to assist in preventing malaria.

Ao Dai: Traditional slit skirt and trousers worn by Vietnamese women.

AO: Area of Operations.

AP Round: An armor piercing round.

APC: Armored Personnel Carrier.

APO: Army Post Office.

ARA: Arial Rocket Artillery; 2.75 millimeter rockets fired from military helicopters.

Arc Light: Code name for the devastating aerial raids of B-52 Strato fortresses against enemy positions in Southeast Asia. The first B-52 Arc Light raid took place on June 18, 1965, on a suspected Viet Cong base north of Saigon. In November 1965, B-52s directly supported American ground forces for the first time and were used regularly for that purpose thereafter.

ARCOM: Army Commendation Medal.

Article 15: Summary administration and disciplinary judgment of a soldier by his commander; may result in fines, confinement in the stockade, and/or a reduction in rank.

Artillery: Large-caliber crew served cannons launching projectiles, usually high explosives against distant enemy targets.

Artillery Fan: The range and distance artillery can fire projectiles. Friendly troops usually operated within this artillery fan. If friendly troops operated outside of the range fan, they could not receive artillery fire support. Occasionally friendly troops were ordered to operate outside of their artillery fan.

ARTY: Artillery.

ARVN: Army of the Republic of Vietnam.

ASA: Army Security Agency.

ASAP: As soon as possible; a request for extreme urgency in a military operation.

Ash and Trash: Helicopter term similar to "Pigs & Rice." Taking on mission flights that are considered noncombative (doesn't mean you aren't going to get shot at) and generally assigned to an area and taking men from field to rear base camp, taking hot food out to the field, evacuating men, etc. The term was perverted to "Ass and Trash" by many in-country aircrews to differentiate between hauling people and supplies.

A Shau Valley: The A Shau Valley is located in Thua Thien Province of I Corps near the Laotian border. The A Shau Valley was one of several valleys and mountains and was one of the principal entry points to South Vietnam via the Ho Chi Minh trail. It was an area that was critical to the North Vietnamese since it was the conduit for supplies, additional troops, and communications for units of the North Vietnamese Army (NVA) and

Viet Cong (VC) operating in I Corps. Because of its importance to the NVA and VC, it was the target of repeated major operations by allied forces, especially the US 101st Airborne Division. Likewise, it was defended vigorously by the NVA and VC. Consequently, the A Shau Valley was the scene of much fighting throughout the war, and it acquired a fearsome reputation for soldiers on both sides. Being a veteran of A Shau Valley operations became a mark of distinction among combat veterans. The most famous battle of the A Shau Valley was known as Hamburger Hill.

Attrition: A military strategy adopted by General Westmoreland to win the Vietnam War; also called body count.

Automatic Ambush: A Claymore mine(s) rigged with a trip wire. The Claymores would fire when the trip wire was tripped.

AWOL: Absent without official leave from the unit or military.

B-40: A Chinese rocket-propelled grenade (RPG).

B-52 BOMBER: The B-52 is regarded by experts as the most successful military aircraft ever produced. Its nickname is BUFF (see *BUFF* below). The B-52 began entering service in the mid-1950s and by 1959 had replaced the awesome but obsolete B-36 as the backbone of Strategic Air Command's (SAC) heavy bomber force. Its primary mission was nuclear deterrence through retaliation. The B-52 has been amazingly adaptable. It was initially designed to achieve very high-altitude penetration of enemy airspace. But when that concept was rendered obsolete by the development of accurate surface-to-air missiles (SAMs), the B-52 was redesigned and reconstructed for low-altitude penetration. It has undergone eight major design changes since first flown in 1952, from B-52A to B-52H. When the Vietnam situation began to deteriorate in 1964, Key SAC commanders began pressing for SAC to get involved in any US action in Vietnam. But the first problem was one of mission. How could a heavy strategic bomber designed to carry nuclear bombs be used in Vietnam? The answer was to modify the B-52 again. Two B-52 units, the 320th Bomb Wing and the 2nd Bomb Wing, had their aircraft modified to carry "iron bombs," conventional high-explosive bombs. After a second modification, each B-52 used in Vietnam could carry eighty-four 500-pound bombs internally and twenty-four 750-pound bombs on underwing racks, for a 3,000-mile nonstop range. The two bomb wings were deployed to operate from Guam as the 133rd Provisional Wing. Later, additional units were deployed to Thailand and Okinawa to reduce in-flight time, and thus warning time. The first B-52 raids against a target in South Vietnam (and the first war action for the B-52) took place on June 18, 1965. The target was a Viet Cong jungle sanctuary. The results were not encouraging. Two B-52s collided in flight to the target and were lost in the Pacific Ocean. The results of the bombing could not be evaluated because the area was controlled by the Viet Cong. Although the press criticized the use of B-52s, ground commanders were much impressed with the potential of the B-52. Previous attempts to use tactical bombers and fighter-bombers to disrupt enemy troop concentrations and supply depots had not been successful. But the B-52 was a veritable flying boxcar, and the effect of a squadron-size attack was to create a virtual Armageddon on the ground. Ironically, the most effective use of the B-52 in Vietnam was for tactical support of ground troops. B-52s were called in to disrupt enemy troop concentrations and supply areas with devastating effect. From June 1965 until August 1973, when operations ceased, B-52s flew 124,532 sorties that successfully dropped their bombloads on target. Thirty-one B-52s were lost: eighteen shot down by the enemy, and thirteen lost to operational problems.

Bac Si: Vietnamese for *doctor* or *medic*.

Baht: Thai unit of currency.

Ba-Ma-Ba: The number for 33 and a popular Vietnamese beer called Tiger Piss.

Bamboo Viper: The small and deadly snake nicknamed the two-stepper. If you were bitten by a bamboo viper, you were told you would die before you take two steps. They were very venomous.

Ban Me Thuot: The largest city in the Central Highlands and the site of a major northern offensive in the spring of 1975.

Banana Clip: Banana-shaped magazine, standard on the AK-47 assault rifle.

BAR: The Browning automatic rifle; a US .30-caliber automatic weapon.

Base Camp: A base camp is a large headquarters that provided fire support, logistics, and other supply items to sustain a combat unit in the field within that unit's tactical areas of responsibility. That combat unit may operate in or away from its base camp. Base camps usually contain all or part of a given unit's support elements. Base camps used firebases to extend their command and control, firepower, and combat influence.

Basic Load: The minimum load of ammunition that a soldier carries. Normally a soldier carried three to four times the basic load.

BDA: Battle damage assessment.

BDE: Brigade.

Beaucoup: Vietnamese/French term for *many* or *lots of.*

Beehive: An antipersonnel direct-fire artillery shell containing several thousand small steel "fleshettes." Each fleshette is about one inch long and looks similar to a finishing nail with four fins. A 105 howitzer projectile contained six thousand fleshettes. Beehives are fired directly at advancing enemy formations. During the Vietnam War, fleshettes were integrated into firebase defense plans. They were superb and used as a primary base camp and firebase defense munition against ground attack.

Berm: A four- to six-foot–high earthen embankment normally around a firebase to prevent direct observation and direct fires.

Bic: Vietnamese for "Do you understand?"

Bien Hoa: A large Vietnamese city and US airfield and military base in III Corps twelve miles north of Saigon.

Big Red One: Nickname for the 1st Infantry Division, based on the red numeral *1* on the division shoulder patch. "If you're going to be one, be a Big Red One!" Also, known as the Bloody One, Bloody Red One, or Big Dead One.

Bingo: Air Force term for the point in a flight in which there's only enough fuel remaining to return to base.

Bipod: Two-legged, supportive stand on the front of many weapons.

Bird Dog: A small Air Force plane used by FACs to request, direct, and control air support.

Bird: An aircraft normally a plane or helicopter.

Black Bird: Nickname of the SR-71 reconnaissance plane and Air Force Special Operations aircraft.

Black Boxes: Sensors dropped from aircraft during the Vietnam War to detect enemy movement.

Black Operation/Mission: A black operation or mission is a covert operation by a government, a government agency, or a military organization. Black operations may be conducted by private companies or groups. Key features of a black operation are that it is a secret and is not attributable to the organization or country conducting the black operation or mission.

Bladder: A heavy-duty rubberized collapsible petroleum drum ranging from two thousand to fifty thousand gallons.

Blasting Cap: A device used to detonate explosive materials.

Bloused Boots: Bloused boots are jungle or other fatigue pants tucked into boots.

Blown Away: To be killed or get really high on drugs.

Blue Leg: Infantryman, a.k.a. "grunt."

Blue Line: A river or stream on a map.

BN: Battalion; a battalion is an organizational institution in the Army and Marine Corps consisting of two to five companies. An infantry battalion in the Vietnam War was commanded by a lieutenant colonel and usually had around five hundred soldiers or marines assigned. An artillery battalion was commanded by a lieutenant colonel and usually had about two hundred personnel assigned. During the Vietnam War, American battalions were usually smaller because of a lack of replacements.

Bo Doi: A uniformed NVA soldier.

Boat People: Refugees fleeing Vietnam by boat after the fall of Saigon in 1975.

Body Bag: A black plastic zip-up bag used to transport dead personnel.

BOHICA: Bend over, here it comes again.

Bok-Bok: Fight/fighting.

Booby Trap: An explosive device used to wound or kill personnel. It is estimated that booby traps accounted for 25–30 percent of injuries to US and allied personnel in Vietnam.

Boom-Boom: A short time with a prostitute.

Boondocks, Boonies, Brush or Bush: Expressions for the jungle, or any remote area away from a base camp or city; sometimes used to refer to any area in Vietnam.

Boonie Rat: An infantryman (grunt).

Boot: Someone fresh out of boot camp or basic training.

BOQ: Bachelor Officers' Quarters.

Bouncing Betty: A conical three-pronged mine that would jump/spring about three feet into the air and explode when triggered.

Brain Bucket: Slang for *helmet* or *steel pot*.

Break Squelch: To send a "click-hiss" signal on a radio by depressing the push-to-talk button without speaking used by LLRPs and others when actually speaking into the microphone might reveal your position.

Brigade: The term *brigade* is a basic military organizational institution smaller than a division and larger than a battalion. During the Vietnam War, a division was organized into three brigades, with each brigade commanded by a colonel. A division consists of approximately ten thousand soldiers. There were also separate infantry brigades functioning in the Vietnam War. The 11th, 196th, and 198th Infantry Brigades fought in the war until 1967, when they were brought together to reconstitute the American Division, or the 23rd Infantry. The 199th Infantry Brigade and the 173rd Airborne Brigade continued to fight as independent entities. A number of combat support brigades, designed to provide supplies, medical care, and maintenance, also functioned in South Vietnam during the 1960s and 1970s.

Bring Smoke: To direct intense artillery or air strikes on an enemy position.

Bro: Short for *brother*.

Bronco: An OV-10 aircraft used as a FAC.

Buddhist: The religion of the majority of the Vietnamese people.

BUFF: Big Ugly Friendly F——; a B-52 heavy USAF bomber.

Butter Bar: A Second Lieutenant.

Buttonhook: A movement technique. The unit moves past the objective then does a U-turn called a buttonhook and moves back to the objective or a night defensive position.

Buy or Bought the Farm: To die, or death.

BX: Base Exchange. A BX is a large variety store for the Navy and Marines; it is about the size of Walmart.

C&C: Command and Control.

CA: Combat Assault; the airlift of troops into a landing zone to conduct a combat operation.

Caca Dau: Vietnamese slang meaning "to kill."

Cal: Caliber.

Cam Ranh Bay: A natural deepwater port, major logistics base, and US air base in II Corps.

Cambodia: A communist country west of South Vietnam and a sanctuary for the NVA.

Cammies: Camouflaged jungle fatigues worn by both friendly and enemy forces in South Vietnam.

Cane pressure mine: Named for the exertion of air on its detonator. The VC/NVA placed this mine in trees to destroy helicopters when dropping off troops and supplies.

Cao Dai: Cao Dai means high tower and is a syncretic faith containing elements of several major religions. Cao Dai originated in the 1920s among civil servants in Saigon and later spread to rural areas near the Cambodian border.

CAP: Combined Action Platoon.

CAR-15: A shorter version of the M-16. CAR-15s were used by Special Forces, Pathfinders, LRRPs, and Saigon commandos. Around 2010, CAR-15s with several modifications began to replace the standard conventional M-16. They are called AT-4s. They are very popular today with civilians and are called assault rifles.

Caribou: A dynamic US Army small fixed wing aircraft used mostly to resupply Special Forces camps. Later, the US Air Force assumed operational control of the Caribou.

CAS: Close Air Support.

CAV: Short for *Cavalry*.

CBU: Cluster Bomb Unit.

CCC: Command and Control Central.

CCN: Command and Control North.

CCS: Command and Control South.

CDS: Container Delivery System; large canister filled with supplies dropped from an aircraft.

Central Highlands: The Central Highlands, a plateau area at the southern edge of the Truong Son Mountains, was a strategically important region of South Vietnam throughout the 1960s and 1970s. Nearly one million people, primarily Montagnard tribesmen, lived in the twenty thousand square miles of the Central Highlands in 1968. The region was economically known for its production of coffee, tea, and vegetables.

CG: Commanding General.

CH-54: US Army heavy cargo helicopter; also called Sky Crane.

Charge: The amount of explosive powder required to fire artillery or blow up a target.

Charlie: The enemy; VC or NVA.

Cherry: A new person in the unit without combat experience.

Chest Breakers: C Ration cigarettes. The worst were Camels.

Chi Lai: Known as Surf City in South Vietnam; also an in-country R & R center.

Chicken Plate: A chest protector (body armor) worn by helicopter pilots and door gunners. Sometimes a pilot and/or door gunners sit on one.

CHICOM: Chinese communist–made weapons, ammunition, equipment, or material.

Chieu Hoi: A program to encourage soldiers from the VC and the NVA to defect to US military or South Vietnam military. A Chieu Hoi is an enemy soldier that defected to South Vietnam and worked and/or cooperated with the US and South Vietnamese government or military.

China Beach: An in-country R & R center located near Da Nang on the coast.

Chinook: The CH-47 medium lift cargo helicopter; also called Shit Hook or Hook.

CHOGIE, CUT A CHOGIE: Move out quickly. Term brought to Vietnam by soldiers who had served in Korea.

Choi Oi: Vietnamese term; exclamation like "Good heavens!" or "What the hell!"

Choke Butter: C ration peanut butter.

Chopper: Term for *helicopter*.

Chuck: The enemy; VC or NVA.

Chunker: M-79 forty-millimeter grenade launcher.

Church Key: A bottle opener.

CI: Counterinsurgency.

CIA: Central Intelligence Agency.

CIB: Combat Infantry Badge. The CIB was awarded to infantry and Special Forces soldiers, NCOs, and officers that engaged the enemy in direct combat in Southeast Asia. An individual must be an infantry officer in the grade of colonel or below, or an enlisted man or warrant officer with an infantry MOS of 11B.

CID: Criminal Investigation Division.

CIDG: Civilian Irregular Defense Group; militia forces trained by Special Forces.

CINCPAC: Commander in Chief, Pacific.

CISO: Counterinsurgency Support Office.

Citadel: A rectangular structure surrounded by walls in Hue.

CJCS: Chairman, Joint Chiefs of Staff.

Clacker: A small handheld generator used to fire the Claymore mine and other electronic demolitions.

Class V: A supply class for ammunition, LAWs, artillery, and mortar rounds and grenades.

Claymore: A popular, concave-shaped antipersonnel land mine. Widely used in Vietnam, the Claymore antipersonnel mine was designed to produce a directional zed, fan-shaped pattern of fragments. The Claymore used a curved block of C-4 explosive, shaped to blow all its force outward in a semicircular pattern. A large number of pellets were embedded in the face of the explosive, creating a devastating blast of fragments similar to the effect of an oversized shotgun. With their directional pattern, Claymores were well-suited as a perimeter-defense weapon. With electronic firing, defenders in bunkers could set Claymores in a pattern to cover all approaches and fire them at will. One problem with this was the tendency of the enemy to use infiltrators to sneak into the defense perimeter before an attack and simply turn the Claymores around. Then when defenders fired the mine, its fragments peppered their own position.

Clean Genes: A term coined by Senator Eugene McCarthy. Senator McCarthy urged his supporters to shed their "hippie" and unkempt look and become more clean-cut in order not to scare voters. The few that cleaned up their act were known as clean genes.

Clover Leaf: A security patrol that departs from a friendly position and moves in a clockwise direction for a few hundred meters and then returns. The route is in a cloverleaf direction similar to a clover leaf.

Cluster Bombs: A generic term for a number of different CBUs: SADEYE/BLU-26B Cluster Bombs, later nicknamed "guava" bombs by the Vietnamese. These one-pound, baseball-sized bombs were usually dropped in lots of six hundred or more. The bomblets were released from a dispenser in such a way as to spread them across a wide area. When they hit the ground, they exploded, sending out smaller steel balls embedded in their cases. There were also CBU-24; CBU-25; Clamshell CBU, which exploded in a donut pattern, creating a circle of fire in a hollow; and CBU-49, a canister of time-delayed, baseball-sized bomblets that go off randomly over a thirty-minute period, each blasting out 250 white-hot ball bearings; and Rockeye CBU, a thermite device used for burning targets.

CMB: Combat Medical Badge.

CNO: Chief of Naval Operations.

CO: Commanding Officer.

CO: Commanding Officer.

COASTIES: Nickname used to identify the United States Coast Guard servicemen and women.

COBRA: The AH-1G attack helicopter. Nicknamed by some as the Shark or Snake. The Cobra carried 2.75 inch air-to-ground rockets, mini-guns, and a forty-millimeter gun mounted in a turret under the nose of the aircraft. There were other configurations also. The old D-model Hueys were phased out and the Cobras used in greater strength around 1968. Most of the Cobras were painted with eyes and big, scary teeth like a shark for psychological impact.

Colon: A French term for a colonial settler in South Vietnam.

Combat Assault: Two or more helicopters landing on an LZ with troops.

Combat Hornet: C-119 USAF medium-lift airplane; also called the flying boxcar.

Combat Pay: An additional $50 to $60 per month paid to the US military serving in South Vietnam.

Comic Book: Also called a funny paper and denotes a military map.

COMMO Check: A communications check on the radio.

COMMO: Communications.

Company: A company is an organizational institution commanded by a captain and consisting of two or more platoons. It varies widely in size according to its mission. An artillery unit is called a battery, and a cavalry unit is called a troop.

Compass Man: This was usually the third soldier in the order of march in the Vietnam War. His duty was to navigate the unit to the objective. A squad leader and platoon leader always checked the compass man.

COMUSMACV: Commander United States Military Assistance Command, Vietnam.

Concertina: Circular wire with razor barbs attached placed outside of bases to assist in impeding or stopping an enemy ground assault.

Cong Bo: Water buffalo.

Cong Khi: Monkey.

Cong Moui: Mosquito.

Contact: Condition of being in contact with the enemy, a firefight, also "in the shit."

CONUS: Continental United States.

Cook-Off: A situation where an automatic weapon has fired so many rounds that the heat has built up enough in the weapon to set off the remaining rounds without using the trigger mech. This was common in the .50 caliber, and the only way to stop it was to rip and break the belt manually.

Cooper-Church Amendment: Passed on December 12, 1969, that prohibited President Nixon from conducting military operations in Southeast Asia without congressional approval.

CORDS: Civil Operations and Revolutionary Development Support teams.

Corps: South Vietnam was divided into four corps tactical zones (CTZs).

> I Corps: The northern five provinces of South Vietnam made up I Corps.

> II Corps: Made up of the fifteen provinces directly south of I Corps.

> III Corps: The ten provinces in III Corps stretched from where the Central Highlands blended into the flat alluvial plain of the northern Mekong Delta to the Delta itself, and from the Cambodian border in the west past Saigon to the South China Sea.

> IV Corps: The entire Mekong Delta south of the Saigon formed IV Corps.

Cost: The Vietnam War cost the US taxpayers approximately 150 billion dollars.

COSVN: Central Office for South Vietnam organized by the North Vietnamese. COSVN was believed to be located in the Fishhook area of Cambodia.

CP: Command Post.

CQ: Charge of Quarters.

Cracker Box: A field ambulance.

Crane: Slang for a CH-54 Sky Crane.

Crew Chief: Helicopter airplane crew member who maintains the aircraft.

Cross Load: Spreading your unit on several trucks or aircraft so that the unit is spread out.

Crosscheck: Everyone checks everyone else for things that are loose, make noise, light up, smell bad, etc.

Crusader: USN F-8 jet used as a reconnaissance aircraft because of its speed and maneuverability.

Cs, C rations, C-rats, Charlie rats, or combat rations: Canned meals used in military operations during the Vietnam War. Ham and lima beans were the worst!

CS: A riot-control gas agent, such as a CS-grenade, used widely to clear out enemy tunnel works.

CSAR: Combat Search and Rescue.

CTZ: Corps tactical zone.

Cu Chi: An important communist base area near the village of Cu Chi. The VC leadership constructed a very large tunnel complex under the city and American units/base camps. Cu Chi was twenty miles northwest of Saigon.

CYA: Cover your ass.

CYCLO: A three-wheel passenger vehicle powered by a human on a bicycle.

C-4: C-4 was a plastic explosive popular among soldiers in Vietnam because of its various properties. It was easy to carry because of its lightweight, stable nature and had a potent explosive power. Malleable with a texture similar to Play-Doh, it could be formed into a shaped charge of infinite configuration. The availability of C-4 reduced the necessity of carrying a variety of explosive charges. C-4 would not explode without use of detonation devices, even when dropped, beaten, shot, or burned. It was not destabilized by water, an important consideration given the Vietnam climate. Because it could be safely burned, C-4 was popular with GIs, who would break off a small piece of it for heating water or C rations. Sometimes they used it in foxholes to warm hands.

Da Nang: City in Quang-Nam Province, I Corps and site of a US air base.

Dac Cong: VC Special Forces Unit.

Daily-Daily: Daily anti-malaria pill.

Daisy Chain: Detonation cord linking several Claymore mines or other explosives together.

Daisy Cutter: A fifteen thousand–pound bomb that would cut down vegetation and trees for three hundred meters from point of impact. Also used to clear a jungle for a two- or three-ship LZ/PZ or to create a clearing for a firebase.

Dai-ta: Vietnamese for *colonel.*

Dap: A stylized, ritualized manner of shaking hands, started by African American troops.

Dapsone: A small pill taken periodically by US troops, ostensibly to prevent malaria but actually to prevent leprosy.

DD Form-4: Enlistment contract with US military.

DD-214: Military transfer or discharge form.

Defoliant: A chemical that is sprayed or dusted on vegetation that causes the leaves to fall off and vegetation to die; also called Agent Orange.

Delta Dagger: US Air Force F-102 jet.

DEROS: Date eligible for return from overseas; the date a person's tour in Vietnam was estimated to end.

Desertion: There were only twenty-four proven cases of battlefield desertion during the Vietnam War.

DESOTO: Destroyer patrols off North Vietnam.

Det Cord: Detonating cord. An "instantaneous fuse" in the form of a long thin flexible tube loaded with explosive (PETN). Det Cord was used to obtain the simultaneous explosion from widely spaced demolitions, such as multiple Claymores. Det Cord burns at twenty-five thousand feet per second. It may also be used to fall trees by wrapping three turns per foot of tree diameter around the tree and firing.

Deuce and a half: A military medium cargo truck that carried personnel and cargo.

Deuce: Two.

Di di mau: Pronounced *dee dee mile*; Vietnamese for "to send" or "get away or get out." Also called Di Di.

Di Wee: Vietnamese for *captain*.

DIA: Defense Intelligence Agency.

Diddy Boppin: Slang term for someone moving carelessly without caution or someone walking without a purpose.

Dime Nickel: A 105 millimeter howitzer.

Dinky Dou: Vietnamese for *crazy*.

Dioxin: The main ingredient of defoliants (Agent Orange) in South Vietnam.

Div: Division. A division is a nearly universal military organization consisting of approximately ten thousand to fourteen thousand troops commanded by a major general. During the Vietnam War, the following US divisions or elements thereof participated in the war. The US Army divisions were the 1st Cavalry Division, 1st, 4th, 9th, 23rd Americal, 25th, and the 101st Airborne Division. US Marine divisions were the 1st, 3rd, and 5th Marine Divisions.

Dixie Station: A fixed point in the South China Sea in international waters off the coast of South Vietnam that served as a staging area for US Navy forces. Dixie Station was located 11 degrees north, 110 degrees east, and it was used from 1965 to 1966 as a reference point for air operations by the US Navy Seventh Fleet Attack Carrier Striking Force, Task Force 77.

DMZ: Demilitarized zone. Boundary established between North and South Vietnam on July 22, 1954, at the 17th parallel.

DOC: Affectionate title for enlisted medical aid man. What the grunts would call medics.

DOD: Department of Defense.

Don Ganh: Shoulder pole on which Vietnamese women carried goods to market.

Dong Ap Bia: Mountain on the Laos border also known as Hamburger Hill.

Dong: Currency of North Vietnam.

Donut Dolly: American Red Cross volunteer—female. Also called Doughnut Dollies. Namesake of World War I counterpart;

helped the morale of the troops. They were also known as Pastry Pigs.

Dope: A term for marijuana and other illicit drugs.

Doper: A person who used illicit drugs.

Doubtfuls: Indigenous personnel who cannot be categorized as either Viet Cong or civil offenders. It also can mean suspect personnel spotted from ground or aircraft.

Dove: A person who is antiwar.

Draft Classification: Civilian draft board status and classification during 1964–1972.

I-A: Available for military service.

I-A-O: Conscientious objector available for noncombatant military service only.

I-C: Member of the Armed Forces of the US, the Coast Guard, and Geodetic Survey, or the Public Health Service.

I-D: Member of reserve component or student taking military training.

I-H: Registrant not currently subject to processing for induction.

I-O: Conscientious objector available for civilian work contributing to the maintenance of the national health, safety, or interest.

I-S: Student deferred by statute (high school).

I-Y: Registrant available for military service, but qualified for military only in the event of war or national emergency.

I-W: Conscientious objector performing civilian work contributing to the maintenance of the national health, safety, or interest.

II-A: Registrant deferred because of civilian occupation (except agriculture or activity in study).

II-C: Registrant deferred because of agricultural occupation.

II-D: Registrant deferred because of study preparing for the ministry.

II-S: Registrant deferred because of activity in study.

III-A: Registrant with a child or children; registrant deferred by reason of extreme hardship to dependents.

IV-A: Registrant who has completed service; sole surviving son.

IV-B: Official deferred by law.

IV-C: Alien.

IV-D: Minister of religion or divinity student.

IV-F: Registrant not qualified for any military service.

IV-G: Registrant exempt from service during peace; surviving son or brother.

IV-W: Conscientious objector who has completed alternate service contributing to the maintenance of the national health, safety, or interest in lieu of induction into the Armed Forces of the United States.

V-A: Registrant over the age of liability for military service.

Drag Bombs: Bombs dropped at low level. They were also known as dumb bombs.

Drag: The last soldier in the order of march. He was responsible for rear security.

Dragonfly: US Air Force A-37 jet.

Dress Whites: The formal lightweight uniform for the US military.

Drum: A circular magazine that holds ammunition until ready to mount on the weapon and "feed" the ammo.

DRV: Democratic Republic of Vietnam (North Vietnam).

Du Mi Ami: Pronounced *Dumammy*. In Vietnamese, it meant Motherf——. This was my radio call sign in South Vietnam and stuck with me for my military career. My peers still call me Dumammy at military reunions.

Dud: Not a live round and slang for an inept soldier.

Duffel Bag: The oblong, unwieldy bag in which troops stored most of their gear. Also, an artillery term for *motion/sound/seismic sensors* placed along suspected enemy trails or areas. Duffel bag sensors contained small radio transmitters that sent a signal to an intelligence unit when triggered. Once triggered, the artillery fired on the "duffel bag" target to intercept or interdict the enemy.

Dung burning detail: A detail of several soldiers burning human waste in fifty-five-gallon drums. It was also called the shit detail.

Dung Lai: A Vietnamese word that meant "stop" or "halt."

Duster: The M-42. It was an automatic twin 40 mm "ack-ack" set up on a tank body. Dusters were WWII tracked vehicles brought to RVN. They were medium size and sported two 40 mm pom-poms plus one M60 machine gun, plus a crew of about four to five with individual weapons. They were used for convoy security and perimeter security for artillery bases each night.

Dustoff: Also called MEDEVAC. *Dustoff* was a nickname for a medical evacuation helicopter or mission. "I need a Dustoff" became an all-too-familiar call on the airwaves of Vietnam. Dustoff missions were medical evacuation missions using helicopters. While the term has been used to apply to all medical evacuation missions, GIs reserved the term for missions flown to pick up wounded soldiers in the field, often under fire. When a soldier was hit, the call went out for a Dustoff, and any helicopter in the area without a higher priority mission could respond. Many of the early helicopters used in Vietnam did not fare well in Dustoff missions due to their lack of maneuverability and relatively slow speed, combined with a small door. The UH-1 Huey excelled in this role, with its wide doors and ability to get in and out quickly. Still, flying Dustoffs took courage on the part of the crew, as ground fire was the rule rather than the exception. The rewards, however, were great. Dustoffs allowed wounded soldiers to be brought to medical facilities much more quickly than in any other war, usually in a matter of minutes, and saved many lives.

DZ: Drop zone. An open and cleared area to receive personnel or supplies dropped by parachute.

E and E: Escape and Evasion.

Eagle Beach: 101st Airborne Division R & R center in I Corps on the South China Sea.

Eagle Flight: A helicopter force of platoon size or larger on standby and ready to be used as an emergency reaction force to reinforce a ground unit in contact with the enemy.

Early Out: Discharge prior to commitment release date.

Easter or Spring Offensive: Was a mass invasion by the NVA into South Vietnam in March 1972 that was initially successful but failed in a few months.

ECM: Electronic countermeasures, radar, and other frequency-jamming equipment.

EEI: Essential Elements of Information.

EENT: End Evening Nautical Twilight. The light from the sky between full night and sunrise.

Egg Beater: Slang name for a Huey or any helicopter.

Elephant Balls: Five hundred–gallon rubber bladder filled with fuel.

Elephant Grass: The tall grassy foliage found in abundance in South Vietnam. It had very sharp edges and could cut through jungle fatigues.

Elephant Valley: Northern part of the Ashau Valley in I Corps.

ELINT: Electronic intelligence.

EM: Enlisted man.

Enlisted men's grades: E1-Trainee, E2-Private, E3-Private First Class, E4-Corporal or Specialist-4, E5-Sergeant, E6-Staff Sergeant, E7-Sergeant First Class, E8-Master Sergeant/First Sargent, E9-Staff Sergeant Major/Command Sergeant Major.

Ensign: Entry-level officer rank in the Navy and Coast Guard.

Entrenching tool: Also called an idiot stick. A small collapsible shovel sometimes carried in a canvas cover.

EOD: Explosive ordinance disposal.

ER: Efficiency report.

ETA: Estimated time of arrival.

ETD: Estimated time of departure.

ETS: Established termination of service.

Exfil: Exfiltration out of area.

Expectant: A term for someone expected to die.

Extend: An administrative agreement to serve in South Vietnam beyond the normal twelve-month tour.

Extraction: The removal of military personnel from the field, firebases, or other areas.

F-100 or HUN: A USAF close air support jet.

F-4 PHANTOM II: The F-4 Phantom II, a twin-engine, all-weather, tactical fighter-bomber was one of the principal aircraft deployed to Southeast Asia. Capable of operating at speeds of more than 1,600 miles per hour and at altitudes approaching sixty thousand feet, the first F-4s were deployed to participate in the air war over Vietnam in August 1964 by the United States Navy. On August 6, 1964, in response to the Gulf of Tonkin incident, five F-4Bs from the USS *Constellation* attacked North Vietnamese patrol boat bases. The F-4 aircraft expanded their operations beginning on April 3, 1965, when fifty F-4Bs attacked a road bridge sixty-five miles south of Hanoi. The first United States Air Force (USAF) F-4s were deployed to Southeast Asia in early 1965 and became involved in significant air operations during the summer. On July 10, 1965, two F-4Cs shot down two MiG-17 fighters over North Vietnam with Sidewinder missiles. In October 1965, the first RF-4s, aircraft equipped with reconnaissance equipment, were deployed to the theater. By March 1966, seven USAF F-4 squadrons were in South Vietnam and three were in Thailand. Buildup of F-4 aircraft and operations continued thereafter, including F-4s from the Marine Corps. A total of 511 F-4s from all services were lost in Southeast Asia from June 6, 1965, through June 29, 1973. Of these, 430 were combat losses, while 81 resulted from aerial or ground accidents. The F-4 was called a lot of things, mostly with respect. It was referred to by some as Fox 4.

FAC (Fack): Forward air controller. The forward air controller (FAC) had the responsibility for calling in air strikes on enemy positions during the Vietnam War. Usually flying a low-level, low-speed aircraft, such as a single-engine Cessna O-1 Bird Dog spotter plane, the FAC identified Viet Cong or North Vietnamese positions and relayed the information to attack aircraft, helicopter gunships, or high-altitude bombers. On the ground, a forward air controller would call in similar information.

Fantail: The stern or aft open area of a ship, also called the afterdeck.

FARMGATE: Clandestine US Air Force unit in South Vietnam during 1964.

Fast Mover: A jet.

Fat Albert: A large USAF cargo aircraft; also called a C-5A.

Fat City: MACV Headquarters in Saigon.

Fatigues: Standard issue uniform of the US Army; usually olive drab.

Firebase: Firebases were temporary and mobile small base camps, fortresses, and LZs that provided artillery, logistics, ammunition, and other support to combat ground units in the field as required. Firebases were mobile and extended commanders' fire and combat power beyond the large permanent base camps. Some firebases also provided aircraft fuel, rockets, and ammunition for helicopters to expedite and facilitate combat operations. The average size of firebases were between three to five acres. Firebases could be round, oval, square, rectangle, star, or a combination. Security consisted of a four- to six-foot dirt berm on the inside closest to the troops and several strands of concertina wire about thirty to fifty meters apart outside the berm. The berm prevented direct enemy observation and direct fire into the firebase. Tangle foot wire interlaced was secured about six inches above the ground between the berm and the first strand of wire. Large sandbag bunkers and individual defensive positions were tactfully placed and located around the berm. A 105 mm and a 155mm artillery battery are located on each end of the firebase. The artillery provided fire support for infantry troops in the field, and during a ground attack, the artillery would lower their tubs and fire point-blank using beehive rounds directly into the advancing enemy. An infantry company usually rotated to the firebase to provide security. Virtually every firebase in South Vietnam received a ground attack and was under constant mortar and rocket attack. Although several enemy regiments attacked specified firebases, the enemy never overran any US firebase. Firebase tactics, techniques, and procedures developed during the Vietnam War remain in use today. Some firebases in South Vietnam are depicted below:

FB Gladiator	FB Dottie	FB Betty
FB Veghel	FB Jack	FB Kathryn

FB Maureen	FB Mooney	FB Rakkasan
FB Bartlett	FB Ripcord	FB Birmingham
FB White	FB Granite	FB Ike
FB Carolyn	FB Jamie	FB Barbara
FB Los Banos	FB Tomahawk	FB Roy
FB Pledge	FB Pistol	FB Brick
FB Spear	FB Normandy	FB Arsenal
FB Eagle	FB Bastogne	FB Sally
FB Jerome	FB Airborne	FB Jay
FB O'Reilly	FB Blaze	FB Tennessee
FB Whip	FB Goodman	FB Bradley
FB Grant	FB Chop Chop	FB Peanuts

FBI: Federal Bureau of Investigation.

Feet Wet: Expression used by pilots to indicate they were over water.

Field of Fire: An area that a weapon or group of weapons can cover effectively with fire from a given position.

Fighting Position: A modified foxhole or position that may have sandbag protection and sometimes an elevated roof of sheet metal, reinforced with sandbags or dirt. Sized for one or two troops, fighting positions might be dispersed around a company or battery area for defensive use during a ground attack.

Fire for effect: When all artillery and mortar ordinance was fired at the enemy in continual firing until ordered to stop.

Fire Mission: A communications format used to call artillery or mortar fire.

Firefight: Exchanging rifle fire with the enemy.

1st Cavalry Division: During the nineteenth century, American cavalry units were horse-mounted troops designed to survey enemy positions and provide screens for incoming infantry units. The horse-mounted cavalry gave way during the twentieth century to armored personnel carriers and tanks. A major innovation of the Vietnam War was the use of air cavalry units where troops are moved into battlefield positions by helicopters. The 1st Cavalry Division was one of the main air cavalry units in Southeast Asia. Originally activated in 1921, the 1st Cavalry

Division fought (dismounted) in the Pacific during World War II and later in Korea. In 1965, the division's flag was taken from Korea and presented to the experimental 11th Air Assault Division, which became the 1st Cavalry Division (Airmobile). The former 1st Cavalry Division, still in Korea, became the new 2nd Infantry Division. The division was deployed to South Vietnam in September 1965 and was the first full division to arrive in the country. It was almost immediately in battle in the Ia Drang Valley. The division won a Presidential Unit Citation for its fierce fighting. During 1966 and 1967, elements of the division were engaged in numerous actions throughout the II Corps tactical zone. Initially committed to operations in Binh Dinh Province in early 1968, the bulk of the division was hurriedly recommitted to the Battle for Hue and then to the relief of the marine position at Khe Sanh. Later in the year, the division served in the A Shau Valley before being shifted to protect the northern and western approaches to Saigon. As the Army's first airmobile division, the 1st Cavalry Division pioneered air assault tactics. It was considered one of the Army's elite units in Vietnam, highly valuable because of its extreme mobility. The division suffered over thirty thousand casualties during the war.

First Shirt: The first sergeant in a company; also called top. This is the guy that made things happen.

Fishhook: A small peninsula of land that extended from Cambodia into South Vietnam in III Corps. It was purported that the COSVN headquarters was located inside of the fishhook. The fishhook area was a major NVA sanctuary.

Fishing Trawlers: The USSR used fishing trawlers in the South China Sea to monitor US Navy operations and to report B-52 bombing missions from Guam directed to North and South Vietnam.

Flak Jacket/Vest: A protective vest worn by US military personnel to protect against light shrapnel.

FLAMING DART: Code name of bombing operations in reprisal for attacks on US forces during the early stages of the Vietnam War.

Flare: Illumination projectile.

Flight time: The flight time from point A to point B.

FLIR: Forward Looking Infrared Radar.

Flower Children: The professed nonviolent hippies of the sixties and seventies.

Flying Boxcar: A USAF C-119 medium lift fixed wing airplane used to transport supplies, cargo, and troops. The Boxcar was also called the Flying Hornet.

Flying Telephone Pole: A North Vietnamese SAM fired at US aircraft. According to pilots, the launched SAMs looked like telephone poles flying.

Flying Telephone Pole: The slang name of the Russian SA-2 surface-to-air rocket used in North Vietnam.

FNG: The most common name for a new guy in Vietnam. FNG translated as f—— new guy.

FO: Forward Observer; the person who calls in and adjusts artillery and mortar fire. An American, British, Canadian, and Australian conference on artillery fire direction in 1966 resulted in changes in US terminology for requesting and adjusting artillery.

Old Term	New Term
1. Azimuth	Direction
2. Barrage	Final protective fire
3. Cease-fire	Check firing
4. Coordinates	Grid

FOB: Forward Operating Base.

Foo Gas: A combination of jet fuel and explosives in fifty-five-gallon drums placed outside firebases to defend perimeters when the enemy attacked.

Formaldehyde: A chemical in beer used as a preservative in Vietnam.

Frag: Short for *fragmentation grenade*. The M67 was the standard hand grenade used by the US military in the Vietnam War. The M67 could be thrown thirty to thirty-five meters by the average soldier and has a four- to five-second fuse. The steel fragments are provided by the grenade body and can produce a casualty radius of fifteen meters with a fatality radius of five meters.

Fragging: When a friendly soldier intentionally kills or maims another friendly soldier using a hand grenade. The grenade could be tossed, thrown, or booby-trapped.

Fratricide: A situation when US and/or allied military are killed by friendly fire, artillery, or air strikes.

Freak: The slang term for a drug-addict, pothead, or society dropout in South Vietnam and the US.

Free Fire Zone: An area of operations where anything moving could be fired upon. All non-US military or allied personnel seen or found in this zone was assumed to be the enemy. Occasionally woodcutters would be seen. We captured them and evacuated them to our rear base camp.

Freedom Bird: A US bound civilian airliner with military aboard flying back to the world.

Freq: Radio frequency.

Friendlies: US military and its allies.

Friendly Fire: Any friendly fire, air, or artillery that was mistakenly directed at American positions.

FTA: Free the Army or "F—— the Army;" a derogatory phrase used by frustrated soldiers or civilians.

FTX: Field Training Exercise.

FUBAR: Short for "F—— Up Beyond All Repair" or "Recognition." To describe impossible situations, equipment, or persons as in, "It is (or They are) totally Fubar!"

Funny Money: US Military Payment Certificate (MPC); also called funny money.

Fuze: Triggering mechanism attached to the nose of an artillery shell or bomb.

FY: Fiscal Year.

FYI: For your information.

G1: Personnel officer on a general staff.

G2: Military Intelligence officer on a general staff.

G3: Operations officer on a general staff.

G4: Supply officer on a general staff.

Ga Mug: Thank you.

Gecko: A small green lizard often kept as a pet by base camp personnel in Vietnam to catch flies and other insects.

Ghost or Ghosting: Goldbricking, sandbagging, or hiding out in the rear as if not seen.

Ghost Riders: The 189th Assault Helicopter Company.

GI: Government Issue.

Globemaster: A USAF heavy cargo fixed wing aircraft in the 1950s and '60s. Also called a C-124.

GO: General officer.

Gomers: North Vietnamese.

Gook: Slang term for *Vietnamese*.

GP Strap: General purpose strap that came off your rucksack. Many uses, but used mainly to replace the sling on an M-16.

GP: General purpose.

GQ: General quarters—battle stations where military personnel are assigned to go ASAP when alarm sounds.

Grease Gun: M-3 submachine gun.

Great Society: President Johnson's ambitious program of social legislation and civil rights. The Vietnam War costs reduced Great Society funding and forced cutbacks.

Green Backs: US currency used in Vietnam usually on the Black Market. You got a better deal if you used Green Backs.

Green Berets: US Army Special Forces.

Green Tracers: The color of enemy tracers.

Green-Eye: Starlight scope. Light amplifying telescope, used to see at night.

Grunt: A popular nickname for an infantryman in Vietnam; supposedly derived from the sound one made from lifting up his rucksack. Also called ground pounder or crunchie.

Grunts: Slang for *infantry troops*.

Guerilla nuts: Slang for the chocolate bars in C rations. Also called John Wayne bars.

Guerilla Warfare: Unconventional warfare used by the VC and NVA in South Vietnam.

Guerrilla: A soldier of a resistance movement who are organized on a military or paramilitary basis.

Gun Trucks: Gun trucks were the trucks that would accompany convoys and provide security. They were usually fitted with a .50 and one or two M-60s, plus individual weapons for a normal crew of four to five.

Gung Ho: A very pro-military person.

Gunship: A helicopter equipped with machine guns, chunkers, and rockets.

GVN: Government of South Vietnam.

H & I: Harassment and interdictory fire, usually artillery and/or mortar fire, fired on suspected enemy locations.

Hai Van Pass: A particularly treacherous pass through the mountains south of Phu Bai and just north of Dang.

HALO: High-Altitude Low Opening free fall parachuting technique.

Ham and Lima Beans: The least favored C ration meal in Vietnam and the military inventory. They really sucked! They were also called Ham 'n' Motherf———.

Hamburger Hill: A major battle fought in the Ashau Valley in May 1969; also called Dong Ap Bia Mountain.

Hamlet: A village in Vietnam.

Hanoi Hannah: The female disc jockey broadcasting propaganda from North Vietnam to US military.

Hanoi Hilton: Hoa Lo prison located in Hanoi and was the major North Vietnam prison where American POWs were kept. Hoa Lo prison had the nickname of the Hanoi Hilton.

Hanoi Jane: Hanoi Jane was a nickname given to Jane Fonda after she visited Hanoi during the war.

Hanoi: The capital of North Vietnam during the war.

Hawk: A pro-war person.

Hawkeye: A USN plane used to direct aerial bombing missions and air interdictions.

HE: High Explosives.

Head: A person who smoked marijuana or used other illicit drugs, also a restroom in the Navy.

HEAT Round: High Explosive, Anti-Tank.

Heat Tab: A blue smokeless chemical tablet used to heat C rations or water. The Heat Tab must be ignited with a match or lighter.

Heavy LRRPs Team: LRRPs usually operated in teams of four to six guys. On occasion, when it was suspected the team was going to deliberately make contact with the enemy, the LRRPs were assigned 10. This was commonly called a heavy team. It was more difficult to hide, but the additional M-60 machine gun and other firepower made the inconvenience worth the trouble.

Height Ashbury: The area in San Francisco that was originally a center of flower power children but turned into a run-down drug area by the end of the sixties.

Helicopter: The US aircraft that was shot down the most; about 4,865 were lost during the Vietnam War.

Herbicide: A chemical substance used to destroy or inhibit the growth of crops, plants, weeds, grasses, and jungle.

Hercules: A USAF C-130 medium cargo four-motor prop airplane.

Highway One: A major north south route/highway from the DMZ to Saigon.

Hippie: The name of those who dropped out of society during the sixties.

Hispanic: The largest minority group on the Vietnam Wall memorial in Washington DC.

Ho Chi Minh Sandals: Sandals made of pieces of vehicle or aircraft tires.

Ho Chi Minh Trail: A network of trails that began in North Vietnam and headed south through Laos and Cambodia ending in South Vietnam.

Ho Chi Minh: Vietnamese statesman who declared Vietnam independence. Ho's real name was Nguyen Ai Quoc.

Hoa Hao: Hoa Hao was an offshoot of Buddhism and the brainchild of the "mad monk" Huynh Phu So, who founded the new faith in the late 1930s.

Hon Tre: An island of the coast of South Vietnam used by US Special Forces for intense Recondo training.

Hooch: A house, living quarters, or a native hut. A poncho shelter was also called hooch.

Hook: Same as a Chinook. A twin-rotor medium helicopter used primary for cargo.

Hope, Bob: A comedian who was known for entertaining US military at Christmastime.

Horn: Any two-way radio.

Hose Down: Intense firing at the enemy.

Hostile(s): The enemy.

Hot: Referred to an LZ or area when enemy troops were in the area shooting at friendly forces.

Howitzer: A relative short range, high angle of fire cannon with usually a 105 or 155 MM shell.

HQ: Headquarters.

Hue: First built by Emperor Gia Long early in the nineteenth century, Hue was the imperial capital of Vietnam between 1802 and 1945. It is located on Highway 1, about 420 miles south of Hanoi and 670 miles north of Saigon, and was an independent municipality under the Republic of Vietnam (RVN). For the Viet Cong and North Vietnamese, Hue was a city with tremendous historical significance. Being the former imperial capital of a united Vietnam, the center of Vietnamese cultural and religious life, and the capital of Thua Thien Province, Hue became an important symbol in the struggle for dominance of Indochina. It was also a difficult city to defend. Isolated by the Annamite mountain chain and bordered by Laos to the west and the demilitarized zone to the north, Hue was without access to a major port for resupply. Still, before the Tet Offensive, Hue was considered secure for South Vietnam. That all ended on January 31, 1968. At 3:40 a.m. that day, North Vietnamese Army (NVA) artillery began pounding the city. Elements of the NVA 6th Regiment simultaneously attacked Military Assistance Command, Vietnam (MACV) headquarters in Hue and ARVN 1st Division headquarters. Other NVA troops blockaded Highway 1 north and south of the city and attacked several hundred other sites in the city. By daylight, the Viet Cong flag was flying atop the Imperial Citadel of the Nguyen emperors. Hue had fallen to the communists. The American and ARVN counterattack on Hue began almost immediately with huge volumes of artillery, naval bombardment, and air strikes, reducing much of Hue to rubble while elements of the First Air Cavalry Division, the 101st Airborne Division, the ARVN 1st Division, the US 1st Marines, and ARVN Rangers and Marines engaged in house-to-house, hand-to-hand combat with NVA troops and Viet Cong. The Imperial Citadel was not recaptured from the communists until February 24, 1968. Hue had been devastated. More than 50 percent of the city had been totally destroyed, and 116,000 people of a total population of 140,000 had been rendered homeless. Nearly 6,000 civilians were dead or missing, and several thousands more were assassinated outright during the Viet Cong occupation. The NVA and Viet Cong suffered 5,000 dead; the United States, 216 dead and 1,364 seriously wounded; and the ARVN, 384 dead and 1,830 seriously wounded. Like the Tet Offensive in general, the battle for Hue was a tactical defeat for the communists. Hue in particular, and Tet in general, was indeed the turning point in the war.

HUEY: Nickname for the UH-series helicopters: "utility helicopter." The Bell UH-1 helicopter is one of aviation's true success stories. Thousands of the aircraft have been made in a number of variations, serving a multitude of roles. Called the Iroquois by the United States Army, the aircraft is much better known by its nickname of Huey, derived from its initial designation of HU-1. In its multitude of roles in Vietnam, the Huey became a familiar sight on the television screens of America. Hardly a night passed without the evening news showing Huey's conducting MEDEVAC or other missions. Bell was chosen in 1955 to provide the Army with a utility helicopter capable of serving as a frontline medical evacuation (see MEDEVAC) aircraft, a general utility aircraft, and an instrument training aircraft. Deliveries to the US Army began in 1959. In 1961, a more powerful version, the UH-1B, was introduced. In 1967, starting with the UH-1D series, the airframe length was increased, giving the Huey a much roomier passenger-cargo compartment capable of carrying more troops or supplies. In 1968, Bell developed a specialized version of the aircraft with a stronger airframe and more powerful engine. The "Huey tug," as it was nicknamed, was capable of lifting loads up to three tons; nearly double that of a conventional Huey. Powered by a 1,400 SHP AVCO Lycoming engine, the Huey had a cruising speed of 127 mph and a range of 318 miles. Fast and highly maneuverable, the Huey proved far superior to the CH-21 or CH-34 as an assault helicopter. Combat troops normally rode in the wide doors on each side of the aircraft and could exit quickly, greatly reducing the time the helicopter was on the ground. Often troops jumped from a Huey just above the ground as it "bounced" in ground effect and then left, with the entire ground time reduced to a matter of seconds.

Hump or Humping: Walking with a rucksack through the jungle, highlands, or the Delta on a military operation.

HUN: A USAF jet used for close air support. Also called an F-100.

Huskie: A USAF HH-43B helicopter used by air rescue teams.

I & I: Slang for intoxication and intercourse. The term was used in lieu of R & R sometimes.

I & R: Intelligence and Reconnaissance patrol.

Idiot Stick: Same as an entrenching tool (small shovel the infantry soldiers carried).

IG: Inspector General.

Illum: Illumination. Flares dropped by aircraft and fired from the ground by hand, artillery, or mortars.

In the Field: Any forward combat area or any area outside of a town or base camp.

Incoming: Enemy artillery/mortar and/or rocket fire that falls within a secure area or friendly positions.

In-country: Being in Vietnam.

Insertion/Inserted: Helicopter placement of combat troops in an operational area.

Intel: Intelligence.

Intruder: USN A-6 aircraft that carried fifteen thousand pounds of payload (bombs).

Iodine Tablet: A tablet placed in a canteen of water to purify water procured from rivers, streams, and bomb craters in the field. If the water source was running and flowing, one tablet was sufficient. However, if the water was murky, two or more tablets were necessary.

IP: Instructor pilot.

Iron Triangle: The nickname of an enemy stronghold fifteen miles north of Saigon.

Irregulars: Armed individuals and groups not members of the regular armed forces, police, or other internal security forces.

Ivy Division: Nickname of the 4th Infantry Division. (Patch has four ivy leaves.)

Jack Benny: Jack Benny was a comedian who always claimed he was thirty-nine years old.

JCRC: Joint Casualty Resolution Center.

JCS: Joint Chiefs of Staff.

Jesus Nut: Main rotor retaining nut that holds the main rotor onto the rest of the helicopter. If it came off, only Jesus could help you.

JOC: Joint Operations Center.

Jody or Jake: Slang for the guy who would steal your girl while you were in the military or Vietnam.

Joint Staff: Staff organization for the Joint Chiefs of Staff.

Jolly Green Giant: A USAF heavy lift helicopter that carried troops and/or cargo. Also used for downed pilot rescue.

Jungle Boots: The military jungle boot was developed and designed for use in jungle warfare and hot, wet, and humid environments because the standard US Army black leather combat boot was unsuitable and not durable. The jungle boot had nylon canvas tops and black leather for the toe and heel. Jungle boot features included water drains to drain the water from the inside, removable ventilating insoles, a stainless steel plate inside the boot's sole to protect from punji stakes, and the Panama mud-clearing Vibram outsole with nylon webbing reinforcement on the uppers. Pilots and aircraft crews did not wear jungle boots. They wore the full-leather boot because in an aircraft crash, the nylon would melt and burn human flesh. Later, many outdoor shoe and boot companies adopted several features from the jungle boot.

Jungle Fatigues: Jungle fatigues were also known as tropical fatigues. More commonly known as jungle fatigues, they were adopted in 1963 and were made of 5.5 ounce cotton poplin dyed Army shade olive green (OG) 107 or OG-107. The first-generation jungle fatigues were easily distinguishable because of exposed buttons on the coat and pants. In 1964, the Army Combat Material Command revised the jungle fatigues. The biggest change to the second pattern was the buttons on the coat and pants were covered to prevent snagging on bushes. The third and final pattern of jungle fatigues were introduced to the military in early 1967. These were a simplified version of the second pattern. Minor adjustments included eliminating the side take-up tabs, gas flap, and shoulder epaulettes. A web-slide take-up tab was added to the waist of the pants. The jungle fatigues provided protection from the sun, insects, and flora. The best feature of jungle fatigues was that they dried quickly when wet. Later, civilian outdoor companies adopted and marketed sportswear based on the jungle fatigue material and design.

Jungle Penetrator: A device lowered from a hovering helicopter to extract a person.

JUWTF: Joint Unconventional Warfare Task Force.

Kak Wheel: Carried on a thick string around an RTO's neck to encrypt map coordinates.

KANZUS: Korean, Australian, New Zealand, and US. The acronym was used on several treaties.

Katyusha Rocket: A motorized or towed rocket system the Viet Minh acquired from the Soviet Union. The Viet Minh employed these rockets against the French at Diem Bien Phu. I did not see or hear of them being used against friendlies in South Vietnam.

K-Bar: Combat knife with a six-inch blade and hard leather handle, used mostly by the Marine Corps.

Khe Sanh: An Army, Marine, Special Forces, and ARVN base that was under siege for seventy-seven days.

Khmer Rouge: Cambodian communists.

Khong Biet: Vietnamese for "I don't know" or "I don't understand."

KIA: Killed in Action.

KISS: Keep It Simple Stupid.

Kit Carson Scout: A former Viet Cong or North Vietnam soldier who surrendered and performed scout duties for the US military under the Chieu Hoi program. They were always suspect and watched closely because some could not always be trusted. Some rallied only to work for the Viet Cong (VC) or NVA as spies. Several Kit Carson scouts led US forces into traps or ambushes. Good Kit Carson scouts were recognized and rewarded. The Kit Carson scouts knew the terrain and culture and understood the VC and NVA tactics. They could recognize enemy booby traps, base camps, and assembly areas. Kit Carson scouts also were able to recognize enemy collaborators in villages and the enemy masquerading as civilians.

KKK: Khmer Kampuchea Krom.

Klick: The term for *one thousand meters*; also known as a kilometer; about 0.62 of a mile.

KP: Kitchen police.

La Vay: Beer.

Lai Dai: Vietnamese for "bring to me" or "come to me."

Lam Son 719: The ARVN campaign to curtail southbound supply shipments on the Ho Chi Minh trail. The military incursion into Laos was conducted February 8 to March 24, 1971.

Land Line: Ground wire communications.

Lao Dung: The party founded by Ho Chi Minh in 1951.

Laser: A laser was a sighting device used to mark targets for air strikes. Lasers used invisible light or radiation to identify enemy targets for follow on air strikes.

LAW: Pronounced *law*. The M72 LAW was a light anti-tank weapon, shoulder-fired, 66-millimeter rocket with a one-time disposable fiberglass launcher. Deemed and proven worthless in a jungle environment.

LBJ: Long Bien Jail. LBJ was the US military prison in the South Vietnamese city of Long Binh.

Leatherneck: Term for Marine. Marines wore a leather neckband 1798–1880 for protection of the neck during sword combat.

Leech: Found on land near the water and in the water. They attached themselves to the human body and engorged on blood. You needed a match or lit cigarette to burn and dislodge them from the flesh.

Leg: Non-airborne personnel.

Lifer: A career military person.

Light Up: To fire on the enemy.

Lima Charlie: A communications term meaning "I hear you loud and clear."

Lima: Flying low level in an aircraft about treetop level.

Lima Site 85: A distinctive mountain in Laos used to land helicopters during the war. The mountain was a key location for a tactical air control and navigation TACON beacon that guided US aircraft to targets in the Red River Delta of North Vietnam.

Linebacker I: The US airpower response to the North Vietnamese Spring offensive in 1972. Operation Linebacker I endured and remains a classic aerial interdiction operation conducted May 10 to October 23, 1972.

Linebacker II: The US airpower response to North Vietnam when they walked out of the Paris peace talks. The aerial bombing campaign was conducted December 18–29, 1972, and forced the North Vietnamese back to the negotiation table.

Linkup: Two separate military units coming together and linking up.

Lister Bag: A large plastic or canvas drinking water container about the size of a duffel bag.

Litter: Canvas or nylon stretched over a folding frame, used to transport wounded, sick, or deceased soldiers in a MEDEVAC.

Little People: A term for the Vietnamese people; friendly or enemy.

LLDB: Luc Luong Dac Biet. LLDB was the Vietnamese Special Forces.

LNO: Liaison Officer.

Loach: Light Observation Helicopter.

LOC: Lines of communication (roads, trails, and paths).

Lock n Load: Load a weapon and prepare to fire.

LOH: Pronounced *Loach*. A LOH is a light observation helicopter.

Long Bien: A large military base near Saigon for personnel replacements and supplies.

LP: Listening position/post: A two- or three-man post placed outside the barbwire surrounding a firebase. Each LP would deploy with Claymore mines and trip flares. The LP would have at least one radio, and the soldiers would take turns listening and observing during the night. They were the early warning for the troops inside the perimeter.

LRRP Rations: Pronounced *Lurp*. LRRP rations were a US Army freeze-dried dehydrated field ration developed in the early 1960s during the Vietnam War. They were designed for Special Forces, LRRPs, Pathfinders, and Navy SEALs that operated deep in enemy territory. LRRP rations aided a soldier's mobility and stealth because they were lighter than C rations. LRRP rations required about 1.5 pints of water to cook and reconstitute the meal for eating. In 1968, conventional forces in the field began receiving LRRP rations during their resupply. Soldiers often mixed C rations with their LRRPs for more variety and extra energy. The eight varieties of LRRP meals included the following:

1.	Beef Stew	Good
2.	Chicken and Rice	Good
3.	Beef Hash	Good
4.	Spaghetti	Good
5.	Chicken Stew	The best
6.	Chili	Good
7.	Beef and Rice	Good
8.	Pork and Scalloped Potatoes	Number 10

LRRP: Long Range Reconnaissance Patrol.

LT: Lieutenant.

LTC: Lieutenant Colonel.

LZ: Landing zone.

M-1: World War II vintage American military rifle/carbine. The 8 shot, .30 caliber M-1 was superseded by the M-14 and subsequently by the 20-round .223 caliber M-16.

M-14: A .308 caliber rifle used by US troops in Vietnam until replaced by the M-16.

M-16: A selective fire semiautomatic or automatic rifle carried by the US military and allies in Vietnam beginning in the late '60s. It was a .223 caliber rifle.

M-60: A belt-fed machine gun used by the US military and allies in Vietnam. The M-60 machine gun still remains the best machine gun in the world.

M-72 LAW: Same as the LAW. A light shoulder-fired rocket used by the military in Vietnam. It was garbage and worthless!

M-79: A single-barreled, break-action grenade launcher that fired 40-millimeter projectiles, nicknamed the Chunker, Blooper, Thumper, or Thumpgun.

M-203: An M-16 rifle with a 40-millimeter grenade launcher (chunker) attached underneath.

MA DEUCE: Slang for .50-caliber machine gun.

MAAG: Military Assistance Advisory Group.

MACV: Military Assistance Command, Vietnam. MACV was the US military headquarters just outside Tan Son Nhut Air Base near Saigon.

MACV-SOG: Military Assistance Command Vietnam Studies and Observation Group.

Mad Man Strategy: President Nixon's strategy to bluff the North Vietnamese into believing that he would use nuclear weapons to end the Vietnam War.

Mad Minute: Everyone usually firing to their front for about a minute to confuse the enemy. A mad minute could be conducted any time but was primarily conducted in the early morning at day light prior to the unit moving out.

Mag: An ammunition magazine for the M-16 and M-14. The magazines were two sizes: 20 rounds and 30 rounds.

MAJ: Major.

Mama San: An older Vietnamese woman.

MAROPS: Maritime Operations.

MARS: Military Affiliate Radio Station. One way a person in the rear on a large base camp could call home.

MASH: Mobile Army Surgical Hospital.

MECH: Mechanized infantry.

Medal of Honor: There were 244 awarded during the Vietnam War. Several are pending approval.

MEDCAP: Medical Civilian Action Projects.

MEDEVAC: MEDEVAC was an acronym for medical evacuation, almost always associated with evacuation of casualties by helicopter during or after a battle. Air medical evacuation was introduced and experimented with during World War II and came into its own during the Korean War. The medevac helicopter was an especially important factor in enhancing and sustaining troop morale in the field. Soldiers knew that if they were wounded, the probability was high that they would be transported quickly to a field hospital. MEDEVAC crews on alert could crank the aircraft and lift off in under three minutes. After picking up the wounded, the average time to the nearest hospital or medical facility was fifteen minutes. MEDEVAC crews occasionally had to fly into "hot" landing zones to evacuate the wounded with no gunship or fire support. Under these conditions, the MEDEVAC crews were at great risk of becoming casualties. The use of the helicopter for medical evacuation contributed substantially to the military performance of American and Allied troops during the Vietnam War, and medevacs resulted in many wounded being saved who might otherwise have died. A few MEDEVACs were armed with M-60 machine guns. A synonym for MEDEVAC was Dustoff. Dustoff referred to a MEDEVAC mission and MEDEVAC helicopters after the death of Lieutenant Paul B. Kelley in 1964 while on a MEDEVAC mission. Dustoff was Kelley's radio call sign. Current MEDEVAC tactics, techniques, and procedures used today were perfected in the Vietnam War. The Vietnam War MEDEVAC procedures migrated to the US after the war, wherein major civilian hospitals established air medical evacuation helicopters. Many Vietnam War veterans assisted in establishing these civilian MEDEVAC agencies and also flew the initial civilian MEDEVACs. Some of these old dinosaurs are still flying civilian MEDEVACs.

Mekong Delta: The Mekong Delta covers 26,000 square miles in the IV Corp area of South Vietnam. The terrain is low and is no more than 10 feet above sea level, extremely fertile, and well suited for wetland rice growing. Mangrove swamps and the U Minh Forest are on the southern end. Both were Viet Minh and Viet Cong base areas and strongholds.

Mekong: The longest river in Vietnam and name of the Delta in Southern South Vietnam.

MIA: Missing in action.

MIC: Microphone.

Midway Island Conference: The first meeting between President Thieu of South Vietnam and President Nixon.

MiG: Soviet built jets used by the North Vietnamese Air Force.

MIKE FORCE, MSF: The Mike Force and Special Forces Mobile Strike Force are interchangeable. They are composed of indigenous personnel with US Green Berets as advisers. They were used primarily as a reaction or reinforcing unit.

Mike or Mikes: A Mike is a minute.

MIKE-MIKE: Millimeters, as in "60 Mike Mike" (60 millimeter mortar).

Military time: Military time is a time format using the 24-hour time system that eliminates the need for the designations of "a.m." and "p.m." Military time leaves less room for confusion than standard time. For this reason, military time is the time format preferred by the scientific, medical, and military communities and is also used by railroads and airlines. Several counties use military time. The military and standard conversion chart is depicted below.

Regular Time	Military Time	Military Time Pronunciation
Midnight	0000 or 0000 hours	Zero-zero-zero-zero
1:00 a.m.	0100 or 0100 hours	Zero one hundred hours
2:00 a.m.	0200 or 0200 hours	Zero two hundred hours
3:00 a.m.	0300 or 0300 hours	Zero three hundred hours
4:00 a.m.	0400 or 0400 hours	Zero four hundred hours
5:00 a.m.	0500 or 0500 hours	Zero five hundred hours
6:00 a.m.	0600 or 0600 hours	Zero six hundred hours
7:00 a.m.	0700 or 0700 hours	Zero seven hundred hours
8:00 a.m.	0800 or 0800 hours	Zero eight hundred hours
9:00 a.m.	0900 or 0900 hours	Zero nine hundred hours
10:00 a.m.	1000 or 1000 hours	Ten hundred hours
11:00 a.m.	1100 or 1100 hours	Eleven hundred hours
Noon	1200 or 1200 hours	Twelve hundred hours
1:00 p.m.	1300 or 1300 hours	Thirteen hundred hours
2:00 p.m.	1400 or 1400 hours	Fourteen hundred hours
3:00 p.m.	1500 or 1500 hours	Fifteen hundred hours
4:00 p.m.	1600 or 1600 hours	Sixteen hundred hours
5:00 p.m.	1700 or 1700 hours	Seventeen hundred hours
6:00 p.m.	1800 or 1800 hours	Eighteen hundred hours
7:00 p.m.	1900 or 1900 hours	Nineteen hundred hours
8:00 p.m.	2000 or 2000 hours	Twenty hundred hours
9:00 p.m.	2100 or 2100 hours	Twenty-one hundred hours
10:00 p.m.	2200 or 2200 hours	Twenty-two hundred hours
11:00 p.m.	2300 or 2300 hours	Twenty-three hundred hours

Millipede: A multilegged creepy crawler with a nasty bite.

Minigun: A Gatling-styled machine gun that could shoot six thousand rounds per minute.

Minorities: There were thirty-seven types of diverse American minorities that served in Vietnam.

Mobile Riverine Force: A joint US Army and Navy force established in 1966 for search-and-destroy operations in the Delta. The river assault force used a variety of boats and was occasionally called the Brown Water Navy.

Mohawk: Was a light reconnaissance fixed wing airplane.

Monday Monday Pill: The weekly anti-malaria pill usually taken on Monday.

Monkey Pod Wood: Easy-to-carve wood from which useful objects were made throughout Southeast Asia.

Monkey: A jungle animal used by the mountain tribes as pets or for food.

Monsoon Season: The rainy season in South Vietnam, usually July–September. The majority of rain (90 percent) occurred during this time. The US military hated the monsoon, but the VC and NVA welcomed the monsoon.

Montagnards: Indigenous people of the highlands of South Vietnam. Our best allies and superb fighters! The Viet Cong also had a Montagnard unit. The unit was called the 122 VC Montagnard battalion.

Mopad: A two-wheeled motorbike used by the South Vietnamese as transportation or for hauling cargo.

MOS: Military Occupation Specialty

MOS 01542: Military Occupation Specialty (MOS) of an Army Infantry Officer.

MOS 71542: Denotes US Army Airborne qualified Infantry Officer.

MOS 31542: Denotes US Army Special Forces qualified Infantry Officer.

MOS O5B: MOS of an Army radiotelephone operator.

MOS O5C: MOS of an Army radio teletype operator.

MOS 11B: MOS of an Army enlisted or NCO infantryman.

MOS 11C: MOS of an Army enlisted or NCO indirect fire weapons (Mortars).

MOS 11F: MOS of Army infantry intelligence and operations.

MOS 11H: MOS of Army infantry direct fire weapons (Recoilless Rifle).

MOS 12A: MOS of an Army apprentice engineer.

MOS 67U: MOS of an Army Chinook repairman.

MOS 91A: MOS of an Army medical NCO.

MOS 91B: MOS of an Army medical corpsman (Medic).

Mosquitoes: They were big, were everywhere, and known as the national bird of South Vietnam.

Moua: Rain.

MPC: Military Payment Certificate; also called funny money; used in lieu of US dollar.

MRF: The Mobile Riverine Force consisted of the 2nd Brigade, 9th Infantry Division, and River Assault Flotilla 1.

Mule: The mule is a light Army vehicle. Its nomenclature is a US military M274 truck, platform, utility, 1/2 ton, 4X4, or "Carrier, light weapons, infantry." The mule was introduced in 1956 to supplement the World War II Jeep. There were 11,240 mules produced between their introduction and 1970. Production of the mule ceased in 1970. They were used with airborne forces as platforms for various weapons systems and for carrying men, supplies, and ammunition during the Vietnam War and in other US military operations until 1980. The mule is a completely open and exposed vehicle. It offered absolutely no protection to the driver. It was mainly uses as a cargo carrier and medium-range infantry support vehicle, rather than a tactical vehicle. The mule was phased out from military usage in the 1980s.

Munich Analogy: An analogy that compared attitudes toward the expansion of communism to the 1930s policy of appeasement championed by the British toward the expansion of Nazi Germany. The Munich analogy dominated the thinking of US policymakers on Vietnam who remembered events preceding World War II and resolved not to repeat those mistakes in Indochina.

My Lai Massacre: Most notorious US military atrocity of the Vietnam War. On March 16, 1968, two hundred to five hundred Vietnamese civilians were massacred by US soldiers of Company C, 1st Battalion, 20th Infantry, 11th Infantry Brigade of the 23rd (Americal) Division. Equally infamous was the cover-up of the incident perpetrated by the brigade and division staff.

Nails: A type of warhead attached to a 2.75 inch spin-stabilized, folding-fin, aerial rocket. Called flechettes, this round was used against personnel targets. It was usually launched from helicopter gunships. Nails were also fired in artillery rounds.

Nam: Slang for *Vietnam*; sometimes called Da Nam.

Napalm B: Napalm B was an improvement of the original napalm. Napalm B was composed of 50 percent polystyrene thickness, 25 percent benzene, and 25 percent gasoline. Developed by Dow Chemical company and tested at Eglin Air Force Base Florida. Napalm B burned hotter than ordinary napalm and covered a wider area.

Napalm/Nape: An incendiary used in Vietnam by French and Americans both as defoliant and antipersonnel weapon. Napalm consisted of a flammable organic solvent, usually gasoline, gelled by soap. Delivered by bombs or flamethrower, napalm clung to the surfaces it touched, holding the burning solvent in place on the target.

NCO: Noncommissioned Officer. Pay grades were E-5 through E-9.

NCOC: Noncommissioned officer candidate school. Graduates were known as shake-'n'-bake or whip-'n'-chills.

NCOIC: Noncommissioned officer in charge.

NDP: Night Defensive Position.

Newbie: Any person with less time in Vietnam than the speaker.

NGO: Nongovernment organization.

Nguyen Ai Quoc: Ho Chi Minh's original name.

Nha Trang: A city on the coast of South Vietnam and the headquarters of the 5th Special Forces Group.

Nickel: The number 5.

Nine Rules of US Conduct: These nine rules were listed on a card and issued by MACV to each military person entering South Vietnam.

Nippa Palm: Very sharp-edged palms that grew in very dense concentrations. Nasty; would cut through your jungle fatigues and cut you.

NKP: Nhakon Phanom Air Base, Thailand. NKP was a major communication and electronic warfare base.

NLF: National Liberation Front, officially the National Front for the Liberation of the South.

No Hear, No See, and No Know: The three no's of the North Vietnamese Army.

No Sweat: Slang for "can do easy."

Non La: Conical hat, part of traditional Vietnamese costume.

Noncom: Slang for NCO.

Nook Dau: Vietnamese for *ice*.

Nook: Vietnamese for *water*.

Nouc Mam: Fermented fish and sauce. It stunk! Rice and Nouc Mam was a food staple for the VC and NVA.

NSC: National Security Council.

Number one: Absolutely the best!

Number Ten Thousand: Very, very bad!

Number ten: Absolutely the worst!

NVA: North Vietnamese Army. They were paid the equivalent of $12.00 US dollars per month, no matter what rank. They were very tough, disciplined, and professional.

O & M: Operations and Management.

O Dark Thirty: Very early in the morning, usually the first light of the day.

O2: Cessna Sky Master, also known as push-me-pull-you. The O2 was a FAC aircraft with twin engines; one fore and one aft of cabin section.

OB: Order of Battle. The intelligence known on an enemy force; includes name, organization, capabilities, location, probable course of action, and any other significant intelligence.

OCS: Officer Candidate School.

OD: Olive drab color, standard "Army green" color. Also meant Officer of the Day.

OIC: Officer in charge.

OJT: On-the-job-training.

Old Man: The company commander.

One-O-Five: A 105 millimeter howitzer.

OP: Observation Post. The same as an LP, only employed/deployed during the day.

OPCON: Operational control.

OPLAN: Operations plan.

OPORD: Operations order.

OSI: The Air Force office of Special Investigations.

OSS: Office of Strategic Services.

Otter: A small US Army fixed wing aircraft used for light transport.

OV-10: Also known as a Bronco. A USAF small aircraft used for as a FAC to mark enemy positions for air strikes.

P, Ps': Piasters, the Vietnamese monetary unit.

P-38: A folding metal can opener that was approximately an inch long that came in C rations. You were issued one, and it was usually carried on your dog tags. The term *dog tag* was changed to *identification tags* in the early 1970s.

Pacification: A MACV proposal to win over the local Vietnamese populace through security, economic, and development programs including local self-government to rural South Vietnam.

Pack: A pack is one soldier.

PACOM: Pacific Command.

Paddy Boot: A newly designed and tested boot for use in the Mekong Delta by the 9th Infantry Division and Riverine Forces. The Paddy Boot resembled the jungle boot but had an open weave synthetic material replacing the leather and canvas toe and heel of the jungle boot. The Paddy Boot was intended to reduce foot diseases.

Papa San: An older Vietnamese male.

Paris Peace Accord: Ended the US involvement in Vietnam. The US Senate never ratified this peace agreement.

Parrot's Beak: A major populated area of Cambodia that protruded into South Vietnam where the communists maintained mobile bases for infiltration into South Vietnam.

Pathet Lao: Laotian communist guerillas, brothers to the North Vietnamese communists.

PAVN: People's Army of Vietnam; also the NVA.

PBR: Patrol Boat River.

Peacenick: An opponent of war and one who participates in antiwar demonstrations.

Pedicab: A common mode of transportation in Vietnam with passengers (two) riding in the front.

Peers Report: Commission of inquiry appointed to investigate the My Lai massacre of March 16, 1968. Lt. General William R. Peers headed the investigation. Eventually, several officers and men were charged with murder and other crimes, and more than a dozen officers were charged with suppression of information relating to the incident.

Pentagon Papers: A secret study requested by President Johnson. The US government disclosure fueled the antiwar sentiment in the US. The writers of this document discouraged US involvement in Vietnam.

Perimeter Defense: A perimeter defense is formed when a military unit moving stops and forms a circular perimeter defense. A perimeter defense is also called a wagon wheel. The perimeter defense was developed and perfected in the early stages of the Vietnam War because the enemy would and could attack from any direction. The perimeter defense developed in South Vietnam is widely used by the US military in current contingency operations.

Peter Pilot: The copilot; usually the less experienced pilot in an aircraft.

PF: South Vietnamese Popular Forces.

PFC: Private First Class.

PH: Purple Heart.

Phantom: Slang for the USAF F-4 fast mover.

Phased Departure: The US government term and plan for the military to gradually withdraw from South Vietnam by specified times.

Phoenix: A classified project conducted by Special Forces to destroy the VC and NVA infrastructure.

Phonetic Alphabet: The current phonetic alphabet was developed and used during the Vietnam War. In preceding wars and conflicts, local words were developed and used to spell difficult words. Different military units used different words and created chaos and confusion. A new phonetic alphabet was developed during the Vietnam War to standardize the phonetic alphabet. Examples are depicted below.

Letter	WW II and Korea	Current
A	Apple, Able	Alpha
B	Bacon, Baker	Bravo
C	Cook	Charlie
D	Dog, Duke	Delta
E	Easy	Echo
F	Fox	Foxtrot
G	George, Girl	Golf
H	How, Hit	Hotel
I	Item, Indian	Indigo
J	Jig, Jump	Juliet
K	King, Kill	Kilo
L	Love, Like	Lima
M	Mike, Mad, Mud	Mike
N	Nancy, Nanny	November
O	Oreo, Ox, October	Oscar
P	Pete, Pepper	Papa
Q	Queen, Quack, Quick	Quebec
R	Roger, Rabbit, Rat	Romeo
S	Sugar, Sage	Sierra
T	Tare, Tuba, Ted	Tango
U	Uncle	Uniform
V	Vick, Victory	Victor
W	White, William	Whiskey
X	X-Ray	Xray
Y	Yoke	Yankee
Z	Zebra	Zulu

Plain of Jars: Rolling plain in Xieng Khouang Province of Northern Laos near the border of Vietnam named for a large number of stone urns or jars of unknown origin.

Plain of Reeds: Located primarily in Kien Phong and Kien Tuong Provinces west of Saigon that was a stronghold for communist guerrilla operations throughout the war.

Platoon: The authorized strength of a light infantry platoon was forty-four soldiers. In the Vietnam War, a platoon's average strength was thirty to thirty-four. A platoon is an organizational unit composed of two or more squads. An infantry platoon is commanded by a second or first lieutenant. A senior staff sergeant or platoon sergeant is usually second-in-command.

PLF: Parachute Landing Fall.

PLT: Platoon (see above).

Point or Point Man: The lead soldier in a unit cutting a path through dense vegetation if needed and constantly exposed to the danger of tripping booby traps or being the first in contact with the enemy. His primary mission was front security, seeing the enemy first, and engaging the enemy first.

POL: Petroleum, oil, and lubricants.

Poncho Liner: The poncho liner consists of two layers of nylon surrounding a polyester filling sewed up along the sides and crosswise to ensure a very tough and durable piece of equipment. The lightweight poncho liner was usually used with the poncho to serve as a makeshift sleeping bag. The poncho liner may also be used as a blanket, pillow, shelter, hammock, camo hide site for concealment, jacket liner, seat cushion, mattress, and a variety of other uses. The poncho liner has been a staple for soldiers deployed since it was first introduced in South Vietnam. Many veterans often opt to keep their poncho liner when they leave the military and claim they lost it, and some just pay for their poncho liner rather than turn it in. Civilians love poncho liners because they think they are cool. Poncho liners may be purchased at any reputable military surplus store.

Poncho: An OD/green military issue rain item supposedly waterproof, used to keep personnel dry during rain.

Pop Smoke: A smoke grenade used to mark a target or an LZ/PZ. During extraction, the inbound helicopter crew would call out the color of the smoke they were seeing, normally yellow, purple, or green. This allowed a unit on the ground to confirm for the chopper that the chopper was "on our smoke" because the enemy would occasionally pop a smoke grenade in an effort to lure the chopper to their location. Many units reserved red smoke grenades for marking targets for gunships.

Poppy: A Southeast Asian plant from which heroin was made.

Port: On the left of the ship or boat when facing forward.

POW: Prisoner of war. The vast majority of prisoners were pilots. The USAF had the most POWs.

PRC-25: Nicknamed the Prick 25. A lightweight infantry field radio carried in a rucksack.

PRC-77: Replaced the majority of PRC-25s. The PRC 77 was an upgraded version of the PRC-25. With some modifications, the PRC-77 could provide secure communications.

Profile: A medical excuse from duty.

Project 100,000: Johnson's Great Society program designed to extend the social and economic benefits of military service to disadvantaged or underqualified Americans. Johnson administration officials hoped that by easing military admission standards, underprivileged young men could gain valuable skills, discipline, and useful benefits that would enhance employment opportunities and help stabilize families. The program was a failure and lowered morale and combat efficiency of the military.

Provinces: South Vietnam is divided into these geographic areas.

PSP: Perforated steel plate. Construction panels, about 3'x8', made of plate steel, punched with 2" holes, and having features on the sides for interlocking together. PSP could be linked together to surface a road, airstrip, etc.; or several sheets could be linked into a large plate to form the roof of a bunker, fighting hole, etc., usually covered with sandbags.

PSYOP: Psychological operations.

PT: Physical training.

PTSD: Post-traumatic stress disorder. PTSD is a psychological condition that occurs and reoccurs after a stressful situation such as war, an accident, rape, or robbery. PTSD is characterized by anxiety, depression, guilt, sorrow, shame, death, anxiety, panic, low self-esteem, rage, or any combination of these. Veterans drop the disorder and say PTS.

Pucker Factor: A common term meaning that the more hairy and scary the situation, the more your rear end tightens up.

***Pueblo* Incident:** An incident involving a US Navy vessel captured by North Korea. Originally a light cargo vessel, the *Pueblo* was refitted as a spy ship, equipped with electronic and cryptographic gear, and manned in addition to its regular crew by communications technicians specially trained in electronic intelligence operations.

Puff: Called Puff the Magic Dragon. Puff was a USAF AC-47 or a C-130 fixed wing aircraft equipped with several mini-guns and flares.

Pugil Stick Training: Four-foot staffs with pads used for bayonet sparing and practice.

Punji Stick/Stake: A sharp wooden or metal stick stuck in the ground and meant to be stepped on by non-VC/NVA personnel to impede or stop US and allied military movement.

PUSH: Referring to a radio frequency (i.e., PUSH 71.67, meaning a frequency of 71.67 megahertz).

PX: Post Exchange. PX is a military variety shopping mall similar to Walmart.

PZ: Pickup zone.

QC: QC is Quan Canh in Vietnamese. QC is the Vietnamese military police.

Quad 50s: A World War II vintage antiaircraft weapon used in Vietnam as an antipersonnel weapon. It consisted of four electric solenoid-fired .50 caliber machine guns mounted in a movable turret, sometimes put on the back of a deuce and a half. It was used for firebase and convoy security.

Quantitative Indices: Body count. This is what Robert McNamara used to run and manage the war.

R & R: Rest-and-recreation; also called Rape and Run. R&R was a vacation taken during a one-year duty tour in Vietnam. Out-of-country R & R was at Bangkok, Hawaii, Tokyo, Australia, Hong Kong, Manila, Penang, Taipei, Kuala Lampur, or Singapore.

In-country R & R locations were at Vung Tau, Cam Rahn Bay, or China Beach.

Ranch Hand Operation: The code name for missions involving the aerial spraying of herbicides.

Rand Corporation: A US government–funded think tank that contemplated various scenarios for nuclear war and for the limited war in Vietnam.

Rappel: A person sliding down a rope with or without a snap link.

Rat: A meat staple that was dried and sold in markets throughout Southeast Asia.

RCT: Regimental Combat Team.

RECCE: Reconnaissance.

Recon: Reconnaissance.

Recondo School: A three- to four-week military troop leading school with emphasis on reconnaissance, patrolling, and small unit tactics. It was a brutal, physically and mentally tough, but a superb leadership school for young soldiers.

Recondo: A graduate of Recondo school.

Reconnaissance in Force: The politically correct term for *search and destroy.*

Red Ball: High-speed trails or roads in Vietnam.

Red Cross: The Red Cross had more women stationed in Vietnam than the military.

Red Hats: US advisers to the South Vietnamese Airborne Division.

Red Legs: Slang for *artillerymen.*

RED LZ: Landing zone under hostile fire; also called a hot LZ.

Red River Delta: Geographical heartland of North Vietnam south of Hanoi.

REMF: Rear Echelon Motherf—— that were often not considered real combat soldiers.

Revetment: Sandbagged or earthen barrier.

RF/PF: Regional and Popular Forces of South Vietnam; also known as Ruff-Puffs. Regional Forces and Popular Forces of the Vietnamese military were somewhat similar in makeup and deployment to the American National Guard of the 1960s. They generally operated in the areas where they were recruited.

Not especially effective, militarily, against main-force, enemy units.

Rice Paddy: The common gardening spot for the major crops grown in Vietnam.

Rice: Main product and staple food of the Vietnamese.

RIF: Reduction in Force.

Ring Knocker: A West Point graduate.

River Rat: Navy and Army patrol boats that operated in the rivers and canals in the Delta.

Rock-n-Roll: Fire a weapon on full automatic.

ROE: Rules of engagement. A rather arbitrary set of rules that seemed to consistently change with politics and commanders.

Roger: Radio or verbal term for *understand* or *agree*.

ROK: Pronounced rock. They were military personnel from the Republic of Korea. They were a great unit and fierce fighters.

ROK: Republic of Korea.

Rolling Thunder: Rolling Thunder was the prolonged US bombing campaign against North Vietnam beginning in 1965 and ending in 1968. The campaign was mediocre at best and failed to achieve its strategic goals.

Roman Catholic: The religion of the people that held 95 percent of the wealth but only comprised about 5 percent of the population in South Vietnam.

Rome Plow: Large bulldozer fitted with large blade used to clear jungles and undergrowth.

RON: Rest overnight. RON is a night defensive position for a unit to sleep and rest while conducting operations in the field.

ROTC: Reserve Officer Training Corps/Course: The principle source of commissioned officers in all services.

Round Eye: Slang term used by American soldiers to describe another American or an individual of European descent.

Route 1: Also known as Highway 1. Highway 1 was the road number of the major highway that ran North and South along the seacoast of South Vietnam northward to Hanoi.

RPD: Communist standard issue machine gun.

RPG Screen: Chain-link fence erected around a valuable position to protect it from RPG attack by causing the enemy rocket to explode on the fence and not on the protected bunker etc.

RPG: Russian-manufactured anti-tank grenade launcher; also, rocket-propelled grenade.

RSSZ: Rung Sat Special Zone south of Saigon.

RT: Recon Team.

RTO: Radio Telephone Operator. An RTO carried the radio for his commander.

Ruck: Slang for *rucksack*.

Ruff Puffs: South Vietnamese military units similar to the US National Guard or militia. They were poorly supplied and supported. They were the closest thing to a grassroots rural security force ever developed in the South Vietnamese military.

Rumor Control: An amazingly accurate source of information prior to an event occurring.

Rusk, Dean: US Secretary of State in 1966.

Russia: Supplied 90 percent of war materials used by the VC and NVA. Russia also monitored B-52 bombing runs from Guam to North Vietnam from fishing trawlers in the Pacific Ocean.

RVN: Republic of Vietnam (South).

SAC: Strategic Air Command.

Saddle Up: The command to put on your rucks and prepare to move.

Saigon: The name of the South Vietnamese capital prior to 1975. Present name is Ho Chi Minh City.

SAM: Surface-to-air missile. These SAM sites were located in North Vietnam.

Sand Pan: A small boat and a common means of river transportation for the Vietnamese in the rivers, especially the Delta.

Sapper: An NVA/VC soldier known for their stealth in attacks on fortifications like firebases.

Sappers: NVA or VC demolition commandos that cleared lanes and gaps in the defenses of firebases prior to an NVA attack.

SAR: Search and rescue.

Satchel Charge: A rectangular explosive device with a strap for throwing, usually used by NVA/VC sappers.

Script: See MPC.

SCU: Special Commando Unit.

Sea Huts: Southeast Asia huts. Standard-designed buildings of corrugated tin roofs, walls of horizontal-louvered boards four feet up from the bottom, and screen from the bottom to the roof inside; some were on concrete pads, and some were on blocks; some had sandbags around them about thirty inches from the wall and waist-high; you could walk inside the sandbags from door to door; wooden walkways between buildings so you didn't have to walk in mud; a few sandbags were placed on the roofs to keep them from blowing away in a hurricane. There were literally tens of thousands of these buildings all over Vietnam and Thailand being used for everything—from offices to living quarters to clubs to PXs to "you name it."

SEAL: Navy special warfare force members.

Search and Destroy: *Search and destroy* was an offensive operational term adopted by the US Military Assistance Command in South Vietnam. The term was widely used in South Vietnam from 1965 to 1968. Search-and-destroy missions and operations involved multi-battalions, aggressively maneuvering through known hostile areas of operations to locate and destroy the enemy, cache sites, logistics sites, command and control centers, base camps, training sites and hospitals. Selected units also called these Zippo missions. The term eventually became associated with negative images of burning villages. Search-and-destroy operations and missions were controversial and often criticized. Following the 1968 Tet, the term *search and destroy* was replaced with the term *reconnaissance in force*. The terms search and destroy and reconnaissance in force was replaced in US Army doctrine with movement to contact during the 1970s.

SEATO: Southeast Asia Treaty Organization.

SEMPER FI: This term was adopted by US Marines; short for *semper fidelis*, Latin for "always faithful."

Seventeenth Parallel: The temporary division line between North and South Vietnam established by the Geneva Accords of 1954.

SFG: Special Forces Group.

SFTG: Special Forces Training Group.

Shackle: Communication messages that were encoded, such as unit locations, in order to be able to send the information securely by radio.

Shadow: A C-119 gunship—7.62 and/or 20-millimeter mini-guns mounted in side windows.

Shake-'n'-Bake: See NCOCS.

Shape Charge: An explosive device that detonates in a predetermined direction.

Shawnee: A USAF light CH-21 helicopter.

Shit Hook: Slang for a Chinook helicopter.

Shit: A catchall multipurpose term (i.e., a firefight was "in the shit," a bad situation was "deep shit," to be well prepared and alert was to have your "shit wired tight").

Short, Short-Time, Short-Timer: An individual with little time remaining in Vietnam. An expression that indicated you were close to your DEROS and the Freedom Bird. In your last couple of weeks, you were so "short" you were invisible.

Shotgun/Shotgunner: Armed guard on or in a vehicle who watches for enemy activity and returns fire if attacked.

Sin Loi: Vietnamese slang for "sorry" or "that's too bad" or "tough luck."

SITREP: Situation Report.

Six: The 6 position is directly behind anyone; 12 is to the front, and 6 is to the rear; 6 is also a term for the commanding officer.

Skated: Having it easy; usually in the rear and interchangeable with ghosting.

SKS: Communist Simonov semiautomatic rifle used by the VC/NVA.

Sky Crane: A US Army CH-54 heavy cargo helicopter.

Skyraider: A small A1E USAF prop fixed wing bomber.

Skyhawk: A USAF jet fighter.

Slack or Slack Man: Second man in a patrol, behind the point man; assists the point man in frontal security.

SLAM: Search, locate, annihilate, and monitor.

Sleeper: An undercover agent or a mole.

Slick: A medium utility helicopter used to lift troops or cargo. The Vietnam War became a helicopter war for American forces, and a common way for an infantryman to go into action was by "slick." *Slick* was the term used to refer to an assault helicopter used to place troops into combat during airmobile operations. The UH-1 became the premier helicopter for this. Troops could ride in the wide doors of the aircraft, normally in two rows on each side, and could exit quickly when landing in a hot LZ—a landing zone under fire. Often a UH-1 would not touch down during slick operations; instead, it would hover a couple of feet above the ground while troops evacuated the aircraft. Troops learned to feel the UH-1 "bounce" as it came in quickly and went into a hover, and would exit on the bounce, so that slicks spent very little time close to the ground.

Sling Load: The external cargo load of a helicopter. The load was usually a net full of cargo on the end of a nylon strap attached to the helicopter.

Slope: A derogatory term used to refer to any Asian.

Slow Mover: A propeller-driven AF fighter aircraft.

Smart Bombs: Smart bombs that flew directly to their targets with the aid of a laser sight.

SMF: Special Mission Force.

Smoke Grenade: A cylinder grenade that provides about thirty-forty seconds of smoke. The popular colors were red, green, white, yellow, and purple.

Smoky: A slick that provides a smoke screen for air assaults.

SNAFU: Situation Normal All F—— Up.

Snake: Slang for Cobra gunship.

Sneaky Pete: A US Army Special Forces soldier.

Snoop 'N' Poop: Patrol recon techniques.

SOCOM: Special Operations Command.

SOD: Special Operations Detachment.

SOG: A joint Special Operations Task Force called Studies and Observation Group. Operations were classified.

SOI: Signal Operating Instructions.

Song Tay Raid: A raid conducted against a North Vietnamese prison camp on November 20–21, 1970, to rescue US prisoners of war. The raid was a success, but no US or allied prisoners were found.

SOP: Standard Operating Procedures.

Sortie: One aircraft taking off to conduct the mission for which it was scheduled.

SOS: Slang for s—— on a shingle and usually served for breakfast in mess halls. This breakfast item was chipped beef on toast.

Soul Brother: US black military personnel

South China Sea: The body of water directly east of Vietnam.

Special Forces or SF: US Army soldiers; also called Green Berets, trained in techniques of unconventional warfare.

Spider Hole: An enemy firing from the opening of a small hole in the ground.

Spooky: A USAF AC-47 or C-130 fixed wing aircraft also known as Puff the Magic Dragon and was equipped with several mini-guns.

Squad: A squad is a basic organizational institution in the United States Army and Marine Corps. A staff sergeant usually supervises and leads the squad. An infantry squad in the Vietnam War was composed of two teams of five men each plus the squad leader. A tank and its crew are considered the squad for an armored unit, as is the howitzer or gun and its crew in an artillery unit.

SR-71: A US top secret spy plane used during the Vietnam War.

ST: Spike Team.

Stand Down: Period of rest and refitting in which all operational activity, except for security, is stopped.

Stand To: A time that all soldiers are awake and in a fighting position ready for an enemy attack.

Star Fighter: A USAF F-104 jet fighter.

Star Lifter: A USAF C-141 heavy lift cargo fixed wing jet.

Starlight Scope: A night-vision telescope used by snipers and base camp defense troops to see in the dark.

Stay Behind: An ambush tactic where a small group is left behind after a unit departs the area. The Stay Behind force ambushes the enemy if he enters the departed area.

Steel Pot: The standard military-issued helmet worn by US combat troops.

Step On (s): A confirmed enemy body KIA. The saying was, "If you can step on him, he is a confirmed enemy KIA."

Sterilized: Restore a site to its original condition before moving out of it, particularly if there was a more-than-remote possibility of enemy troops coming across where American troops had been. This included not leaving any C ration cans, bending bushes back that may have been leaned on, brushing the ground free of footprints or other impressions left by sitting or lying, etc. This was not always possible; but it was worth the effort because six (and even ten) men could be, and often were, outnumbered. Success (survival) depended upon not being discovered by their counterparts.

STOL: Short takeoff and landing. C-123 and C-130 aircraft were noted for using little runway when not overloaded.

STRAK: Adherence to strict military code, SOP, regulations, and dress.

Strap Hanger: Anyone who is not a regular member of a unit but is along for the ride and awards.

Super Sabre: A USAF F-100 jet fighter and bomber.

Swift Boat: US Navy patrol boat, designated PCF (patrol craft fast), part of operation Market Time, used to patrol coastal waters and rivers of Vietnam.

TA-50: TA-50 is the clothing and web gear a soldier wears and carries.

Tabasco Sauce: Also called hot sauce. Tabasco sauce was a US condiment used by combat troops to spice up and kill the taste of Cs.

TAC AIR: An air strike flown by fixed wing airplanes.

TACC: Tactical Air Control Center.

Tail Boom: Tail boom is the back 1/3 of a Huey helicopter.

Tally Ho, or Just "Tally": Acknowledgement by a pilot that he had visually acquired another aircraft or ground target that had been called to his attention.

Tangle Foot: Barbed wire stretched in one foot squares about six inches above the ground outside of firebases to impede or stop an enemy ground attack.

TAOR: Tactical area of responsibility.

Tarmac: The hard surface of landing strips, helipads, and asphalt.

TDY: Temporary duty.

Tee-Tee: Very small or little.

Tet: Tet is a traditional Vietnamese Buddhist holiday. Tet celebrates the beginning of the lunar New Year, January 30–31. Tet is Buddha's birthday.

TF: Task Force. A TF is two or more nondifferent units working together.

The World: The USA.

THUD: F-105 aircraft.

Thump Gun: An M-79 grenade launcher; also called Chunker or Thump Gun.

Thunder Chief: A USAFF-105 jet fighter and bomber.

Tiger Fatigues: A tiger-striped uniform worn by US and South Vietnamese elite military units.

TO & E: Table of organization and equipment for US military.

TOC: Tactical Operations Center. The command and control bunker on firebases.

Toe Popper: A US small antipersonnel mine designed to injure the toes or foot.

Tommy Gun: .45-caliber submachine gun, fully automatic shoulder-fired weapon.

Tonkin Gulf Incident: Two US Navy destroyers, the USS *Maddox* and USS *Turner Joy* were fired upon by North Vietnamese PT boats on August 2, 1964. This was justification for President Johnson to conduct limited bombing of the North.

Top: Slang for *top sergeant*; normally the first sergeant of a military unit. Also called First Shirt.

TOT: Time on Target. Multi-artillery units fire at the same target at the same time.

Tracer: A bullet or shell that leaves a trail of smoke or fire when shot or fired.

Tri Border: The area where Vietnam, Cambodia, and Laos meet.

Triage: The medical term meaning "sorting for treatment of wounded," often performed by nurses in South Vietnam.

Trip Flare: An early warning flare placed in front of your position and activated by a trip wire.

Trip Wire: A thin wire used by both sides strung across an area someone may walk through. A trip wire was usually attached to a mine, flare, or booby traps.

Triple Canopy: Very thick jungle. The plants grew at three levels: ground, intermediate, and high levels.

Troops: US troop strength at the peak of the Vietnam War was 542,000 in-country personnel.

TRP: Target Reference Point.

Trung Wee: Vietnamese sergeant.

Tu Dai: A big concern in-country was booby traps. The VC used to warn the locals of booby-trapped areas by posting little wooden signs with those words on it just at the edge of the wood line. Ironically it was pronounced "to die." The term "Tu Dai Area" was used in sitreps.

Tunnel Rat: A small US military person who crawled into and navigated a VC/NVA tunnel or tunnel systems with a flashlight and pistol. Tunnel rats detected tunnel booby traps, engaged the enemy underground, and recorded and mapped tunnel systems.

Two Stepper: The name of the small and deadly snake called bamboo viper. The reputation was you only had two steps after you were bitten before you died.

Typhoon: Asian/Pacific name for a hurricane.

U Minh Forrest: A major VC stronghold south of Saigon and deep in the Delta.

US: United States.

U2: A US spy plane located in Saigon and used to photograph SAM sites and other military targets in North Vietnam.

UA: Unauthorized absence. (See AWOL)

UCMJ: Uniform Code of Military Justice.

Uncle Ho: Ho Chi Minh, the leader of North Vietnam.

USA: United States of America or United States Army.

USAF: United States Air Force.

USAID: US Agency for International Development.

USARPAC: United States Army, Pacific.

USARV: United States Army Vietnam.

USCG: United States Coast Guard.

USMC: United States Marine Corps.

USN: United States Navy.

USO: United Service Organization.

USS *New Jersey*: The only US battleship to serve in the Vietnam War.

USSF: United States Special Forces

UW: Unconventional Warfare.

Valley Forge Hospital: A military hospital in Pennsylvania where many Vietnam War wounded were sent.

VC/NVA: The average VC/NVA soldier was five feet and three inches tall, weighed 115–120 pounds, was Buddhist, and single.

VC: Viet Cong.

VCI: Viet Cong Infrastructure; the VC's cadre. VC leaders, guides, ammo, and food storage site providers, safe house providers, and local tacticians. Render Ineffective the VCI was the second of eight pacification program goals for 1969. The Phoenix Program grew out of this effort.

VFW: Veterans of Foreign Wars.

Viet Bac: Also called northern Viet. A party proposal and concept to create a liberated area in the mountains of northern Vietnam near the Sino-Vietnamese as a base of operations against the French.

Viet Cong: Communist forces fighting the South Vietnamese government.

Viet Minh: Ho Chi Minh created this party in 1941.

Viet Minh: Viet Nam Doc Lap Dong Minh Hoi or the Vietnamese Independence League.

Vietnam Veterans Memorial: After watching the film *The Deer Hunter* in 1979, Vietnam veteran Jan C. Scruggs first conceived the idea for a Vietnam Veterans Memorial. A Yale architectural student, Maya Lin, submitted the winning design. The memorial was built in Constitution Gardens in Washington DC, through private donations from the public, and dedicated in 1982. The memorial is referred to as the Wall.

Vietnam Wall: A monument in Washington DC with the US military KIAs in the Vietnam War listed.

Vietnam Women's Memorial: Diane Carlson Evans, RN, is the founder of this memorial project. She served in the Army Nurse Corps from 1966 to 1972 and was in Vietnam from 1968–69. The sculptor is Glenna Goodacre, who created the Women's Memorial in bronze. The memorial was dedicated over the Veterans Day weekend of November 10–12, 1993, and stands near the Wall.

Vietnamization: The plan by President Nixon to turn the war over to the South Vietnamese while the US withdrew from the war with honor.

Ville: Ostensibly *village*, but used to refer to any group of hooches.

VN: Vietnam.

VNAF: Vietnamese Air Force.

Voo Doo: A US Air Force high-flying jet used to photograph North Vietnam military targets.

VR: Visual reconnaissance.

VT: Variable Time artillery fuse incorporated a small radar transceiver, used to obtain a reliable twenty-meter airburst.

VVA: Vietnam Veterans of America.

WAC: Woman's Army Corp. WACs were US, Army females not in the medical branches. All US Army nurses in South Vietnam were assigned to the 44th Medical Brigade.

Wagon Wheel: A circular perimeter defensive position.

Wait-a-Minute Vines or Bushes: A vine or bush that snagged or caught your boot, leg, web gear, or weapon as you were rucking or patrolling through an area. These vines and bushes impeded soldiers' movement through an area. Although wait-a-minute vines or bushes only slowed you for a few seconds, they were a distraction.

War Powers Act: The US congressional effort in 1973 to limit presidential war-making powers and to ensure more legislative control of the nation's military.

War Zone C: An NVA stronghold north of Tay Ninh. It was the main PAVN approach from Cambodia to Saigon. War Zone C contained command posts, logistic bases, hospitals, and several tunnels.

War Zone D: An NVA and VC stronghold north of Bien Hoa. It was the main avenue of approach from the central part of South Vietnam to Saigon.

Warthog: A-10 aircraft named Warthog because of its "ugly" appearance.

Waste: Kill.

Watergate: Term given to a vast array of abuses of power during Nixon's administration.

Web Gear: Web gear was the cotton/canvas fighting equipment a soldier wore while conducting combat operations in South Vietnam. Every soldier wore his web gear in different arrays while in the field. Web gear includes a pistol belt, two ammunition pouches, two canteens with covers, a first aid packet, and a compass packet. These were held together and supported by an H harness that helped distribute the weight. The initial web gear for soldiers during the early years of the Vietnam War was designed for soldiers carrying the M-14 rifle. The web gear was cotton and heavy. During 1968, new nylon web gear began replacing the passé gear. The new web gear was lighter, and ammunition pouches were redesigned for the new M-16 magazines and had grenade pouches on their sides to store and protect grenades. The H harness was eliminated and replaced with a Y harness. The Y harness eliminated one harness strap.

White Mice: South Vietnamese police. The nickname came from their uniform white helmets and gloves.

White Star: White Star was the US military aid program in Laos from 1955 to 1961 managed by the Program Evaluation Office, which was attached to the economic aid mission in Vientiane. The majority of the military was US Special Forces.

Whitewalls: A military haircut that was short on top and very close on the sides.

WIA: Wounded in action.

Wild Weasel: A USAF aircraft, usually an F-105 that was equipped with special electronic countermeasures that could detect SAM sites. After detection, the pilot would attack the SAM site.

Willie Peter, Willie Pete, Willie Papa, and WP: A white phosphorus grenade, mortar, or artillery round. The best artillery round we could fire. The enemy hated it and usually broke contact immediately.

Wise Men: An informal senior adviser group to President Johnson.

WO: Warrant officer.

Wobbly One: A new warrant officer.

WOC: Warrant officer candidate.

Women: A total of eleven thousand US military women served in Vietnam during the war. They were prohibited from direct combat during the Vietnam War.

- 1Lt Hegwig (Heddy) Orlowski, a nurse, was killed in Vietnam on November 30, 1967, along with two other nurses in the same helicopter crash.
- 36 US Marine women served in Vietnam from 1965 through 1973; the least of any service.
- 8 US military women are on the Vietnam Wall memorial.
- No US military women deserted from service during the Viet War.
- The average age of the US military woman in Vietnam was 23.
- The US Air Force had the most females to serve in Vietnam.
- All US Army nurses were assigned to the 44th Medical Brigade in Vietnam.
- US military female classifications were nurses or administrative.

WORLD: The United States or any place outside of Vietnam.

WWII: World War II.

Xin Loi or Xoine Loi: Pronounced by GIs as *Sin Loy*, meaning "too bad," "tough shit," "sorry about that." The literal translation is "excuse me."

XM-203: The XM-203 was an M-16 with a short M-79 barrel on the bottom that fired 40-millimeter shells. This weapon was experimental and tested in South Vietnam.

XO: Executive officer and usually second-in-command of a military unit.

X-Ray Team: A communications relay unit.

Yankee Station: A fixed point in international waters off the coast of North Vietnam in the South China Sea, located at 17 degrees 30' north and 108 degrees 30' east. Yankee Station was the staging area for the US Navy's Seventh Fleet Attack Carrier Strike Force.

Yard(s): Montagnard soldiers.

Yippee: Yippee was the Youth International Party. They were the radical antiwar group led by Jerry Rubin and Abbie Hoffman.

Zama: A military hospital in Camp Zama, Japan. Usually the first stop of a MEDEVAC aircraft returning to the United States.

Zap: Kill.

Zippo: Flamethrower. Also refers to the popular cigarette lighter of that brand name and specified search-and-destroy missions.

ZULU: The phonetic pronunciation of the letter *Z*.

4 Deuce: A US heavy mortar.

7 Mountains: An NVA and VC stronghold on the Cambodian border in IV Corps. The area consisted of seven mountains.

.50 Cal: US military heavy machine gun.

.51 Cal: A communist heavy machine gun, 1 mm larger than US .50 cal.

81: A US medium mortar.

122-Millimeter Rocket: A Viet Cong (VC or North Vietnamese Army [NVA]) rocket with a range of about twenty-two kilometers.

201 File: US Army soldier personnel file.

A Vignette to Demonstrate Our Lingo

Saddle up. We are humping three klicks after resupply to a PZ to conduct a CA. The CO has designated us as first in order of march. Roberts point, Hartley slack, Smith compass, and Roy drag. Chunkers get a double basic load. RTOs get extra batteries, monitor the horn, and ensure we are on the old man's push. No strap hangers. Idiot Sticks will be tied down; two LAWs per man. Five slicks and two snakes will meet us at 1030 on the PZ. C & C bird will be on station. The ACL for the slicks will be six packs. Squads will cross load. We will LIMA LIMA to the LZ in the ASHAU. ETA to LZ will be about fourteen mikes. If the LZ is hot and there is beaucoup Charlie, we will light them up and go into a wagon wheel. I will get on the horn and request BUFF, Spooky, Fast Movers, and Willie Peter from the firebase. After contact, we will do some clover leafs. Do not cross the Blue Line or Red Ball on patrol. Search for some Chicom weapons and capture some NVA. No diddy bopping or ghosting. If no contact, we will hump about two klicks, move into the triple canopy, and maybe link up with the CIDG for a search-and-destroy operation. The CIDG will have a yard company attached. Report any WIAs/KIAs and POWs to me immediately. MEDEVAC is about twenty mikes away. All WIA/KIAs will go to the MASH. Watch out for two steppers, Bouncing Betties, and toe poppers. Do not lose your comic book. Captured P will be turned in. About an hour prior to EENT, we will move and select a RON site. We will use the buttonhook technique to move into the RON site. Each squad will post an OP/LP immediately and then put out Claymores and trip flares. First squad will place an AA on the trail to their front. Second squad put nails in the 90. No Cs prior to dark, and no chest breakers after dark. Stand to is O-Dark Thirty. Be prepared for a mad minute twenty minutes later. Cherries will stay with their squad leader during the OP. Prepare your AARs and SITREPs prior to dark. We have a new butter bar, and he will issue a new OPORD at 0800 tomorrow. I will recommend a few ARCOMs if needed for the operation. We have a Chieu Hoi attached and BN 4 deuces are in direct support. Top will be with us. Questions.

APPENDIX B

Principals and Key Personnel in/of the Vietnam War

You can't tell the players without a scorecard.

South Vietnam

Bao Dai: Dai was crowned emperor by France in 1925 at age twelve. He collaborated with the Japanese during the Second World War, served Ho Chi Minh briefly as an adviser in 1945, and was restored as chief of state by the French. He was never interested in governing; he was supplanted in 1955 by Ngo Dinh Diem. For nearly three decades, the former emperor was attended by a volunteer equerry, Bui Tuong Minh, nicknamed Tommy.

Bui Diem: Diem was a son of a scholarly northern family, served as South Vietnam's ambassador to the United States from 1966 to 1972. During the 1968 election, he worked with Anna Chennault to persuade Thieu that Nixon would offer him better peace terms than Humphrey.

Duong Van Minh: Minh was known as Big Minh because he stood six feet tall, led the Revolutionary Military Council that overthrew Diem in November 1963. He himself was sent into exile after the January 1964 coup of Nguyen Khanh.

Hoang Duc Nha: Nha was educated in the United States and became an influential adviser to his cousin Nguyen Van Thieu.

Ngo Dinh Diem: Diem returned to Saigon from self-imposed exile in the United States to become prime minister of South Vietnam in 1954 after the Geneva agreement divided the country. He replaced Emperor Bao Dai as head of government in 1955 and thwarted the planned unification elections of 1956. After US complaints about his autocratic rule, he was deposed by a junta of his generals and murdered on November 1963 along with Ngo Dinh Nhu, his brother and adviser.

Ngo Din Nhu: Nhu was Diem's younger brother. He became unpopular with the South Vietnamese people and with Americans in Washington and the US embassy in Saigon for his influence over Diem.

Nguyen Cao Ky: Ky was born in 1930 and became prime minister of South Vietnam in 1965 and its vice president under Nguyen Van Thieu in 1967. Trained by the French military, he broke with Thieu in 1971 and fled the country in April 1975.

Nguyen Khanh: Khanh overthrew the leaders of the coup against Diem three months later in January 1964. He proved to be an inept leader and was sent into exile early in 1965.

Nguyen Van Thieu: Thieu was a general trained in the US who fought for the French and served as president of South Vietnam from 1967 until the communists took the country in 1975.

Tran Kim Tuyen: Tuyen was a Catholic with medical and law degrees from French schools in Hanoi. He was sent South in 1954 to run Nhu's secret police. Exiled and then jailed for plotting against Diem, he lived until 1975 under house arrest in Saigon before escaping to England.

Tri Quang: Quang was a Buddhist dissident in South Vietnam and helped to bring down Diem in 1963. He was also a leader in the Struggle Movement against Ky in 1966. The struggle failed, and he withdrew to the An Quang pagoda in Saigon.

North Vietnam

Bui Tin: Tin was a fifty-year-old journalist who was also an officer in North Vietnam's PAVN, accepted Minh's surrender at the Independence Hall on April 30, 1975.

Dang Vu Hiep: Hiep was a veteran of Dien Bien Phu and a political officer in the North Vietnamese Army. He served as an adviser to the Viet Cong in the Central Highlands where he remained for ten years. In 1965, Hiep took part in the attacks on Pleiku on February 7 and Qui Nhon barracks three days later.

Ho Chi Minh: Minh was born in 1890 with the name of Nguyen Sinh Cung in the central Vietnamese province of Nghe Tinh. He joined the French Communist Party in 1920 and formed the Indochinese Communist Party in the early 1930s and a nationalist alliance called the Viet Minh in May 1941. The founder of the Democratic Republic of Vietnam, Ho was revered in the North for his commitment to independence and unity.

Le Duan: Duan first enlisted in Ho's youth movement in 1928 and rose in the communist ranks. He replaced Truong Chinh as acting general secretary of the Hanoi politburo in 1956, the same year his pamphlet "The Path of Revolution in the South" inspired the resistance to Diem. Even before Ho's death, Le Duan had emerged as the driving force for southern independence.

Le Duc Tho: Tho became Hanoi's leading negotiator at the Paris peace talks. He declined the honor when he and Kissinger were awarded the 1973 Nobel Peace Prize because, he said, "peace had not yet been established."

Lu Doan Huynh: Huynh joined Giap's Army as a seventeen-year-old and held posts in Hanoi's Foreign Ministry in Southeast Asia before becoming an intelligence analyst for the Department of US Affairs. Huynh was a member of the five-person team that drafted documents for peace talks with the United States.

Nguyen Chi Thanh: Thanh commanded North Vietnamese operations in South Vietnam from 1965 until he died of a heart attack in July 1967.

Nguyen Huu Tho: Tho was a southerner and was named chairman of the National Liberation Front in December 1960. He took his orders from the Hanoi politburo.

Nguyen Khac Huynh: Huynh was an analyst in Hanoi with the Foreign Ministry when communist soldiers entered Saigon in 1975.

Nguyen Minh Vy: Vy joined with Ho in 1945 and governed the Fifth Zone during the war with France, overseeing the four coastal provinces south of Hue.

Nguyen Thi Dinh: Dinh spent three years in the French Poulo Condore prison, where her husband had died. She led an early resistance to Diem in the Mekong Delta's Ben Tre province. In 1965, she became deputy commander of the South Vietnam Liberation Forces, the highest combat position held by a woman in the Viet Cong.

Nguyen Thi Ngoc Dung: Dung was an effective speaker on behalf of the National Liberation Front throughout Europe. She ran away in the mid-1940s to join the resistance to the French in the Mekong Delta. After marrying and having children, she spent the next decades separated from her family because she worked for the Vietminh and then the Viet Cong.

Ta Minh Kham: Kham was born in Ben Tre, South Vietnam, and joined Ho's forces before he was twenty. He fought the French for nine years and became commander of a Viet Minh battalion. After studying at the Beijing Military Institute from 1954–1957, Kham was sent to South Vietnam in 1961 to organize resistance to Diem and the Americans.

Phan Van Dong: Dong was North Vietnam's premier from 1955 to 1975 and the premier of the Socialist Republic of Vietnam until 1986. With Ho and Giap, he ruled the country until Le Duan became increasingly influential.

Tran Bach Dang: Dang was the ranking communist political officer in Saigon and helped to plan the Tet Offensive of 1968.

Tran Quang Co: Co was a twenty-six-year-old Viet Minh at Dien Bien Phu and was assigned to the camp with Giap's prisoners of war. From 1966–1968, Co assisted in drafting Hanoi's negotiating terms to prepare for a possible peace conference.

Tran Van Tra: Tra was a military leader of the National Liberation Front and was a lieutenant general in the North Vietnamese Army. As chairman of the Central Office for South Vietnam (COSVN), he coordinated the assault on Saigon during the 1968 Tet Offensive.

Truong Chinh: Chinh was born Dan Xuan Khu but changed his name—because Truong Chinh meant "long march"—to show his solidarity with Mao. After making a bloody botch of Hanoi's land reform program, he was forced to step down as general secretary of the Indochinese Communist Party.

Van Tien Dung: Dung replaced Giap as commander of the People's Army of Vietnam and was the commanding general who led the PAVN to victory in April 1975.

Vo Nguyen Giap: Giap was born in 1911 and was the founder and commander of the People's Army of Vietnam until 1972. Giap was a member of the Communist Party from his midteens and led the siege that defeated the French at Dien Bien Phu.

Xuan Thuy: Thuy was Hanoi's foreign minister in the mid-1960s and then chief delegate to the Paris peace talks although Le Duc Tho was the more powerful figure.

Cambodia

Lon Nol: Nol with Sirik Matak organized the successful coup against Norodom Sihanouk in March 1970. His troops were defeated by the Khmer Rouge communist rebels, and Nol fled to Indonesia when the communists took Cambodia on April 17, 1975.

Pol Pot: Pot was head of the communist Khmer Rouge. He was born Saloth Sar to a family connected to Sihanouk's royal line. His forces defeated Lon Nol in 1975, and as prime minister, Pol Pot's policies were responsible for the death of 1.5 million Cambodians. His regime was overthrown by an Army from the Socialist Republic of Vietnam in 1978.

Norodom Sihanouk: Sihanouk was a former prince of Cambodia and abdicated the throne in 1954 to form a popular political party. After his overthrow in 1970, Sihanouk went into exile in Beijing and supported the Khmer Rouge.

Laos

Kong Le: Le was a Lao Army captain and headed the coup in August 1960 that overthrew the government backed by the United States and returned neutralist Prince Souvanna Phouma to power.

Phoumi Nosavan: Nosavan was a right-wing minister of defense supported in the late 1950s by the CIA.

Souphanouvong: Souphanouvong was the younger half brother of Prince Souvanna Phouma and became a political leader of the Pathet Lao communist movement.

Souvanna Phouma: Phouma was prime minister of Laos at various times from 1951 to 1975. He tried to steer a neutral course but permitted US bombing of communist supply routes from 1963 to 1973.

China

Mao Zedong: Zedong was president of the People's Republic of China and broke with the Soviets in the 1960s and welcomed Richard Nixon to China on February 21, 1972.

Zhou Enlai: Enlai was premier of the People's Republic of China for twenty-seven years from 1949 until his death in 1976. He endorsed an unfavorable settlement for the North Vietnamese at the Geneva conference of 1954.

USSR

Leonid Brezhnev: Brezhnev replaced Nikita Khrushchev as first secretary-general of the Soviet Communist Party in 1964 and retained the position until his death in 1982. To offset China's military aid to North Vietnam, Brezhnev promoted and increased the Soviet Union's support in high-technology equipment as radar and surface-to-air missiles.

Anatoly Dobrynin: Dobrynin was Soviet ambassador to the United States from 1962 to 1986 and was a go-between for Robert Kennedy and the Kremlin during the Cuban missile crisis of 1962.

Nikita Khrushchev: Khrushchev was secretary-general of the Soviet Communist Party and premier of the USSR from 1958 to 1964. He was removed and replaced by Brezhnev and Kosygin.

Alexei Kosygin: Kosygin was prime minister of the Soviet Union from 1964 to 1980. He traveled to Hanoi early in 1965 to urge that the North Vietnamese negotiate with the United States, but the US bombing of North Vietnam after the Viet Cong attack on Pleiku led Kosygin to approve military aid for the North.

United States

Creighton Abrams: Abrams replaced William Westmoreland as commander of the Military Assistance Command Vietnam in July 1968 and oversaw withdrawal of US forces. He was selected to be the Army chief of staff in 1972.

Dean Acheson: Acheson was appointed Truman's secretary of state in 1949 and was a hardline adviser to both Kennedy and Johnson as one of the Wise Men, but on March 26, 1968, he reversed his policy and called for negotiation with North Vietnam.

Everett Alvarez Jr.: Alvarez was a Navy lieutenant and was the first US pilot taken prisoner by the North Vietnamese.

George W. Ball: Ball was US undersecretary of state from 1961 to September 1966 and was the most outspoken dissenter from the escalations of Kennedy and Johnson.

Chester Bowles: Bowles was US undersecretary of state in 1961 but dislodged from that job. He was made a roving ambassador and then sent for his second tour as ambassador to India from 1963 until 1969. Bowles was punished by the Kennedy brothers for his public criticism of the Bay of Pigs invasion in Cuba.

McGeorge Bundy: Bundy was the president's assistant for national affairs under Kennedy and until February 28, 1966, under Johnson. A former dean of the faculty at Harvard College, Bundy was a major proponent of the Vietnam War.

William L. Calley Jr.: Calley was a twenty-five-year-old second lieu-tenant from the 1st Battalion, 32nd Infantry of the American

Division when he oversaw the massacre of Vietnamese civilians on March 16, 1968. Convicted by a court-martial of premeditated murder and sentenced to life in prison, Calley benefited from Nixon's intervention and was paroled in November 1974.

Clark Clifford: Clifford was an attorney who advised Johnson privately and became secretary of defense in 1968. He almost immediately recommended disengaging from the war.

William Colby: Colby was the CIA's Saigon station chief from 1959 to 1962. He became involved in the late 1960s in civilian operations and also the Phoenix anti-guerrilla program. He was appointed CIA director in 1973.

Chester Cooper: Cooper was a CIA analyst until 1964 when he moved to the White House as a member of the National Security Council. He worked with Averell Harriman repeatedly to end the war through negotiation.

Allen Dulles: Dulles was director of the CIA from 1953 until Kennedy replaced him after the Bay of Pigs.

John Foster Dulles: Dulles was Eisenhower's secretary of state and organized the Southeast Asia Treaty Organization. He resisted the Geneva conference of 1954 but became an enthusiastic backer of Diem.

Elbridge Durbrow: Durbrow was a career foreign service officer. He was appointed ambassador to South Vietnam by Eisenhower in 1957. Kennedy replaced him with Frederick Nolting in 1961.

Daniel Ellsberg: Ellsberg went to South Vietnam in 1961 and returned from 1966 to 1967 as a senior liaison officer to the American embassy and the following year as assistant to the ambassador. Later Ellsberg turned against the war and leaked the documents known as the *Pentagon Papers* to the *New York Times*. Charged with conspiracy, theft, and violation of espionage laws, Ellsberg was freed when the federal judge found the White House break-in of Ellsberg's psychiatrist's office to be government misconduct.

Michael Forrestal: Forrestal was appointed by Kennedy to the staff of the National Security Council in 1962 and was involved in drafting the August 24, 1963, cable to Lodge that set off acrimonious debate in the White House.

J. William Fulbright: Fulbright was a Democrat senator from Arkansas and chairman of the Senate Foreign Relations Committee. He won approval for the Tonkin Gulf Resolution in August 1964, but by early 1966 chaired hearings to give a platform to antiwar spokesmen.

John Kenneth Galbraith: Galbraith was a Harvard economist appointed as ambassador to India by Kennedy. He was an early witty critic of the Vietnam effort.

Leslie Gelb: Gelb was a deputy director of the Defense Department's policy planning and was assigned by McNamara in June 1967 to write a history of the US involvement in Vietnam.

Arthur J. Goldberg: Goldberg was named secretary of labor and then associate Supreme Court justice by Kennedy. Johnson persuaded him to leave the Court in 1965 to replace Adlai Stevenson as ambassador to the United Nations.

Ernest Gruening: Gruening was a Democrat senator from Alaska. He joined Wayne Morse of Oregon in casting the two votes against the Tonkin Gulf Resolution of 1964.

Philip Habib: Habib was a counselor for political affairs in the American embassy in Saigon in 1965. He briefed the Wise Men at the March 1968 meeting that left most of them opposed to the war. In 1968, Habib went to Paris as part of Harriman's team and stayed on under Nixon until July 1970.

Alexander M. Haig: Haig was wounded while commanding a battalion in Vietnam in the midsixties. As Kissinger's military aide in the National Security Council, Haig was rapidly promoted by Nixon and finally named White House chief of staff in April 1973.

Paul D. Harkins: Harkins became the first commander of the US Military Assistance Command, Vietnam on February 13, 1962, when Kennedy expanded the US military role in South Vietnam. His support for Diem was complete and uncritical.

W. Averell Harriman: Harriman was a former governor of New York and was appointed by Kennedy as ambassador-at-large and, later in 1961, as assistant secretary of state for Far Eastern affairs. He moved on under Kennedy and Johnson to become undersecretary of state for political affairs and ambassador-at-large for Southeast Asia. Harriman negotiated the neutrality for Laos in Geneva in 1962 and headed the first Paris peace team in 1968.

Roger Hilsman: Hilsman was active in counterinsurgency in World War II. He warned against reliance on only-military solutions in Vietnam. From his posts in the State Department, Hilsman worked to replace Diem and drafted the August 24, 1963, memorandum that was seen as encouraging a military coup.

Harold K. Johnson: Johnson was jumped past forty-three senior generals by President Johnson to replace General Earle Wheeler in July 1964 as Army chief of staff. The following year, General Johnson was among those who recommended sending American combat troops to South Vietnam. General Westmoreland replaced him as Army chief of staff in 1968.

Lyndon B. Johnson: Johnson succeeded to the presidency by the assassination of President Kennedy. He escalated the war in 1965 both by bombing North Vietnam and by introducing US combat troops in the South. Antiwar sentiment led him to announce on March 31, 1968, that he would not be a candidate for reelection.

U. Alexis Johnson: Johnson was a US Foreign Service officer. He went to Saigon as Maxwell Taylor's deputy ambassador in 1964.

John F. Kennedy: Kennedy was president of the United States from 1961 to 1963. He expressed misgivings about the war, but his administration increased the number of American advisers in South Vietnam from seven hundred to fifteen thousand.

Robert Kennedy: Robert Kennedy was John Kennedy's brother and his attorney general. He was elected to the US Senate from New York in 1964 and was a candidate for president.

Henry Kissinger: Kissinger was born in Germany in 1923. He was teaching international relations at Harvard University when Richard Nixon chose him as his national security adviser in 1969. After years of negotiation, Kissinger and North Vietnam's Le Duc Tho signed a peace agreement in Paris on January 27,

MAJOR (RETIRED) STEVEN E COOK

1973. In September, Kissinger replaced William P. Rogers as secretary of state.

William Kohlmann: Kohlmann was assigned to the CIA's Saigon station for much of the 1960s, cultivating Buddhists and other political leaders on behalf of the agency.

Robert W. Komer: Komer was a senior analyst with the CIA and went to Saigon in 1966 as Johnson's special assistant for pacification. Before his departure in 1968, Komer oversaw the Phoenix Program.

Melvin R. Laird: Laird was a politically adept Wisconsin congressman. He was Nixon's secretary of defense from 1968 to 1973. Laird framed the US effort to return the brunt of the fighting to the ARVN Vietnamization.

Edward G. Lansdale: Lansdale was a former advertising man. He worked for the CIA in the Philippines before going to South Vietnam in June 1954 to bolster Diem's government.

Curtis LeMay: LeMay was US Air Force of chief of staff from 1961 to 1965. He was an early proponent of bombing the North and said in late 1963 that the US should bomb the country "back into the Stone Age." LeMay became George Wallace's vice president candidate in 1968.

Lyman Lemnitzer: Lemnitzer predicted the invasion into the South by the North Vietnamese. He was chairman of the Joint Chiefs of Staff from 1960 to 1962. In 1962, Kennedy named him NATO commander.

Henry Cabot Lodge Jr.: Lodge replaced Frederick Nolting as ambassador to South Vietnam. After supporting the coup that led to Diem's murder, Lodge returned to the US in 1964 to work against the Republican nomination of Barry Goldwater. He went back for a second stint as ambassador in 1965–1966. Nixon sent him in 1969 to replace Harriman as head of the US delegation at the Paris peace talks.

Graham A. Martin: Martin replaced Ellsworth Bunker and was the last US ambassador to South Vietnam. Martin's refusal to heed warnings about North Vietnamese intentions thwarted an orderly withdrawal of Americans and friendly Vietnamese from the country and led to the chaos of late April 1975.

Eugene J. McCarthy: McCarthy was a Minnesota senator and challenged Johnson for the Democrat Party's nomination in 1968 as an antiwar candidate. His strong support in the New Hampshire primary encouraged Robert Kennedy to enter the race.

John McCone: McCone was director of the CIA from 1961 to 1965. He strongly supported Diem and arguing after the coup that a stable government in the South was unlikely. He also opposed retaliation bombing raids against North Vietnam.

George McGovern: McGovern was a Democrat senator from South Dakota and was a leading critic of the Vietnam War. When he ran for president in 1972, McGovern was easily defeated by Nixon.

Robert S. McNamara: McNamara was briefly the president of Ford Motor Company. He served as secretary of defense from 1961 to 1968. Publicly optimistic, he slowly became convinced that the war could not be won in South Vietnam.

John T. McNaughton: McNaughton was McNamara's influential assistant secretary of defense for international security affairs. He backed the bombing of North Vietnam and increased American military involvement. Before his death in a plane crash in July 1967, he had decided losing South Vietnam would not jeopardize the US position in the world.

John Mitchell: Mitchell was Nixon's US attorney general until he resigned to become chairman of his reelection campaign. In 1975, he served eighteen months in prison for his role in the Watergate break-in and cover-up.

Wayne L. Morse: Morse was a Democrat from Oregon and was the only senator to vote with Senator Ernest Gruening against the Gulf of Tonkin Resolution in 1964.

Frederick E. Nolting: Nolting was ambassador to South Vietnam from 1961 to 1963. He was heavily criticized for apologizing for Diem's shortcomings.

John H. Richardson: Richardson went to Saigon as CIA station chief in 1962. Lodge had him recalled on October 5, 1963, for being too close to Diem and Nhu.

Franklin Delano Roosevelt: Roosevelt was US president from 1933 to 1945. He spoke of making Indochina a trusteeship leading to independence but died before implementing his vision.

Walter W. Rostow: Rostow worked on McGeorge Bundy's national security team from 1961 until he was named to head the policy planning office at the State Department.

Dean Rusk: Rusk was assistant secretary of state for Far Eastern affairs during the Truman administration. As secretary of state, he ceded strategy for Vietnam to Robert McNamara at the Pentagon.

James Schlesinger: Schlesinger served as Nixon's CIA director until he replaced Elliot Richardson, who had briefly succeeded Laird as secretary of defense in 1973.

Ulysses S. Grant Sharp Jr.: Sharp was deeply committed to the Vietnam War. He succeeded Admiral Harry Felt in June 1964 as the Navy's Commander in Chief, Pacific before retiring in 1968.

William H. Sullivan: Sullivan was a career foreign service officer. He was Harriman's chief aide at the 1962 Geneva conference, which neutralized Laos. Later he became the US ambassador to Laos.

Maxwell D. Taylor: Taylor was a four-star Army general brought back from retirement by President John Kennedy. He chaired the Joint Chiefs of Staff before Johnson appointed him as ambassador to South Vietnam in 1964.

Cyrus R. Vance: Vance was secretary of the Army from 1962 to 1963 and then McNamara's deputy secretary of defense until 1967.

John Paul Vann: Vann was disgusted with the cautious approach of Diem's generals to fighting the Viet Cong. He was a senior US Army official in the Mekong Delta who provided newsmen in the early 1960s with accurate accounts of ARVN failures.

William Westmoreland: Westmoreland replaced General Harkins and commanded US forces in South Vietnam from 1964 to

1968; then he became the US Army chief of staff for the next four years.

Earle G. Wheeler: Wheeler was appointed US Army chief of staff in 1962 by Kennedy. Two years later, Johnson appointed him to the office of chairman of the Joint Chiefs. He supported sending more American combat troops and increasing the bombing of the North.

Questions for Reflection

1. Compare and contrast Bao Dai to Ngo Dinh Diem.
2. Compare and contrast Ho Chi Minh to LeDuan.
3. Describe General Vo Nguyen Giap's leadership style.
4. What role did Zhou Enlai have at the Geneva conference in 1954 that had a negative impact against the North Vietnamese?
5. Describe the aid that Alexei Kosygin provided to North Vietnam.
6. Compare and contrast General Westmoreland's leadership style to General Abrams.
7. Why did President Nixon parole Second Lieutenant Calley?
8. Who was Daniel Ellsberg, and why was he charged with conspiracy?
9. Who was Henry Kissinger, and what was his role during the Paris Peace Accords?
10. Who was Robert S. McNamara, and why did he suddenly stop supporting the war?

APPENDIX C

Chronological Events of the Vietnam War

These early years set the stage for the Second Indochina War.

1944

Communist activist Ho Chi Minh secretly returns to Vietnam after thirty years in exile and organizes a nationalist organization known as the Viet Minh. After Japanese troops occupy Vietnam during World War II, the US military intelligence agency Office of Strategic Services (OSS) allies with Ho Chi Minh and his Viet Minh guerillas to harass Japanese troops in the jungles and to help rescue downed American pilots.

1945

March 9: Amid rumors of a possible American invasion, Japanese oust the French colonial government, which had been operating independently, and seize control of Vietnam, installing Bao Dai as their puppet ruler.

June–July: Severe famine strikes Hanoi and surrounding areas, eventually resulting in two million deaths from starvation out of a population of ten million. The famine generates political unrest and peasant revolts against the Japanese and remnants of French colonial society. Ho Chi Minh capitalizes on the turmoil by successfully campaigning for his Viet Minh movement.

July: Following defeat of Nazi Germany, World War II Allies including the US, Britain, and Soviet Union hold the Potsdam Conference in Germany to plan the postwar world. Vietnam is considered a minor item on the agenda. In order to disarm the Japanese in Vietnam, the Allies divide the country in half at the 17th parallel. Chinese Nationalists will move in and disarm the Japanese north of the parallel while the British will move in and do the same in the South. During the conference, representatives from France request the return of all French prewar colonies in Southeast Asia. Their request is granted. The countries of Laos, Vietnam, and Cambodia will once again become French colonies following the removal of the Japanese.

August: Japanese surrender unconditionally. Vietnam's puppet emperor, Bao Dai, abdicates. Ho Chi Minh's guerrillas now occupy Hanoi and proclaim a provisional government.

September: Japanese sign the surrender agreement in Tokyo Bay formally ending World War II in the Pacific. On this same day, Ho Chi Minh proclaims the independence of Vietnam by quoting from the text of the American Declaration of Independence, which has been supplied to him by the OSS: "We hold the truth that all men are created equal, that they are endowed by their Creator with certain unalienable rights, among them life, liberty and the pursuit of happiness." This immortal statement is extracted from the Declaration of Independence of the United States of America in 1776. These are undeniable truths.

Ho declares himself president of the Democratic Republic of Vietnam and pursues American recognition but is repeatedly ignored by President Harry Truman.

September: Reclaiming Indochina colonies after World War II, France rebuffs demands for independent Vietnam but allows Democratic Republic of Vietnam, founded by revolutionary leader Ho Chi Minh, to become a "free state" within the French Union.

September 13: British forces arrive in Saigon, South Vietnam.

September: French troops return to Vietnam; battles break out between French and communist Viet Minh and Chinese Nationalist forces.

September 14: In North Vietnam, 150,000 Chinese Nationalist soldiers, consisting mainly of poor peasants, arrive in Hanoi after looting Vietnamese villages during their entire march down from China. They then proceed to loot Hanoi.

September 22: In South Vietnam, 1,400 French soldiers released by the British from former Japanese internment camps enter Saigon aided by French civilians and go on a deadly rampage, attacking Viet Minh and killing innocent civilians including children. An estimated twenty thousand French civilians lived in Saigon.

September 24: In Saigon, Viet Minh successfully organized a general strike shutting down all commerce along with electricity and water supplies. In a suburb of Saigon, members of Binh Xuyen, a Vietnamese criminal organization, massacre 150 French and Eurasian civilians including children.

September 26: The first American death in Vietnam occurs, during the unrest in Saigon, as OSS officer Lieutenant Colonel Peter Dewey is killed by Viet Minh guerillas who mistook him for a French officer. Before his death, Dewey had filed a report on the deepening crisis in Vietnam, stating his opinion that the US "ought to clear out of Southeast Asia."

October: French soldiers numbering thirty-five thousand, under the command of World War II General Jacques Philippe Leclerc, arrive in South Vietnam to restore French rule. Viet Minh immediately begin a guerrilla campaign to harass them. The French then succeed in expelling the Viet Minh from Saigon.

1946
The Beginning of the First Indochina War

February: The Chinese under Chiang Kai-Shek agree to withdraw from North Vietnam and allow the French to return in exchange for French concessions in Shanghai and other Chinese ports.

March: Ho Chi Minh agrees to permit French troops to return to Hanoi temporarily in exchange for French recognition of his Democratic Republic of Vietnam. Chinese troops then depart.

France formally recognizes the free state, Democratic Republic of Vietnam, within the French union and as part of the French Indochina Union.

May–September: Ho Chi Minh spends four months in France attempting to negotiate full independence and unity for Vietnam, but fails to obtain any guarantee from the French.

June: In a major affront to Ho Chi Minh, the French high commissioner for Indochina proclaims a separatist French-controlled government for South Vietnam. The new government and country will be called the Republic of Chochinchina.

November: After a series of violent clashes with Viet Minh, French forces bombard Haiphong harbor and occupy Hanoi, forcing Ho Chi Minh and his Viet Minh forces to retreat into the jungle.

December: In Hanoi, thirty thousand Viet Minh launch their first large-scale attack against the French. Thus begins an eight-year struggle known as the First Indochina War. "The resistance will be long and arduous, but our cause is just and we will surely triumph," declares Viet Minh military commander Vo Nguyen Giap. "If these people want a fight, they'll get it," French commander General Etrienne Valluy states.

1947

October: The French conduct Operation Lea, a series of attacks on Viet Minh guerrilla positions in North Vietnam near the Chinese border. Although the Viet Minh suffer nine thousand casualties, most of the forty thousand–strong Viet Minh force slips away through gaps in the French Lines.

1949

March 8: France establishes an independent Vietnam and names Emperor Bao Dai as puppet head of state in South Vietnam.

July: The French establish the South Vietnamese National Army.

July: Laos is recognized as an independent state but with special ties to France.

October: Mao Zedong's communist forces defeat Chiang Kai-shek's Nationalist Army in the Chinese civil war. Mao's victory ignites American anticommunist sentiment regarding Southeast Asia and will result in a White House foreign policy goal of "containment" of communist expansion in the region.

November: Cambodia follows the Laos pattern and establishes special ties to France.

1950

January: The People's Republic of China and the Soviet Union recognize Ho Chi Minh's Democratic Republic of Vietnam. China then begins sending military advisers and modern weapons to the Viet Minh, including automatic weapons, mortars, howitzers, and trucks. Much of the equipment is American made and had belonged to the Chinese Nationalists before their defeat by Mao. With the influx of new equipment and Chinese advisers, General Giap transforms his guerrilla fighters into conventional Army units, including five light infantry divisions and one heavy division.

February: The United States and Britain recognize Bao Dai's French-controlled South Vietnam government. Viet Minh begin an offensive against French outposts in North Vietnam near the Chinese border.

February: In America, the era of "McCarthyism" erupts as Senator Joseph R. McCarthy of Wisconsin gives a speech claiming the US State Department harbors communists. As a consequence of McCarthyism, no US politician is willing to appear to be soft on communism.

March: The US makes its first financial aid to pro-French Vietnam; aid is channeled through France.

June: The first US military advisers are sent to Vietnam. They are called MAAG (Military Assistance Advisory Group).

June 30: President Harry S. Truman orders US ground troops into Korea following communist North Korea's invasion of the South. In his message to the American people, Truman describes the invasion as a Moscow-backed attack by monolithic world communism.

July 26: United States military involvement in Vietnam begins as President Truman authorizes $15 million in military aid to the French. American military advisers will accompany the flow of US tanks, planes, artillery, and other supplies to Vietnam. Over the next four years, the US will spend $3 billion on the French war and, by 1954, will provide 80 percent of all war supplies used by the French.

September 16: General Giap begins his main attack against French outposts near the Chinese border. As the outposts fall, the French lose six thousand men and large stores of military equipment to the Viet Minh.

September 27: The US establishes a Military Assistance Advisory Group in Saigon to aid the French Army.

1951

January 13: General Giap and twenty thousand Viet Minh begin a series of attacks on fortified French positions in the Red River Delta. The open areas of the Delta, in contrast to the jungle, allow French troops under the new command of General Jean de Lattre to strike back with devastating results from the De Lattre Line, which encircles the region. Later, six thousand Viet Minh die while assaulting the town of Vinh near Hanoi in the first attack, causing Giap to withdraw.

March 23–28: In the second attack, Giap targets the Mao Khe outpost near Haiphong. Giap withdraws after being pounded by French naval gunfire and air strikes. Giap loses three thousand Viet Minh.

May 29–June 18: Giap makes yet another attempt to break through the De Lattre Line, this time in the Day River area southeast of Hanoi. French reinforcements, combined with air strikes and armed boat attacks result in another defeat for Giap, with ten thousand killed and wounded. Among the French casualties is Bernard de Lattre, the only son of General De Lattre.

June 9: Giap begins a general withdrawal of Viet Minh troops from the Red River Delta.

September: General De Lattre travels to Washington seeking more aid from the Pentagon. Additional aid is approved and includes military equipment.

November 16: French forces link up at Hoa Binh southwest of Hanoi as General De Lattre attempts to seize the momentum and lure Giap into a major battle.

November 20: Stricken by cancer, ailing General De Lattre is replaced by General Raoul Salan. De Lattre returns home and dies in Paris two months later just after being raised to marshal.

December 9: Giap begins a careful counteroffensive by attacking the French outpost at Tu Vu on the Black River. Giap now avoids conventional warfare and instead wages hit-and-run attacks followed by a retreat into the dense jungles. His goal is to cut French supply lines.

By year's end, French casualties in Vietnam surpass ninety thousand.

1952

January–December: French troops equipped with US materiel fight an increasingly aggressive Viet Minh. The period is marked by terrorist attacks in various cities including Hanoi and Saigon.

January 12: French supply lines to Hoa Binh along the Black River are cut. The road along Route Coloniale 6 is also cut.

February 22–26: The French withdraw from the Hoa Binh back to the De Lattre Line, aided by a thirty thousand-round artillery barrage. Casualties for each side surpassed five thousand during the Black River skirmishes.

October 11: Giap now attempts to draw the French out from the De Lattre Line by attacking along the Fan Si Pan mountain range between the Red and Black Rivers.

October 29: The French counter Giap's move by launching Operation Lorraine, targeting major Viet Minh supply bases in the Viet Bac region. But Giap outsmarts the French by ignoring their maneuvers and maintains his position along the Black River.

November 14–17: The French cancel Operation Loraine and withdraw back toward the De Lattre Line but must first fight off a Viet Minh ambush at Chan Muong.

1953

January 20: Dwight D. Eisenhower, former five-star Army general and Allied commander in Europe during World War II, is inaugurated as the thirty-fourth president of the United States. During his term, Eisenhower will greatly increase US aid to the French in Vietnam to prevent a communist victory. US military advisers will continue to accompany American supplies sent to Vietnam. To justify America's financial commitment, Eisenhower will cite a domino theory in which a communist victory in Vietnam would result in surrounding countries falling one after another like a "falling row of dominoes." The domino theory will be used by a succession of presidents and their advisers to justify ever-deepening US involvement in Vietnam.

March 5: Soviet leader Josef Stalin dies. The outspoken Nikita Khrushchev succeeds him.

July 27: The Korean War ends as an armistice, and the signing divides the country at the 38th parallel into Communist North and Democratic South. The armistice is seen by many in the international community as a potential model for resolving the ongoing conflict in Vietnam.

November 20: The French, under their new commander General Henri Navarre, begin Operation Castor, the construction of a series of entrenched outposts protecting a small air base in the isolated jungle valley at Dien Bien Phu in northwest Vietnam.

General Giap immediately begins massing Viet Minh troops and artillery in the area. He sensed the potential for a decisive blow against the French. Giap's troops manually drag two hundred heavy howitzers up rugged mountainsides to target the French air base. The French, aware of Giap's intentions, mass their own troops and artillery, preparing for a showdown, but the French grossly underestimated Giap's strength.

1954

March 13: Outnumbering the French five to one, fifty thousand Viet Minh under Giap begin their assault against fortified hills protecting the Dien Bien Phu air base. Giap's artillery pounds the French and shuts down the only runway, thus forcing the French to rely on risky parachute drops for resupply. Giap's troops then take out their shovels and begin construction of a maze of tunnels and trenches, slowly inching their way toward the main French position and surrounding it.

March 13–May 1: The siege at Dien Bien Phu occurs as nearly ten thousand French soldiers are trapped by forty-five thousand Viet Minh. The French troops soon run out of fresh water and medical supplies. The French urgently appeal to Washington for help. The US Joint Chiefs of Staff now consider three possible options: sending American combat troops to the rescue; a massive conventional air strike by B-29 bombers; the use of tactical atomic weapons. President Eisenhower dismisses the conventional air raid and the nuclear option after getting a strong negative response to such actions from America's chief ally, Britain. Eisenhower also decided against sending US ground troops to rescue the French, citing the likelihood of high casualty rates in the jungles around Dien Bien Phu.

May 7: At 5:30 p.m., 10,000 French soldiers surrender at Dien Bien Phu. By now, an estimated 8,000 Viet Minh and 1,500 French have died. The French survivors are marched for up to 60 days to prison camps 500 miles away. Nearly half die during the march or in captivity. France proceeds to withdraw completely from Vietnam, ending a bitter eight-year struggle against the Viet Minh in which 400,000 soldiers and civilians from all sides had perished.

May 8: The Geneva conference on Indochina begins, attended by the US, Britain, China, the Soviet Union, Vietnam, Cambodia, and Laos—all meeting to negotiate a solution for Southeast Asia.

June: Ngo Dinh Diem, appointed prime minister by Bao Dai, arrives in Vietnam.

July 21: The Geneva Accords divide Vietnam in half at the 17th parallel, with Ho Chi Minh's communists ceded the North, while Bao Dai's regime is granted the South. The accords also provide for elections to be held in all of Vietnam within two years to reunify the country. The US opposes the unifying elections, fearing a likely victory by Ho Chi Minh. The US and South Vietnam do not sign the agreements. The International Control Commission (ICC) is appointed to oversee compliance.

August: Refuges estimated at more than one million leave North Vietnam for the South.

September: Southeast Asia Treaty Organization (SEATO) is formed to contain communist expansion in the area.

October: Following the French departure from Hanoi, Ho Chi Minh returns after spending eight years hiding in the jungle and formally takes control of North Vietnam.

In the South, Bao Dai has installed Ngo Dinh Diem as his prime minister. The US now pins its hopes on anticommunist Diem for a democratic South Vietnam. It is Diem, however, who predicts "another more deadly war" will erupt over the future of Vietnam.

Diem, a Roman Catholic in an overwhelmingly Buddhist country, encourages Vietnamese Catholics living in communist North Vietnam to flee south. Nearly one million leave. At the same time, some ninety thousand communists in the South go North, although nearly ten thousand Viet Minh fighters are instructed by Hanoi to quietly remain behind as moles in South Vietnam.

October: President Eisenhower gives aid directly to South Vietnam, bypassing the French channel.

October: French military forces depart Hanoi, and the Viet Minh control North Vietnam

1955

January: The first shipment of US military aid arrives in Saigon. The US also offers to train the fledging South Vietnam Army.

February: US advisers begin direct training of South Vietnamese military, though French advisers are also involved.

March: Diem confronts Binh Xuyen, certain religious sects, and other secret societies. Hundreds are killed by Diem's forces, and by midyear, the opposition was defeated.

May: Prime Minister Diem wages a violent crackdown against the Binh Xuyen organized crime group in Saigon, which operates casinos, brothels, and opium dens.

July: Ho Chi Minh visits Moscow and agrees to accept Soviet aid.

July: Diem refuses to participate in all Vietnam elections, saying free elections in the North are not possible.

October 23: Bao Dai is ousted from power, defeated by Prime Minister Diem in a US-backed plebiscite, which was rigged. Diem is advised on consolidating power by US Air Force Colonel Edward G. Lansdale, who is attached to the Central Intelligence Agency. Diem becomes the unchallenged president of South Vietnam.

October 26: The Republic of South Vietnam is proclaimed with Diem as its first president. In America, President Eisenhower pledges his support for the new government and offers military aid.

Diem assigns most high-level government positions to close friends and family members including his younger brother Ngo Dinh Nhu, who will be his chief adviser. Diem's style of leadership, aloof and autocratic, will create future political problems for him despite the best efforts of his American advisers to popularize him via American-style political rallies and tours of the countryside.

December: In North Vietnam, radical land reforms by communists result in land owners being hauled before "people's tribunals." Thousands are executed or sent to forced labor camps during this period of ideological cleansing by Ho Chi Minh.

In South Vietnam, President Diem rewards Catholic support by giving them land seized from Buddhist peasants, arousing their anger and eroding his support among them. Diem also allows big land owners to retain their holdings, disappointing peasants hoping for land reform.

1956

January: Diem launches a brutal crackdown against Viet Minh suspects in the countryside. Those arrested are denied counsel and hauled before "security committees" with many suspects tortured or executed under the guise of "shot while attempting escape."

March: General assembly elections are held in South Vietnam with a major victory for Diem party members.

April 28: The last French soldier leaves South Vietnam. The French high command for Indochina is then dissolved. US advisers take over full training duties of the South Vietnamese Army.

July: The deadline passes for the unifying elections set by the Geneva Conference. Diem, backed by the US, had refused to participate.

July: US Vice President Nixon visits South Vietnam.

October: Three US installations in Saigon are bombed.

November: Peasant unrest in North Vietnam resulting from oppressive land reforms is put down by communist force with more than six thousand killed or deported.

1957

January: The Soviet Union proposes permanent division of Vietnam into North and South, with the two nations admitted separately to the United Nations. The US rejects the proposal, unwilling to recognize communist North Vietnam.

January: The ICC complains that neither North nor South Vietnam is complying with Geneva Accords.

May 8–18: Diem pays a state visit to Washington where President Eisenhower labels him the "miracle man" of Asia and reaffirms US commitment. "The cost of defending freedom, of defending America, must be paid in many forms and in many places . . . military as well as economic help is currently needed in Vietnam," Eisenhower states.

Diem's government, however, with its main focus on security, spends little on schools, medical care, or other badly needed social services in the countryside. Communist guerrillas and propagandists in the countryside capitalize on this by making simple promises of land reform and a better standard of living to gain popular support among peasants.

June: The last French military advisers leave South Vietnam.

June–Aug: Personnel from the 1st Special Forces Group on Okinawa first enter South Vietnam. They establish a training center at Nha Trang and train fifty-eight South Vietnamese soldiers in Special Forces tactics, techniques, and procedures.

October: Viet Minh guerillas begin a widespread campaign of terror in South Vietnam, including bombings and assassinations. By year's end, over four hundred South Vietnamese officials are killed.

November: Ho Chi Minh visits the USSR and Europe.

1958

January: Communist forces attack a plantation near Saigon, the latest in an increasing level of insurgency in the South.

June: A coordinated command structure is formed by communists in the Mekong Delta where thirty-seven armed companies are being organized.

December: Message exchanges are intercepted in which North Vietnam says it will undertake overt insurgency in the South.

1959
The Beginning of the Second Indochina War

January: The Second Indochina War begins when North Vietnam's Central Executive Committee issues Resolution 15, changing its strategy toward South Vietnam from political struggle to armed conflict. The armed revolution begins as Ho Chi Minh declares a People's War to unite all of Vietnam under his leadership. His politburo now orders a changeover to an all-out military struggle.

April 4: President Eisenhower makes his first commitment to maintain South Vietnam as a separate national state.

May: North Vietnamese establish the Central Office of South Vietnam (COSVN) to oversee the coming war in the South. The suspected location of COSVN is in the Fishhook area of Cambodia. North Vietnam organizes Group 559 to begin enlargement of the Ho Chi Minh trail. The trail eventually expand into a 1,500-mile-long network of jungle and mountain passes extending from North Vietnam's coast along Vietnam's western border through Laos, parts of Cambodia, funneling a constant stream of soldiers and supplies into the highlands of South Vietnam. In 1959, it takes six months to make the journey; by 1968, it will take only six weeks due to road improvements by North Vietnamese laborers, many of whom are women. In the 1970s, a parallel fuel pipeline will be added.

May: North Vietnamese central committee resolution calls for "armed struggle" to reunite Vietnam, codifying Hanoi's support for the overthrow of the Saigon regime by National Liberation Front (NLF), or Viet Cong. The North Vietnamese establish the Central Office of South Vietnam (COSVN) to command and control the war in the South. Construction of the Ho Chi Minh trail begins.

July: An estimated four thousand Viet Minh guerillas, originally born in the South, are sent from North Vietnam to infiltrate South Vietnam. North Vietnam organizes Logistical Group 759 to oversee movement of men and logistics from North Vietnam to the South.

July 8: Two US military advisers, Major Dale Buis and Sergeant Chester Ovnard, are killed by Viet Minh guerillas at Bien Hoa, South Vietnam. They are the first Americans killed in the Second Indochina War, which Americans will come to know simply as the Vietnam War.

October: Heavy communist casualties are reported after South Vietnamese government's military campaign in Camau peninsula.

1960

January: Largest communist insurgency operation to date over-throws a Vietnamese Army installation in Tay Ninh province; captures weapons and ammunition.

April: Universal military conscription is imposed in North Vietnam. Tour of duty is indefinite. Eighteen distinguished nationalists in South Vietnam send a petition to President Diem advocating that he reform his rigid, family-run, and increasingly corrupt government. Diem ignores their advice and instead closes several opposition newspapers and arrests journalists and intellectuals.

November: A failed coup against President Diem by disgruntled South Vietnamese Army officers brings a harsh crackdown against all perceived "enemies of the state." Over fifty thousand are arrested by police controlled by Diem's brother Nhu with many innocent civilians tortured then executed. This results in further erosion of popular support for Diem. Thousands who fear arrest flee to North Vietnam. Ho Chi Minh will later send many back to infiltrate South Vietnam as part of his People's Liberation Armed Forces. Diem calls the infiltrators Viet Cong, meaning communist Vietnamese. Ho's guerillas blend into the countryside, indistinguishable from South Vietnamese, while working to undermine Diem's government.

November: John F. Kennedy is elected President of US.

December 20: The National Liberation Front is established by Hanoi as its communist political organization for Viet Cong guerillas in South Vietnam.

1961

January: Soviet Premier Nikita Khrushchev pledges support for "wars of national liberation" throughout the world. His statement greatly encourages communists in North Vietnam to escalate their armed struggle to unify Vietnam under Ho Chi Minh.

January 20: John Fitzgerald Kennedy is inaugurated as the thirty-fifth US president and declares, "We shall pay any price, bear any burden, meet any hardship, support any friend, and oppose any foe, to insure the survival and the success of liberty." Privately, outgoing President Eisenhower tells him, "I think you're going to have to send troops," to Southeast Asia.

The youthful Kennedy administration is inexperienced in matters regarding Southeast Asia. Kennedy's Secretary of Defense, forty-four-year-old Robert McNamara, along with civilian planners recruited from the academic community, will play a crucial role in deciding White House strategy for Vietnam over the next several years. Under their leadership, the United States will wage a limited war to force a political settlement.

However, the US will be opposed by an enemy dedicated to total military victory "whatever the sacrifices, however long the struggle . . . until Vietnam is fully independent and reunified," as stated by Ho Chi Minh.

April: Diem is elected president by overwhelming majority.

May: Vice President Lyndon B. Johnson visits President Diem in South Vietnam and hails the embattled leader as the Winston Churchill of Asia. President Kennedy sends four hundred American Green Beret "special advisors" to South Vietnam to train South Vietnamese soldiers in methods of "counterinsurgency" in the fight against Viet Cong guerrillas. The role of the Green Berets soon expands to include the establishment of Civilian Irregular Defense Groups (CIDG) made up of fierce mountain men known as the Montagnards. These groups establish a series of fortified camps strung out along the mountains to thwart infiltration by North Vietnamese.

June: President Kennedy and Premier Khrushchev meet in Vienna.

September: A Viet Cong force seizes a provincial capital only fifty miles from Saigon. Later, the conflict widens as twenty-six thousand Viet Cong launch several successful attacks on South Vietnamese troops. Diem then requests more military aid from the Kennedy administration.

October: To get a firsthand look at the deteriorating military situation, top Kennedy aides, Maxwell Taylor and Walt Rostow, visit Vietnam. "If Vietnam goes, it will be exceedingly difficult to hold Southeast Asia," Taylor reports to the president and advises Kennedy to expand the number of US military advisers and to send eight thousand combat soldiers.

October 24: On the sixth anniversary of the Republic of South Vietnam, President Kennedy sends a letter to President Diem and pledges, "The United States is determined to help Vietnam preserve its independence."

November: President Kennedy then sends additional military advisers along with American helicopter units to transport and direct South Vietnamese troops in battle, thus involving Americans in combat operations. Kennedy justifies the expanding US military role as a means "to prevent a communist takeover of Vietnam which is in accordance with a policy our government has followed since 1954." The number of military advisers sent by Kennedy will eventually surpass sixteen thousand.

December: Viet Cong guerrillas now control much of the countryside in South Vietnam and frequently ambush South Vietnamese troops. The cost to America of maintaining South Vietnam's sagging two hundred thousand–man Army and managing the overall conflict in Vietnam rises to a million dollars per day.

1962

January: Defoliation begins.

January 11: During his State of the Union address, President Kennedy states, "Few generations in all of history have been granted the role of being the great defender of freedom in its maximum hour of danger. This is our good fortune."

January 15: During a press conference, President Kennedy is asked if any Americans in Vietnam are engaged in the fighting. "No," the president responds without further comment.

February: Strategic Hamlet program is inaugurated.

February: MACV, the US Military Assistance Command for Vietnam, is formed. It replaces MAAG Vietnam, the Military Assistance Advisory Group, which had been established in 1950.

February 27: The presidential palace in Saigon is bombed by two renegade South Vietnamese pilots flying American-made World War II–era fighter planes. President Diem and his brother Nhu escape unharmed. Diem attributes his survival to "divine protection."

March: Operation Sunrise begins the Strategic Hamlet resettlement program in which scattered rural populations in South Vietnam are uprooted from their ancestral farmlands and resettled into fortified villages defended by local militias. However, over fifty of the hamlets are soon infiltrated and easily taken over by Viet Cong who kill or intimidate village leaders. As a result, Diem orders bombing raids against suspected Viet Cong–controlled hamlets. The air strikes by the South Vietnamese Air Force are supported by US pilots, who also conduct some of the bombings. Civilian casualties erode popular support for Diem and result in growing peasant hostility toward America, which is largely blamed for the unpopular resettlement program as well as the bombings.

May: Viet Cong organize themselves into battalion-sized units operating in central Vietnam. Defense Secretary McNamara visits South Vietnam and reports, "We are winning the war."

July 23: The Declaration on the Neutrality of Laos signed in Geneva by the US and thirteen other nations prohibits US invasion of portions of the Ho Chi Minh trail inside eastern Laos.

August 1: President Kennedy signs the Foreign Assistance Act of 1962, which provides "military assistance to countries which are on the rim of the communist world and under direct attack." A US Special Forces camp is set up at Khe Sanh to monitor North Vietnamese Army (NVA) infiltration down the Ho Chi Minh trail.

August: Troops from Australia are assigned to South Vietnam

October: The Cuban missile crisis begins.

December: US troops in South Vietnam increase to eleven thousand.

1963

January 3: A Viet Cong victory in the Battle of Ap Bac makes front-page news in America as 350 Viet Cong fighters defeat a large force of American-equipped South Vietnamese troops attempting to seize a radio transmitter. Three American helicopter crew members are killed. The South Vietnamese Army is run by officers personally chosen by President Diem, not for their competence, but for their loyalty to him. Diem has instructed his officers to avoid casualties. Their primary mission, he has told them, is to protect him from any coups in Saigon.

May: Buddhists riot in South Vietnam after they are denied the right to display religious flags during their celebration of Buddha's birthday. In Hue, South Vietnamese police and Army troops shoot at Buddhist demonstrators, resulting in the deaths of one woman and eight children. Political pressure now mounts on the Kennedy administration to disassociate itself from Diem's repressive, family-run government. "You are responsible for the present trouble because you back Diem and his government of ignoramuses," a leading Buddhist tells US officials in Saigon.

June–August: Buddhist demonstrations spread. Several Buddhist monks publicly burn themselves to death as an act of protest. The immolations are captured on film by news photographers and shock the American public as well as President Kennedy. Diem responds to the deepening unrest by imposing martial law. South Vietnamese Special Forces originally trained by the

US and now controlled by Diem's younger brother Nhu wage violent crackdowns against Buddhist sanctuaries in Saigon, Hue, and other cities. Nhu's crackdowns spark widespread anti-Diem demonstrations. Meanwhile, during an American TV interview, Nhu's wife, the flamboyant Madame Nhu, coldly refers to the Buddhist immolations as a "barbecue." As the overall situation worsens, high-level talks at the White House focus on the need to force Diem to reform.

June: President Kennedy names Henry Cabot Lodge as ambassador to South Vietnam.

July 4: South Vietnamese General Tran Van Don, a Buddhist, contacts the CIA in Saigon about the possibility of staging a coup against Diem.

August: President de Gaulle of France says Vietnamese must free themselves from foreign influence. His remarks are interpreted as an attempt to get France back into Vietnam.

August 22: The new US ambassador Henry Cabot Lodge arrives in South Vietnam.

August 24: A US State Department message sent to Ambassador Lodge is interpreted by Lodge to indicate he should encourage the military coup against President Diem.

August 26: Ambassador Lodge meets President Diem for the first time. Under instructions from President Kennedy, Lodge tells Diem to fire his brother, the much-hated Nhu, and to reform his government. But Diem arrogantly refuses even to discuss such matters with Lodge. President Kennedy and top aides begin three days of heated discussions over whether the US should in fact support the military coup against Diem.

August 29: Lodge sends a message to Washington, stating "There is no possibility, in my view, that the war can be won under a Diem administration." President Kennedy then gives Lodge a free hand to manage the unfolding events in Saigon. However, the coup against Diem fizzles due to mistrust and suspicion within the ranks of the military conspirators.

September: Kennedy sends Defense Secretary McNamara and Maxwell Taylor to Vietnam. Visit lasts until October 10.

September 2: During a TV news interview with Walter Cronkite, President Kennedy describes Diem as "out of touch with the people" and adds that South Vietnam's government might regain popular support "with changes in policy and perhaps in personnel." Also during the interview, Kennedy comments on America's commitment to Vietnam: "If we withdrew from Vietnam, the communists would control Vietnam. Pretty soon, Thailand, Cambodia, Laos, Malaya, would go."

October 2: President Kennedy sends Ambassador Lodge a mixed message that "no initiative should now be taken to give any encouragement to a coup" but that Lodge should "identify and build contacts with possible leadership as and when it appears."

October 5: Lodge informs President Kennedy that the coup against Diem appears to be on again. The rebel generals, led by Duong Van "Big" Minh, first ask for assurances that US aid to South Vietnam will continue after Diem's removal and that the US will not interfere with the actual coup. This scenario suits the White House well, in that the generals will appear to be acting on their own without any direct US involvement. President Kennedy gives his approval. The CIA in Saigon then signals the conspirators that the United States will not interfere with the overthrow of President Diem.

October 25: Prompted by concerns over public relations fallout if the coup fails, a worried White House seeks reassurances from Ambassador Lodge that the coup will succeed.

October 28: Ambassador Lodge reports a coup is "imminent."

October 29: An increasingly nervous White House now instructs Lodge to postpone the coup. Lodge responds it can only be stopped by betraying the conspirators to Diem.

November 1: Lodge has a routine meeting with Diem from 10:00 a.m. until noon at the presidential palace, and then departs. At 1:30 p.m., during the traditional siesta time, the coup begins as mutinous troops roar into Saigon, surround the presidential palace, and also seize police headquarters. Diem and his brother Nhu are trapped inside the palace and reject all appeals to surrender. Diem telephones the rebel generals and attempts, but fails, to talk them out of the coup. Diem then calls Lodge and asks, "What is the attitude of the United States?" Lodge responds, "It is four thirty a.m. in Washington, and the US government cannot possibly have a view." Lodge then expresses concern for Diem's safety, to which Diem responds, "I am trying to restore order." At 8:00 p.m., Diem and Nhu slip out of the presidential palace unnoticed and go to a safe house in the suburbs that belongs to a wealthy Chinese merchant.

November 2: At 3:00 a.m., one of Diem's aides betrays his location to the generals. The hunt for Diem and Nhu now begins. At 6:00 a.m., Diem telephones the generals. Realizing the situation is hopeless, Diem and Nhu offer to surrender from inside a Catholic church. Diem and Nhu are then taken into custody by rebel officers and placed in the back of an armored personnel carrier. While traveling to Saigon, the vehicle stops, and Diem and Nhu are assassinated. At the White House, a meeting is interrupted with the news of Diem's death. According to witnesses, President Kennedy's face turns a ghostly shade of white, and he immediately leaves the room. Later, the president records in his private diary, "I feel that we must bear a good deal of responsibility for it." Saigon celebrates the downfall of Diem's regime. But the coup results in a power vacuum in which a series of military and civilian governments seize control of South Vietnam, a country that becomes totally dependent on the United States for its existence. Viet Cong use the unstable political situation to increase their hold over the rural population of South Vietnam to nearly 40 percent.

November 22: President John F. Kennedy is assassinated in Dallas. Lyndon B. Johnson is sworn in as the thirty-sixth US president. He is the fourth president coping with Vietnam and will oversee massive escalation of the war while utilizing many of the same policy advisers who served Kennedy.

November 24: President Johnson declares he will not "lose Vietnam" during a meeting with Ambassador Lodge in Washington. By year's end, there are 16,300 American military advisers in South Vietnam, which received $500 million in US aid during 1963.

December: McNamara visit Saigon to check progress in war under South Vietnam's new leadership.

1964

January: Communists begin a new period of combat in South Vietnam with the objective of annihilating ARVN forces. North Vietnam's Resolution 9 secretly authorizes massive combat operations for the NVA below the 17th parallel.

January 16: MACV Studies and Observation Group (SOG) begins its highly classified clandestine operations throughout Southeast Asia. It's Detachment B-52, 5th Special Forces Group, and the Air Force's 1st Flight Detachment receives the Presidential Unit Citation for actions beginning January 24.

January 17–18: At the battle of Thanh Phu Island, six crewmen of MACV's Utility Tactical Company are KIA when their UH-1B Helicopter is shot down in the Mekong Delta.

January 30: General Minh is ousted from power in a bloodless coup led by General Nguyen Khanh, who becomes the new leader of South Vietnam.

February 16: Marine Captain Donald E. Koelper of the MAAG Naval Advisory Group is KIA in a blast at the Kinh-Do Theater in Saigon.

March: Secret US-backed bombing raids begin against the Ho Chi Minh trail inside Laos, conducted by mercenaries flying old American fighter planes.

March 6: Defense Secretary McNamara visits South Vietnam and states that General Khanh "has our admiration, our respect and our complete support" and adds, "We'll stay for as long as it takes. We shall provide whatever help is required to win the battle against the communist insurgents." Following his visit, McNamara advises President Johnson to increase military aid to shore up the sagging South Vietnamese Army. McNamara and other Johnson policymakers now become focused on the need to prevent a communist victory in South Vietnam, believing it would damage the credibility of the US globally. The war in

Vietnam thus becomes a test of US resolve in fighting communism with America's prestige and President Johnson's reputation on the line. The cost to America of maintaining South Vietnam's Army and managing the overall conflict in Vietnam now rises to two million dollars per day.

March 17: The US National Security Council recommends the bombing of North Vietnam. President Johnson approves only the planning phase by the Pentagon.

April 10–13: The VC stand their ground against ARVN forces in the U Minh Forest and Mekong Delta with heavy casualties on both sides. This is the longest battle to date.

April: General William Westmoreland succeeds General Paul Harkins as US commander in South Vietnam.

May: President Johnson's aides begin work on a Congressional resolution supporting the president's war policy in Vietnam. The resolution is shelved temporarily due to lack of support in the Senate, but will later be used as the basis of the Gulf of Tonkin resolution.

Summer: As fifty-six thousand Viet Cong spread their successful guerrilla war throughout South Vietnam, they are reinforced by North Vietnamese Army (NVA) regulars pouring in via the Ho Chi Minh trail. Responding to this escalation, President Johnson approves Operation Plan 34A, CIA-run covert operations using South Vietnamese commandos in speedboats to harass radar sites along the coastline of North Vietnam. The raids are supported by US Navy warships in the Gulf of Tonkin, including the destroyer USS *Maddox*, which conducts electronic surveillance to pinpoint the radar locations.

July: New Zealand sends troops to South Vietnam.

July 1: General Maxwell D. Taylor, chairman of the Joint Chiefs of Staff, is appointed by President Johnson as the new US ambassador to South Vietnam. During his one-year tenure, Taylor will have to deal with five successive governments in politically unstable South Vietnam. President Johnson also appoints Lt. Gen. William C. Westmoreland to be the new US military commander in Vietnam. Westmoreland is a West Point graduate and a highly decorated veteran of World War II and Korea.

July 16–17: Senator Barry Goldwater is chosen as the Republican nominee for president at the Republican National Convention in San Francisco. During his acceptance speech, Goldwater declares, "Extremism in the defense of liberty is no vice." Goldwater is a staunch conservative and virulent anti-Communist whose campaign rhetoric will impact coming White House decisions concerning Vietnam. Above all, Johnson's aides do not want the president to appear to be soft on communism and thus risk losing the November presidential election. But at the same time, they also want the president to avoid being labeled a warmonger concerning Vietnam.

July 31: In the Gulf of Tonkin, as part of Operation Plan 34A, South Vietnamese commandos in unmarked speedboats raid two North Vietnamese military bases located on islands just off the coast. In the vicinity is the destroyer USS *Maddox*.

August 2: Three North Vietnamese patrol boats attack the American destroyer USS *Maddox* in the Gulf of Tonkin ten miles off the coast of North Vietnam. They fire three torpedoes and machine guns, but only a single machine gun round actually strikes the *Maddox* with no casualties. US Navy fighters from the carrier *Ticonderoga*, led by Commander James Stockdale, attack the patrol boats, sinking one and damaging the other two.

At the White House, it is Sunday morning (twelve hours behind Vietnam time). President Johnson, reacting cautiously to reports of the incident, decides against retaliation. Instead, he sends a diplomatic message to Hanoi warning of "grave consequences" from any further "unprovoked" attacks. Johnson then orders the *Maddox* to resume operations in the Gulf of Tonkin in the same vicinity where the attack had occurred. Meanwhile, the Joints Chiefs of Staff put US combat troops on alert and also select targets in North Vietnam for a possible bombing raid, should the need arise.

August 3: The *Maddox*, joined by a second destroyer, USS *Turner Joy*, begin a series of vigorous zigzags in the Gulf of Tonkin, sailing to within eight miles of North Vietnam's coast, while at the same time, South Vietnamese commandos in speedboats harass North Vietnamese defenses along the coastline. By nightfall, thunderstorms roll in, affecting the accuracy of electronic instruments on the destroyers. Crew members reading their instruments believe they have come under torpedo attack from North Vietnamese patrol boats. Both destroyers open fire on numerous apparent targets, but there are no actual sightings of any attacking boats.

August 4: Although immediate doubts arise concerning the validity of the second attack, the Joint Chiefs of Staff strongly recommend a retaliatory bombing raid against North Vietnam. Press reports in America greatly embellish the second attack with spectacular eyewitness accounts although no journalists had been on board the destroyers. At the White House, President Johnson decides to retaliate. Thus, the first bombing of North Vietnam by the United States occurs as oil facilities and naval targets are attacked without warning by sixty-four US Navy fighter-bombers. "Our response for the present will be limited and fitting," President Johnson tells Americans during a midnight TV appearance, an hour after the attack began. "We Americans know, although others appear to forget, the risk of spreading conflict. We still seek no wider war." Two Navy jets are shot down during the bombing raids, resulting in the first American prisoner of war, Lt. Everett Alvarez of San Jose, California, who is taken to an internment center in Hanoi, later dubbed the Hanoi Hilton by the nearly six hundred American airmen who become POWs.

August 5: Opinion polls indicate 85 percent of Americans support President Johnson's bombing decision. Numerous newspaper editorials also come out in support of the president. Johnson's aides, including Defense Secretary McNamara, now lobby Congress to pass a White House resolution that will give the president a free hand in Vietnam.

August 6: During a meeting in the Senate, McNamara is confronted by Senator Wayne Morse of Oregon, who had been tipped off by someone in the Pentagon that the *Maddox* had in fact been involved in the South Vietnamese commando raids against North Vietnam and thus was not the victim of an "unprovoked" attack. McNamara responds that the US Navy "played absolutely no part in, was not associated with, and was not aware of, any South Vietnamese actions, if there were any."

August 7: In response to the two incidents involving the *Maddox* and *Turner Joy*, the US Congress, at the behest of President Johnson, overwhelmingly passes the Gulf of Tonkin Resolution put forward by the White House, allowing the president "to take all necessary steps, including the use of armed force" to prevent further attacks against US forces. The resolution, passed unanimously in the House and 98–2 in the Senate, grants enormous power to President Johnson to wage an undeclared war in Vietnam from the White House. The only senators voting against the resolution are Wayne Morse and Ernest Gruening of Alaska, who said, "All Vietnam is not worth the life of a single American boy."

August 21: In Saigon, students and Buddhist militants begin a series of escalating protests against General Khanh's military regime. As a result, Khanh resigns as sole leader in favor of a triumvirate that includes himself, General Minh, and General Khiem. The streets of Saigon soon disintegrate into chaos and mob violence amid the government's gross instability.

August 26: President Johnson is nominated at the Democratic National Convention. During his campaign, he declares, "We are not about to send American boys nine or ten thousand miles away from home to do what Asian boys ought to be doing for themselves."

September 13: South Korean troops arrive in South Vietnam. The initial force consists of thirty-four officers and ninety-six enlisted men in a mobile hospital unit. The Korean force will grow to about fifty thousand eventually.

September 7: President Johnson assembles his top aides at the White House to ponder the future course of action in Vietnam.

September 13: Two disgruntled South Vietnamese generals stage an unsuccessful coup in Saigon.

October 1: The US Army 5th Special Forces Group based in Fort Bragg, North Carolina, is assigned to South Vietnam to oversee Green Beret operations.

October 8: A military group from the Republic of China arrives in South Vietnam to provide advice on political warfare and assist with medical care.

October 14: Soviet leader Nikita Khrushchev is ousted from power, replaced by Leonid Brezhnev as leader of the USSR.

October 16: China tests its first atomic bomb. China, by this time, has also amassed troops along its border with Vietnam, responding to US escalation.

November 1: The first attack by Viet Cong against Americans in Vietnam occurs at Bien Hoa Air Base, twelve miles north of Saigon. A predawn mortar assault kills five Americans, two South Vietnamese, and wounds nearly a hundred others. President Johnson dismisses all recommendations for a retaliatory air strike against North Vietnam.

November 3: With 61 percent of the popular vote, Democrat Lyndon B. Johnson is reelected as president of the United States in a landslide victory, the biggest to date in US history, defeating Republican Barry Goldwater by 16 million votes. The Democrats also achieve big majorities in both the US House and Senate.

December 1: Ten thousand NVA soldiers arrive in the Central Highlands of South Vietnam via the Ho Chi Minh trail, carrying sophisticated weapons provided by China and the Soviet Union. They shore up Viet Cong battalions with the weapons and also provide experienced soldiers as leaders. At the White House, President Johnson's top aides—including Secretary of State Dean Rusk, National Security Advisor McGeorge Bundy, and Defense Secretary McNamara—recommend a policy of gradual escalation of US military involvement in Vietnam.

December 20: Another military coup occurs in Saigon by the South Vietnamese Army. This time General Khanh and young officers, led by Nguyen Cao Ky and Nguyen Van Thieu, oust older generals including General Minh from the government and seize control.

December 21: An angry Ambassador Taylor summons the young officers to the US embassy then scolds them like schoolboys over the continuing instability and endless intrigues plaguing South Vietnam's government. "Americans," he had already warned them, "are tired of coups." Taylor's behavior greatly offends the young officers. General Khanh retaliates by lashing out in the press against Taylor and the US, stating that America is reverting to "colonialism" in its treatment of South Vietnam.

December 24: Viet Cong terrorists set off a car bomb explosion at the Brinks Hotel, an American officers' residence in downtown Saigon. The bomb is timed to detonate at 5:45 p.m., during happy hour in the bar. Two Americans are killed and fifty-eight wounded. President Johnson dismisses all recommendations for a retaliatory air strike against North Vietnam. By year's end, the number of American military advisers in South Vietnam is 23,000. There are now an estimated 170,000 Viet Cong/NVA fighters in the People's Revolutionary Army, which has begun waging coordinated battalion-sized attacks against South Vietnamese troops in villages around Saigon.

1965

This was the year that US conventional ground combat operations really began. The Gulf of Tonkin Resolution gave President Johnson authority to increase US military involvement in South Vietnam. The first US ground troops landed in South Vietnam. In 1965, major confrontations occurred between the US military and the enemy.

January: South Korean troops arrive in South Vietnam.
January: Buddhist demonstrations disrupt life in major cities. A Buddhist nun commits fiery suicide; the first since 1963.

January 20: Lyndon B. Johnson takes the oath as president and declares, "We can never again stand aside, prideful in isolation. Terrific dangers and troubles that we once called 'foreign' now constantly live among us."

January 27: General Khanh seizes full control of South Vietnam's government. Johnson aides, National Security Adviser McGeorge Bundy and Defense Secretary Robert McNamara, send a memo to the president stating that America's limited military involvement in Vietnam is not succeeding and that the US has reached a "fork in the road" in Vietnam and must either soon escalate or withdraw.

January: Operation Game Warden begins US Navy river patrols on South Vietnam's three thousand nautical miles of inland waterways.

February 4: National Security Adviser McGeorge Bundy visits South Vietnam for the first time. In North Vietnam, Soviet prime minister Aleksei Kosygin coincidentally arrives in Hanoi.

February 6: Viet Cong guerrillas attack the US military compound at Pleiku in the Central Highlands, killing eight Americans, wounding 126, and destroying ten aircraft.

February 7–8: "I've had enough of this," President Johnson tells his National Security advisers. He then approves Operation Flaming Dart, the bombing of a North Vietnamese Army camp near Dong Hoi by US Navy jets from the carrier Ranger. Johnson makes no speeches or public statements concerning his decision. Opinion polls taken in the US shortly after the bombing indicate a 70 percent approval rating for the president and an 80 percent approval of US military involvement in Vietnam. Johnson now agrees to a long-standing recommendation from his advisers for a sustained bombing campaign against North Vietnam. In Hanoi, Soviet prime minister Kosygin is pressured by the North Vietnamese to provide unlimited military aid to counter the American "aggression." Kosygin gives in to their demands. As a result, sophisticated Soviet surface-to-air missiles (SAMs) begin arriving in Hanoi within weeks.

February 18: Another military coup in Saigon results in General Khanh finally ousted from power and a new military/civilian government installed, led by Dr. Phan Huy Quat.

February 22: General Westmoreland requests two battalions of US Marines to protect the American air base at Da Nang from six thousand Viet Cong massed in the vicinity. The president approves his request, despite the "grave reservations" of Ambassador Taylor in Vietnam who warns that America may be about to repeat the same mistakes made by the French in sending ever-increasing numbers of soldiers into the Asian forests and jungles of a "hostile foreign country" where friend and foe are indistinguishable.

March 2: Operation Rolling Thunder begins as over one hundred American fighter-bombers attack targets in North Vietnam. Scheduled to last eight weeks, Rolling Thunder will instead go on for three years. The first US air strikes also occur against the Ho Chi Minh trail. Throughout the war, the trail is heavily bombed by American jets with little actual success in halting the tremendous flow of soldiers and supplies from the North. Over five hundred American jets will be lost attacking the trail. After each attack, bomb damage along the trail is repaired by female construction crews. During the entire war, the US will fly three million sorties and drop nearly 8 million tons of bombs, four times the tonnage dropped during all of World War II, in the largest display of firepower in the history of warfare. The majority of bombs are dropped in South Vietnam against Viet Cong and North Vietnamese Army positions, resulting in 3 million civilian refugees due to the destruction of numerous villages. In North Vietnam, military targets include fuel depots and factories. The North Vietnamese react to the air strikes by decentralizing their factories and supply bases, thus minimizing their vulnerability to bomb damage.

March 8: The first US combat troops arrive in Vietnam as 3,500 Marines land at China Beach to defend the American air base at Da Nang. They join 23,000 American military advisers already in Vietnam.

March 9: President Johnson authorizes the use of napalm, a petroleum-based jelly organic solvent explosive.

March 11: Operation Market Time, a joint effort between the US Navy and South Vietnamese Navy, commences to disrupt North Vietnamese sea routes used to funnel supplies into the South. The operation is highly successful in cutting off coastal supply lines and results in the North Vietnamese shifting to the more difficult land route along the Ho Chi Minh trail.

March 29: Viet Cong terrorists bomb the US embassy in Saigon.

April 1: At the White House, President Johnson authorizes sending two more Marine battalions and up to twenty thousand logistical personnel to Vietnam. The president also authorizes American combat troops to conduct patrols to root out Viet Cong in the countryside. His decision to allow offensive operations is kept secret from the American press and public for two months.

April 7: President Johnson delivers his "Peace without Conquest" speech at Johns Hopkins University offering Hanoi "unconditional discussions" to stop the war in return for massive economic assistance in modernizing Vietnam. "Old Ho can't turn that down," Johnson privately tells his aides. But Johnson's peace overture is quickly rejected.

April 15: A thousand tons of bombs are dropped on Viet Cong positions by US and South Vietnamese fighter-bombers.

April 17: In Washington, fifteen thousand students gather to protest the US bombing campaign. Student demonstrators will often refer to President Johnson, his advisers, the Pentagon, Washington bureaucrats, and weapons manufacturers simply as the Establishment.

April 20: In Honolulu, Johnson's top aides—including McNamara, General Westmoreland, General Wheeler, William Bundy, and Ambassador Taylor—meet and agree to recommend to the president sending another forty thousand combat soldiers to Vietnam.

April 24: President Johnson announces Americans in Vietnam are eligible for combat pay.

May 3: The first US Army combat troops, 3,500 men of the 173rd Airborne Brigade, arrive in Vietnam.

May 11: Viet Cong overrun South Vietnamese troops in Phuoc Long Province north of Saigon and also attack in central South Vietnam.

May 13: The first bombing pause is announced by the US in the hope that Hanoi will now negotiate. There will be six more pauses during the Rolling Thunder bombing campaign, all with the same intention. However, each time, the North Vietnamese ignore the peace overtures and instead use the pause to repair air defenses and send more troops and supplies into the South via the Ho Chi Minh trail. Viet Cong attack the US Special Forces camp in Phuoc Long. During the fighting, 2nd Lt. Charles Williams earns the Medal of Honor by knocking out a Viet Cong machine gun then guiding rescue helicopters, while wounded four times.

May 19: US bombing of North Vietnam resumes.

June 18: Nguyen Cao Ky takes power in South Vietnam as the new prime minister with Nguyen Van Thieu functioning as official chief of state. They lead the tenth government in twenty months.

July 1: Viet Cong stage a mortar attack against Da Nang air base and destroy three aircraft.

July 8: Henry Cabot Lodge is reappointed as US ambassador to South Vietnam.

July 21–28: President Johnson meets with top aides to decide the future course of action in Vietnam.

July 28: During a noontime press conference, President Johnson announces he will send forty-four combat battalions to Vietnam, increasing the US military presence to 125,000 men. Monthly draft calls are doubled to thirty-five thousand. "I have asked the commanding general, General Westmoreland, what more he needs to meet this mounting aggression. He has told me. And we will meet his needs. We cannot be defeated by force of arms. We will stand in Vietnam." "I do not find it easy to send the flower of our youth, our finest young men, into battle.

I have spoken to you today of the divisions and the forces and the battalions and the units, but I know them all, every one. I have seen them in a thousand streets, of a hundred towns, in every state in this union-working and laughing and building, and filled with hope and life. I think I know, too, how their mothers weep and how their families sorrow."

August: Combined Action Platoons are formed by US Marines utilizing South Vietnamese militia units to protect villages and conduct patrols to root out Viet Cong guerrillas.

August 3: The destruction of suspected Viet Cong villages near Da Nang by a US Marine rifle company is shown on CBS TV and generates controversy in America. Earlier, seven Marines had been killed nearby while searching for Viet Cong following a mortar attack against the air base at Da Nang.

August 4: President Johnson asks Congress for an additional $1.7 billion for the war.

August 5: Viet Cong destroy two million gallons of fuel in storage tanks near Da Nang.

August 8: The US conducts major air strikes against the Viet Cong.

August 18–24: Operation Starlite begins the first major US ground operation in Vietnam as US Marines wage a preemptive strike against 1,500 Viet Cong planning to assault the American airfield at Chu Lai. The Marines arrive by helicopter and by sea following heavy artillery and air bombardment of Viet Cong positions. Marines suffer 45 killed and 120 wounded. Viet Cong suffer 614 dead and 9 taken prisoner. This decisive first victory gives a big boost to US troop morale.

August 31: President Johnson signs a law criminalizing draft card burning. Although it may result in a five-year prison sentence and $1,000 fine, the burnings become common during antiwar rallies and often attract the attention of news media.

October 16: Antiwar rallies occur in forty American cities and in international cities including London and Rome.

October 19: North Vietnamese Army troops attack the US Special Forces camp at Plei Me in a prelude to the Battle of Ia Drang Valley in South Vietnam's Central Highlands.

October 30: Twenty-five thousand march in Washington in support of US involvement in Vietnam. The marchers are led by five Medal of Honor recipients.

November 14–16: The Battle of Ia Drang Valley marks the first major ground battle between US troops and North Vietnamese Army regulars (NVA) inside South Vietnam. American Army troops of the 1st Cavalry Division (Airmobile) respond to the NVA threat by using helicopters to fly directly into the battle zone. Upon landing, the troops quickly disembark then engage in fierce firefights, supported by heavy artillery and B-52 air strikes, marking the first use of B-52s to assist combat troops. The two-day battle ends with NVA retreating into the jungle. Americans lose 79 KIA and 121 wounded. NVA losses are estimated at 2,000.

November 17: The American success at Ia Drang is marred by a deadly ambush against 400 soldiers of the US 7th Cavalry sent on foot to occupy nearby landing zone Albany. NVA troops that had been held in reserve during Ia Drang, along with troops that had retreated, kill 155 Americans and wound 124.

November 27: In Washington, thirty-five thousand antiwar protesters circle the White House then march on to the Washington Monument for a rally.

November 30: After visiting Vietnam, Defense Secretary McNamara privately warns that American casualty rates of up to one thousand dead per month could be expected.

December 4: In Saigon, Viet Cong terrorists bomb a hotel used by US military personnel, killing eight and wounding 137.

December 7: Defense Secretary McNamara tells President Johnson that the North Vietnamese apparently "believe that the war will be a long one, that time is their ally, and that their staying power is superior to ours."

December 9: The *New York Times* reveals the US is unable to stop the flow of North Vietnamese soldiers and supplies into the South despite extensive bombing.

December 18–20: President Johnson and top aides meet to decide the future course of action.

December 25: The second pause in the bombing of North Vietnam occurs. This will last for thirty-seven days while the US attempts to pressure North Vietnam into a negotiated peace. However, the North Vietnamese denounce the bombing halt as a "trick" and continue Viet Cong terrorist activities in the South. By year's end, the US troop levels in Vietnam reached 184,300. An estimated 90,000 South Vietnamese soldiers deserted in 1965, while an estimated 35,000 soldiers from North Vietnam infiltrated the South via the Ho Chi Minh trail. Up to 50 percent of the countryside in South Vietnam is now under some degree of Viet Cong control. *Time* magazine chooses General William Westmoreland as 1965's Man of the Year.

1966

January 12: During his State of the Union address before Congress, President Johnson comments that the war in Vietnam is unlike America's previous wars, "yet, finally, war is always the same. It is young men dying in the fullness of their promise. It is trying to kill a man that you do not even know well enough to hate . . . therefore, to know war is to know that there is still madness in this world."

January 28–March 6: Operation Masher marks the beginning of large-scale US search-and-destroy operations against Viet Cong and NVA troop encampments. However, President Johnson orders the name changed to the less-aggressive-sounding White Wing over concern for US public opinion. During the forty-two-day operation in South Vietnam's Bon Son Plain near the coast, troopers of the US 1st Cavalry Division (Airmobile) once again fly by helicopters directly into battle zones and engage in heavy fighting. The US military has 228 Americans killed in action and 788 wounded. NVA losses are put at 1,342. The term *search and destroy* is used by the media to describe everything from large-scale airmobile troop movements to small patrols rooting out Viet Cong in tiny hamlets. The term eventually becomes associated with negative images of Americans burning villages.

January 31: Citing Hanoi's failure to respond to his peace overtures during the thirty-seven-day bombing pause, President Johnson announces bombing of North Vietnam will resume. Senator Robert F. Kennedy criticizes President Johnson's decision to resume the bombing, stating that the "US may be headed on a road from which there is no turning back, a road that leads to catastrophe for all mankind." His comments infuriate the president.

February: The Senate Foreign Relations Committee, chaired by Senator J. William Fulbright, holds televised hearings examining America's policy in Vietnam. Appearing before the committee, Defense Secretary McNamara states that US objectives in Vietnam are "not to destroy or overthrow the communist government of North Vietnam. They are limited to the destruction of the insurrection and aggression directed by North Vietnamese against the political institutions of South Vietnam."

February 3: Influential newspaper columnist Walter Lippmann lambastes President Johnson's strategy in Vietnam, stating, "Gestures, propaganda, public relations and bombing and more bombing will not work." Lippmann predicts Vietnam will divide America as combat casualties mount.

February 6–9: President Johnson and South Vietnam's prime minister Nguyen Cao Ky meet in Honolulu.

March 1: An attempt to repeal the Gulf of Tonkin Resolution fails in the US Senate by a vote of 92 to 5. The attempt was led by Sen. Wayne Morse.

March 9: The US reveals that twenty thousand acres of food crops have been destroyed in suspected Viet Cong villages. The admission generates harsh criticism from the American academic community.

March 10: South Vietnamese Buddhists begin a violent campaign to oust Prime Minister Ky following his dismissal of a top Buddhist general. This marks the beginning of a period of extreme unrest in several cities in South Vietnam including Saigon, Da Nang, and Hue as political squabbling spills out into the streets and interferes with US military operations.

March 26: Antiwar protests are held in New York, Washington DC, Chicago, Philadelphia, Boston, and San Francisco.

April 12: B-52 bombers are used for the first time against North Vietnam. Each B-52 carries up to one hundred bombs, dropped from an altitude of about six miles. Target selections are closely supervised by the White House. There are six main target categories: power facilities, war support facilities, transportation lines, military complexes, fuel storage, and air defense installations.

April 13: Viet Cong attack Tan Son Nhut airport in Saigon, causing 140 casualties while destroying 12 US helicopters and 9 aircraft.

May: Thousands in Washington DC demonstrate against the war.

May 2: Secretary of Defense McNamara privately reports the North Vietnamese are infiltrating 4,500 men per month into the South.

May 14: Political unrest intensifies as South Vietnamese troops loyal to Prime Minister Ky overrun renegade South Vietnamese Buddhist troops in Da Nang. Ky's troops then move on to Hue to oust renegades there. Ky's actions result in a new series of immolations by Buddhist monks and nuns as an act of protest against his Saigon regime and its American backers. Buddhist leader Tri Quang blames President Johnson personally for the situation. Johnson responds by labeling the immolations as "tragic and unnecessary."

June 4: A three-page antiwar advertisement appears in the *New York Times* signed by 6,400 teachers and professors.

June 25: Political unrest in South Vietnam abates following the crackdown on Buddhist rebels by Prime Minister Ky, including the arrest of Buddhist leader Tri Quang. Ky now appeals for calm.

June 29: Citing increased infiltration of communist guerrillas from North Vietnam into the South, the US bombs oil depots around Hanoi and Haiphong, ending a self-imposed moratorium. The US is very cautious about targeting the city of Hanoi itself over concerns for the reactions of North Vietnam's military allies, China and the Soviet Union. This concern also prevents any US ground invasion of North Vietnam, despite such recommendations by a few military planners in Washington.

July 6: Hanoi radio reports that captured American pilots have been paraded through the streets of Hanoi through jeering crowds.

July 11: The US intensifies bombing raids against portions of the Ho Chi Minh trail winding through Laos.

July 15: Operation Hastings is launched by US Marines and South Vietnamese troops against ten thousand NVA in Quang Tri Province. This is the largest combined military operation to date in the war.

July 30: For the first time, the US bombs NVA troops in the demilitarized zone, the buffer area separating North and South Vietnam.

August 9: US jets attack two South Vietnamese villages by mistake, killing sixty-three civilians and wounding over one hundred.

August 30: Hanoi announces China will provide economic and technical assistance.

September 1: During a visit to neighboring Cambodia, French president Charles de Gaulle calls for US withdrawal from Vietnam.

September 12: The heaviest air raid of the war to date occurs as five hundred US jets attack NVA supply lines and coastal targets.

September 14–November 24: Operation Attleboro begins involving 20,000 US and South Vietnamese soldiers in a successful search-and-destroy mission 50 miles north of Saigon near the Cambodian border. During the fighting, an enormous weapons cache is uncovered in a hidden base camp in the jungle. Americans lose 155 KIA and 494 are wounded. North Vietnamese losses are 1,106.

September 23: The US reveals jungles near the demilitarized zone are being defoliated by sprayed chemicals.

October 2–24: The US 1st Air Cavalry Division conducts Operation Irving to clear NVA from mountainous areas near Qui Nhon.

October 3: The Soviet Union announces it will provide military and economic assistance to North Vietnam.

October 25: President Johnson conducts a conference in Manila with America's Vietnam Allies: Australia, Philippines, Thailand, New Zealand, South Korea, and South Vietnam. The Allies pledge to withdraw from Vietnam within six months if North Vietnam will withdraw completely from the South.

October 26: President Johnson visits US troops at Cam Ranh Bay. This is the first of two visits to Vietnam made during his presidency.

November 7: Defense Secretary McNamara is confronted by student protesters during a visit to Harvard University.

November 12: The *New York Times* reports that 40 percent of US economic aid sent to Saigon is stolen or winds up on the black market.

December 8–9: North Vietnam rejects a proposal by President Johnson for discussions concerning treatment of POWs and a possible exchange.

December 13–14: The village of Caudat near Hanoi is leveled by US bombers resulting in harsh criticism from the international community.

December 26: Facing increased scrutiny from journalists over mounting civilian casualties in North Vietnam, the US Defense Department now admits civilians may have been bombed accidentally.

December 27: The US mounts a large-scale air assault against suspected Viet Cong positions in the Mekong Delta using napalm and hundreds of tons of bombs.

By year's end, US troop levels reach 389,000, with 5,008 combat deaths and 30,093 wounded. Over half of the American casualties are caused by snipers and small-arms fire during Viet Cong ambushes, along with handmade booby traps and mines planted everywhere in the countryside by Viet Cong. American allies fighting in Vietnam include 45,000 soldiers from South Korea and 7,000 Australians. An estimated 89,000 soldiers from North Vietnam infiltrated the South via the Ho Chi Minh trail in 1966.

1967

January 2: Operation Bolo occurs as 28 US Air Force F-4 Phantom jets lure North Vietnamese MIG-21's interceptors into a dogfight over Hanoi and shoot down seven of them. This leaves only nine MIG-21s operational for the North Vietnamese. American pilots, however, are prohibited by Washington from attacking MIG air bases in North Vietnam.

January 8–26: Operation Cedar Falls occurs. It is the largest combined offensive to date and involves sixteen thousand American and fourteen thousand South Vietnamese soldiers clearing out Viet Cong from the Iron Triangle area twenty-five miles northwest of Saigon. The Viet Cong choose not to fight and instead melt away into the jungle. Americans then uncover an extensive network of tunnels and, for the first time, use "tunnel rats," the nickname given to specially trained volunteers who explore the maze of tunnels. After the American and South Vietnamese troops leave the area, Viet Cong return and rebuild their sanctuary. This pattern is repeated throughout the war as Americans utilize in-and-out tactics in which troops arrive by helicopters, secure an area, and then depart by helicopters.

January 10: UN Secretary-General U Thant expresses doubts that Vietnam is essential to the security of the West. On this same day, during his State of the Union address before Congress, President Johnson once again declares, "We will stand firm in Vietnam."

January 23: Senator J. William Fulbright publishes *The Arrogance of Power*, a book critical of American war policy in Vietnam advocating direct peace talks between the South Vietnamese government and the Viet Cong. By this time, Fulbright and President Johnson are no longer on speaking terms. Instead, the president uses the news media to deride Fulbright, Robert Kennedy, and a growing number of critics in Congress as "nervous Nellies" and "sunshine patriots."

February 2: President Johnson states there are no "serious indications that the other side is ready to stop the war."

February 8–10: American religious groups stage a nationwide Fast for Peace.

February 8–12: A truce occurs during Tet, the lunar New Year, and a traditional Vietnamese holiday.

February 13: Following the failure of diplomatic peace efforts, President Johnson announces the US will resume full-scale bombing of North Vietnam.

February 22–May 14: The largest US military offensive of the war occurs. Operation Junction City involves 22 US and 4 South Vietnamese battalions attempting to destroy the NVA's Central Office headquarters in South Vietnam. The offensive includes the only parachute assault by US troops during the entire war. During the fighting at Ap Gu, US 1st Battalion, 26th Infantry is commanded by Lt. Gen. Alexander M. Haig, who will later become an influential White House aide. Junction City ends with 2,728 Viet Cong killed and 34 captured. American losses are 282 killed and 1,576 wounded. NVA relocate their central office headquarters inside Cambodia, thus avoiding capture.

March: Ellsworth Bunker is named successor to Lodge as US ambassador to South Vietnam.

March 8: Congress authorizes $4.5 billion for the war.

March 19–21: President Johnson meets in Guam with South Vietnam's prime minister Ky and pressures Ky to hold national elections.

April 6: Quang Tri City is attacked by 2,500 Viet Cong and NVA.

April 14: Richard M. Nixon visits Saigon and states that antiwar protests back in the US are "prolonging the war."

April 15: Antiwar demonstrations occur in New York and San Francisco, involving nearly two hundred thousand protesters. Rev. Martin Luther King declares that the war is undermining President Johnson's Great Society social reform programs: "The pursuit of this widened war has narrowed the promised dimensions of the domestic welfare programs, making the poor white and negro bear the heaviest burdens both at the front and at home."

April 20: US bombers target Haiphong harbor in North Vietnam for the first time.

April 24-May 11: Hill fights rage at Khe Sanh between US 3rd Marines and the North Vietnamese Army, resulting in 940 NVA killed. American losses are 155 killed and 425 wounded. The isolated air base is located in mountainous terrain less than 10 miles from North Vietnam near the border of Laos. General Westmoreland condemns antiwar demonstrators saying they give the North Vietnamese soldier "hope that he can win politically that which he cannot accomplish militarily." Privately, he has already warned President Johnson "the war could go on indefinitely."

May 1: Ellsworth Bunker replaces Henry Cabot Lodge as US ambassador to South Vietnam.

May 2: The US is condemned during a mock war crimes tribunal held in Stockholm, organized by British philosopher Bertrand Russell.

May 9: Robert W. Komer, a former CIA analyst, is appointed by President Johnson as deputy commander of MACV to form a new agency called Civil Operations and Revolutionary Development Support (CORDS) to pacify the population of South Vietnam. Nearly 60 percent of rural villages in South Vietnam are now under Viet Cong control. $850 million in food, medical supplies, machinery, and numerous other household items will be distributed through CORDS to the population in order to regain their loyalty in the struggle for the "hearts and minds" of common villagers. CORDS also train local militias to protect their villages from the Viet Cong.

May 13: In New York City, seventy thousand march in support of the war, led by a New York City fire captain.

May 18–26: US and South Vietnamese troops enter the demilitarized zone for the first time and engage in a series of firefights with NVA. Both sides suffer heavy losses.

May 22: President Johnson publicly urges North Vietnam to accept a peace compromise.

June: Johnson and Kosygin meet to discuss Vietnam peace. No progress is made.

June: The Mobile Riverine Force becomes operational utilizing US Navy Swift boats combined with Army troop support to halt Viet Cong usage of inland waterways in the Mekong Delta.

July: General Westmoreland requests an additional 200,000 reinforcements on top of the 475,000 soldiers already scheduled to be sent to Vietnam, which would bring the US total in Vietnam to 675,000. President Johnson agrees only to an extra 45,000.

July 7: North Vietnam's politburo makes the decision to launch a widespread offensive against South Vietnam. Conceived in three phases, the first phase involves attacks against remote border areas in an effort to lure American troops away from South Vietnam's cities. The second phase (Tet Offensive) will be an attack against the cities themselves by Viet Cong forces aided by NVA troops, in the hope of igniting a "general uprising" to overthrow the government of South Vietnam. The third phase involves the actual invasion of South Vietnam by NVA troops coming from North Vietnam.

July 29: A fire resulting from a punctured fuel tank kills 134 US crewmen aboard the USS *Forestall* in the Gulf of Tonkin, in the worst naval accident since World War II.

August 9: The Senate Armed Services Committee begins closed-door hearings concerning the influence of civilian advisers on military planning. During the hearings, Defense Secretary McNamara testifies that the extensive and costly US bombing campaign in Vietnam is failing to impact North Vietnam's war-making ability in South Vietnam and that nothing short of "the virtual annihilation of North Vietnam and its people" through bombing would ever succeed.

August 18: California governor Ronald Reagan says the US should get out of Vietnam, citing the difficulties of winning a war when "too many qualified targets have been put off limits to bombing."

August 21: The Chinese shoot down two US fighter-bombers that accidentally crossed their border during air raids in North Vietnam along the Chinese border.

September: Troops from Thailand arrive in South Vietnam.

September 1: North Vietnamese prime minister Pham Van Dong publicly states Hanoi will "continue to fight."

September 3: National elections are held in South Vietnam. With 80 percent of eligible voters participating, Nguyen Van Thieu is elected president with Nguyen Cao Ky as his vice president, the pair winning just 35 percent of the vote.

September 11–October 31: US Marines are besieged by NVA at Con Thien, located two miles south of the demilitarized zone. A massive long-range artillery duel then erupts between NVA and US guns during the siege as NVA fire 42,000 rounds at the Marines while the US responds with 281,000 rounds and B-52 air strikes to lift the siege. NVA losses are estimated at over 2,000.

October: A public opinion poll indicates 46 percent of Americans now believe US military involvement in Vietnam to be a "mistake." However, most Americans also believe that the US should "win or get out" of Vietnam. Also in October, *Life* magazine renounces its earlier support of President Johnson's war policies.

October 5: Hanoi accuses the US of hitting a school in North Vietnam with antipersonnel bombs.

October 21–23: March on the Pentagon draws fifty-five thousand protesters. In London, protesters try to storm the US embassy.

October 31: President Johnson reaffirms his commitment to maintain US involvement in South Vietnam.

November 3–December 1: The Battle of Dak To occurs in the mountainous terrain along the border of Cambodia and Laos as the US 4th Infantry Division heads off a planned NVA attack against the Special Forces camp located there. Massive air strikes combined with US and South Vietnamese ground attacks result in an NVA withdrawal into Laos and Cambodia. NVA losses are put at 1,644. US troops suffer 289 killed. "Along with the gallantry and tenacity of our soldiers, our tremendously successful air logistic operation was the key to the victory," states General Westmoreland.

November 11: President Johnson makes another peace overture, but it is soon rejected by Hanoi.

November 17: Following an optimistic briefing in the White House by General Westmoreland, Ambassador Bunker, and Robert Komer, President Johnson tells the American public on TV, "We are inflicting greater losses than we're taking . . . We are making progress." In a *Time* magazine interview, General Westmoreland taunts the Viet Cong, saying, "I hope they try something because we are looking for a fight."

November 29: An emotional Robert McNamara announces his resignation as Defense Secretary during a press briefing, stating, "Mr. President . . . I cannot find words to express what lies in my heart today" Behind closed doors, he had begun regularly expressing doubts over Johnson's war strategy, angering the president. McNamara joins a growing list of Johnson's top aides who resigned over the war, including Bill Moyers, McGeorge Bundy, and George Ball.

November 30: Antiwar Democrat Eugene McCarthy announces he will be a candidate for president opposing Lyndon Johnson, stating, "We are involved in a very deep crisis of leadership, a crisis of direction and a crisis of national purpose . . . the entire history of this war in Vietnam, no matter what we call it, has been one of continued error and misjudgment."

December 4: Four days of antiwar protests begin in New York. Among the 585 protesters arrested is renowned "baby doctor" Dr. Benjamin Spock.

December 6: The US reports Viet Cong murdered 252 civilians in the hamlet of Dak Son.

December 23: Upon arrival at Cam Ranh Bay in Vietnam, President Johnson declares, "All the challenges have been met. The enemy is not beaten, but he knows that he has met his master in the field." This is the president's second and final trip to Vietnam during his presidency. By year's end, US troop levels reach 463,000, with 16,000 combat deaths to date. By this time, over a million American soldiers have rotated through Vietnam, with length of service for draftees being one year, and most Americans serving in support units. An estimated 90,000 soldiers from North Vietnam infiltrated into the South via the Ho Chi Minh trail in 1967. Overall, Viet Cong/NVA troop strength throughout South Vietnam is now estimated up to 300,000 men.

1968

January 5: Operation Niagara I to map NVA positions around Khe Sanh begins.

January 21: Twenty thousand NVA troops under the command of General Giap attack the American air base at Khe Sanh. A seventy-seven-day siege begins as five thousand US Marines in the isolated outpost are encircled. The siege attracts enormous media attention back in America, with many comparisons made to the 1954 Battle of Dien Bien Phu in which the French were surrounded then defeated. "I don't want another damn Dien Bien Phu," an anxious President Johnson tells Joint Chiefs Chairman Gen. Earle Wheeler. As Johnson personally sends off Marine reinforcements, he states, "The eyes of the nation and the eyes of the entire world, the eyes of all of history itself, are on that little brave band of defenders who hold the pass at Khe Sanh." Johnson issues presidential orders to the Marines to hold the base and demands a guarantee "signed in blood" from the Joint Chiefs of Staff that they will succeed. Operation Niagara II then begins a massive aerial supply effort to the besieged Marines along with heavy B-52 bombardment of NVA troop positions. At the peak of the battle, NVA soldiers are hit round-the-clock every ninety minutes by groups of three B-52s, which drop over 110,000 tons of bombs during the siege, the heaviest bombardment of a small area in the history of warfare.

January 31: The turning point of the war occurs as eighty-four thousand Viet Cong guerrillas aided by NVA troops launch the Tet Offensive, attacking a hundred cities and towns throughout South Vietnam. The surprise offensive is closely observed by American TV news crews in Vietnam, which film the US embassy in Saigon being attacked by seventeen Viet Cong commandos, along with bloody scenes from battle areas showing American soldiers under fire, dead, and wounded. The graphic color film footage is then quickly relayed back to the states for broadcast on nightly news programs. Americans at home thus have a front-row seat in their living rooms to the Viet Cong/NVA assaults against their fathers, sons, and brothers, ten thousand miles away. "The whole thing stinks, really," says a Marine under fire at Hue after more than one hundred Marines are killed.

January 31–March 7: In the Battle for Saigon during Tet, thirty-five NVA and Viet Cong battalions are defeated by fifty battalions of American and Allied troops that had been positioned to protect the city on a hunch by Lt. Gen. Fred C. Weyand, a veteran of World War II in the Pacific. Nicknamed the Savior of Saigon, Weyand had sensed the coming attack, prepared his troops, and on February 1 launched a decisive counterattack against the Viet Cong at Tan Son Nhut airport, thus protecting nearby MACV and South Vietnamese military headquarters from possible capture.

January 31–March 2: In the Battle for Hue during Tet, twelve thousand NVA and Viet Cong troops storm the lightly defended historical city and begin systematic executions of over three thousand "enemies of the people," including South Vietnamese government officials, and captured South Vietnamese officers and Catholic priests. South Vietnamese troops and three US Marine battalions counterattack and engage in the heaviest fighting of the entire Tet Offensive. They retake the old imperial city, house by house, street by street, aided by American air and artillery strikes. On February 24, US Marines occupy the Imperial Palace in the heart of the citadel, and the battle soon ends with a North Vietnamese defeat. American losses are 142 Marines killed and 857 wounded, 74 US Army killed and

507 wounded. South Vietnamese suffer 384 killed and 1,830 wounded. NVA killed are over 5,000.

February 1: In Saigon during Tet, a suspected Viet Cong guerrilla is shot in the head by South Vietnam's police chief Gen. Nguyen Ngoc Loan, in full view of an NBC news cameraman and an Associated Press still photographer. The haunting AP photo taken by Eddie Adams appears on the front page of most American newspapers the next morning. Americans also observe the filmed execution on NBC-TV. Another controversy during Tet, and one of the most controversial statements of the entire war, is made by an American officer who states, "We had to destroy it, in order to save it," referring to a small city near Saigon leveled by American bombs. His statement is later used by many as a metaphor for the American experience in Vietnam.

February 2: President Johnson labels the Tet Offensive "a complete failure." For the North Vietnamese, the Tet Offensive is both a military and political failure in Vietnam. The "general uprising" they had hoped to ignite among South Vietnamese peasants against the Saigon government never materialized. The Viet Cong, who had also come out of hiding to do most of the actual fighting, suffered devastating losses and never regained their former strength. As a result, most of the fighting will be taken over by North Vietnamese regulars fighting a conventional war. Tet's only success, and an unexpected one, was in eroding grassroots support among Americans and in Congress for continuing the war indefinitely.

February 8: Twenty-one US Marines are killed by NVA at Khe Sanh.

February 27: Influential CBS-TV news anchorman Walter Cronkite, who just returned from Saigon, tells Americans during his *CBS Evening News* broadcast that he is certain "the bloody experience of Vietnam is to end in a stalemate."

February 28: Joint Chiefs Chairman General Wheeler, at the behest of General Westmoreland, asks President Johnson for an additional 206,000 soldiers and mobilization of reserve units in the US.

March: The battle for Hue ends with NVA repulsed.

March 1: Clark Clifford, renowned Washington lawyer and an old friend of the president, becomes the new US Secretary of Defense. For the next few days, Clifford conducts an intensive study of the entire situation in Vietnam, discovers there is no concept or overall plan anywhere in Washington for achieving victory in Vietnam, then reports to President Johnson that the United States should not escalate the war. "The time has come to decide where we go from here," he tells Johnson.

March 2: Forty-eight US Army soldiers are killed during an ambush at Tan Son Nhut airport in Saigon.

March 10: The *New York Times* breaks the news of Westmoreland's 206,000 troop request. The *Times* story is denied by the White House. Secretary of State Dean Rusk is then called before the Senate Foreign Relations Committee and grilled for two days on live TV about the troop request and the overall effectiveness of Johnson's war strategy.

March 11: Operation Quyet Thang begins a twenty-eight-day offensive by thirty-three US and South Vietnamese battalions in the Saigon region.

March 12: By a very slim margin of just three hundred votes, President Johnson defeats antiwar Democrat Eugene McCarthy in the New Hampshire Democratic primary election. This indicates that political support for Johnson is seriously eroding. Public opinion polls taken after the Tet Offensive revealed Johnson's overall approval rating has slipped to 36 percent, while approval of his Vietnam War policy slipped to 26 percent.

March 14: Senator Robert F. Kennedy offers President Johnson a confidential political proposition. Kennedy will agree to stay out of the presidential race if Johnson will renounce his earlier Vietnam strategy and appoint a committee, including Kennedy, to chart a new course in Vietnam. Johnson spurns the offer.

March 16: Robert F. Kennedy announces his candidacy for the presidency. Polls indicate Kennedy is now more popular than the president. During his campaign, Kennedy addresses the issue of his participation in forming President John F. Kennedy's

Vietnam policy by stating, "Past error is no excuse for its own perpetuation."

March 16: Over three hundred Vietnamese civilians are slaughtered in My Lai hamlet by members of Charlie Company, 1st Battalion, 20th Infantry US Army, while participating in an air assault against suspected Viet Cong encampments in Quang Ngai Province. Upon entering My Lai and finding no Viet Cong, the Americans begin killing every civilian in sight, interrupted only by helicopter pilot Hugh Thompson, who lands and begins evacuating civilians after realizing what is happening.

March 23: During a secret meeting in the Philippines, General Wheeler informs General Westmoreland that President Johnson will approve only 13,500 additional soldiers out of the original 206,000 requested. General Wheeler also instructs Westmoreland to urge the South Vietnamese to expand their own war effort.

March 25: Clark Clifford convenes the Wise Men, a dozen distinguished elder statesmen and soldiers, including former Secretary of State Dean Acheson and World War II general Omar Bradley at the State Department for dinner. They are given a blunt assessment of the situation in Vietnam, including the widespread corruption of the Saigon government and the unlikely prospect for military victory "under the present circumstances."

March 26: The Wise Men gather at the White House for lunch with the president. They now advocate US withdrawal from Vietnam, with only four of those present dissenting from that opinion.

March 28: The initial report by participants at My Lai states that sixty-nine Viet Cong soldiers were killed and makes no mention of civilian casualties. The My Lai massacre is successfully concealed for a year, until a series of letters from Vietnam veteran Ronald Ridenhour spark an official Army investigation that results in Charlie Company commander, Capt. Ernest L. Medina, First Platoon Leader, Lt. William Calley, and fourteen others being brought to trial by the Army. A news photo of the carnage—showing a mass of dead children, women, and old men—remains one of the most enduring images of America's involvement in Vietnam.

March 31: President Johnson stuns the world by announcing his surprise decision not to seek reelection. He also announces a partial bombing halt and urges Hanoi to begin peace talks. "We are prepared to move immediately toward peace through negotiations." As a result, peace talks soon begin. The bombing halt only affects targets north of the 20th parallel, including Hanoi.

April: General Creighton W. Abrams named to succeed General Westmoreland in South Vietnam.

April 1: The US 1st Cavalry Division (Airmobile) begins Operation Pegasus to reopen Route 9, the relief route to the besieged Marines at Khe Sanh.

April 4: Civil rights leader Rev. Dr. Martin Luther King is assassinated in Memphis. Racial unrest then erupts in over one hundred American cities.

April 8: The siege of Khe Sanh ends with the withdrawal of NVA troops from the area as a result of intensive American bombing and the reopening of Route 9. NVA losses during the siege are estimated up to 15,000. US Marines suffered 199 killed and 830 wounded. 1st Cavalry suffered 92 killed and 629 wounded reopening Route 9. The US command then secretly shuts down the Khe Sanh air base and withdraws the Marines. Commenting on the heroism of US troops that defended Khe Sanh, President Johnson states, "They vividly demonstrated to the enemy the utter futility of his attempts to win a military victory in the South." A North Vietnamese official labels the closing of Khe Sanh air base as America's "gravest defeat" so far.

April 11: Defense Secretary Clifford announces General Westmoreland's request for 206,000 additional soldiers will not be granted.

April 23: Antiwar activists at Columbia University seize five buildings.

April 27: In New York, two hundred thousand students refuse to attend classes as a protest.

April 30-May 3: The Battle of Dai Do occurs along the demilitarized zone as NVA troops seek to open an invasion corridor into South Vietnam. They are halted by a battalion of US Marines nicknamed the Magnificent Bastards, under the command of Lt. Col. William Weise. Aided by heavy artillery and air strikes, NVA suffers 1,568 killed. There are 81 Marines killed and 297 wounded. The US Army loses 29 KIA supporting the Marines and 130 wounded. For the time being, this defeat ends North Vietnam's hope of successfully invading the South. They will wait four years, until 1972, before trying again, after most of the Americans have gone. It will actually take seven years, until 1975, for them to succeed.

May 5: Viet Cong launch Mini Tet, a series of rocket and mortar attacks against Saigon and 119 cities and military installations throughout South Vietnam. The US responds with air strikes using napalm and high explosives.

May 10: An NVA battalion attacks the Special Forces camp at Kham Duc along the border of Laos. The isolated camp had been established in 1963 to monitor North Vietnamese infiltration. Now encircled by NVA, the decision is made to evacuate via C-130 transport planes. At the conclusion of the successful airlift, it is discovered that three US Air Force controllers have accidentally been left behind. Although the camp is now overrun by NVA and two C-130s have already been shot down, Lt. Col. Joe M. Jackson pilots a C-123 Provider, lands on the airstrip under intense fire, gathers all three controllers, then takes off. For heroic action, Jackson is awarded the Medal of Honor.

May 10: Peace talks begin in Paris but soon stall as the US insists that North Vietnamese troops withdraw from the South, while the North Vietnamese insist on Viet Cong participation in a coalition government in South Vietnam. This marks the beginning of five years of on-again, off-again official talks between the US and North Vietnam in Paris.

June 5: Robert F. Kennedy is shot and mortally wounded in Los Angeles just after winning the California Democratic presidential primary election.

June: At the end of June, Le Duc Tho, chief negotiator, leaves the Paris peace talks and returns to Hanoi.

July: Congress passes a 10 percent income tax surcharge to defray the ballooning costs of the war.

July 1: General Westmoreland is replaced as US commander in Vietnam by General Creighton W. Abrams. The Phoenix Program is established to crush the secret Viet Cong infrastructure (VCI) in South Vietnam. The VCI, estimated at up to seventy thousand communist guerrillas, has been responsible for a long-standing campaign of terror against Americans, South Vietnamese government officials, village leaders, and innocent civilians. However, the Phoenix Program, which is controlled through CORDS under the direction of Robert Komer, generates huge controversy in America concerning numerous alleged assassinations of suspected Viet Cong operatives by South Vietnamese trained by the US. The controversy, generated in part through North Vietnamese propaganda, eventually results in Congressional hearings. Testifying in 1971 before Congress, Komer's successor William E. Colby states, "The Phoenix Program was not a program of assassination. The Phoenix Program was a part of the overall pacification program." Colby admits that 20,587 Viet Cong had been killed "mostly in combat situations . . . by regular or paramilitary forces."

July 3: Three American prisoners of war are released by Hanoi.

July 19: President Johnson and South Vietnam's president Thieu meet in Hawaii.

August 8: Richard M. Nixon is chosen as the Republican presidential candidate and promises "an honorable end to the war in Vietnam."

August 28: During the Democratic national convention in Chicago, 10,000 antiwar protesters gather on downtown streets and are then confronted by 26,000 police and national guardsmen. The brutal crackdown is covered live on network television. Over 800 demonstrators are injured. The United States is now experiencing a level of social unrest unseen since the American Civil

War era, a hundred years earlier. There have been 221 student protests at 101 colleges and universities thus far in 1968.

September 30: The nine hundredth US aircraft is shot down over North Vietnam.

October: Operation Sealord begins the largest combined naval operation of the entire war as over 1,200 US Navy and South Vietnamese Navy gunboats and warships target NVA supply lines extending from Cambodia into the Mekong Delta. NVA supply camps in the Delta and along other waterways are also successfully disrupted during the two-year operation.

October 21: The US releases fourteen North Vietnamese POWs.

October 27: In London, fifty thousand protest the war.

October 31: Operation Rolling Thunder ends as President Johnson announces a complete halt of US bombing of North Vietnam in the hope of restarting the peace talks. Throughout the three-and-a-half-year bombing campaign, the US flew over 300,000 sorties and dropped a million tons of bombs on North Vietnam. The equivalent of 800 tons of bombs was dropped per day, with little actual success in halting the flow of soldiers and supplies into the South or in damaging North Vietnamese morale. In fact, the opposite has occurred as the North Vietnamese have patriotically rallied around their communist leaders as a result of the onslaught. By now, many towns south of Hanoi have been leveled with a US estimate of 52,000 civilian deaths. During Operation Rolling Thunder, North Vietnam's sophisticated, Soviet-supplied air defense system managed to shoot down 922 US aircraft.

November: Le Duc Tho returns to Paris for peace talks.

November: William E. Colby replaces Robert Komer as head of CORDS.

November 5: Republican Richard M. Nixon narrowly defeats Democrat Hubert Humphrey in the US presidential election.

November 27: President-elect Nixon asks Harvard professor Henry Kissinger to be his national security advisor. Kissinger accepts. By year's end, US troop levels reached 495,000 with 30,000 American deaths to date. In 1968, over a thousand a month were killed. An estimated 150,000 soldiers from North Vietnam infiltrated the South via the Ho Chi Minh trail in 1968. Although the US conducted 200 air strikes each day against the trail in late 1968, up to 10,000 NVA supply trucks are en route at any given time.

December: North Vietnamese negotiators at the Paris peace conference squabble over the shape of the conference table.

1969

January 1: Henry Cabot Lodge, former American ambassador to South Vietnam, is nominated by President-elect Nixon to be the senior US negotiator at the Paris peace talks.

January 20: Richard M. Nixon is inaugurated as the thirty-seventh US president and declares, "The greatest honor history can bestow is the title of peacemaker. This honor now beckons America." He is the fifth president coping with Vietnam and had successfully campaigned on a pledge of "peace with honor."

January 22: Operation Dewey Canyon, the last major operation by US Marines, begins in the Da Krong valley.

January 25: Paris peace talks open with the US, South Vietnam, North Vietnam, and the Viet Cong all in attendance.

February 23: Viet Cong attack 110 targets throughout South Vietnam including Saigon.

February 25: NVA raid a Marine Base Camp near the demilitarized zone and kill thirty-six US Marines.

March 4: President Nixon threatens to resume bombing North Vietnam in retaliation for Viet Cong offenses in the South.

March 15: US troops go on the offensive inside the demilitarized zone for the first time since 1968.

March: Letters from Vietnam veteran Ronald Ridenhour result in a US Army investigation into the My Lai massacre.

March 17: President Nixon authorizes Operation Menu, the secret bombing of Cambodia by B-52s, targeting North Vietnamese supply sanctuaries located along the border of Vietnam.

March: Mass graves of hundreds of executed civilians are uncovered in Hue.

April 9: An estimated three hundred antiwar students at Harvard University seize the administration building, throw out eight deans, then lock themselves in. They are later forcibly ejected.

April 30: US troop levels peak at 543,400. There have been 33,641 Americans killed by now, a total greater than the Korean War.

May: The *New York Times* breaks the news of the secret bombing of Cambodia. As a result, Nixon orders FBI wiretaps on the telephones of four journalists, along with thirteen government officials to determine the source of the news leak.

May 10–May 20: Forty-six men of the 101st Airborne die, and another four hundred are wounded during a fierce ten-day battle at Hamburger Hill in the A Shau Valley near Hue. After the hill is taken, the troops are then ordered to abandon it by their commander. NVA then move in and take back the hill unopposed. The costly assault and its confused aftermath provoke a political outcry back in the US that American lives are being wasted in Vietnam. One senator labels the assault "senseless and irresponsible." It is the beginning of the end for America in Vietnam as Washington now orders MACV commander Gen. Creighton Abrams to avoid such encounters in the future. Hamburger Hill is the last major search-and-destroy mission by US troops during the war. Small unit actions will now be used instead. A long period of decline in morale and discipline begins among American draftees serving in Vietnam involuntarily. Drug usage becomes rampant as nearly 50 percent experiment with marijuana, opium, or heroin, which is easy to obtain on the streets of Saigon. US military hospitals later become deluged with drug-related cases as drug abuse casualties far outnumber casualties of war.

May 14: During his first TV speech on Vietnam, President Nixon presents a peace plan in which America and North Vietnam would simultaneously pull out of South Vietnam over the next year. The offer is rejected by Hanoi.

June: Bombing of North Vietnam resumes briefly in retaliation for the loss of a US reconnaissance plane.

June 8: President Nixon meets South Vietnam's president Nguyen Van Thieu at Midway Island and informs him US troop levels are going to be sharply reduced. During a press briefing with Thieu, Nixon announces Vietnamization of the war and a US troop withdrawal of twenty-five thousand men.

June 27: *Life* magazine displays portrait photos of all 242 Americans killed in Vietnam during the previous week, including the 46 killed at Hamburger Hill. The photos have a stunning impact on Americans nationwide as they view the once smiling young faces of the dead.

July: President Nixon, through a French emissary, sends a secret letter to Ho Chi Minh urging him to settle the war, while at the same time threatening to resume bombing if peace talks remain stalled as of November 1. In August, Hanoi responds by repeating earlier demands for Viet Cong participation in a coalition government in South Vietnam.

July 8: The very first US troop withdrawal occurs as eight hundred men from the 9th Infantry Division are sent home. The phased troop withdrawal will occur in fourteen stages from July 1969 through November 1972.

July 17: Secretary of State William Rogers accuses Hanoi of "lacking humanity" in the treatment of American POWs.

July 25: The Nixon Doctrine is made public. It advocates US military and economic assistance to nations around the world struggling against communism, but no more Vietnam-style ground wars involving American troops. The emphasis is thus placed on local military self-sufficiency, backed by US airpower and technical assistance to assure security.

July 30: President Nixon visits US troops and President Thieu in Vietnam. This is Nixon's only trip to Vietnam during his presidency.

August 4: Henry Kissinger conducts his first secret meeting in Paris with representatives from Hanoi.

August 12: Viet Cong begin a new offensive attacking 150 targets throughout South Vietnam.

September 2: Ho Chi Minh dies of a heart attack at age seventy-nine. He is succeeded by Le Duan, who publicly reads the last will of Ho Chi Minh urging the North Vietnamese to fight on "until the last Yankee has gone."

September 5: The US Army brings murder charges against Lt. William Calley concerning the massacre of Vietnamese civilians at My Lai in March of 1968.

September 16: President Nixon orders the withdrawal of thirty-five thousand soldiers from Vietnam and a reduction in draft calls.

October: An opinion poll indicates 71 percent of Americans approve of President Nixon's Vietnam policy.

October 15: The Moratorium peace demonstration is held in Washington and several US cities. Demonstration organiz- ers had received praises from North Vietnam's prime minister Pham Van Dong, who stated in a letter to them, "May your fall offensive succeed splendidly," marking the first time Hanoi publicly acknowledged the American antiwar movement. Dong's comments infuriate American conservatives, including Vice President Spiro Agnew, who lambastes the protesters as communist "dupes" comprised of "an effete corps of impudent snobs who characterize themselves as intellectuals."

November 3: President Nixon delivers a major TV speech asking for support from "the great silent majority of my fellow Americans" for his Vietnam strategy. "The more divided we are at home, the less likely the enemy is to negotiate at Paris . . . North Vietnam cannot defeat or humiliate the United States. Only Americans can do that."

November 15: The Mobilization peace demonstration draws an esti- mated 250,000 in Washington for the largest antiwar protest in US history.

November 16: For the first time, the US Army publicly discusses events surrounding the My Lai massacre.

December 1: The first draft lottery since World War II is held in New York City. Each day of the year is randomly assigned a number from 1–365. Those with birthdays on days that wind up with a low number will likely be drafted.

December 15: President Nixon orders an additional fifty thousand soldiers out of Vietnam.

December 20: A frustrated Henry Cabot Lodge quits his post as chief US negotiator at the Paris peace talks. By year's end, America's fighting strength in Vietnam has been reduced by 115,000 men. Americans have lost 40,024 military killed in Vietnam. Over the next few years, the South Vietnamese Army will be boosted to over 500,000 men in accordance with Vietnamization of the war in which they will take over the fighting from Americans.

1970

February 2: B-52 bombers strike the Ho Chi Minh trail in retaliation for the increasing number of Viet Cong raids throughout the South.

February 21: Although the official peace talks remain deadlocked in Paris, behind the scenes, Henry Kissinger begins a series of secret talks with North Vietnam's Le Duc Tho, which will go on for two years.

March 18: Prince Sihanouk of Cambodia is deposed by General Lon Nol. Sihanouk, who had been out of the country at the time of the coup, then aligns with Cambodian communists, known as the Khmer Rouge, in an effort to oust Lon Nol's regime. The Khmer Rouge are led by an unknown figure named Pol Pot, who eagerly capitalizes on the enormous prestige and popularity of Prince Sihanouk to increase support for his Khmer Rouge movement among Cambodians. Pol Pot will later violently oust Lon Nol then begin a radical experiment to create an agrarian utopia, resulting in the deaths of 25 percent of the country's population (2 million persons) from starvation, overwork, and systematic executions.

March 20: Cambodian troops under Gen. Lon Nol attack Khmer Rouge and North Vietnamese forces inside Cambodia. At the

White House, Nixon and top aides discuss plans to assist Lon Nol's pro-American regime.

March 31: The US Army brings murder charges against Captain Ernest L. Medina concerning the massacre of Vietnamese civilians at My Lai in March of 1968.

April 20: President Nixon announces the withdrawal of another 150,000 Americans from Vietnam within a year.

April 30: President Nixon stuns Americans by announcing US and South Vietnamese incursion into Cambodia, "not for the purpose of expanding the war into Cambodia but for the purpose of ending the war in Vietnam and winning the just peace we desire." The announcement generates a tidal wave of protest by politicians, the press, students, professors, clergy members, business leaders, and many average Americans against Nixon and the Vietnam War. The incursion is in response to continuing communist gains against Lon Nol's forces and is also intended to weaken overall NVA military strength as a prelude to US departure from Vietnam.

May 1: May Day, the traditional communist holiday. A combined force of fifteen thousand US and South Vietnamese soldiers attack NVA supply bases inside Cambodia. However, throughout this offensive, NVA and Viet Cong carefully avoid large-scale battles and instead withdraw westward, farther into Cambodia, leaving behind their base camps containing huge stores of weapons and ammunition.

May 1: President Nixon calls antiwar students "bums blowing up campuses."

May 2: American college campuses erupt in protest over the invasion of Cambodia.

May 4: At Kent State University in Ohio, National Guardsmen shoot and kill four student protesters and wound nine. In response to the killings, over four hundred colleges and universities across America shut down. In Washington, nearly one hundred thousand protesters surround various government buildings including the White House and historical monuments. On an impulse, President Nixon exits the White House and pays a late-night surprise visit to the Lincoln Memorial and chats with young protesters.

May 6: In Saigon over the past week, 450 civilians were killed during Viet Cong terrorist raids throughout the city, the highest weekly death toll to date.

June 3: NVA begin a new offensive toward Phnom Penh in Cambodia. The US provides air strikes to prevent the defeat of Lon Nol's inexperienced young troops.

June 22: American usage of jungle defoliants in Vietnam is halted.

June 24: The US Senate repeals the 1964 Gulf of Tonkin Resolution.

June 30: US troops withdraw from Cambodia. Over 350 Americans died during the incursion.

August 11: South Vietnamese troops take over the defense of border positions from US troops.

August 24: Heavy B-52 bombing raids occur along the demilitarized zone.

September 5: Operation Jefferson Glenn, the last US offensive in Vietnam, begins in Thua Thien Province.

October 7: During a TV speech, President Nixon proposes a "stand-still" cease-fire in which all troops would stop shooting and remain in place pending a formal peace agreement. Hanoi does not respond.

October 24: South Vietnamese troops begin a new offensive into Cambodia.

November 12: The military trial of Lt. William Calley begins at Fort Benning, Georgia, concerning the massacre of Vietnamese civilians at My Lai.

November 20: American troop levels drop to 334,600.

November 20–21: The Son Tay raid was a US Special Forces raid on a prison camp near the North Vietnamese village of Son Tay to rescue US prisoners of war. Although no prisoners were found, the raid was considered a tactical success. Following the Son Tay raid, the North Vietnamese closed the outlying prisoner camps and consolidated all POWs in Ha Noi. Ha Noi was known as the Hanoi Hilton. The Son Tay raid boosted POWs' morale.

December 10: President Nixon warns Hanoi that more bombing raids may occur if North Vietnamese attacks continue against the South.

December 22: The Cooper-Church amendment to the US defense appropriations bill forbids the use of any US ground forces in Laos or Cambodia. American troop levels drop to 280,000 by year's end. During the year, an estimated sixty thousand soldiers experimented with drugs, according to the US command. There were also over two hundred incidents of "fragging" in which unpopular officers were attacked with fragmentation grenades by men under their command. In addition, many units are now plagued by racial unrest, reflecting the disharmony back home.

1971

January 4: President Nixon announces "the end is in sight."

January 19: US fighter-bombers launch heavy air strikes against NVA supply camps in Laos and Cambodia.

January 30–April 6: Operation Lam Son 719, an all-South Vietnamese ground offensive, occurs as 17,000 South Vietnamese soldiers attack 22,000 NVA inside Laos in an attempt to sever the Ho Chi Minh trail. Aided by heavy US artillery and air strikes, along with American helicopter lifts, South Vietnamese troops advance to their first objective but then stall, thus allowing the NVA time to bring in massive troop reinforcements. By battle's end, 40,000 NVA pursue 8,000 South Vietnamese survivors back across the border. The South Vietnamese suffer 7,682 casualties, nearly half the original force. The US suffers 215 killed, over 100 helicopters lost, and over 600 damaged while supporting the offensive. NVA losses are estimated up to 20,000 as a result of the intense American bombardment. Also among those killed was *Life* magazine photographer Larry Burrows, who had been working in Vietnam for ten years. Although an upbeat President Nixon declares after the battle that "Vietnamization has succeeded," the failed offensive indicates true Vietnamization of the war may be difficult to achieve.

March: Opinion polls indicate Nixon's approval rating among Americans has dropped to 50 percent, while approval of his Vietnam strategy has slipped to just 34 percent. Half of all Americans polled believe the war in Vietnam to be "morally wrong."

March 1: The Capitol building in Washington is damaged by a bomb apparently planted in protest of the invasion of Laos.

March 10: China pledges complete support for North Vietnam's struggle against the US

March 29: Lt. William Calley is found guilty of the murder of twenty-two My Lai civilians. He is sentenced to life imprisonment with hard labor; however, the sentence is later reduced to twenty years, then ten years. Out of sixteen military personnel charged with offenses concerning the My Lai massacre, only five were actually court-martialed, and only Calley was ever found guilty.

April 1: President Nixon orders Calley released pending his appeal.

April 19: Vietnam Veterans against the War begin a week of nationwide protests.

April 24: Another mass demonstration is held in Washington, attracting nearly two hundred thousand.

April 29: Total American deaths in Vietnam surpass forty-five thousand.

April 30: The last US Marine combat units depart Vietnam.

May: Paris peace talks enter their fourth year still in deadlock.

May 3–5: A mass arrest of twelve thousand protesters occurs in Washington.

June: During a college commencement speech, Senator Mike Mansfield labels the Vietnam War "a tragic mistake."

June 13: The *New York Times* begins publication of the *Pentagon Papers*, a secret Defense Department archive of the paperwork involved in decisions made by previous White House administrations concerning Vietnam. Publication of the classified documents infuriates President Nixon.

June 15: Nixon attempts to stop further publication of the *Pentagon Papers* through legal action against the *Times* in the US District Court.

June 18: The *Washington Post* begins its publication of the *Pentagon Papers*. The *Times* and *Post* now become involved in legal wrangling with the Nixon administration, which soon winds up before the US Supreme Court.

June 22: A nonbinding resolution passed in the US Senate urges the removal of all American troops from Vietnam by year's end.

June 28: The source of the *Pentagon Papers* leak, Daniel Ellsberg, surrenders to police.

June 30: The US Supreme Court rules 6–3 in favor of the *New York Times* and *Washington Post* publication of the *Pentagon Papers*.

June: George Jackson replaces William Colby as head of CORDS.

July 1: 6,100 American soldiers depart Vietnam, a daily record.

July 15: President Nixon announces he will visit communist China in 1972, a major diplomatic breakthrough.

July 17: The Plumbers unit is established in the White House by Nixon aides John Ehrlichman and Charles Colson to investigate Daniel Ellsberg and to "plug" various news leaks. Colson also compiles an "enemies list" featuring the names of two hundred prominent Americans considered to be anti-Nixon.

August 2: The US admits there are some thirty thousand CIA-sponsored irregulars operating in Laos.

August 18: Australia and New Zealand announce the pending withdrawal of their troops from Vietnam.

September 22: Captain Ernest L. Medina is acquitted of all charges concerning the massacre of Vietnamese civilians at My Lai.

October 3: Running unopposed, President Thieu of South Vietnam is reelected.

October 9: Members of the US 1st Air Cavalry Division refuses an assignment to go out on patrol by expressing "a desire not to go." This is one in a series of American ground troops engaging in "combat refusal."

October 31: The first Viet Cong POWs are released by Saigon. There are nearly three thousand Viet Cong prisoners.

December 17: US troop levels drop to 156,800.

December 26–30: The first bombing north of the 20th parallel is conducted in response to the buildup of North Vietnamese forces. These bombing missions are against military installations in North Vietnam citing violations of the agreements surrounding the 1968 bombing halt.

1972

January 25: President Nixon announces a proposed eight-point peace plan for Vietnam and also reveals that Kissinger has been secretly negotiating with the North Vietnamese. However, Hanoi rejects Nixon's peace overture. Nixon also announces additional US troop reductions.

February 21–28: President Nixon visits China and meets with Mao Zedong and Prime Minister Zhou Enlai to forge new diplomatic relations with the communist nation. Nixon's visit causes great concern in Hanoi that their wartime ally China might be inclined to agree to an unfavorable settlement of the war to improve Chinese relations with the US.

March 10: The US 101st Airborne Division is withdrawn from Vietnam.

March 23: The US stages a boycott of the Paris peace talks as President Nixon accuses Hanoi of refusing to "negotiate seriously."

March-September: The Eastertide Offensive occurs as two hundred thousand North Vietnamese soldiers under the command of General Vo Nguyen Giap wage an all-out attempt to conquer South Vietnam. The offensive is a tremendous gamble by Giap and is undertaken as a result of US troop withdrawal, the strength of the antiwar movement in America likely preventing a US retaliatory response, and the poor performance of South Vietnam's Army during Operation Lam Son 719 in 1971. Giap's immediate strategy involves the capture of Quang Tri in the northern part of South Vietnam, Kontum in the midsection, and An Loc in the south. North Vietnam's communist leaders also hope a successful offensive will harm Richard Nixon politically during this presidential election year in America, much as President Lyndon Johnson had suffered as a result of the 1968

Tet Offensive. The communists believe Nixon's removal would disrupt American aid to South Vietnam.

March 30: NVA Eastertide attack on Quang Tri begins.

April 2: In response to the Eastertide Offensive, President Nixon authorizes the US 7th Fleet to target NVA troops massed around the demilitarized zone with air strikes and naval gunfire.

April 4: In a further response to Eastertide, President Nixon authorizes a massive bombing campaign targeting all NVA troops invading South Vietnam along with B-52 air strikes against North Vietnam. "The bastards have never been bombed like they're going to be bombed this time," Nixon privately declares.

April 10: Heavy B-52 bombardments ranging 145 miles into North Vietnam begin.

April 12: NVA Eastertide attack on Kontum begins in central South Vietnam. If the attack succeeds, South Vietnam will effectively be cut in two.

April 15: Hanoi and Haiphong harbor are bombed by the US.

April 15–20: Protests against the bombings erupt in America.

April 19: NVA Eastertide attack on An Loc begins.

April 27: Paris peace talks resume.

April 30: US troop levels drop to sixty-nine thousand.

May: Secret meetings between Kissinger and Le Duc Tho resume.

May 1: South Vietnamese abandon Quang Tri City to the NVA.

May 4: The US and South Vietnam suspend participation in the Paris peace talks indefinitely; 125 additional US warplanes are ordered to Vietnam.

May 8: In response to the ongoing NVA Eastertide Offensive, President Nixon announces Operation Linebacker I, the mining of North Vietnam's harbors along with intensified bombing of roads, bridges, and oil facilities. The announcement brings international condemnation of the US and ignites more antiwar protests in America. During an air strike conducted by South Vietnamese pilots, napalm bombs are accidentally dropped on South Vietnamese civilians, including children. Filmed footage and a still photo of a badly burned nude girl fleeing the destruction of her hamlet becomes yet another enduring image of the war.

May 9: Operation Linebacker I commences with US jets laying mines in Haiphong harbor.

May 1: NVA capture Quang Tri City.

May 15: The headquarters for the US Army in Vietnam is decommissioned.

May 17: According to US reports, Operation Linebacker I is damaging North Vietnam's ability to supply NVA troops engaged in the Eastertide Offensive.

May 22–30: President Nixon visits the Soviet Union and meets with Leonid Brezhnev to forge new diplomatic relations with the communist nation. Nixon's visit causes great concern in Hanoi that their Soviet ally might be inclined to agree to an unfavorable settlement of the war to improve Soviet relations with the US.

May 30: NVA attack on Kontum is thwarted by South Vietnamese troops, aided by massive US air strikes.

June 1: Hanoi admits Operation Linebacker I is causing severe disruptions.

June 9: Senior US military adviser John Paul Vann is killed in a helicopter crash near Pleiku. He had been assisting South Vietnamese troops in the defense of Kontum.

June 17: Five burglars are arrested inside the Watergate building in Washington while attempting to plant hidden microphones in the Democratic National Committee offices. Subsequent investigations will reveal they have ties to the Nixon White House.

June 28: South Vietnamese troops begin a counteroffensive to retake Quang Tri Province, aided by US Navy gunfire and B-52 bombardments.

June 30: General Frederick C. Weyand replaces General Abrams as MACV commander in Vietnam.

July 11: NVA attack on An Loc is thwarted by South Vietnamese troops aided by B-52 air strikes.

July 13: Paris peace talks resume.

July 14: The Democrats choose Senator George McGovern of South Dakota as their presidential nominee. McGovern, an outspoken critic of the war, advocates "immediate and complete withdrawal."

July 18: During a visit to Hanoi, actress Jane Fonda broadcasts antiwar messages via Radio Hanoi.

July 19: South Vietnamese troops begin a major counteroffensive against NVA in Binh Dinh province.

August 1: Henry Kissinger meets again with Le Duc Tho in Paris.

August 23: The last US combat troops depart Vietnam.

September 16: Quang Tri City is recaptured by South Vietnamese troops.

September 29: Heavy US air raids against airfields in North Vietnam destroy 10 percent of their air force.

October 8: The long-standing diplomatic stalemate between Henry Kissinger and Le Duc Tho finally ends as both sides agree to major concessions. The US will allow North Vietnamese troops already in South Vietnam to remain there, while North Vietnam drops its demand for the removal of South Vietnam's President Thieu and the dissolution of his government. Although Kissinger's staff members privately express concerns over allowing NVA troops to remain in the South, Kissinger rebuffs them, saying, "I want to end this war before the election."

October 22: In Saigon, Kissinger visits President Thieu to discuss the peace proposal. Meetings between Kissinger and Thieu go badly as an emotional Thieu adamantly opposes allowing North Vietnamese troops to remain indefinitely in South Vietnam. An angry Kissinger reports Thieu's reaction to President Nixon, who then threatens Thieu with a total cut-off of all American aid. But Thieu does not back down. Kissinger then returns to Washington.

October 22: Operation Linebacker I ends. US warplanes flew 40,000 sorties and dropped over 125,000 tons of bombs during the bombing campaign, which effectively disrupted North Vietnam's Eastertide Offensive. During the failed offensive, the North suffered an estimated 100,000 military casualties and lost half its tanks and artillery. Leader of the offensive, legendary General Vo Nguyen Giap, the victor at Dien Bien Phu, was then quietly ousted in favor of his deputy Gen. Van Tien Dung. South Vietnam lost 40,000 soldiers stopping the offensive, in the heaviest fighting of the entire war.

October 24: President Thieu publicly denounces Kissinger's peace proposal.

October 26: Radio Hanoi reveals terms of the peace proposal and accuses the US of attempting to sabotage the settlement. At the White House, now a week before the presidential election, Henry Kissinger holds a press briefing and declares, "We believe that peace is at hand. We believe that an agreement is in sight."

November 7: Richard M. Nixon wins the presidential election in the biggest landslide to date in US history.

November 14: President Nixon sends a letter to President Thieu secretly pledging "to take swift and severe retaliatory action" if North Vietnam violates the proposed peace treaty.

November 30: American troop withdrawal from Vietnam is completed, although there are still sixteen thousand Army advisers and administrators remaining to assist South Vietnam's military forces.

December 13: In Paris, peace negotiations between Kissinger and Le Duc Tho collapse after Kissinger presents a list of sixty-nine changes demanded by President Thieu. President Nixon now issues an ultimatum to North Vietnam that serious negotiations must resume within seventy-two hours. Hanoi does not respond. As a result, Nixon orders Operation Linebacker II, eleven days and nights of maximum force bombing against military targets in Hanoi by B-52 bombers.

December 18: Operation Linebacker II begins. The so-called Christmas bombings are widely denounced by American politicians, the media, and various world leaders including the pope. North Vietnamese filmed footage of civilian casualties further increase the outrage. In addition, a few downed B-52 pilots made public statements in North Vietnam against the bombing.

December 26: North Vietnam agrees to continue peace negotiations within five days of the end of bombing.

December 29: Operation Linebacker II ends what has been the most intensive bombing campaign of the entire war with over 100,000 bombs dropped on Hanoi and Haiphong. Fifteen of the 121 B-52s participating were shot down by the North Vietnamese who fired 1,200 SAMs. There were 1,318 civilian deaths from the bombing, according to Hanoi.

1973

January 8: Kissinger and Le Duc Tho resume negotiations in Paris.

January 9: All remaining differences are resolved between Kissinger and Le Duc Tho. President Thieu, once again threatened by Nixon with a total cut-off of American aid to South Vietnam, now unwillingly accepts the peace agreement, which still allows North Vietnamese troops to remain in South Vietnam. Thieu labels the terms "tantamount to surrender" for South Vietnam.

January 23: President Nixon announces that an agreement has been reached, which will "end the war and bring peace with honor."

January 27: The Paris Peace Accords are signed by the US, North Vietnam, South Vietnam, and the Viet Cong. Under the terms, the US agrees to immediately halt all military activities and withdraw all remaining military personnel within sixty days. The North Vietnamese agree to an immediate cease-fire and the release of all American POWs within sixty days. An estimated 150,000 North Vietnamese soldiers presently in South Vietnam are allowed to remain. Vietnam is still divided. South Vietnam is considered to be one country with two governments, one led by President Thieu, the other led by Viet Cong, pending future reconciliation.

January 27: Secretary of Defense Melvin Laird announces the draft is ended in favor of voluntary enlistment.

January 27: The last American soldier to die in combat in Vietnam, Lt. Col. William B. Nolde, is killed.

February 12: Operation Homecoming begins the release of 591 American POWs from Hanoi.

March 29: The last remaining American troops withdraw from Vietnam as President Nixon declares, *"The* day we have all worked and prayed for has finally come." America's longest war concludes. During 15 years of military involvement, over 2 million Americans served in Vietnam with 500,000 seeing actual combat. About 47,244 were killed in action, including 8,000 airmen. There were 10,446 noncombat deaths. There were 153,329 seriously wounded, including 10,000 amputees. Over 2,400 American POWs/MIAs were unaccounted for as of 1973.

April: President Nixon and President Thieu meet at San Clemente, California. Nixon renews his earlier secret pledge to respond militarily if North Vietnam violates the peace agreement.

April 1: Captain Robert White, the last known American POW, is released.

April 30: The Watergate scandal results in the resignation of top Nixon aides H. R. Haldeman and John Ehrlichman.

June 19: The US Congress passes the Case-Church Amendment, which forbids any further US military involvement in Southeast Asia, effective August 15, 1973. The veto-proof vote is 278–124 in the House and 64–26 in the Senate. The Amendment paves the way for North Vietnam to wage yet another invasion of the South, this time without fear of US bombing.

June 24: Graham Martin becomes the new US ambassador to South Vietnam.

July: The US Navy removes mines from ports in North Vietnam which had been installed during Operation Linebacker.

July 16: The US Senate Armed Forces Committee begins hearings into the secret bombing of Cambodia during 1969–70.

July 17: Secretary of Defense James Schlesinger testifies before the Armed Forces Committee that 3,500 bombing raids were launched into Cambodia to protect American troops by targeting NVA positions. The extent of Nixon's secret bombing campaign angers many in Congress and results in the first call for Nixon's impeachment.

August 14: US bombing activities in Cambodia are halted in accordance with the Congressional ban resulting from the Case-Church Amendment.

August 22: Henry Kissinger is appointed by President Nixon as the new Secretary of State, replacing William Rogers.

September 22: South Vietnamese troops assault NVA near Pleiku.

October 10: Political scandal results in the resignation of Vice President Spiro T. Agnew. He is replaced by Congressman Gerald R. Ford.

November 7: Congress passes the War Powers Resolution requiring the president to obtain the support of Congress within ninety days of sending American troops abroad.

December 3: Viet Cong destroy 18 million gallons of fuel stored near Saigon.

1974

January: Fighting continues between the NVA and South Vietnamese forces. In October, the politburo in the North decides to launch an invasion of South Vietnam in 1975. During December, the North violates the Parris peace treaty and tests President Ford's resolve by attacking Phuoc Long province in South Vietnam. President Ford can only respond with diplomatic protests because of the congressional ban on all US military activity in Southeast Asia.

May 9: Congress begins impeachment proceedings against President Nixon stemming from the Watergate scandal.

August 9: Richard M. Nixon resigns the presidency as result of Watergate. Gerald R. Ford is sworn in as the thirty-eighth US president, becoming the sixth president coping with Vietnam.

September: The US Congress appropriates only $700 million for South Vietnam. This leaves the South Vietnamese Army underfunded and results in a decline of military readiness and morale.

September 16: President Gerald R. Ford announces a clemency program for draft evaders and military deserters. The program runs through March 31, 1975, and requires fugitives to take an oath of allegiance and also perform up to two years of community service. Out of an estimated 124,000 men eligible, about 22,500 take advantage of the offer.

October: The politburo in North Vietnam decides to launch an invasion of South Vietnam in 1975.

November 19: William Calley is freed after serving three and a half years under house arrest following his conviction for the murder of twenty-two My Lai civilians.

December 13: North Vietnam violates the Paris peace treaty and tests President Ford's resolve by attacking Phuoc Long province in South Vietnam. President Ford responds with diplomatic protests but no military force in compliance with the Congressional ban on all US military activity in Southeast Asia.

December 18: North Vietnam's leaders meet in Hanoi to form a plan for final victory.

1975

January: Phuoc Long falls to the NVA.

January 8: NVA general staff plan for the invasion of South Vietnam by twenty divisions is approved by North Vietnam's politburo. By now, the Soviet-supplied North Vietnamese Army is the fifth largest in the world. It anticipates a two-year struggle for victory. But in reality, South Vietnam's forces will collapse in only fifty-five days.

January 14: Testifying before Congress, Secretary of Defense James Schlesinger states that the US is not living up to its earlier promise to South Vietnam's President Thieu of "severe retaliatory action" in the event North Vietnam violated the Paris peace treaty.

January 21: During a press conference, President Ford states the US is unwilling to reenter the war.

February 5: NVA military leader General Van Tien Dung secretly crosses into South Vietnam to take command of the final offensive.

March 10: The final offensive begins as twenty-five thousand NVA attack Ban Me Thuot located in the Central Highlands.

March 11: Ban Me Thuot falls after half of the four thousand South Vietnamese soldiers defending it surrender or desert.

March 13: President Thieu decides to abandon the Highlands region and two Northern provinces to the NVA. This results in a mass exodus of civilians and soldiers, clogging roads, and bringing general chaos. NVA then shell the disorganized retreat, which becomes known as "the convoy of tears."

March 18: Realizing the South Vietnamese Army is nearing collapse, NVA leaders meet and decide to accelerate their offensive to achieve total victory before May 1.

March 19: Quang Tri City falls to NVA.

March 24: Tam Ky overrun by NVA.

March 25: Hue falls without resistance after a three-day siege. South Vietnamese troops now break and run from other threatened areas. Millions of refugees flee south.

March 26: Chu Lai is evacuated.

March 28: Da Nang is shelled as thirty-five thousand NVA prepare to attack.

March 30: Da Nang falls as one hundred thousand South Vietnamese soldiers surrender after being abandoned by their commanding officers.

March 31: NVA begin the Ho Chi Minh Campaign, the final push toward Saigon.

April 9: NVA close in on Xuan Loc, thirty-eight miles from Saigon. Over forty thousand NVA attack the city and, for the first time, encounter stiff resistance from South Vietnamese troops.

April 20: US Ambassador Graham Martin meets with President Thieu and pressures him to resign given the gravity of the situation and the unlikelihood that Thieu could ever negotiate with the communists.

April 21: A bitter, tearful President Thieu resigns during a nine-ty-minute rambling TV speech to the people of South Vietnam. Thieu reads from the letter sent by Nixon in 1972 pledging "severe retaliatory action" if South Vietnam was threatened. Thieu condemns the Paris Peace Accords, Henry Kissinger, and the US: "The United States has not respected its promises. It is inhumane. It is untrustworthy. It is irresponsible." He is then ushered into exile in Taiwan, aided by the CIA.

April 22: Xuan Loc falls to the NVA after a two-week battle with South Vietnam's 18th Army Division, which inflicted over five thousand NVA casualties and delayed the Ho Chi Minh Campaign for two weeks.

April 23: One hundred thousand NVA soldiers advance on Saigon, which is now overflowing with refugees. On this same day, President Ford gives a speech at Tulane University stating the conflict in Vietnam is "a war that is finished as far as America is concerned."

April 27: Saigon is encircled. Thirty thousand South Vietnamese soldiers are inside the city but are leaderless. NVA fire rockets into downtown civilian areas as the city erupts into chaos and widespread looting.

April 28: "Neutralist" General Duong Van "Big" Minh becomes the new president of South Vietnam and appeals for a cease-fire. His appeal is ignored.

April 29: NVA shell Tan Son Nhut air base in Saigon, killing two US Marines at the compound gate. Conditions then deteriorate as South Vietnamese civilians loot the air base. President Ford now orders Operation Frequent Wind, the helicopter evacuation of seven thousand Americans and South Vietnamese from Saigon, which begins with the radio broadcast of the song "White Christmas" as a prearranged code signal. At Tan Son Nhut, frantic civilians begin swarming the helicopters. The evacuation is then shifted to the walled-in American embassy, which is secured by US Marines in full combat gear. But the scene there also deteriorates, as thousands of civilians attempt to get into the compound. Three US aircraft carriers stand by off the coast of Vietnam to handle incoming Americans and South Vietnamese refugees. Many South Vietnamese pilots also land on the carriers, flying American-made helicopters, which are then pushed overboard to make room for more arrivals. Filmed footage of the $250,000 choppers being tossed into the sea becomes an enduring image of the war's end.

April 30: At 8:35 a.m., the last Americans, ten Marines from the embassy, depart Saigon, concluding the United States presence in Vietnam. North Vietnamese troops pour into Saigon and encounter little resistance. By 11:00 a.m., the red and blue Viet Cong flag flies from the presidential palace. President Minh broadcasts a message of unconditional surrender. The Second Indochina War is over, and the Third Indochina War begins almost immediately.

Appendix D

Lesson Outline

Why would anyone want to teach anything
about the Second Indochina War?

I. Methodology
II. Lexicon
III. Corps Tactical Zones
    A. Location
    B. Geography
IV. Operational Hot Spots
    A. Ashau Valley
    B. Fishhook
    C. Parrots Peak
    D. Elephant Ear
    E. Seven Mountains
    F. War Zone C
    G. War Zone D
    H. Iron Triangle
V. US Military Organization and Location
    A. Military Assistance Command Vietnam
    B. I Field Force
    C. II Field Force
    D. Army Divisions and Locations
        1. 1st Infantry Division
        2. 1st Cavalry Division

3. 4th Infantry Division

4. 9th Infantry Division

5. 25th Infantry Division

6. 82nd Airborne Division, 3rd Brigade

7. 101st Airborne Division

8. Americal Infantry Division

9. 173rd Airborne Brigade

E. Unit Organization

    1. Division

    2. Brigade

    3. Battalion

    4. Company

    5. Platoon

    6. Squad

F. Areas of Operations

G. Command and Control

VI.   Firebases

A. Types

    1. Oval

    2. Circle

    3. Rectangle

    4. Square

    5. Triangle

    6. Star

B. Construction

    1. Field of fire

    2. Berm

    3. Concertina Wire

    4. Tangle Foot

    5. Bunkers

    6. RPG Screen

    7. Trip Flares

    8. Claymores

    9. Foo Gas

C. Organization

    1. Infantry

       2. Artillery

       3. Tactical Operations Center (TOC)

       4. Mortars

       5. Logistics Pad

       6. Aid Station

       7. Gates

    D. Sappers

VII. Weapons

    A. Allied

       1. M-16

       2. Car-15

       3. M-14

       4. M-79 (Chunker)

       5. M-60

       6. .50 Cal.

       7. 81 MM Mortar

       8. 4.2 Mortar

       9. Hand Grenade

       10. .45 Cal. Pistol

       11. .38 Cal. Pistol

       12. Light Anti-Tank Weapon (LAW)

       13. 105 MM Howitzer

       14. 155 MM Howitzer

       15. 8 Inch Artillery

       16. Smoke Grenade

    B. Threat/Enemy

       1. AK-47

       2. SKS

       3. Rocket Propelled Grenade (RPG)

       4. RPD

VIII. Aircraft

    A. Rotor Wing

       1. UH-1 (Slick)

       2. AH-64 (Cobra)

       3. Light Observation Helicopter (LOH)

       4. CH-47 (Hook)

        5. CH-54 (Crane)
    B. Fixed Wing
        1. L-19 (Bird Dog)
        2. OV-10 (Bronco)
        3. C7A (Caribou)
        4. C-123
        5. C-130
        6. C-47 (Puff and Spooky)
    C. Fast Movers
        1. F-100
        2. F-4 (Phantom)
        3. A-1E (Skyraider)
        4. B-52 (BUFF)
IX. Uniforms
    A. Allied
        1. Camies
        2. Tigers
        3. Jungle Fatigues
        4. Boots
        5. No Underwear, Tee Shirt, or Socks
    B. Threat/Enemy
        1. Black Cotton
        2. US
        3. Khaki
        4. Mix
X. Equipment
    A. Allied
        1. Web Gear
        2. Helmet
        3. Rucksack
        4. Poncho
        5. Poncho Liner
    B. Threat/Enemy
        1. Web Gear
        2. Belt
        3. Hammock

        4. Map Case
        5. US Gear
        6. Mix
XI. Military Operations
    A. Combat Assault (CA)
        1. Select LZ/PZ
        2. Pickup Formations
            a. PZ
            b. Landing Formations
            c. LZ
        3. ACL
        4. Cross Load
        5. Fire Support
    B. Search and Destroy
        1. AM (Midnight to 6:00 a.m.)
            a. Stand To
            b. Chow
            c. Pack Up
            d. Operations Order (OPORD) Briefing
                (1) Situation
                    (a) Friendly
                    (b) Enemy
                (2) Mission
                    -Who
                    -What
                    -When
                    -Where
                    -Why
                (3) Execution
                (4) Logistics
                (5) Command and Signal
            e. Movement Techniques, Breaks, Contact with the
               Enemy
        2. PM
                (a) Big break
                (b) Day ambush

(c) Resupply
(d) Water Run
f. Evening about 1600–1700, Decide RON or Ambush
  (1) RON Site
    (a) RON Selection
      - Visual
      - Map Recon
    (b) RON Techniques
      - Button Hook
      - Stop and Go
    (c) RON Organization
      -Direction of Movement Is 12
      -North Is 12
      -Squad Sectors
    (d) Post Security
      -Check or Cut Fields of Fire
      -Claymores and Trip Flares Out
      -Guard Roster
      -Place MGs
      -Prepare Range Cards
      -Establish One TRP
      -Chow
  (2) Ambush
    (a) Select Site and Conduct a Recon
      -Trail
      -Road
    (b) Issue OPORD (Modified)
      -Kill Zone
      -Positions
      -Weapons
      -Claymores
      -Rear Security
      - Fire Support
      -Search teams
      -POW teams

XII. Threat/Enemy Tactics, Techniques, and Procedures
    A. Organization
        1. NVA
            -Regiments
            -Battalions
            -Companies
            -Platoons
            -Squads
        2. Viet Cong
            a. Hard Corps Military
                -Battalions
                -Companies
                -Platoons
                -Squads
            b. Paramilitary
                -Sniper Teams
                -Trail Watchers
                -Small Unit Patrols
                -Early Warning Teams
            c. Underground
                -Combat Teams
                -Intelligence Teams
                -NVA Staff
                -Shadow Government
                -Logistics
    B. Combat Operations
        1. Ambush
            a. Roads
            b. Trails
            c. LZs
        2. Raids
            a. Villages
            b. Small Allied Outposts
            c. Firebases
            d. Rear Areas/Base Camps
    C. Base Areas/Camps

1. South Vietnam
   a. Jungle
   b. Village
   c. Cities
2. Safe Areas (Off-Limits)
   a. Cambodia
   b. Laos
3. Tunnel Complexes

XV. Pathfinder Operations
  A. Mission
  B. Organization
    1. Detachment
    2. Company
  C. Adviser Duties
    1. US Aviation
    2. US Infantry
    3. US Firebases
    4. ARVN
      -Army
      -Marines
      -Airborne Units
      -Rangers
  D. Recovery Operations
    1. Down Aircraft
    2. Personnel/Units
    3. Equipment

XVI. US Special Forces
  A. Mission
  B. Organization
    1. Group Headquarters
    2. Companies
      -Headquarters Company; Battalion Size
      -A Company; Battalion Size
      -B Company; Battalion Size
      -C Company; Battalion Size
      -D Company; Battalion Size

RECOMMENDED READING LIST

A Better War: The Unexamined Victories and Final Tragedy of America's Last Years in Vietnam by Lewis Sorley

A Soldier Reports by General William C. Westmoreland

A Time for War by Robert Schulzinger

Abuse of Power: The New Nixon Tapes by Stanley Kutler

American Reckoning by Christian G. Appy

America and the Indochina Wars by Lester Brune and Richard D. Burns

An American Ordeal: The Antiwar Movement of the Vietnam Era by Charles DeBenedetti and

Charles Chatfield

Antiwar Movement by Adam Garfinkle

Arrogance of Power: The Secret World of Richard Nixon by Anthony Summers

Ashes to Ashes: The Phoenix Program and the Vietnam War by Dale Andrade

Backfire: The CIA's Secret War in Laos and Its Link to the War in Vietnam by Roger Warner

Campus Wars: The Peace Movement at American State Universities in the Vietnam Era by

Kenneth Heinman

China and the Vietnam Wars by Qiang Zhai

China's Involvement in the Vietnam War, 1964–1969 by Chen Jian

Close Quarters by Larry Heinemann

Conflict of Myths by Larry Cable

Dereliction of Duty: Lyndon Johnson, Robert McNamara, the Joint Chiefs of Staff, and the Lies

That Led to Vietnam by H. R. McMaster

Dog Soldiers by Robert Stone

Encyclopedia of the Vietnam War by Stanley I. Kutler

Flawed Giant: Lyndon Johnson and His Times by Robert Dallek

Guerrilla Diplomacy by Robert K. Brigham

Ho Chi Minh, biography by Duiker

How We Lost the Vietnam War by Nguyen Cao Ky

Inside the Viet Cong and the North Vietnamese Army by Michael Lanning and Dan Cragg

Johnson, Nixon and Doves by Melvin Small

Matterhorn by Karl Marlantes

Mission on the Ho Chi Minh Trail: Myth and the War in Vietnam by Richard L. Stevens

On Strategy by Harry G. Summers

Our Endless War, memoirs by Tran Van Don

Paper Soldiers: The American Press and the Vietnam War by Clarence R. Wyatt

Platoon Leader by Colonel James R. McDonough, USA (Ret.)

Report or Distort by Glenn MacDonald

Setup: What the Air Force Did in Vietnam and Why by Earl H. Tilford Jr.

South Vietnam: Nation under Stress by Robert Scigliano

Stolen Valor by B. G. Burkett

Telltale Hearts: The Origins and Impact of the Vietnam Antiwar Movement by Adam Garfinckle

TET by Don Oberdorfer

The 13th Valley by John Del Vecchio

The Counterinsurgency Era: US Doctrines and Performances by Douglas S. Blaufarb

The Limits of Air Power: The Bombing of North Vietnam by Mark Clodfelter

The Pentagon Papers *as Published by the* New York Times by Neil Sheehan

The Soviet Union and the Vietnam War by Ilya V. Gaiduk

The TET Offensive by Marc J. Gilbert and William Head

The Things They Carried by Tim O'Brian

The Vietnam Wars, 1945–1990 by Marilyn Young

The War Within: America's Battle over Vietnam by Tom Wells
Trapped by Success: The Eisenhower Administration and Vietnam by
   David Anderson
Twenty Years and Twenty Days, memoirs by Nguyen Cao Ky
Victory at Any Cost: The Genius of Vietnam's General Vo Nguyen Giap
   by Cecil Currey
Vietnam in Military Statistics by Michael Clodfelter
We Were Soldiers Once . . . and Young by Lieutenant General Hal
   Moore, USA (Ret.), and Joseph
H. Gallow
Where We Were in Vietnam by Michael P. Kelley

BIBLIOGRAPHY

Adair, Gilbert. *Hollywood's Vietnam*. London: Proteus, 1981.

Adams, Sam. "Vietnam Cover-Up: Playing War with Numbers." *Harper's Magazine*, May 1975.

Alan, Louis. *The End of the War in Asia*. London: Hart-Davis MacGibbon, 1976.

Alonso, Harriet Hyman. *Peace as a Woman's Issue: A History of the US Movement for World Peace and Women's Rights*. Syracuse University Press, 1993.

Alexander, Joseph and Merrrill L. Bantlett. *Amphibious Warfare and the Vietnam War*. 1984.

Ambrose, Stephen E. *Nixon*. 1987.

Andrade, Dale. *Ashes to Ashes: The Phoenix Program and the Vietnam War*. Lexington, MA: D. C. Heath, 1990.

Austin, Anthony. *The President's War: The Story of the Tonkin Gulf Resolution and How the Nation Was Trapped in Vietnam*.

Barrett, David M. *Uncertain Warriors: Lyndon Johnson and His Vietnam Advisors*. 1993.

Becket, Brian. *The Illustrated History of the Vietnam War*. 1985.

Bell, Dana. *Vietnam Warbirds in Action*. 1986.

Berger, Carl. *US Air Force in Southeast Asia: 1961–1973*. 1984.

Berman, Harvey P. *The Agent Orange Payment Program*. 1990.

Blaufarb, Douglas S. "The Counter-Insurgency Era." 2003.

Bonds, Ray. *The Vietnam War*. Crown Publishers, 1979.

Bosiljevac, T. L. *SEALs: UDT/SEAL Operations in South Vietnam*. 1990.

Bowers, Ray. *The US Force in Southeast Asia: Tactical Aircraft*. 1983.

Burchett, Wilfred. *Inside Story of the Guerrilla War*. International Publishers, 1965.

Buttinger, Joseph. "A Political History." 1968.

Cable, Larry. *Conflict of Myths: The Development of Counter-Insurgency Doctrine and the Vietnam War.* 1988.

Cable, Larry. *US and the Wars in Vietnam, 1965–68.*

Clarke, Jeffery J. *Advice and Support.* 1988.

Clodfelter, Mark. *The American Bombing of North Vietnam.* 1989.

Colby, William, with James McCargar. *Lost Victory.* 1989.

Collins, James L. *The Development and Training of the South Vietnamese Army, 1950–1972.* 1975.

Collins, James Lawton and Robert S. Larson. *Vietnam Studies: Allied Participation in Vietnam.*

Cooper, Chester A. *The Last Crusade.* 1973.

Croizat, Victor J. *The Brown Water Navy: The River and Coastal War in Indochina and Vietnam, 1940–1972.* Blandford Press, 1984.

Croizat, Victor J. *Vietnamese Naval Forces.* 1973.

Cutler, Thomas J. *Brown Water, Black Berets: Coastal and Riverine Warfare in Vietnam.* 1988.

Davidson, Phillip B. "Vietnam at War: The History, 1946–1975."

De Mark, Brian Van. *Into the Quagmire, Lyndon Johnson and the Escalation of the Vietnam War.* 1991.

Donovan, David. *Once a Warrior King.* 1985.

Duiker, William J. "The Rise of Nationalism in Vietnam." 1976.

Duiker, William J. "Sacred War." 1995.

Dunn, Carroll H. *Base Development in South Vietnam.* 1972.

Dunstan, Simon. *Vietnam Choppers, 1950–1975.* 1988.

Eckhardt, George S. *Command and Control.* 1974.

Eschmann, Karl J. *Linebacker: The Untold Story of the Air Raids over North Vietnam.* Ivy Books, 1989.

Fisher, Charles A. "Southeast Asia: A Social Economic and Political Geography." 1966.

Francilion, Rene J. *The Tonkin Gulf Yacht Club: US Carrier Operations off Vietnam.* 1988.

Fulton, William B. *Riverine Operations, 1966–1969.* Pentagon, 1985.

Genovese, Michael A. *The Nixon Presidency: Power and Politics in Turbulent Times.* Greenwood Press, 1990.

Gitlin, Todd. *The Sixties: Years of Hope, Days of Rage.* Bantam Books, 1987.

Gross, Charges. *A Different Breed of Cats: The Air National Guard and the 1968 Reserve Mobilizations.* 1983.

Guenter, Lewy. *Territorial Forces.* 1981.

Herring, George C. "America's Longest War." 1986.

Hughes, Ken. *Chasing Shadows: The Nixon Tapes, the Chennault Affair and the Origins of Watergate.* 1980.

Kamps, Charles T. Jr. *The History of the Vietnam War.* Exeter Books, 1987.

Kaplan, Hyman R. *US Coast Guard in South Vietnam.* 1971.

Karnow, Stanley. "Vietnam: A History." 1983.

Katcher, P. *Armies of the Vietnam War 1962–75, Men-at-Arms Series.* Reed International Books.

Kelly, Colonel Francis J. *Vietnam Studies, US Special Forces, 1961–1971.* 1985.

King, Peter. *Australia in the Second Indo China-War.* 1983.

Kinnard, Douglas. *The War Managers.* 1985.

Krepinevich, Andrew Jr. *US Army and Vietnam.* 1986.

Kutler, Stanley L. *Encyclopedia of the Vietnam War.* 1996.

Lanning, Michael and Dan Cragg. *Inside the VC and the NVA.* Ballantine Books, 1992.

Lanning, Michael and Dan Cragg. *NVA Infantryman Advancing Inside the VC and the NVA.* Ballantine Books, 1992.

Larzelere, Alex. *The Coast Guard at War in Vietnam.* 1997.

Lewy, Guenter. *America in Vietnam.* Oxford University Press, 1978.

Lippman, Walter. *The Cold War: A Study in US Foreign Policy.* Harper and Row, 1947.

Littauer, R. *The Air War in Indochina.* Cornell University study. Beacon Press, 1971.

Maclear, Michael. "Vietnam: A Complete Photographic History." 1981.

Marolda, Edward J. and Oscar Fitzgerald. *The US Navy and the Vietnam Conflict.* 1986.

McMaster, H. R. *Dereliction of Duty: Lyndon Johnson, Robert McNamara, the Joint Chiefs of Staff and the Lies That Led to Vietnam.* HarperCollins, 1997.

Melson, Charles D. *US Marines in Vietnam, 1954–1973: Headquarters, US Marine Headquarters.* 1985.

Minear, Larry. *Private Aid and Public Policy.* 1988.

Momyer, General William W. *Airpower in Three Wars.* 1979.

Morris, Roger Haig. *Uncertain Greatness: Henry Kissinger and American Foreign Policy.* Harper and Row, 1977.

Morrocco, John. *Rain of Fire: Air War.* 1986.

Nguyen, Lien-Hang T. "Hanoi's War." 2012.

Nixon, Richard M. *No More Vietnams.* 1985.

Olson, James S. *Dictionary of the Vietnam War.* Greenwood Press, 1988.

Palmer, Bruce Jr. *The 25 Year War.* 1984.

Piotrowski, General. *Basic Airman to General: The Secret War and Other Conflicts.* 2014.

Shulimson, Jack and Major Charles M. Johnson. *US Marine Corps, US Marines in Vietnam.* 1965.

Simmons, Edwin H. *The US Marines in Vietnam.* 1996.

Son, Phan Van. *The Viet Cong Tet Offensive.* 1989.

Spector, Ronald H. *Advice and Support: The Early Years.* 1983.

Stevens, Richard Linn. *The Trail: A History of the Ho Chi Minh Trail.* Garland, 1993.

Stockdale, James A. *A Vietnam Experience: Ten Years of Reflection.* 1984.

Sutherland, Ian D. W. *Special Forces of the US Army, 1952–1982.* 1990.

Tucker, Spencer C. "The Encyclopedia of the Vietnam War." 1998.

Vien, Cao Van. *The US Advisor.* 1980.

Vinh, Pham Kim. "The Vietnamese Culture." 1994.

Weiner, Tim. *One Man against the World: The Tragedy of Richard Nixon.* 1990.

Westmoreland, William C. *Report on Operations in South Vietnam, January 1964–June 1968.* 1969.

Westmoreland, William C. *A Soldier Reports*. New York: Doubleday, 1976.

Westmoreland, William C. *A War of Attrition*. New York: Crane-Russak, 1977.

Wirtz, James. *The Tet Offensive: Intelligence Failure in War*. Cornell University Press, 1991.

Wyatt, Clearance R. *Paper Soldiers: The American Press and the Vietnam War*. University of Chicago Press, 1993.

Zhai, Qiang. "China and the Vietnam Wars." 2000.

More Sources

After-Action Report, "Operation Rolling Thunder I & II"

Congressional Stolen Valor Act

MACV Handbook for Advisors

Magazine, US Military Officers Association of America article dated 2014

Personal interviews with various military soldiers, noncommissioned officers, company grade officers, and field officers.

The Pentagon Papers. Gravel Edition. Boston: Beacon Press, 1972.

US Military Code of Conduct Graphic Training Aid Card 21–50, 1958

US Military Officers Association of America article dated 2014

US Military Operations Plan 34-A, Declassified

Various US Military Field and Technical Manuals

Various US Military Standing Operating Procedures

Veterans of Foreign Wars Magazine, August 2014

Veterans of Foreign Wars Magazine, May 2014

Vietnam Veterans of America Magazine, May/June 2012

Wikipedia

About the Author

Major Steven Eugene "Dumammy" Cook, United States Army (retired), was born August 21, 1947, in Elkins, West Virginia (WV). He enlisted in the US Army in 1965 under the Airborne Infantry unassigned option. His first assignment after graduating from Airborne School was with the 101st Airborne Division Reconnaissance Company. As a Private First Class and later as a Fire team leader, he developed, tested,  and codified long-range patrolling doctrine and standard operating procedures for infantry reconnaissance units in South Vietnam. In 1967, he volunteered for the newly activated 3rd Battalion, 506th Airborne Infantry, which had been earmarked to conduct combat operations in South Vietnam. As a squad leader in Company B, he trained his squad for combat in Vietnam. Sergeant Cook completed his first combat tour in October 1968. For his exceptional combat leadership and other dynamic contributions, Sergeant Cook was selected as a Distinguished Member of the 506 Airborne Infantry Regiment in April 2014.

In October 1968, Sergeant Cook extended for another combat tour in the 145th Pathfinder Detachment of the 1st Aviation Brigade. As a Pathfinder team sergeant, he coordinated and provided aviation, air assault, reconnaissance, and infantry advisor support to US and allied forces in III and IV Corps South Vietnam. These Pathfinder missions were performed almost daily and consisted of organizing US and allied forces for air assaults into unknown landing zones (LZ). Sergeant Cook accompanied these units into the LZ and ground guided the follow-on air flights into the LZ. Sergeant Cook remained on the ground with these units and provided artillery, gunships, air strikes, MEDEVACs, and other support as needed.

In May 1969, Sergeant Cook extended his combat tour again and was reassigned to the 11th Pathfinder Company, 1st Cavalry Division. As a Pathfinder, he provided empirical air assault, reconnaissance, and infantry expertise to US and allied forces in III Corps. Sergeant Cook was promoted to staff sergeant in November 1969 and was assigned as team sergeant of Team 1. Because of critical personnel shortages, Staff Sergeant Cook personally led many Pathfinder missions and air assaults into new LZs. As team sergeant, he led two artillery raids into Cambodia. Later, Staff Sergeant Cook accompanied a South Vietnam Airborne Infantry Battalion into the Fishhook area of Cambodia during the spring invasion. For several days he was the senior enlisted infantry adviser in several of the Airborne Infantry companies and provided artillery, gunship, air strikes, MEDEVAC, and other support as needed.

After graduating Infantry Officer Candidate School at Fort Benning, Georgia, in 1971, Second Lieutenant Cook successfully performed the duties of an Infantry Rifle Platoon Leader and company executive officer of Company A, 2nd Battalion, 508th Airborne Infantry, 82nd Airborne Division. He was also an active skydiver in the 82nd Sport Parachute Club and Demonstration Team.

In January 1973, First Lieutenant Cook was assigned as executive officer of Special Forces Operational Detachment Alpha (SFODA) 531 (later renumbered to 571) Company A, 3rd Battalion (Delta Packet), 5th Special Forces Group (SFG), Fort Bragg, North Carolina. As executive officer, he was an assault team leader and trained his assault team for worldwide direct action contingency missions.

In February 1974, First Lieutenant Cook was assigned as executive officer of SFODA-3 (HALO) Company A, 1st Battalion 10th

SFG in West Germany. He tested and perfected nonstandard high-altitude low-opening (HALO) parachutes, equipment, and procedures for US and allied Special Forces.

Captain Cook was assigned as commander of SFODA-9 (Scout Swim) Company B, 1st Battalion 10th SFG in February 1975. He developed and perfected long-range surface-swim and small-boat infiltration techniques for US and allies Special Forces. Captain Cook successfully led his detachment in four theater-level unconventional warfare field training exercises (FTX).

After graduating from the Infantry Officer Advanced Course in 1978, Captain Cook was assigned to the Infantry School, teaching 550 hours of criterion-referenced light infantry, airborne, and air assault tactics, techniques, and procedures to newly commissioned officers in the Infantry Officer Basic Course (IOBC).

In 1979, Captain Cook was assigned to the US Army Airborne Department serving as a company commander, S3, and acting Pathfinder committee chief. As company commander, he ensured the training of three hundred to five hundred basic airborne students daily. Later as the battalion operations officer, he planned, monitored, and ensured the safe and professional training of approximately twenty-one thousand US and allied basic airborne students and approximately five hundred US and allied Pathfinder students annually. As acting Pathfinder committee chief, Captain Cook instructed and graded Pathfinder classes, developed, codified, and published Pathfinder tactics, techniques, and procedures that are still used in training and worldwide Pathfinder operations.

In 1982, Major Cook was assigned outside his infantry specialty as executive officer of the 2nd Battalion, US Army Intelligence School at Fort Devens. As the only officer on the battalion staff, he managed the administration, accountability, operations, planning, training, security, and logistics of a 1,200 coed student and permanent party battalion.

In October 1983, Major Cook was personally selected by the 10th Special Forces Group (SFG) commander to command Company C, 3rd Battalion 10th SFG. As commander, he monitored seven strategic war plans and ensured his detachments were prepared for unconventional warfare for any European contingency.

In October 1985, Major Cook was reassigned as the executive officer of the 3rd Battalion, 10th SFG. As executive officer and chief of staff, he supervised the battalion administration, intelligence matters, training, logistics, and communications. In February 1986, Major Cook retired from active duty as the executive officer of 3rd Battalion 10th SFG.

After retirement, Mr. Cook was among the first civilian Civil Service Instructors selected to teach in the elite Special Forces Operations and Intelligence Course at Fort Bragg. He instructed Special Forces basic, advanced, and classified subjects to US and Allied Special Forces, Special Mission Unit personnel, agencies, and law enforcement organizations.

In 1988, Mr. Cook was reassigned to the Combat Developments Directorate of the Special Warfare Center and School (SWCS). He was a test and development officer that managed the development and testing of new and nonstandard Special Forces weapons, equipment, and air items.

From 1989 through 2000, Mr. Cook was the Deputy Chief of the Joint Army and Special Operations Forces (SOF) Division, Directorate of Training and Doctrine, SWCS. During this assignment, he managed the writing teams and subject matter experts that developed and reviewed SOF doctrine and training field manuals, publications, and literature. He integrated Army SOF doctrine into army, multiservice, and joint publications. Mr. Cook developed and wrote the Special Operations Command and Control Element (SOCCE), Special Operations Coordination Element (SOCOORD), and the Terminal Guidance Operations (TGO) handbooks and the first draft of Field Manual 31-20-2 and 2A (classified), Unconventional Warfare Tactics, Techniques, and Procedures for Special Forces. He was selected as SWCS Supervisor of the Year in 1993 and 1998.

From 2000 to 2003, Mr. Cook served as a training specialist and command manager on the US Army Staff in the Pentagon and was awarded the US Army Staff Identification Badge in 2004. He is a survivor of the 9/11 Pentagon terrorism attack. Mr. Cook retired in 2006 while serving as the executive officer of a requirements division on the Army Staff.

Although Mr. Cook is retired, he continues to support Special Forces. Because of his exceptional, extraordinary, and exemplary personal contributions, training Special Forces and rare and unique leadership above and beyond the call of duty, Major Cook was selected as a Distinguished Member of the 1st Special Forces Regiment in 2017.

Major Cook is an active member of the Davis Memorial Presbyterian Church in Elkins and is a Wednesday night Bible study leader. Major Cook lectures and provides empirical military expertise and vignettes during Vietnamese history classes, with an emphasis on the Second Indochina War at Davis and Elkins (D & E) College in Elkins. He developed, wrote, and published a student handbook, *Dynamics of the Vietnam War*, for D & E students to better understand the military aspects of the Vietnam War. He also lectures to various groups, including veterans, family members, professional organizations, federal agencies, clubs, associations, college students, and educators on the Vietnam War. His first-person, no-spin lectures include an overview of conventional Special Forces and Pathfinder operations in South Vietnam during the Second Indochina War. Major Cook provides political science and history counseling and tutoring to high school and college students.

His awards include the Combat Infantry Badge, Expert Infantry Badge, Special Forces Tab, Bronze Star (5), Purple Heart (4), Vietnam Service Medal with 9 campaign stars, Military Free Fall Jumpmaster Badge, SCUBA Badge, Pathfinder Badge, Master Parachutists Badge, US Army Staff Identification Badge, South Vietnamese Parachutist Badge, German Parachutist Badge, Spanish Parachutist Badge, Danish Parachutist Badge, French Parachutist Badge, Italian Parachutist Badge, Belgium Parachutist Badge, South African Parachutist Badge, Laos Parachutist Badge, 2nd Battalion 19th Special Forces Ridge Runner Wings # 14, 101st Airborne Division Parachute Gold Wings # 609, 82nd Airborne Division Century Parachute Wings # 597, United States Sport Parachute Association (USPA) D-License #

6795, USPA 3000 Parachute Jump Badge #1507, USPA 36 hours in Free Fall Badge # 1432, and USPA Jumpmaster and Instructor ratings. He has numerous other American and foreign decorations and awards.

Major Cook resides with his wife, Deborah, in Elkins, West Virginia.

CPSIA information can be obtained
at www.ICGtesting.com
Printed in the USA
BVHW090609180519
548308BV00002B/2/P

9 781643 494340